Western Intellectuals and the Soviet Union, 1920–40

THE UNIVERSITY OF
WINCHESTER

Despite the
Western int
supporters (
seemingly i
prominent '
ser, G.B. Sl
and Elsa Ti
Previously
scenes' ope
intellectual:
various offi
Association
tural Relati
the Soviet '
priority for
seducing sc

Ludmila S
the Univers
Studies, an
and French
preting (Au

To be returned on or before the day marked above, subject to recall.

BASEES/Routledge Series on Russian and East European Studies

Series editor

Richard Sakwa
Department of Politics and International Relations, University of Kent

Editorial Committee:

Julian Cooper
Centre for Russian and East European Studies, University of Birmingham
Terry Cox
Department of Central and East European Studies, University of Glasgow
Rosalind Marsh
Department of European Studies and Modern Languages, University of Bath
David Moon
Department of History, University of Durham
Hilary Pilkington
Department of Sociology, University of Warwick
Stephen White
Department of Politics, University of Glasgow

Founding Editorial Committee Member:

George Blazyca
Centre for Contemporary European Studies, University of Paisley

This series is published on behalf of BASEES (the British Association for Slavonic and East European Studies). The series comprises original, high-quality, research-level work by both new and established scholars on all aspects of Russian, Soviet, post-Soviet and East European Studies in humanities and social science subjects.

Western Intellectuals and the Soviet Union, 1920–40

From Red Square to the Left Bank

Ludmila Stern

LONDON AND NEW YORK

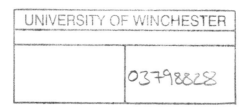
First published 2007
by Routledge
2 Park Square, Milton Park, Abingdon, Oxon OX14 4RN

Simultaneously published in the USA and Canada by Routledge
270 Madison Ave, New York NY 10016

Routledge is an imprint of the Taylor & Francis Group

Transferred to Digital Printing 2009

Typeset in Times New Roman by
Prepress Projects Ltd, Perth, UK

British Library Cataloguing in Publication Data
A catalogue record for this book is available from the British Library

Library of Congress Cataloging in Publication Data
Stern, Ludmila.
  Western intellectuals and the Soviet Union, : 1920-40 : from Red Square
to the Left Bank / Ludmila Stern.
  p. cm. — (BASEES/Routledge series on Russian and East European
Studies ; 31)
  Includes bibliographical references and index.
  ISBN 0–415–36005–6 (hardback : alk. paper) 1. Communism and
intellectuals—History—20th century. 2. Soviet Union—Politics and
government—1917–1936—Foreign public opinion. 3. Intellectuals—
Attitudes—History—20th century. 4. Communism—History—20th
century. 5. Intellectuals—Europe, Western. 6. Intellectuals—United
States. I. Title. II. Series.
  HX528.S74 2006
  305.5'52094709042—dc22
                                                       2006011021

ISBN10: 0–415–36005–6 (hbk)
ISBN10: 0–415–54585–4 (pbk)
ISBN10: 0–203–00814–6 (ebk)

ISBN13: 978–0–415–36005–0 (hbk)
ISBN13: 978–0–415–54585–3 (pbk)
ISBN13: 978–0–203–00814–0 (ebk)

To my grandparents

These writers have to be governed in such a way that they don't feel that directives may be coming from Moscow. In other words, they have to be influenced in such a way that <u>they</u> say what we want to hear.

Johannes Becher

Contents

Acknowledgements

This book is an extended adaptation of my PhD thesis *French Intellectuals and Soviet Cultural Organisations in the 1920s–30s* (2000). I was supported by a Postdoctoral Writing Grant from the Faculty of Arts and Social Sciences at the University of New South Wales, Sydney.

I would like to express my gratitude to my Australian and overseas colleagues, and friends and family, especially Jerome, who assisted me during the painstaking task of writing this book. My special thanks go to Claude Bloch, who generously gave me her time and shared her memories. I thank my editor, Andrew McDonald, for his patience and support beyond the call of duty.

Above all, this book would not have been written without my grandparents, Moisey and Hanka Salman. They are at the source of my family's history, the inspiration for this book.

Explanatory note

This book is based on the mainly unpublished Soviet and, to a lesser degree, French archival sources. The English translations of the Russian and French originals are, for the most part, my own. In the absence of adequate English translations of some of the Russian or French terms and expressions, and in order to reproduce the exact names of organisations, I have provided the original terms, italicised and in brackets.

I have adopted the following principles for the transliteration of Russian proper names. I have used conventional transliteration for names of well-known figures (e.g. Trotsky, Gorky and Fadeev). I have used the British Standards Institution transliteration for less familiar names (e.g. Tret'yakov, Kol'tsov, Pil'nyak), with the exception of surnames ending in *-skiy*, which are transliterated as *-sky* (e.g. Mayakovsky).

In the bibliography and footnotes, authors' names, book titles, and articles and publishers' place names have all been transliterated, followed in brackets by the English translation. Where the same titles are referred to further in the text, only the English translation of the title is used.

When quoting, I have tried to preserve the style of the original. If words in the original text were underlined, I have done the same.

Introduction

My mother, Colette Salman, was born in 1934 in the women's prison at Fresnes, near Paris.

Her parents, my grandparents, were Polish-born Jews who had studied medicine in Paris in the late 1920s and early 1930s. Like so many young people in those days, they became Communists; later, they joined an illegal organisation that conducted industrial espionage for the Soviet Union. This network, in which my grandmother was a courier, infiltrated French society to the very top, including the government and the army. The network was exposed in December 1933 and that is how my grandmother, already pregnant, found herself in jail.

When she was released in 1936, she and my two-year-old mother followed my grandfather to the only place they wanted to be, the Soviet Union. There, they found not a socialist paradise but a country poisoned by fear and suspicion. When they spoke French in the street, passers-by accused them of being foreign spies. One by one, their fellow political migrants were arrested. My grandfather, who was sure it would soon be his turn, was indeed taken away in 1937.

In the Butyrka jail in Moscow, in a cell overcrowded with both Russian and foreign political prisoners, he watched inmates being brought back from interrogation, destroyed and barely alive; at night, he was regularly woken by the cries of the beaten and tortured. His greatest fear was that my grandmother would be arrested and that my mother would disappear into one of the orphanages for 'little Trotskyites', never to be found again. During the months he spent in jail, the five-rouble note he was allowed to receive monthly was the only sign that my grandmother was still free.

My grandfather was released without charge eighteen months later. At that time, Nikolay Yezhov, the Head of the People's Commissariat for Internal Affairs or NKVD, became a victim of the terror himself and was replaced by an even more sinister figure, Lavrenty Beria.

The release of my grandfather from jail was not the end of my grandparents' nightmare. In 1949, Stalin's so-called anti-cosmopolitan campaign was directed against the Jewish intelligentsia. My grandfather, a Sorbonne graduate with a postgraduate degree from the Moscow Medical Faculty, was fired from his position and denied the right to practise or teach medicine. He was unemployed for years, desperately seeking work in provincial towns. With the 'white robes affair' in 1953, in which doctors, principally Jewish, were accused of wanting to kill Stalin and other Communist leaders, my grandfather was in great danger of being arrested again.

Possibly worst of all, my grandparents were trapped, unable to contemplate ever being released to the West. How they blamed themselves for their youthful folly! Even though the threats to their lives diminished somewhat after Stalin's death, they were to be forever affected by the fear of arrest and the loss of family members. They had no illusions left about the Soviet system and no hope for the future. They lived in the Soviet Union until they were able to leave for Australia in 1982.

Growing up in Moscow in the 1960s and 1970s and seeing my grandparents' rejection of everything Soviet, I tried to understand what had caused them, years earlier, to be drawn to the Soviet Union, even going so far as to become spies. They gave me different explanations. 'We were Communists!' said my grandmother, as if this were self-explanatory. My more reflective grandfather elaborated on how they had pictured the Soviet Union from afar in those days. He spoke of being affected by the romantic side of the Revolution; he recalled the pathos of Soviet films such as *Battleship Potemkin* and *Chapayev*, whose heroes gave their lives to create a better world. My grandfather and his left-wing friends believed that a more just world was coming into existence in the Soviet Union. Their dream was to help build this new and better world, thus hastening what Paul Vaillant-Couturier, the Communist writer, called *les lendemains qui chantent*.

My grandparents were unanimous on one aspect: that despite being attracted to the Soviet Union and being members of the Communist Party, they had never volunteered to spy. However, their desire to help the Soviet Union was exploited. Pressure came partly from the French Communist Party (FCP) and partly from agencies and individuals whom they never named because they had been sworn to secrecy. My grandparents never spoke of their experiences and, even in old age, they only hinted at isolated episodes from their past.

The story of my grandparents' involvement with the Soviet Union is not unique. Many of their friends – Polish, French, German and Austrian – shared their history. Moreover, as well as these ordinary young people, the greatest Western intellectuals gravitated towards Communism in the 1920s and 1930s and gave support to the Soviet Union. I have known the names of those who were seen as having been the Soviet Union's great friends in the West since childhood: the British writers H.G. Wells and George Bernard Shaw, the American Theodore Dreiser, and the Germans Heinrich Mann and Lion Feuchtwanger. The largest group were the French writers, whose names were known to every Soviet reader: Anatole France, Henri Barbusse, Romain Rolland, Louis Aragon and Elsa Triolet. In the Soviet Union, these writers were revered and their works, translated into Russian, could be found in people's homes and in every Soviet library.

As I was growing up, I found it difficult to understand why these leading intellectuals had been attracted to the USSR. Why were intelligent individuals seized by the religious fervour of neophytes, refusing to tolerate any evidence which suggested that their picture of the Soviet Union might not be accurate? How could they have promoted and blindly supported what is now known to be a lie, a myth? Didn't they know what Stalin was doing? Hadn't they heard about the famine in the 1930s, the arrests and trials, the deportations and executions? Unbelievably, they seemed to be ignorant of the fact that the Soviet Union was a repressive and, indeed, a criminal regime. Worse, they had legitimised it by lending it their names and defending it in their own countries. In order to understand the nature of Western intellectuals' involvement with the USSR, I began to research these relationships. Later, this became the subject of my Masters and then my PhD thesis.

I discovered a large volume of literature on the subject. David Caute, Paul Hollander, Tony Judt and other historians have examined the reasons for the attraction of Western intellectuals to the Soviet Union. The historical roots lie in the tradition of the French Revolution, the pursuit of *liberté, égalité, fraternité*. Contemporary circumstances also made them receptive. Following World War I, Western intellectuals were demoralised and bitter. They felt alienated from a society based on social inequality and an ineffectual parliamentary system, and during the Depression they became even more disillusioned. Their real fear, however, was of a rise of Fascism all over Europe and the threat of war emanating from Nazi Germany.

Against this backdrop, the existence of the Soviet Union inspired hope. In the 1920s, Paul Langevin called the Russian Revolution 'the first realisation of hopes for universal liberation'; by the 1930s, the Soviet Union came to represent, in Stephen Spender's words, 'a struggle of light against darkness'. In the 1920s, these observations stirred Western intellectuals to defend the first socialist state; in the 1930s, they viewed the Soviet Union as the only moral and military stronghold against Fascism. Beyond this, the Soviet Union in the 1930s represented a new, superior, civilisation. It was the land of the Five-Year Plan, industrialisation, collectivisation and unparalleled social reforms, and its programmes for universal literacy and full employment, free medicine and child protection seemed without parallel in Western countries. The Soviet Union, the promised land of socialism, also seemed to revolutionise the idea of culture; culture became a vital element of life, and artists and writers an integral part of society. The Soviet Union had already given the world avant-garde in film by Eisenstein, theatre by Meyerhold and literature by Mayakovsky, and had realised the town-planning and design dreams of Walter Gropius and the Bauhaus. André Gide, inspired by the cultural opportunities offered in the Soviet Union, spoke for many other intellectuals when he proclaimed, 'The fate of culture, from now on, depends on the USSR. We shall defend it.'

And they certainly did. Throughout the 1920s and 1930s, Western intellectuals promoted, defended and justified the USSR against hostile opinion and diplomatic isolation. Reading the press of that time, I found countless statements, articles and appeals by Henri Barbusse and Romain Rolland in defence of the Soviet Union. I unearthed numerous accounts of Louis Aragon, André Gide and many others defending the Soviet Union at public rallies and international congresses. I read accounts by Louis Fischer and H.G. Wells of their trips to the USSR, in which they conveyed the greatness of the Soviet experiment. In the American John Reed Clubs and the British Left Book Club, Mike Gold, Victor Gollancz and Sidney Webb promoted Soviet civilisation as being superior.

I also discovered – and this came as a surprise – that many sympathisers tended to publicise only positive information while overlooking or suppressing the negative. Some simply lied. In the early to mid-1930s, Walter Duranty and G.B. Shaw publicly denied that the USSR had experienced devastating famine. Bloch and Rolland excused the lack of political freedoms. Paul Robeson and Lion Feuchtwanger were fooled by the official Soviet version of the 1936–37 show trials and condoned the subsequent executions. I was shocked to discover that Western writers had conducted orchestrated campaigns against fellow intellectuals who criticised the USSR. The Communists hounded Panaït Istrati in the French press, and writers of various orientations tried to prevent André Gide from publishing his critical *Return from the USSR*. André Malraux cynically refused to discredit the USSR because it was helping the Republicans during the Spanish Civil War. Some intellectuals justified the 1939 Molotov–Ribbentrop Non-Aggression Pact between the Soviet Union and Nazi Germany and the 1940 Soviet invasion of Finland. This seemed even more shocking to me because it showed that they supported not some set of principles for which the Soviet state might have been believed to stand but the interests of that state itself.

Support of the Soviet Union from the opinion leaders Theodore Dreiser and George Bernard Shaw, the physicists Paul Langevin and Frédéric Joliot-Curie, and the politicians Edouard Herriot and Sidney Webb inspired a great number of other supporters, drawn mainly from the ranks of the liberal professions. The extent of the intelligentsia's involvement with the USSR during this time was unprecedented. It happened not only in France, where intellectuals had a tradition of political involvement known as *engagement*, but also in England, where intellectuals had previously dissociated themselves from public life and politics; in this period, they considered themselves as, to quote Stephen Spender, 'honorary French intellectuals'. After 1933, many German and Austrian intellectuals had been forced into exile and quite a few found refuge in France, for example Walter Benjamin, Heinrich Mann and Lion Feuchtwanger. The headquarters of the KPD, the German Communist Party, was located in Paris from 1933 to 1935, when it moved to Moscow, and it was in France that Willi Münzenberg worked on the German Popular Front with non-Communist intellectuals. Consequently, France became a home for and centre of European involvement with the Soviet Union.

The enchantment of left-wing Western intellectuals with the Soviet Union has been described at length in fiction and in the non-fiction works *Homage to Catalonia*, *The God that Failed* and *Darkness at Noon*. However, after years of extensive research in the 1980s, I felt that there was more to this enchantment than had been documented. I knew that the Soviet system must have played a considerable part in seducing Western intellectuals and turning them into supporters and I had no doubt that Western intellectuals had been used and manipulated, but how? There was no evidence documenting the ways in which this had been achieved.

The collapse of the USSR and the opening of the Soviet archives gave me a chance to look for answers. My most significant finding was that support from Western intellectuals was not always spontaneous and that the Soviet Union had indeed influenced and manipulated intellectuals for its own benefit. I could now identify the mechanisms by which Western intellectuals had been led to accept the Soviet myth and to act as they did. My work in the Moscow archives between 1995 and 2004 led me to discover the methods by which the Soviet Union had attracted large parts of the Western intelligentsia and guided their sympathies into actions for the benefit of the USSR. Just as importantly, I discovered that the common perception that their actions were idealistic and disinterested was no more than a myth.

Initially, in 1919–20, the individual leaders – Lenin, Trotsky, Zinov'yev – acted in an unfocussed way regarding propaganda matters. Around 1923–26, major organisations began to develop cultural methods to add to the existing apparatus of political propaganda; the main goal was to gain the sympathies of the Western intelligentsia. These organisations included: the Comintern or Third Communist International; the Russian Communist Party or RKP(b); and the body representing the Soviet state, the All-Union Central Executive Committee or TsIK. I found the evidence for this development in the Comintern records kept at the former Communist Party Archives (RGASPI),[1] and in the records of TsIK in the State Archive of the Russian Federation (GARF),[2] then only recently opened.

Ironically, these organisations had conflicting goals. The Comintern, the highest body of international Communist parties, had its headquarters in, and was dominated by, Moscow; it wished to destabilise Western regimes through subversion and revolutionary actions. At the same time, the Soviet state (represented by TsIK) tried to gain recognition in the West and to establish diplomatic and trade relations. Comintern leaders such as the Hungarians Bela Kun and Bela Illesh, who worked in Moscow, openly proposed propaganda techniques in their reports and correspondence. Meanwhile, anonymous Soviet state bureaucrats only hinted at the exercise of the Soviet political influence under the cover of cultural relations. Regardless of the differences, these organisations shared the basic strategy of seducing foreign intellectuals and surreptitiously leading them to act in a way that would benefit the USSR. The German writer Johannes Becher summed up the deception:

> These writers have to be governed in such a way that they don't feel that there may be directives from Moscow. . . . they have to be influenced in such a way that they say what we want to hear.

As I discovered, the actual work on the ground of engaging and influencing Western intellectuals, and finally leading them into action, was delegated to smaller 'cultural' organisations that were created for that purpose. Three of these organisations seemed particularly important: the International Association of Revolutionary Writers (MORP), the All-Union Society for Cultural Relations with Foreign Countries (VOKS) and the Foreign Commission of the Praesidium of the Soviet Writers' Union. All three organisations involved themselves with writers and other intellectuals whose political views ranged from 'left bourgeois' to Communist. I could see that these 'cultural' organisations operated differently; they used different methods and, consequently, obtained different results, even from the same targets. For example, when two or three organisations targeted Henri Barbusse, Romain Rolland and Lion Feuchtwanger, each organisation had its own way of treating the same writer.

MORP was established 'from below' by revolutionary writers, most of whom were not Russian but who lived in the USSR. They wished to create the literary branch of the Comintern, Litintern. Initially called the International Bureau of Revolutionary Literature (1926), it was renamed in 1930.[3] Among these founding writers were the Poles Bruno Yasensky and Stanislaw Liudkiewicz, the Germans Alfred Kurella and Johannes Becher, and the Hungarian Antal Hidas. These writers, forced into exile for their revolutionary activities, acted in a dogmatic and coercive way towards their peers, other Communist and pro-Communist writers in their home countries. They were unforgiving of any ideological deviation and, in the late 1920s, implemented the party line of 'class against class'.

MORP tried to create national branches in order to engage foreign revolutionary writers in different countries and to bring them into line with Soviet policies and agendas. In Germany, this branch was called the League of Proletarian Revolutionary Writers (BPRS, 1928) and in France, the Association of Revolutionary Writers and Artists (AEAR, 1932). In America, MORP took over the John Reed Clubs, an existing network of writers' associations, and proclaimed them MORP branches. The writers in these organisations, under pressure from MORP, were to produce ideological materials in support of the USSR and publish them in both the Soviet multilingual journal *International Literature* (*Internatsional'naya literatura*)[4] and the foreign Communist press such as the French *l'Humanité*, the German *Rote Fahne* and the British *Daily Worker*.

MORP's ideological rigidity was counterproductive. Through the records of its meetings, I could see that it was both unable and unwilling to engage uncommitted writers. What is more, it alienated old allies. Its attempts to manipulate and control writers were effective with younger writers such as Louis Aragon or with those who, like Jean Fréville, already shared MORP's goals. MORP failed to dominate eminent writers, for example Rolland and Barbusse, and instead drove them away. In 1932–34, the Soviet Union's political goals changed and it urgently needed to engage a broader circle of uncommitted writers in order to create a united anti-Fascist front; however, MORP was unable to adopt a more tolerant approach and became ineffective. To make the situation worse, MORP's patron, the Comintern, was losing its political strength. As a result, MORP was closed in 1935.

In contrast to MORP, the All-Union Society of Cultural Relations with Foreign Countries, or VOKS, targeted the non-Communist intelligentsia. For this reason, it adopted an entirely different *modus operandi*.[5] Founded in 1925 'from above' by the RKP(b) and TsIK,[6] VOKS was given a monopoly on Soviet relations with foreign intelligentsia. VOKS claimed to do no more than establish cultural relations and tried not to be seen to be associated with either the Soviet government or the Communist movement. Its archival documents, however, prove that it pursued the same goals as the Comintern but by more sophisticated means. VOKS developed subtle methods of enticing potential sympathisers. It acted as a helpful and hospitable organisation supplying information about the USSR to foreigners and inviting them to visit and discover 'the truth about the USSR'. VOKS's activities were supported by the People's Commissariat of Foreign Affairs (NKID), including personal support from its Commissar, Maxim Litvinov.

The heart and soul of VOKS's operations in the 1920s was Olga Kameneva, its first Chair (1925–29), Lev Trotsky's sister and Lev Kamenev's ex-wife. I could find almost no information about her outside of the VOKS archives and my impressions of her are based on the letters she wrote to her staff and colleagues. Well connected to the leading figures in the Soviet government, the Bolshevik Party and the Comintern, Kameneva was a person of political flair, energy, initiative and confident decision-making. She inspired VOKS's strategies and operations and was personally involved in the process of establishing a network of Western intellectual support. She operated from her Moscow headquarters, which was nicknamed 'the Kameneva Institute' by Walter Benjamin. Its departments and sectors were staffed by bilingual officers in charge of foreign countries (*referenty*) and by interpreter/guides. She personally supervised VOKS's plenipotentiary representatives abroad (*upolnomochennyy*), who were usually diplomats from the Soviet embassies (and thus NKID employees). The correspondence among the VOKS staff provided me with an insight into previously unknown VOKS operations and tactics.

One of Kameneva's central goals was to identify individual Western intellectuals who were susceptible to becoming Soviet 'conduits of influence' (*provodniki nashego vliyaniya*). From my research, it appears that Kameneva used two tactics to manipulate them. One, her pet project, was to create a network of Cultural Rapprochement Societies in foreign countries. On the surface, they existed to screen Soviet films and perform Soviet music, and to be supplied with what seemed to be informative materials about the USSR. Kameneva seemed to interfere in the running of these societies, although this could be attributed to her enthusiasm. Her second tactic was to bring intellectuals to the USSR, apparently for the enjoyment of Soviet hospitality and sightseeing. The writers Georges Duhamel and Theodore Dreiser were invited in 1927 for the tenth anniversary celebrations of the October Revolution and I found no evidence of any demands made on them.

After Hitler came to power and with the rise of pro-Soviet feelings in the West, the extent of VOKS's operations increased dramatically. It was at this time that Aleksandr Arosev, a former diplomat, was appointed Chair of VOKS (1934–37).[7] Arosev's active nature and his contacts with foreigners were right for the time. He had previously worked in France and other European countries; he personally knew Romain Rolland, Albert Marquet and Maurice Ravel and encouraged their visits to the USSR. Arosev believed in developing flexible and unobtrusive methods of propaganda;[8] he especially emphasised the reception of foreigners and saw himself as a 'hospitable and smiling' *maître d'hôtel*.[9]

Indeed, by then, VOKS's hospitality had grown to be a sizeable industry that

effectively attracted, encouraged, seduced, influenced and rewarded foreign intellectuals. VOKS perfected the art of hospitality; it developed standard activity
and sightseeing programmes and, in the case of eminent intellectuals, individual
plans that would appeal to their personal interests. Visitors were offered luxurious
accommodation and travel including holidays on the Black Sea and sightseeing
trips. They were honoured by the Soviet government and fellow intellectuals, their
literary works were translated into Russian and published in runs of hundreds of
thousands, and they were invited to address large audiences of admirers. Before
leaving the Soviet Union, the visitors usually gave appreciative interviews. On
their return home, they issued enthusiastic statements (like Albert Marquet) or
made impassioned appeals in defence of the USSR (like Romain Rolland). André
Malraux's participation in congresses also resulted from a trip, as did Sidney and
Beatrice Webb's activities in the British Society for Cultural Relations with the
USSR. These varied forms of support were all a clear result of VOKS's influence.

VOKS's decline began in 1936. The USSR had developed into a strong industrial and military power and the Soviet leadership relied less and less on support from the West.[10] The atmosphere of fear and the arrests and trials made it
dangerous for Soviet citizens to have relationships with foreigners. Following
the NKVD's calls for vigilance, Arosev encouraged suspicion and denunciations
among VOKS employees. Interpreter/guides, whom Arosev described as 'barrage
detachments' (*zagraditel'nyye otryady*), were held responsible for the opinions
and actions of visitors in their charge. Arosev instructed them to fill what had
been proforma reports with 'more literary fiction' (*pobol'she belletristiki*). None
of these changes was obvious on the surface and, in 1937–39, VOKS managed
to organise further successful visits from such important guests as the sociologist
Georges Friedmann, the publisher Victor Gollancz, the writer Lion Feuchtwanger
and the linguist Marcel Cohen.

Around 1937, as the stream of foreign visitors began to slow down, a third
cultural organisation influenced relations between Western writers and the Soviet
Union. The Foreign Commission of the Soviet Writers' Union, created in 1935 to
replace MORP, picked up many of the contacts previously established by MORP
and VOKS and maintained them using a new method, correspondence. I found the
files of the Foreign Commission at the Russian State Archives of Literature and
Art (RGALI) in Moscow.[11]

The Foreign Commission built its approach on VOKS's tactics of non-coercive
relations and it turned subtle influence into a fine art. It encouraged personal ties
with Western intellectuals, showering them with favours and gifts in the hope
of being repaid at some stage. Its Chair, the literary bureaucrat Mikhail Apletin,
who had previously worked for both MORP and VOKS, developed the art of
charming and friendly service even further. He corresponded with foreign writers,
sent them birthday cards and gifts, praised and flattered them, arranged publication of their works and let them know about their popularity within the Soviet
Union. He encouraged them to correspond with Soviet writers and created an
illusion of genuine friendship. These illusions and favours, sustained entirely by

an exchange of letters, brought about warm relationships with Western writers and scholars such as André Malraux, Georges Friedmann, Jean-Richard Bloch and others. The Western writers felt loyal, indebted and dependent; indeed, they provided a variety of services and favours in return.

The 1939 Ribbentrop–Molotov Pact, followed by the 1940 Soviet invasion of Finland, marked the end of a chapter during which Soviet cultural organisations had stage-managed support from Western intellectuals. Many long-term supporters, such as Paul Langevin and Joliot-Curie and the Communist writer Paul Nizan, broke with the USSR, shocked by its betrayal of the international anti-Fascist movement. However, some other eminent supporters, for example Rolland, Malraux and Gollancz, although deeply troubled and disapproving, never publicly condemned the USSR. A minority of others, such as Aragon and Bloch, remained unconditionally loyal. At the end of World War II, when the victorious Soviet Union decided to re-establish relations with the Western intellectual world, this handful of writers made it possible to mend the broken links and open a new chapter in the history of Western intellectuals' support of the Soviet Union.

1 The Soviet myth and Western intellectuals

From attraction to action

> Now, the fire from Moscow. From now on, within each man there is an inner dialogue in which Moscow is inevitably one of the interlocutors.
>
> Pierre Drieu La Rochelle

The signing of the Non-Aggression Pact between the USSR and Nazi Germany in August 1939 produced a cataclysm among supporters of the Soviet Union in the West. Overnight, the Soviet-led anti-Fascist front was no more and Western intellectuals' faith in the USSR collapsed. For many, this meant the end of almost two decades of involvement with the Soviet Union, a time of loyalty and uncritical support. Today, we need to understand why Western intellectuals had been so enthusiastic about the Soviet Union and trusted it so much. What made them believe that the Soviet Union represented a society of the future, a society culturally and politically superior to the West and the only hope against Fascism? We need to understand not only why Western intellectuals were held captive by this attractive and unrealistic myth but also why they helped to promote it. Cultural discourse played an important part in their seduction and in the way they helped to perpetuate this myth. How then was this myth constructed and how, under its sway, did Western intellectuals defend the Soviet Union in the 1920s and 1930s?

First images of Russia

In the first few years after the October Revolution, Western perceptions of the new Russia were mixed. Russia was remembered as it used to be under the Tsars, poor and backward, yet at the same time impressions of a new Russia began to trickle in, brought by a handful of Western visitors. Their impressions differed considerably. Lincoln Steffens may have said in 1919 'I have seen the future and it works', but, a year later, Bertrand Russell pessimistically described his trip to Russia as a 'continually increasing nightmare'.[1]

Although getting to Russia in those years was difficult, if not dangerous, and life there harsh, travellers' tales had a distinct tendency to be sympathetic. After the publication of John Reed's 1919 best-seller, *Ten Days that Shook the World*, other supportive eye-witness accounts followed: articles such as 'What we saw in Russia' by French Communist leaders M. Cachin and L.-O. Frossard[2] and books such as *And the Last Fight Let Us Face (Six Months in Soviet Russia)* by Madeleine Marx.[3] Sympathy towards Russia even generated a stream of pulp fiction such as *Verochka* by Francis Carco, *Ma Petite Bolchévique* by Moussa de Courtial and *L'Amour en Russie* by Claude Anet.

A desire to help Russia survive civil war, foreign intervention and famine stirred Western intellectuals into action. At public rallies and meetings, they roused large audiences with passion and pathos; they used language that was persuasive, if not openly propagandist. Public addresses were inspired by both the underlying images of pre-revolutionary 'Holy Russia' and the suffering of the post-revolutionary Russian people. A natural disaster, the 1919–22 Volga famine, fitted this image. At a public rally, Paul Vaillant-Couturier made an impassioned appeal for people to come to the aid of Russia. In his speech, the famine became a symbol of the self-sacrifice made by the Russian people for a better future for all humankind.

> This great people is suffering ills of all kinds for the betterment of humanity. During my recent journey to Moscow, the Russians shared with me their hope of seeing their suffering help in the triumph of Communism.[4]

In those days, when the spoken word was often as influential as periodicals in shaping opinion, rallies in France drew audiences of thousands. Public gatherings in support of Russia extended from the working-class 'red belt' of Paris to the notoriously right-wing military school of Saint-Cyr, and from the cultured Salle des Sociétés Savantes to bourgeois Versailles. Fridtjof Nansen's conference on the famine, held in Paris on 17 February 1922, drew an audience of 5,000. At the conference, a film on the Volga region was screened and *L'Album de la Famine,* a collection of photographs with an introduction by Anatole France, was on sale.[5]

Sympathetic public opinion was mobilised through committees and organisations. These committees and organisations became so numerous that, in 1921–23, the French police created a file called *Comités et Organisations pour l'Aide à la Russie.*[6] Committee leaders often invited illustrious figures to join them as celebrity attractions. The very first appeal for aid launched by the Soviet government was written by Maxim Gorky. The Red Cross engaged the support of the living legend, Anatole France, who issued the rallying cry 'Au secours des enfants russes!'[7] Willi Münzenberg, a brilliant propagandist and entrepreneur, assembled a German committee 'to protect the Soviet experience and assure its survival'. His committee included intellectuals and artists, among them Albert Einstein and Käthe Kollwitz. Within two months, Münzenberg's Committee was sending a boatload of food supplies to Russia.

Another widespread idea, frequently voiced in appeals and speeches, was that revolutionary terror was unavoidable to ensure the survival of the Revolution and the Republic – a distinct mindset inherited from the French Revolution. Henri

Barbusse, the pacifist and author of *Under Fire*, had no misgivings about defending the brutal methods of the 'dictatorship of Reason'.

> Not only are they right in their orthodoxy, they are also right to impose their authoritarian means. The men in Moscow were right, if indeed they did so, to maintain by force, for the past three years, the dictatorship of Reason. Every revolution imposes a constitution by force . . .
> They are right in saying that if you want to abolish classes you should want to impose a dictatorship of the proletariat. To believe that there is a different way of realising social equality for all is not only naive but criminal.[8]

Non-Communists also supported revolutionary terror. Edouard Herriot, the mayor of Lyon, visited the USSR in 1922. Two years later, as Chairman of the Council of the French government, Herriot would engineer recognition of the USSR by France; in 1922, he publicly justified the existing system in the context of Russia's historic social inequality and injustice.[9]

In the mid- to late 1920s, more diverse and attractive images of a new, developing Russia began to spread.

The birth of the Soviet cultural myth

Russian scholar Efim Etkind once referred to Soviet culture in the 1920s and 1930s as a distorting mirror (*krivoye zerkalo*) that the Western intelligentsia had mistaken for an accurate reflection of Soviet reality. Indeed, the Western intelligentsia took a keen interest in Soviet literature and arts, partly because they saw it, to quote Paul Nizan, as a 'tool of knowledge' (*instrument de connaissance*) of Soviet society.[10] Unable to distinguish between reality and fiction and particularly sensitive to cultural issues, Western intellectuals constructed a cultural myth of the Soviet Union. They both were subject to this myth and helped to promote it.

Soviet culture began to reach the West in about the mid-1920s, shortly after the end of the Civil War and the introduction of the New Economic Policy. The Soviet works of art that became known in the West reinforced memories of the 1905–10 Russian avant-garde, familiar to Western viewers of the *Ballets russes* and Stanislavsky's theatre. At the 1925 Paris International Exhibition of Decorative Arts, the Soviet Union attracted much attention with its strikingly original pavilion by Melnikov, Aleksandr Rodchenko's avant-garde photography, and El Lissitzky's constructivist posters. Later, Meyerhold's and Tairov's experimental theatres and films by Eisenstein, Pudovkin and Vertov drew an enthusiastic response from the left-wing intelligentsia.

Growing interest in the Soviet Union was reflected in reviews and articles that appeared daily in the USA in the general periodicals *New York Evening Post* and *New Masses* and the literary *New York Times Book Review* and *Books Abroad*. The French Communist *l'Humanité* regularly featured articles about Soviet cultural life and published excerpts by Soviet writers in its regular columns *La vie intel-*

lectuelle and *Les littératures étrangères*. As well as the Communist and left-wing press, periodicals such as the British *New Statesman and Nation* and the French *NRF* also wrote about Soviet cultural life.

Periodicals of the time featured notices announcing forthcoming Soviet books, concerts and talks about Russia. Articles and reviews by Western and Soviet authors praised Soviet literature and art for its artistic achievement. 'Whenever we could,' recalled British writer Stephen Spender,

> we went to see those Russian films which were shown often in Berlin at this period: *Earth, The General Line, The Mother, Potemkin, Ten Days that Shook the World, The Way into Life*, etc. These films . . . excited us because they had the modernism, the poetic sensibility, the satire, the visual beauty, all those qualities we found most exciting in other forms of modern art, but they also conveyed a message of hope.[11]

Not all of the products of Russian culture were met with equal interest. The classics – Turgenev, Dostoyevsky, Tolstoy and Chekhov – were still translated and read for their timeless value but they also stood for the Russia of the past, as did the Russian émigré writers. The left-wing intelligentsia avoided the *grande dame* of émigré literature, Zinaïda Hippius, and the future Nobel Prize winner Ivan Bunin. Even Stanislavsky's Moscow Art Theatre was now regarded as old-fashioned and conventional. 'This theatrical art has dated, as has Chekhov's dramatic art,' wrote the literary critic Boris de Schloetzer.[12] The audience wanted the new art of the new Russia.

The up-and-coming Soviet literature included a mixture of high-quality works by Blok, Zamyatin, Babel and Pil'nyak, and works by second- or third-rate authors, many of whom have long since been forgotten: Gladkov, Serafimovich, Panferov. Films of popular appeal, such as *Chapayev* (1934, Vasil'yev brothers), were screened alongside intellectual cinematic masterpieces by Eisenstein and Dziga Vertov. These works were mostly inspired by the Revolution and, later, by socialist construction and labour.

It is intriguing to consider the picture of the Soviet Union created by these Soviet cultural artefacts and the way in which they were interpreted by both little-known reviewers and major writers. Assuming that works of fiction were accurate documents, reviewers praised Protazanov's film *Polikushka* for painting a picture of destitution in pre-revolutionary Russia, and *Peter the Great* for depicting the first national hero. Reviewers were enthusiastic about films and novels depicting the Revolution and the Civil War – *Chapayev*, A. Tolstoy's *The Road to Calvary*, A. Neverov's *Tashkent, City of Bread* – but also saw them as documentary chronicles of Russia's tragic yet heroic times. Ilya Ehrenburg was one of the favourite writers because of his quasi-documentary style. 'A good novel. And a good documentary,' wrote Pierre Abraham,[13] comparing Ehrenburg to a modern-day Balzac. Indeed, Western writers read Soviet fiction as preparation for their trips to the USSR: André Gide based his ideas of Soviet society on Ehrenburg's *The Second Day of Creation*,[14] and Jean-Richard Bloch on Sholokhov's *Virgin Lands*

Upturned.[15] After all, Bloch had already said that he treated history as a novel, and the novel as historical material.[16]

The absolute favourites of both audiences and reviewers were stories inspired by the Revolution and the Civil War. Reviews, particularly French, were full of praise for these books and films. Victor Shklovsky's *Sentimental Journey* was said to be 'a moving and impartial history of the Russian Revolution', and the string of epithets that unfailingly followed the all-time favourite *Chapayev* said more about what the audience looked for in a film than it said about the film itself. *Chapayev* was called 'an authentic masterpiece', 'the crown of the Russian cinema', 'a great, moving and heroic film'; it was declared to 'have a soul'.[17] It made a very strong impression on Gide.

One of the common beliefs generated by Soviet art and culture was that the Russian Revolution, like the 1789 French Revolution, had produced a new culture and rejuvenated the nation. This idea was particularly dear to intellectuals. They compared Russia with their own decaying 'old world', which they contrasted with the technologically advanced American civilisation and the culturally superior Communist one. A common perception was that Soviet art and culture were leading the world. Film represented the avant-garde more than any other art form. André Malraux, modernist writer, art historian and a future Minister for Culture, wrote, 'Isn't it true that the real expression of Communist art is not literature but film?'[18] British writers of the 1930s welcomed the aesthetics of mechanisation and found that 'Sovkino techniques were precisely poetry's way forward'.[19]

Sergey Eisenstein was particularly in vogue. Once his *Battleship Potemkin* had been banned in a number of European countries for its subversive influence, it was impossible to get a seat at the club screenings run by left-wing and Communist circles. 'There is not an educated mind in France that would not be aware of the productions of this director, undeniably one of the first in today's world,' wrote the major literary journal *NRF.*[20] Eisenstein was recognised as a director who altered the traditional role of the cinema in Western society by introducing 'the incomparably expressive medium reviled by the bourgeois economy'.[21] His influence on intellectuals was immense. The German theatre director Erwin Piscator wanted to incorporate excerpts from the still unfinished *October* into one of his stage productions. Walter Benjamin spoke of the major influence Eisenstein's *montage* had had on his conceptual thinking.

Another popular icon was the Soviet writer and artist; he was believed to be nothing like the decadent bourgeois Western intellectual. Like Gorky, this composite Soviet writer overcame his destitute background and the hardships of pre-revolutionary Russia. Like Shklovsky and Babel, he fought in the Revolution and the Civil War. Like Mayakovsky, he worked for the creation of the new society as a technician, a labourer of the Revolution, and like Ostrovsky, the author of *How Steel was Tempered*, he sacrificed his health and even life itself to build a new society.

> One does not hesitate to identify Ostrovsky with his hero . . . We know that Ostrovsky, worn out and sick, lost his sight, the use of his arm and his legs,

and then of the other arm. Only then did he become a writer, so that he could continue to serve his cause. In effect, his autobiographical book is at once narrative and action.[22]

In the minds of Western intellectuals, the ultimate appeal of being a Soviet writer was his unprecedented, privileged place in society. After all, Stalin himself proclaimed writers to be 'the engineers of the human soul'. 'The proletarian revolution gives writers, artists and scholars their dignity by breaking the hypocritical slavery of neutrality in art and science,' declared Vaillant-Couturier.[23] What could be closer to the hearts of Western intellectuals, particularly French and German, who aspired to be seen as educators and advisers by society? Eminent Western writers echoed this notion. 'Never has a great writer played a more exalted role,' wrote Romain Rolland on Gorky's death. 'It is as if he were in charge of literature, the arts and sciences in the USSR, their mentor, their most severe judge and their defender.'[24] Rolland even attributed a role to Gorky in the creation of the 1936 Soviet Constitution ('to which his ideas most certainly must have contributed').

Ilya Ehrenburg, who had lived in France since 1910 and become part of the Parisian intellectual elite, helped to shape this exalted idea of the artist.[25] His work was translated and published across Europe, and he dedicated his *The Second Day of Creation* to André Gide, 'a great writer and a great man'. In the West, Ehrenburg spoke of his own experiences as a mentor to the younger generation of Soviet people, his responsibility towards them and the educational value young people derived from literature. 'Our young people . . . have a particular love for literature. For them, a writer is more than a man who writes novels. He is an older comrade, a friend and a teacher who can teach them how to live.'[26]

In the late 1920s and particularly the 1930s, as official literature and art began to take over the artistic 'Great Experiment' and with socialist realism looming as the only officially accepted artistic method, reviewers became more critical. The Soviet cinema in 1930 was found by Simone de Beauvoir and her friends to be bland and simplistic. 'We regretted not finding this complexity in Russian film any more. It became completely didactic, and we carefully avoided films glorifying collective farms.'[27] Gide was bored by Gladkov's *Cement*, and the literature of the 1930s added nothing to the appeal that the USSR held for him.

The ubiquitous propaganda was one of the major disillusionments. 'This propaganda is childish; . . . I really wish Russian film could be more independent of this propaganda,'[28] wrote an *NRF* critic. 'You cannot even describe as propaganda a story that, above all, can do no more than preach to the converted,'[29] commented another. The lack of originality was even more disappointing. Serafimovich, Gladkov and even Gorky were criticised for oversimplification and the imitative nature of their writing. The same was true of film. 'But we were already familiar with their lighting effects, the camera lingering on the vast landscapes and those faces imaged as still lifes.'[30] Soviet artistic production was now considered repetitive and ineffective. 'The Russians no longer invent anything . . . . It's all the same . . . . The story doesn't touch us . . . . The pathos of it does not affect us.'[31]

Paradoxical as it may seem, this disenchantment actually expressed the Western audience's faith in Soviet civilisation. When the reviewers wrote, 'We expected more',[32] their disappointment stemmed from their high expectations of the USSR, 'a country that no longer has the right to mediocrity and cannot afford any flaws of taste'.[33] Andre Malraux, the sternest critic among friends, continued to acknowledge the unique criteria by which Soviet literature ought to be judged. 'The values which we apply to the Western European novel cannot be applied to the Soviet novel.'[34] While uncompromisingly critical of the very principle of socialist realism and the schematic nature of Soviet literature, Malraux excused these artistic weaknesses as being typical of a new society and reiterated the expectations of Soviet art in the West. 'The world expects of you not just the image of what you are, but of what outstrips you.'

I came, I saw, I was conquered: the USSR through visitors' eyes

In the late 1920s and 1930s, countless Western intellectuals travelled to the Soviet Union. 'The entire British intelligentsia has been to Russia this summer,'[35] wrote Kingsley Martin in 1932, with some exaggeration. The real peak of international pilgrimage to the 'Soviet Mecca' was reached in the mid-1930s, with as many as 200 intellectuals from France alone visiting Russia in 1935.

For Communists and fellow-travellers – non-party members sympathetic to the Communist cause – the trip to the USSR indeed had an air of sanctity about it. For the as yet unconverted, it was a quest for truth, 'a matter of intellectual integrity'.[36] The impact of the Soviet Union on foreigners was unlike that of any other country. 'I came back from the USSR a different man,' Aragon told his fellow American writers.[37] 'The spectacle of Soviet Russia has deeply moved me,' echoed Waldo Frank. 'Every modern must be moved by Russia as a man would be if he were faced with his own future.'[38]

Visits to the USSR inspired an outpouring of published and unpublished accounts. Fred Kupferman lists 125 French accounts from this period.[39] Louis Fischer alone published five books and countless articles in the American and international press. Visitors felt a need to document their trips and share their emotions, prompting them to write letters and diaries and to give interviews while in the Soviet Union. Many published articles, books and poems on their return home. In these writings they bore witness, preached, persuaded and posed as experts, even after short visits. They all wanted to find *le mot juste* about the Soviet Union.

Sympathetic accounts prevailed throughout most of the 1930s. The West was far more receptive to positive than to negative accounts of the USSR, and Marc Ferro comments on the creation of 'a wall of denial' towards any negative information.[40] Supporters, especially Communists, eagerly spread the word through public lectures and rallies, addresses at universities and participation in cultural societies. Paul Nizan went on a lecture tour of France. 'It was only fair to bear witness to what we had seen in order to show that we deserved this privilege . . . . He [Nizan] simply related the achievements we had seen,'[41] recalled Nizan's widow,

Henriette. But nothing compared with the neophytic zeal of those who became converted during a visit. 'I was determined to give my testimony about the USSR. Thus, I did not refuse a single invitation,'[42] wrote Jean-Richard Bloch on his return from Russia in January 1935. Bloch, who had been somewhat hesitant before going to Russia, displayed boundless enthusiasm during his trip and, according to Wolfgang Klein, represents a case of someone who became a believer.[43]

To show how these trips influenced Western intellectuals so strongly and shaped their perceptions, we will follow the journey of Jean-Richard Bloch and his wife Marguerite, who went to the USSR for the First Congress of the Soviet Writers' Union in August 1934. During their trip, both the Blochs wrote daily letters to their children, which remain unpublished and are kept in the Bibliothèque Nationale de France in Paris.[44] Known as *Journal du voyage en URSS*, these letters reflect the process by which Bloch, an influential figure in French left-wing intellectual circles, became politically involved and one of the most devoted supporters of the Soviet Union. Day by day and step by step, these letters reconstruct the events of the Blochs' trip and their responses to them. Stressing their public intention, Francis Cohen, the son of Bloch's best friend, Marcel Cohen, recalled 'They were written in order to be circulated.'[45] The detailed observations make this *Journal* an extremely valuable historical document and Marguerite Bloch's lively and humorous style provides enjoyable reading. It is understandable that the Blochs treasured their *Journal*. Before the Nazi invasion of France, they buried it under a tree near their country house, la Mérigote, near Poitiers. Though damaged by dampness and rodents, it was one of the very few of the Blochs' treasured possessions that survived the war.

J.-R. Bloch had not always been an active fellow-traveller. Although interested in the Soviet experiment, he avoided any direct political involvement with it in the mid- to late 1920s and was very critical of its politics in the early 1930s. However, Hitler's rise to power and the attempted Fascist coup in France on 6 February 1934 changed his views. The USSR once again became the object of his close consideration. When Ilya Ehrenburg, a self-appointed intermediary between the USSR and Western writers, invited Bloch to attend the Writers' Congress in Moscow, Bloch was keen to go. After all, it was a cultural and not a political occasion and all the eminent writers were going. With Malraux, Aragon, Pozner and Nizan, Bloch was one of five French delegates to the Congress; he was the oldest and possibly the most respected. On the eve of his departure, Bloch felt an 'immense affection' for the USSR although it was 'coupled with a strong critical wariness'. He was warned about pickpockets, and procrastination by Soviet officials delayed the visas, tickets and their departure.[46] However, in August, Bloch and his wife left for Moscow.

As soon as Jean-Richard and Marguerite Bloch entered the USSR, their caution evaporated. They were immediately won over by an unexpectedly warm and hospitable welcome. 'They do perform miracles for their guests,'[47] wrote Marguerite Bloch about their hosts in one of the first letters. A sleek, impressive, black Lincoln whisked the Blochs to the Metropol, 'a hotel for foreigners in all its glory', with their room more like a 'real nabob's quarters: a drawing room, a piano, a bathroom'.[48] The *camarades* took care of everything, including the trip, the welcome at the station and their stay.[49] 'We're not paying anything. . . . One is never treated so well as when one pays nothing.'

From the start, Jean-Richard Bloch was in the limelight. 'Papa is besieged by journalists,'[50] continued Marguerite. Newspapers publicised his visit and were filled with his photographs. Later, to illustrate their letters, the Blochs attached cuttings of articles and photographs from Soviet newspapers dedicated to the visit of the 'eminent French writer'. It was no wonder that, wherever he went, he was recognised by ordinary people, including inmates at the Bolshevo commune, a show penal colony.

> And he [an inmate] was a former thief, maybe a murderer, a simple worker at the Bolshevo factory, in a village 45 kilometres from Moscow. Quite extraordinary, is it not, as evidence of the general interest here, and the desire that they have developed in everyone to educate and better themselves.[51]

As with many other visitors, a combination of factors shaped the Blochs' impressions of the USSR. As well as the privileged treatment, there were numerous excursions and sightseeing tours. Not so interested in the 'extraordinary riches'[52] of the Kremlin, the Blochs preferred to visit places 'which make [the Soviets] the most proud and which one cannot miss', such as the Bolshevo commune for the re-education of young criminals or the construction of the Moscow Metro. To the Blochs, these sights represented the real Soviet society. Their tours were full of surprises. One discovery, particularly dear to the Blochs' hearts, was that education and culture formed part of every aspect of Soviet life. At the Park of Culture, along with the colourful flower beds, they saw 'a theatre, an enormous conference hall'; there were also 'geographic consultants . . . medical consultants, consultants on current German politics and economy, on the politics of Japan, legal consultants, musical ones'.[53] They were impressed to discover that the Red Army was not a place where young people were brutalised. At the barracks where the Blochs were taken, a charming general (*le naturel même*[54]) explained to them the educational role of the Army in forming the personalities of its soldiers. 'They have libraries, reading and writing halls, an orchestra, a theatre, but above all, outside the service, their superiors are their *tovarischi* [comrades], like everybody else.'

What Bloch saw confirmed what he had read about the USSR at home. One night, Ehrenburg took the Blochs to an unforgettable literary evening in the park. There, writers met their audience, 'peasants who only left their village a year ago' and were now labourers. Ehrenburg's novel *The Second Day of Creation* provoked an animated discussion, and the audience kept Ehrenburg back, questioning him avidly about both the heroes of his book and his impressions of France. Ehrenburg later told Bloch that 'this direct communication with the popular audience [was] the most significant [thing]' for him as a writer. 'Nothing can be more productive for a writer than this close contact with the masses,' Bloch said later in an interview for *l'Humanité*.[55]

The writer's unique role as a mentor in Soviet society was also fully in evidence at the Writers' Congress. Everybody seemed to follow the events of the Congress. The massive media coverage,[56] the spontaneous gathering of large crowds at its doors, the 'extraordinary delegations' of workers and peasants who attended[57] and the requests that they made for writers to create a particular type of literature that they needed all reinforced the Blochs' conviction of the seriousness with which Soviet society treated literature and writers.

From the things that they saw and people they met, the Blochs concluded that education and culture played a formative part in the creation of the new Soviet man, 'the product of the Revolution', often of humble origin and now a professional: 'a mining engineer, just a young woman',[58] a supervisor at the Metro construction site or a factory director.[59] Older people's consciousness was also transformed, with a volunteer supervisor of a canteen quoting Lenin: 'Every cook should know how to run the State.'[60] According to the Blochs' observations at the Congress, the regime made sure that ethnic minorities benefited from the 'civilising' effect of education; it treated them as part of a new Soviet nation and not as vestiges of an old multinational empire which had dominated and Russified them.

> Imagine the phenomena we see, such as a young Samoyed woman who, ten years ago, was a cannibal and now is doctor of philosophy at the Leningrad University. There is a Samoyed woman at the Central Committee. And they also translate Swift into Mordovian, which has the most backward population amongst all the Soviet republics.[61]

For the Blochs, Soviet culture and art were both inspirational and informative. They had already based their views of the USSR on Soviet books and films; now, the new films and plays that they saw confirmed their previous beliefs that these artistic constructions were 'real things . . . often as revealing as the truth'.[62] Their hosts organised many special film screenings for them, from a documentary on Chelyuskin's heroic exploits in the Arctic to Dovzhenko's *The Earth*, which the Blochs found 'extremely beautiful . . . in the great tradition of Soviet cinema'.[63] When the Theatre Festival followed the Writers' Congress, they attended plays by Meyerhold and Stanislavsky and, like many of their compatriots, were most passionate about Vishnevsky's *The Optimistic Tragedy*, a play about the Civil War.

Among the Blochs' letters there are original and unpublished photographs of Soviet and foreign writers at various Congress-related events: Malraux, Rafael Alberti, Ehrenburg, Babel and Lidin. These group photographs capture the festive atmosphere of the Congress and excursions, and serve to confirm how influential the company of others was to the way in which J.-R. Bloch responded to his stay in the Soviet Union. He immensely enjoyed being part of an international writers' brotherhood at the Congress, constantly stimulated and engaged in discussion and debate. No wonder his wife Marguerite wrote, 'Papa feels like a fish in a pond.'[64] The Blochs formed a close-knit community with the Aragons, the Nizans, the Malraux and the Moussinacs, eating, discussing and travelling together. All of this contributed to an atmosphere which Marguerite described as 'terribly intellectual'.[65]

Even more stimulating and engaging for Bloch was the company of the Soviet cultural elite. Many of them spoke French or German so communication was direct and spontaneous. 'God, there are so many intelligent people here!'[66] exclaimed Marguerite. Her list of people that they met – Babel, Sholokhov, Stanislavsky, Tret'yakov – is adorned with enthusiastic epithets. The Blochs had a 'very interesting' lunch with the Chair of VOKS, Aleksandr Arosev,[67] and were charmed by the Chairman of the Writers' Organising Committee, Mikhail Kol'tsov, a 'fantastic chap'.[68] Bloch spoke about art with Eisenstein, 'a man whose conversation is as good as his films',[69] and Meyerhold, 'an old revolutionary . . . in politics and art'.[70] Bloch felt welcome and included, as he was invited to stay on to make a film or write scripts. Indeed, for the next few months, Bloch explored the possibility of playing a personal part in this Great Experiment and spoke to film studios with a view to making a film.

Marguerite and Jean-Richard Bloch's *Journal* is more than a list of activities and impressions. More importantly, it reveals the influences that they encountered, their responses to the events of their stay and how these led Bloch directly to promote the USSR. His hosts, who took such good care of him and grew to be his friends, became a source of opinions he trusted unconditionally. What could be better than having Ehrenburg as a guide?[71] It was thanks to him that Bloch learned so much about Soviet cultural life, information that he would shortly present in *l'Humanité*. It was Tret'yakov, 'the most obliging man in the world',[72] who told Bloch about the goals of the second Five-Year Plan and industrialisation. This information, initially related in letters, found its way into Bloch's two articles for *Marianne*.[73] Their trust in the people around them naively led the Blochs to repeat opinions on matters about which they knew nothing. 'There are still prisons here,' wrote Marguerite Bloch, 'and despite everything, they are still not charming places. But I believe they are nothing like those in capitalist countries.'[74]

The effect of these influences on the Blochs was to make them see the failures of the socialist system as merely relative, and to misread the real reasons for these failures.[75] Thus, they quoted Ilya Ehrenburg to support their opinion that life in the Soviet Union had improved dramatically.

> When I see people laugh and sing, I am not used to it yet; I say to myself, 'It was worth it, no one is hungry, no one is in rags and everyone feels like dancing and singing. Two or three years ago, this wasn't the case.'[76]

Aragon's Russian wife, Elsa Triolet, 'with her pretty Russian accent and her charming smile',[77] confirmed this opinion: ' "Just think," said Elsa . . . , "two years ago all the shop windows were empty. There were endless queues in front of bread stores, and not one . . . ornament or even clothing for sale. Whereas now, the shops are filled with goods." '[78]

The Blochs' hosts, companions and Congress organisers all played their part in significantly misinterpreting the real historical causes of what the visitors saw. According to them, the Soviet Union was still overcoming the devastation of the revolutionary era. Poverty, starvation and even homeless children in the streets in 1934 were said to be remnants of the *ancien régime* and the Civil War which had ended thirteen years earlier. Readers of the Blochs' letters would never have suspected that the devastation was caused by forced collectivisation and the recent Great Famine. However, apart from being systematically misled, the Blochs' own wishful thinking was important in their interpretation of Soviet reality. What allowed the usually modest Blochs to enjoy their 'unbelievably comfortable situation' and be 'less bothered by it than [they would have been] elsewhere'?[79] Having been in the homes of Kol'tsov, the Congress organiser, and Meyerhold, who invited the Blochs for dinner, they concluded that the Soviet population, and especially writers, also lived well. We might have expected a more critical attitude, even after they were taken to Gorky's *dacha*, 'a small palace given to him by the government'.[80] Judging from their letters, one would conclude that they remained unaware of the crisis in housing and the actual living conditions of the rest of the population.[81] In the year when rationing ended, statements from the Blochs such as 'Moscow is really beginning to be well supplied'[82] were based on impressions made by the buffet at the opening of the Congress and by the endless banquets, including a feast of 'incredible luxury and abundance' organised for the visiting writers at Gorky's dacha.

Their letters often express, directly or indirectly, approval and justification of the Soviet system. Bloch approved of the ubiquity of official organisations and government officials that characterised his trip. For a French writer like Bloch, being a guest of the government was a privilege and another sign of the writer's high status in the USSR.[83] 'The highest authorities are going to receive us at the Kremlin on the 3rd. We are then being offered a trip to Leningrad, and the Armenian government has invited Mama and me to come and pay them a visit.'[84] The Blochs were thrilled and flattered when members of the government – Molotov, Voroshilov, Kaganovich, Bubnov, Bukharin, Radek and others – unexpectedly turned up at the writers' party at Gorky's country house. How naive Marguerite Bloch's description of the officials' arrival at the party 'with such simplicity, warmth and merriment, like children on holiday' seems today.[85] The Blochs did not see this intrusion as an indication of the state's hold over literature and the arts. On the contrary, they approved of the fact that 'everything comes from the top',[86] and Jean-Richard Bloch, that staunch defender of the writer's right to individualism, expressed admiration for the Communist Party's 'phenomenal' control and characterised as 'childish' the reactions of those who complained about the lack of freedom of the press.

On 17 September, Marguerite and Jean-Richard Bloch left Moscow for the Caucasus to witness, as the telegram of invitation from the Armenian government put it, the 'grandiose achievements' of the national republics.[87] They continued to be spoilt, like other foreign writers. While they were travelling to the Caucasus, Louis Aragon was offered treatment at a Black Sea spa, which would have been beyond his means at home in France,[88] and Paul Nizan travelled to Central Asia. Mikhail Kol'tsov provided the Blochs with his private railway carriage, which had a library, a study, a kitchen, a cook and two attendants. The carriage could be uncoupled so that the visitors could stop for a while along the way or even rejoin elsewhere if they wished to travel for a time by car.

The Blochs enjoyed travelling in style. They watched the countryside from the window of the train carriage, bought fruit from peasants at halts along the way and admired the spectacular beauty of the Caucasus from an open car. They also had time to digest their earlier impressions, reflect on the Soviet system and pass on their views in their letters. One major theme, which developed as the Blochs' trip progressed, was their admiration for socialist construction. 'It's an enormous construction site with extraordinary activity and unparalleled courage, where you can see the building grow taller from one hour to the next, but it is still a construction site. . . . Isn't building, though, the most beautiful thing?'[89]

The trip confirmed Bloch's belief in the creative role of the Soviet regime in the national republics. Backward Armenia was not on the margin of an empire dominated by the metropolis but a place with 'the most concentrated example of socialist construction'.[90] Jean-Richard Bloch noted the 'miraculous rebirth . . . of the Turkish [sic] desert, which they are currently transforming into a magnificent garden'.[91] He saw none of the aridity and misery that was the reality but admired the construction sites, the 'Babylonian foundations'[92] and 'immense electrification and irrigation works'.[93] These construction sites, made of pink stone, were the promised vision of the city of the future, with its fountains, theatres and university. He also saw a new nation being born: Bloch wrote about the Soviet people with great feeling, calling them 'manly, courageous, intelligent, selfless, active, always ready to learn and to forge ahead, who came directly from the proletariat and were able to obtain the education to which their merits entitled them'.[94] These people imparted their vision to Bloch.

> This [New] World is more exhilarating than [anything] I have ever seen. . . .
> The assets of this country include the new ideal of a man which it is in the process of creating, joined with the deep cultural past (artistic, poetic, etc.) upon which it is building . . . . The thought of what this scientific civilisation is going to produce upon such fertile human soil, on such a planetary space gives the imagination a sense of strange excitement.[95]

The fact that this task was so enormous enabled Bloch to explain and justify any deficiencies of the system: 'the struggle is terribly hard';[96] 'the poverty is still major';[97] 'in fifteen years you cannot pull . . . 150,000,000 human beings out of the grime and the Middle Ages'.[98] The emotion of Bloch's letters shows that he was wholly won over by the utopian vision of the future, even allocating his own children a place in it.

> They [the Soviet people] want to raise the level of human life, intellectual and material, above everything that capitalism has reserved for its financial oligarchy. . . . I don't think a greater task has ever been attempted since the origins of humankind. [. . .]

I don't think that the scientific and human development of a young man
can be, from now on, complete without a thorough exploration of the USSR.
The second half of the twentieth century will have its centre of gravity here.
— Make sure you study Russian![99]

Like many other intellectuals, Jean-Richard Bloch became a passionate spokesman for the Soviet Union on his return to France. His enthusiasm unexpectedly
met a demand and he found himself in fashion, *l'homme à la mode*. In addition
to talking privately to friends and colleagues – Roger Martin du Gard, Romain
Rolland and Marcel Cohen – he received countless invitations to speak in public.
'From 15 January until 28 February, after the success of my first talks swelled
the flood [of invitations], I gave at least fifteen, all to different and very varied
audiences.'

As I read the Blochs' diary, I felt myself being seduced by the glorious picture
they had painted. I also recognised that, right down to its smallest details, Bloch's
tour of the USSR and his reactions to it bore an uncanny similarity to visits made
by other foreigners at the time: George Bernard Shaw and Sidney Webb, Emil
Ludwig and Lion Feuchtwanger, and Barbusse and Rolland. Like Bloch, they were
invited on these trips, offered excursions and taken to celebrations and parties.
They were also given a great deal of attention by Soviet officials and intellectuals,
many of whom became personal friends. The visitors were themselves revered
as creative and public intellectuals and made to feel important. Like Bloch, they
believed that they were witnessing the birth of a new, superior society in which
they had a personal part to play. This cemented a rapport with the Soviet Union
that was much stronger than mere attraction; it was a rapport of deep involvement
and loyalty on the visitors' part.

And so, for Bloch and the others, the journey through the Soviet Union became
a direct path to promoting and supporting the USSR abroad. Dreiser, Shaw, Webb
and Feuchtwanger, like Bloch, defended the Soviet Union against attack and criticism. But Bloch's unshakable devotion to the USSR also created a point of no
return for him. He became unable to extricate himself from the unconditional role
he had assumed as a defender of the Soviet Union – a position aptly recognised
by his old friend Martin du Gard. 'I will continue to follow you into this life that
is more and more active and missionary, towards which you seem to have turned
and from which it already appears that you may never be able to detach yourself,
even if you wished.'[100]

Defending the Soviet Union

Western visitors who returned from the USSR did not reveal everything they
had learned. In their accounts, many avoided mention of what Maurer ironically
called 'shadows of no historical importance'.[101] What exactly did Bloch's daughter Claude mean when she said, 'My father knew'?[102] Private documents and recollections of friends provide some of the answers. Marguerite Bloch's *Carnet*

de voyage en URSS en 1934, her little black leather-covered notebook that went everywhere with her in Russia, is filled with her handwritten notes that never appeared in her letters or J.-R. Bloch's articles.[103] Rolland's 1935 personal diary, *Voyage à Moscou*, was banned from publication for fifty years; he kept his innermost thoughts to his private correspondence and his conversations with Bloch. Malraux, who displayed 'quasi-Stalinist conformism' when speaking publicly about the USSR,[104] said quite different things in conversation with friends.

The adoption of this doublespeak, whereby private discourse differed from public in content and tone, allowed Western intellectuals to carefully protect the wholesome public image of the USSR that they had created and in which they wanted the West to believe. As we examine their actions more closely, we discover that the discourse they assumed in defence of the Soviet Union was not so much a result of what Jelen called deliberate blindness (*cécité volontaire*)[105] but rather a choice of deliberate silence.

Hiding the bad news

Until approximately 1935–36, the international climate was favourable to the endorsement and glorification of Soviet policies. The peak of this international acceptance came in 1935 with a number of key events: the signing of the French–Soviet Mutual Assistance Pact, the visit of the British Foreign Secretary Anthony Eden to Moscow, the staging of the International Writers' Congress for the Defence of Culture in Paris and the rise of the Popular Front. Later Beauvoir would write in *La Force de l'âge*,

> Suddenly the barrier that used to separate the petite bourgeoisie from the socialist and Communist workers collapsed. Newspapers of all persuasions . . . started publishing a great many sympathetic reports about Moscow and the powerful Red Army.[106]

At this time, many fellow-travellers praised the Soviet system, transferring their admiration of social and cultural achievements onto the Soviet political system. While Paul Robeson called the Soviet Union the only country that gave him the opportunity for creative work, Aragon lent his support to the Belomorcanal construction labour camp and to the 1930 trial of Prompartiya, the Industrial Party.[107] G.B. Shaw wrote in the visitors' book at the Metropol Hotel, 'Tomorrow I leave this land of hope and return to our Western countries of despair.'[108]

Eulogising Stalin, whom Barbusse described as 'the Lenin of today', was central to praising the USSR.[109] Those writers who had been granted an audience with Stalin – Emil Ludwig, H.G. Wells, G.B. Shaw, R. Rolland and Lion Feuchtwanger – were, without exception, under his spell as a man and a state leader. They published, or tried to obtain permission to publish, the transcripts of their interviews with Stalin; Wells, despite his disagreements with 'the ruling brain of the Kremlin', described Stalin as 'candid, fair and honest'.[110]

However, dealing with the failures of the Soviet Union was problematic for fellow-travellers. It was difficult for them to admit that catastrophic events such as collectivisation and famine were happening in the Soviet Union. These intellectuals, who were in the public eye, experienced the conflict between what they knew and what they were prepared to reveal.

Collectivisation, the campaign of forcefully bringing peasants and their goods onto collective farms, started in 1929. The peasants' resistance to the confiscation of their land and animals provoked violent retaliation by the state including execution and deportation of the kulaks, the supposedly wealthy peasants. The Great Famine, *Holodomor*, in which millions died, mainly in the Ukraine in 1931–33, was caused by a combination of bad crops and the destruction of traditional farming, including the confiscation of grain intended for sowing. Unlike the famine of the 1920s, which was used by the government to generate sympathy for the USSR, the Great Famine was denied and no official reports were issued about it. Western left-wing intellectuals also chose to ignore it; the Blochs barely mentioned collectivisation in their letters and the *New York Times* correspondent Walter Duranty, who travelled across the Soviet countryside in 1933, denied any evidence of famine.

Marguerite Bloch's private *Carnet* is revealing in two ways. It shows that the Blochs fully accepted and supported the Soviet version of collectivisation and also that, even though they did, they never mentioned this in public. Marguerite Bloch presents the brutality towards the kulaks as necessary for suppressing their resistance, and her account of their physical destruction is alarmingly unquestioning.

> The Ukraine and the North Caucasus particularly resisted collectivisation, in their own way. In the Northern Caucasus (the Russian Vendée, according to Aragon) the kulaks established themselves as leaders of the collective farms to exploit them, or else were thrown out of them. And they refused to give the grain to the state. They were forced to, by being denied food supplies. [. . .]
>
> Now, the sanctions are harsh. But at that point they were forced to shoot the entire population. They now consider the liquidation of the kulaks complete, but not until recently. And it was hard, with the children on the streets.[111]

Similarly, Walter Duranty avoided the term 'collectivisation', replacing it with the euphemism 'socialisation', and also condoned state terror. For him, 'the crux of the struggle came in the villages, where an attempt was being made to socialise, virtually overnight, a hundred million of the stubbornest and most ignorant peasants in the world'.[112]

Aragon, one of Blochs' sources, quoted the Army commander Vitaly Primakov, the then husband of Elsa Triolet's sister Lili Brik; Primakov, who had been to the Caucasus to suppress the kulaks, described them as a danger to the state and those who fought them, including himself, as heroes.

> When Aragon was telling us about the difficulties of collectivisation in the Northern Caucasus, he said that when Primakov was going around, he was

always escorted by three other officials, and that when he walked into a meeting or a room with many people, he kept his back to the wall, facing the public without ever turning his back to them. An enormous number of workers and soldiers were found dead from being stabbed in the back.[113]

Blochs' other source, Malraux, relied on Isaak Babel, according to whom the regime's ruthless actions were the only way of suppressing a virtual peasant war. Marguerite Bloch describes these actions as exhibiting courage and strength.

> One million dead in the Ukraine? – In any case, everyone speaks about it with horror. And all those kulaks in Siberia (those who aren't dead yet) still frighten them, in the event of war with Japan. More homeless children. But courage generates further courage and action. They know that they have to get organised after having been put to the test in this way. And then the singleness of purpose, and the ability to think about everything, is incredible. The Party has so much power, authority and courage. All these guns, which make people laugh, prove that sabotage was indeed something to fear.[114]

Duranty consciously hid what he knew. In a private conversation with William Strang of the Foreign Office, he admitted that not one million but 'as many as 10 million people may have died directly or indirectly from lack of food in the Soviet Union during the past year'.[115] In the press, however, he maintained that 'there is no actual starvation or deaths from starvation, but there is widespread mortality from diseases due to malnutrition'.[116] Bloch's silence regarding collectivisation and famine and Duranty's deliberate refusal to discuss these issues were early examples of fellow-travellers sweeping negative information under the carpet. The actions of intellectuals during the Victor Serge case give a better insight into this separation between private and public discourse.

Victor Serge, a Belgian-born Trotskyite and descendant of a well-known nineteenth-century Russian revolutionary, had lived in the USSR since the early 1920s. In 1929, with Panaït Istrati and Boris Souvarine, the disillusioned Serge published the three-volume *Vers l'autre flamme*, a critical account of the Soviet system. Forbidden to return to the West, he was exiled from Leningrad to the city of Orenburg, where he led a miserable existence; his mentally ill wife had been left behind in Leningrad. The French Left opposition, under Madeleine Paz, led a campaign to free Serge, engaging the support of Duhamel, Barbusse, Rolland and Bloch to intervene with the Soviet government.

These writers agreed, rather unwillingly, to assist. 'I share your and Barbusse's way of looking at things, when it comes to V.S.,' wrote Rolland to Bloch. 'Like you and Barbusse, I haven't the slightest regard for S., even though I admire his talent.'[117] With only limited compassion for Serge, Bloch and Rolland mainly channelled their energy into protecting the Soviet reputation in France. 'For a year, the S. case has done disproportionate damage to Western public opinion, growing worse with each passing month,'[118] Rolland wrote. Both Bloch and Rolland were confident that the Soviet government would help Serge if they requested it.

Bloch intervened first while in the USSR in 1934. He reported optimistically on meeting the Comintern official Manouil'sky who, 'with warmth and spontaneity', promised to conduct a full and speedy investigation of the case.[119] However, even though Bloch delayed his departure in anticipation of Manouil'sky's response, he was still waiting in vain even after he had returned to France. 'Still no news from Manouilsky,' he noted on 1 January 1935. Rolland intervened during his 1935 trip to the USSR; having written earlier to Gorky and his wife for help, he made his appeal to Yagoda, the People's Commissar for Internal Affairs. He was left reassured that Serge's living conditions were adequate.

> His sentence is not so harsh as that given to political prisoners .... I was given indisputable information on this matter by various people who lived or still live in Orenburg, including a French teacher who had taught there for fifteen years and who still had fond memories of the place. Yagoda sent me a telegram, received on the 12th of July from the Orenburg police, which states that Serge was repeatedly offered work with various institutions including the municipal services (Gorkomkhoz), but that he refused because he had no intention of working for Soviet institutions. Apparently he was recently offered teaching work which he turned down. They say that his material needs are well provided for.[120]

Rolland was prepared to acknowledge the negative role of the Soviet leadership in damaging their own reputation. 'At least, let them shed some light! Don't let them childishly hide the motives for which they condemned Serge and are stealing his literary work! It is below our great friends' dignity. If they want to be harsh, let them, but openly!'[121] However, Bloch displaced the blame onto Serge's supporters: these 'rabid enemies of the present-day Soviet Union'[122] and their 'argument based on a crude, leftist anti-Soviet demagogy'.[123] He was deeply embarrassed when Soviet writers spoke in a clumsy, counter-productive way in defence of their official position at the 1935 International Writers' Congress for the Defence of Culture in Paris.

> It doesn't alter the fact that our Soviet friends are on the wrong track in the Serge case. Their replies to Madeleine Paz were pathetic (Kirshon, Tikhonov, Ehrenburg), immature and ostentatiously lofty; arguments fit enough for Siberian muzhiks ten years ago, but hardly fit for Parisian intellectuals and workers today.[124]

Whoever it was – Duhamel, Rolland, Bloch or even Barbusse – whose intervention counted for most, their requests were seemingly heard and Serge was released in 1936. However, it had been done by exercising the influence of insiders while, in public, maintaining a façade of solidarity with the USSR.

Damning the renegades: Panaït Istrati and André Gide

Though fellow-travellers may have been able to choose what to reveal and what to hide in order to protect the Soviet Union, they had limited power against negative information from other sources. Renegades – that is, former supporters turned heretics – were considered the worst source of slander and, against this, the tactic of supporters was to publicly discredit them or to stifle their voices. Panaït Istrati was one such renegade.

Istrati, the 'Gorky of the Balkans', was the Romanian author of *Kira Kiralina*, a book of romantic stories about the search for freedom. Istrati enjoyed Rolland's patronage and was initially enthusiastic about the Soviet Union, spending over a year travelling there between 1927 and 1929. However, in *Vers l'autre flamme: après seize mois de l'URSS*[125] (1929), the disillusioned Istrati denounced Soviet society as corrupt and run by power-hungry officials who used Communist ideology to exercise dictatorship and control of the masses by cultivating blind obedience and mutual denunciation.

> They [the officials] deliberately introduced injustice into their country. They corrupted numerous social groups, particularly the poor, so they could win majorities and govern. Their corruption is the most brutal: *if you want to eat, even frugally, you have to toe the line and denounce the comrade who refuses to submit.*[126]

Naively hoping that his revelations would help the USSR to overcome its deficiencies, Istrati still considered himself to be a friend. However, his criticism was not tolerated. When Istrati's book was published, he became an instant *persona non grata* among the French Left. Even his protector Rolland was upset by Istrati's alleged exaggerations because the USSR 'deserves to be saved, defended and exalted'.

However, when *l'Humanité* went back to its hounding of Istrati in 1935, accusing him of lies and pouring abuse onto him, this went too far even for Rolland.[127] Francis Jourdain referred to Istrati as 'a patriot, anti-Semite, Fascist'; Barbusse called him 'a rabid dog'; and Vladimir Pozner described *Vers l'autre flamme* as 'a gratuitous insult', 'the most abject slander' and 'a war machine against the USSR'.[128] This hounding followed Istrati beyond the grave. He was proclaimed to have died 'as the Fascist he always was'; he was accused of having 'a vain and petty soul' and his book was compared slightingly with the reports of real friends of the USSR.

> The impressive achievements of socialism and the birth of the new man went over his head. From his trip – one of those trips from which someone like Henri Barbusse, Luc Durtain, Malraux, Francis Jourdain, J.-R. Bloch and others would have drawn inspiration for an impassioned body of work and fruitful action – Istrati only brought back never-ending complaints because he'd had to share a kitchen! Once he had returned to France, he lumped together his pathetic resentments and paltry details into several volumes that ooze hate and bad faith.[129]

A year later, an even greater scandal erupted. It was caused by the publication of *Return from the USSR* by André Gide, possibly the most influential French writer of the interwar period. While in the Soviet Union, where he had been highly acclaimed and lavishly welcomed, Gide reacted enthusiastically, praising the USSR and dedicating *Les nourritures terrestres* to the Soviet youth. But then, Gide shocked the world by publishing the unexpectedly critical *Return from the USSR*. Like Istrati before him, he claimed that he had written the book as a friend and a well-wisher.

Rumours about the damaging book had begun to circulate even before it was published, triggering united efforts to prevent its publication.[130] Ehrenburg tried to find out what was in Gide's forthcoming book. Aragon was reported to have been working on the Dutch Communist, Jef Last, to ask him to persuade Gide to postpone publication; in a telegram, Last indeed implored Gide to do so. Gide's travelling companions, Guilloux and Schiffrin, tried to persuade him, at the very least, to change the initial text, 'to bring out the positive aspects' of the USSR.[131]

No sooner had the book come out on 13 November 1936 than Gide's fellow countrymen attacked. Unlike the case of Istrati, lying about the USSR was not the prime accusation against Gide. In fact, those who were aware of Soviet deficiencies found that Gide's book contributed nothing new. 'Everything discreditable that Gide has told us about Soviet life we have long known through a mountain of reports and documentaries.'[132] Gide's change of opinion was regarded as too sudden to be trustworthy. 'Gide has been too eager to change his mind for us to take his *Return from the USSR* seriously.'[133]

The concerted action of supporters of the USSR who attacked Gide in the left-wing press was unprecedented. Regular Communist visitors to the USSR used their authority to discredit Gide's views as being superficial and inaccurate. 'Not everything is wrong, but almost everything is misinterpreted in the absence of real knowledge,' commented Paul Nizan on the pages of *Vendredi*,[134] citing Soviet cultural achievements to counter Gide's criticisms.[135] In *Europe*, the scholar Georges Friedmann accused Gide of coming to hasty conclusions and, like the arguments of Rolland and Bloch in relation to Serge, denied that Gide's so-called 'truth' could heal. 'You haven't brought back "the truth" from the USSR. The truth is harder to conquer. It requires patience and self-restraint. Your little book only "wounded" without being able to heal.'[136]

The Communist press was, as always, the most virulent. In *Commune*, Louis Aragon linked Gide's book to the anti-Soviet campaign orchestrated by the Gestapo on the occasion of the twentieth anniversary of the October Revolution.[137] Even the non-Communist Rolland published a diatribe in *l'Humanité* that was designed to destroy both Gide and his book.

> This bad book is in fact a mediocre book, an incredibly trivial, superficial and immature book full of contradictions. If the book has created a considerable stir, it is definitely not because of its worth – it is worthless – but because of the rumours that surround Gide's name and the exploitation of his fame by the enemies of the USSR, always on the lookout and ready to use any weapon against it that falls into their malicious hands.[138]

In this torrent of insults and accusations, the most prominent theme was Soviet support of Republican Spain, now a major item to the credit of the USSR. At a time when Western powers did nothing to oppose the victory of Fascism, the USSR was seen as the only country that was both willing and able to bring it to a halt. 'And France did nothing,' recalled Simone de Beauvoir. 'Fortunately the USSR made up its mind; it sent tanks, planes and machine-guns; and the militia, with the help of the International Brigades, saved Madrid.'[139] Soviet support for Republican Spain made many consider Gide's publication untimely; this included Pierre Herbart, another of Gide's travelling companions.

> The USSR had just denounced the non-intervention pact in Spain and was preparing to help the people of Spain fight Fascism. I thought it was harmful, in the weeks in which the fate of the Spanish proletariat would be decided, to heap abuse on the only country that was trying to save it (we were unaware of Mexico's fraternal assistance, which was given without fuss or any thought for personal acclaim).[140]

Malraux's position was similar. In 1936, his abhorrence of Fascism had determined his public loyalty to the USSR, despite criticisms made in private. 'I doubt that *Return from the USSR* shocked him,' recalled Raymond Aron. 'However, he may have considered untimely a polemic against the USSR in the heyday of anti-Fascism.'[141] Aragon expressed this point of view more explicitly, pointing to the need to protect the Soviet reputation so as not to weaken the anti-Fascist camp.

> I am convinced that it is our absolute duty at this time to avoid anything that might in any way shake people's resolve or serve, even against our will, the cause of Fascism. At present the only true ally of the heroic Spanish people is the Soviet Union and we must avoid by all means anything that might tarnish the prestige of this ally.[142]

The campaign against Gide was probably the last striking example of unanimity and orchestrated public action amongst Soviet supporters. The Soviet camp was never again as united, especially as the period of the Gide affair was followed by the Moscow show trials.

The trials: from silence to separation

From 1937, the amount of publicity in the West that was favourable to the USSR declined noticeably. There were fewer supporters. Barbusse had died in 1935 and Vaillant-Couturier in 1937. Aragon, Malraux and Nizan were kept away by events in Spain, fighting on the side of the Republicans. At the same time, confusing and incomprehensible rumours about the Moscow trials began to circulate in the West. There were rumours about old Bolsheviks and government leaders being arrested and tried for treason, for plotting with Trotsky and the Gestapo against Stalin.

These stories mentioned public confessions by the accused and fiery demands for death sentences by the chief prosecutor, Vyshinsky.

The fact that the USSR was seen as the only force that could be depended on to oppose Hitler continued to be a major deterrent to criticism. Marc Ferro claims that democrats and socialists were prepared to turn a blind eye to Stalinist terror out of fear of the Fascist threat.[143] 'Between Fascism and Communism, I have no hesitation, I have chosen Communism and . . . I firmly stand by my decision,' wrote the otherwise apolitical Eugène Dabit.[144]

Today, it may seem unimaginable that many supporters initially accepted the official Soviet version of the trials; and yet, they had been continually justifying state violence. As Bloch had written at the time of the repressions that followed Kirov's assassination in 1934, 'A world cannot be created without errors, regrets, sacrifice nor even without victims.'[145] In 1937, fellow-travellers were prepared to take a similar position. 'From what I have already seen of the workings of the Soviet Government,' said Paul Robeson, 'I can only say that anybody who lifts his hand against it ought to be shot!'[146] British lawyer and writer D.N. Pritt legitimated the trials by saying that 'the charge was true, the confessions correct and the prosecution fairly conducted'. Even the initially sceptical Lion Feuchtwanger, who sat in the Moscow courtroom in January 1937, supported the show trials in his notorious *Moscow 1937*. As the accused made public admissions of their guilt, Rolland refused to believe that the trials had been staged,[147] and he reaffirmed his faith in the USSR in possibly his strongest public statement ever.

> It is now, when hatred pours from fascism of all stripes, and every kind of rabid reaction is aimed at the USSR – in this hour when the USSR is suffering from treacherous and wild attacks, even from countries of the socialist camp that should be proud to fight alongside the USSR, which seek instead to discredit it out of the fear and envy provoked by its enormous successes and its peaceful conquest of minds throughout the world – it is now that I want to pledge to the Soviet Union my loyalty and my unshakeable attachment to its great people and its leaders.
>
> Dead or alive, I shall always be with the youth and people of the USSR in their ordeals and battles, their joys and pains, in their Herculean labours, cleaning up the quagmire of the ancient world to build a new world on a purified land. I shall also be with them when the final victory unites them with the peoples of the world.[148]

However, the trials continued into 1938 when the party favourite, Bukharin, the former NKVD chief, Yagoda, and the former ambassador to Paris, Rakovsky, were put on trial for treason. Worse still, by 1939 many of the Soviet intellectuals personally known to Western visitors had been arrested: Meyerhold, Kol'tsov, Babel, Tret'yakov and Arosev, to name only a few.

Even Western Communists were now disturbed. British Communist writer Edward Upward, admired by the likes of Spender and W.H. Auden, replied to any questions about the trials, 'What trials? I've given up thinking about such things ages ago.'[149] Paul Nizan refused to discuss the trials, even with his friends

Sartre and de Beauvoir.[150] Some intellectuals began to find it impossible to defend the USSR without lying or to justify Soviet actions by the past victories of the USSR.[151] 'Today there is too much corroborating evidence, which no longer permits me to doubt my own. Nor to keep it to myself any longer,'[152] wrote Pierre Herbart. Communists who left the party did so quietly, without public statements. Shocked by the Stalinist persecutions in Spain, Arthur Koestler resigned in 1938 by writing a personal letter to the party. At the same time, he remained loyal to the USSR. 'Whoever goes against the Soviet Union goes against the future.'[153] When Willi Münzenberg distanced himself from the German Communist Party, he condemned neither Stalin nor the USSR, 'the first country where socialism has been constructed'.[154]

Those who were not in the party also distanced themselves quietly, almost reluctantly. After Malraux observed Stalinist methods in Spain in the summer of 1937,[155] he reached the end of his *compagnonnage intellectuel* with the Communists. He did not break with his former allies altogether[156] and avoided making any adverse public statement; rather, he reduced his involvement with the USSR and discontinued any public support. According to Lacouture, this distancing took place in 1938.[157]

Even for Bloch and Rolland, it was a struggle to remain uncritical. Reluctant to condemn or even to publicly discuss the trials, they resorted to a new tactic of self-censorship and self-silencing over matters of which they disapproved, making both writers appear to condone Soviet actions. Between 1936 and 1938, the growing anxiety that Bloch and Rolland experienced over the escalation of the trials was carefully kept to their private correspondence.[158] Bloch wrote to Rolland:

> How shady and embarrassingly mysterious this Moscow trial still appears to be! So many unexplained things . . . so many secretive and underhand attacks! . . . After nineteen years of struggle, these obscure accusations, these implausible hearings, these mass executions, the vanishing of all Lenin's companions, greatly disturb me.[159]

In fact, even correspondence became too open for Rolland. 'The Moscow trial is excruciating,' he wrote at the time of the third trial in 1938. 'I don't want to write here about the matter, we'll talk about it.'[160]

Both Bloch and Rolland were concerned about the damage that bad publicity over the trials would inflict on the world political scene. 'But the effects on the whole world, especially France and America, will be disastrous,'[161] wrote Rolland. However, unlike his response in the Serge case, Rolland was now clearly concerned about the fate of the victims, people he knew personally. He actually wrote to Stalin, imploring him to pardon Bukharin; this idea of quiet diplomacy came from his earlier experience of getting Serge released through intervention with the Soviet leadership. After all, as he wrote to Bloch, it was not only the Soviet reputation at stake but also a united anti-Nazi front.

> Wouldn't the best friends of the USSR deem it urgent to send by the quickest possible means a message (a closed message, not to be published) to the Soviet

authorities, imploring them to consider the disastrous political consequences – for the Popular Front, for the reconciliation of the socialist and communist parties, for the common defence of Spain – of a sentence condemning the accused to capital punishment? At a time when the French Communist Party is doing everything to form a united front among workers of all persuasions, all its efforts could be wiped out by the moral repercussions of such a judgment. It would however seem possible (and wise) to begin with a banishment which would render the condemned harmless, without over-exciting public opinion, which is already deeply disturbed. . . . Mention this to Francis Jourdain if you can![162]

Like Malraux, Rolland withdrew his support for the Soviet Union in 1938 because of the trials. Like Malraux, he did so without any public announcement or open break. According to Bernard Duchatelet, Rolland distanced himself 'not from the Revolution – in which he still believed – but from Stalin's Russia'.[163]

As in the case of Serge, Bloch refused to join the protests of the opposition. 'I certainly do not share the offended protests of our good old leftist Jesuits, who believe that a revolution happens like a spring festival for the delicate pleasure of virtuous souls.'[164] At the end of his inner struggle, Bloch remained on the side of the Revolution and the Soviet state. Lest further discussions hurt the Soviet Union, he made a vow of silence.

I remain silent out of respect for the admirable work done in the USSR and because the credit side of the balance sheet of the Bolshevik Revolution so far exceeds the debit side that one shouldn't do or say anything that might be turned against the bloc that is the socialist state. This does not mean that thought and reflection are absent; they roam freely and gnaw at me.[165]

The end of an alliance?

On 23 August 1939, Stalin signed the Non-Aggression Pact with Hitler. For the first time, there was a public wave of protest against Stalin's hypocrisy by intellectuals. The leading scholars Paul Langevin, Irène Joliot-Curie and Frédéric Joliot, and other members of the *Union des intellectuels français*, signed a manifesto, in *L'Oeuvre* of 30 August, expressing their shock at the reconciliation of the Soviet and German leaderships. Rolland resigned from all his posts in pro-Soviet organisations, and Luc Durtain and René Lalou resigned from the editorial board of *Europe*. *Europe*'s editor-in-chief, Jean Cassou, announced the magazine's 'temporary and silent' closure. The current and former Communists Arthur Koestler, Manes Sperber and Willi Münzenberg called Stalin a traitor, declaring that 'Socialist Russia is no more.'[166] Nizan publicly resigned from the FCP.

Only very few sought openly to excuse the USSR. In *Ce soir*, Aragon claimed that the agreement delayed the war, and publication of an article by Bloch that presented a similar view was prevented only by the closure of the newspaper on 25 August.[167] The closure of the left-wing press by the government in September

1939 marked the end of the intellectuals' pre-war public support for the USSR. When the Soviet Union invaded Finland in the following year, only a very few lonely figures, such as G.B. Shaw and D.N. Pritt, still justified the Soviet action compared with the long lists of signatures condemning the invasion on new petitions by Western intellectuals.

The Soviet contribution

Attempts to explain Western intellectuals' attraction to the Soviet Union are incomplete as long as they exclude the Soviet Union's contribution to these relations. The commonly accepted view, that this attraction was spontaneous and that the support of intellectuals was inspired from within, overlooks the fact that, to a large extent, these relations were instigated and manipulated by the USSR. It has been recognised that the Soviet Union had a vested interest in attracting and influencing its foreign friends; however, it has not been adequately understood how the Soviets manufactured this support.

Some visitors knew, at the time of their trip, that they were being lured and seduced. Istrati bluntly stated that the hospitality and generosity served as a bribe that induced visitors to praise the system; for him, the bribes included trips, exclusive contracts and translations of his books in tens of thousands of copies. 'Don't you think that made it well worth yelling "Long live Communism"?'[168] How could visitors appear ungrateful after they had been treated so well? Stefan Zweig was 'carried on waves of warmth' that gave him the wish to repay the hospitality. 'It is no more than natural to wish to reciprocate generosity with generosity, rapture with rapture. I must admit that I myself in many a moment in Russia came near to crying hosanna and to becoming exalted from the exaltation.'[169] These privileges made visitors close their eyes to many of the deficiencies of the system. 'The staging, the demagogy, the dishonesty, the fraternal cruelty, betrayed themselves so blatantly. But everyone treated us so well! Why not turn a blind eye and say, "Oh well, it will pass!"'[170] recalled Victor Serge. The Nizans would later concur, 'It was an extremely corrupting stay.'[171]

This special treatment and, at the same time, manipulation were part of Soviet foreign policy, which used Soviet socio-cultural achievements to create sympathy towards the USSR and to convert non-Communist foreigners into Soviet allies. Years ago, F. Barghoorn pointed to the entire 'Soviet machinery of guidance of cultural contacts' with organisations such as VOKS and Intourist.[172] The historians Hollander and Margoulies have shown how these and other organisations used hospitality and personal attention ('the ego massage') to manipulate foreign intellectuals. However, theirs is a view from the outside. In the past few years, Western[173] and Russian[174] scholars have gained access to the documents of these organisations and begun to examine how they operated. This examination has opened up vast opportunities.

To understand the precise means by which the Soviet Union attracted Western intellectuals' support and to appreciate their complex responses to the array of pressures, excitements, seductions and inducements provided by the Soviet Union, we shall enter the world of Soviet cultural organisations and examine their inner workings. We shall discover who wrote the proposals and instructions that were designed to entice Western intellectuals, and who implemented these proposals and acted upon the instructions. We shall also see how Western intellectuals – writers, scholars and members of the rank-and-file intelligentsia – responded differently to these actions and gain a better understanding of the reasons for the kind of support described in this chapter.

2 Comintern

The origins of Soviet cultural propaganda

In the years after the Revolution, Soviet relations with the West were driven by two differing imperatives. The first was the survival of the Soviet state through achieving recognition as a diplomatic and commercial partner, a goal pursued by the Soviet government through various People's Commissariats (Soviet Ministries). The second was to spread world revolution through the Third [Communist] International, known as the Comintern. These divided aims produced conflicting interests and, until 1921, the Commissariats and the Comintern acted quite independently and according to differing logics. The Commissariat of Foreign Affairs, which negotiated with capitalist countries on behalf of the Soviet government, even complained that the Comintern's subversive methods hindered its diplomatic operations. But, after 1921, when it had become clear that the revolution would not spread quickly to the rest of Europe, the Comintern changed its tactics. It abandoned its aggressive actions, turning instead to winning the Western masses through the creation of a large movement of public opinion favourable to the USSR.[1] Both the Soviet government and the Comintern began to use cultural propaganda as a means of paying court to Western intellectuals to gain their support for Soviet policies.

The plan to engage foreign intellectuals and the origins of cultural propaganda can be traced back to 1923–24. Starting in 1923, the All-Union Central Executive Committee (TsIK), the highest legislative body of the Soviet Union, created successive organisations to establish official cultural contacts with foreign countries; the purpose of these organisations was to assist in the recognition and promotion of the USSR abroad. The Comintern, on the other hand, developed unofficial policies on how to appeal to Western intellectuals and use cultural propaganda. The development of these policies is discussed in its internal correspondence.

Through TsIK, the Soviet government founded the first Soviet organisation for cultural relations with the West, the Commission for the Establishment of Cultural Relations with Other Countries (*Komissiya po organizatsii kul'turnoy svyazi s drugimi stranami*),[2] on 20 November 1924.[3] It was designed to organise and supervise cultural exchange with other countries;[4] its main emphasis was on the export of Soviet culture, in particular promoting life in the USSR to foreign states and organising Soviet cultural events in those countries.[5] The Commission was the immediate predecessor of VOKS, the All-Union Society for Cultural Relations with Foreign Countries, which will be discussed in Chapters 5–7.

However, the Comintern and another organisation that was created under its auspices, the International Association of Revolutionary Writers (or MORP, discussed in Chapters 3 and 4), were also involved with Western intellectuals and cultural exchange. This chapter will examine the Comintern's internal correspondence, in which its leaders openly discuss how to use art and culture for political purposes and how to appeal to Western intellectuals. This correspondence provides an insight, not previously available, into the operations of a variety of cultural organisations, including those that were created later in the interwar period.

The Comintern: promoting the USSR abroad

The Comintern was founded by Lenin in Moscow in 1919. From the start, it was intended to be the undisputed leader of the world Communist movement. The Comintern instigated the creation of many Communist parties in countries other than Russia, for example the FCP, founded in 1920; parties that already existed, such as the German KPD, founded in 1918, joined the Comintern shortly after its creation. These parties were designated as branches within the Comintern and were strictly subordinated to the Russian Communist Party based in Moscow.[6] Lenin summarised the Comintern's leadership in relation to foreign parties as 'passing . . . Russian experience to foreigners',[7] and the Third Comintern Congress proclaimed that 'the unconditional support of the Soviet Republic remains . . . the cardinal duty of Communists in all countries'.[8] In the eyes of the West, the Comintern was a subversive organisation whose image was associated with illegal activities and which aimed to overthrow existing Western governments and regimes.

As official Soviet policy in the early 1920s swung towards the creation of a united front among its Western allies, it became imperative to win over the Western masses by means that were seen to be legal. Therefore, in the period 1924–27, the Comintern developed tactics to gain sympathy for the USSR from the Western masses. The often semi-legal status of national Communist parties in the 1920s and early 1930s was a hindrance in the struggle for recognition of the USSR by Western nations. This was the case in France, where the Communist Party suffered the incarceration of its leaders and the temporary closure of its journal. Therefore, in addition to overt revolutionary agitation and propaganda in foreign countries, Comintern began to develop less conspicuous tactics to dissociate the image of the USSR from the world Communist movement. Part of this plan was the attempt to reach intellectuals, and the use of various forms of cultural propaganda. The Comintern's resolutions, proposals, Comintern members' reports and various correspondence contain discussions of how to refine old propaganda methods. Today, these documents can be found in RGASPI, the former Party Archives in Moscow (Fond 495).

Cultural propaganda within Comintern

Most of the policies on cultural propaganda and the engagement of foreign intellectuals emanated from the Department of Agitation and Propaganda (known as Agitprop), within the Comintern Executive Committee (IKKI).[9] Although the Chairman of IKKI between 1919 and 1926 was a Russian – a senior Soviet leader, Grigory Zinov'yev – both IKKI and Agitprop had a strong international flavour. Many Comintern members were Western Communists with first-hand knowledge of Western societies. The Head of Agitprop, Bela Kun, was a founding member and leader of the Hungarian Communist Party. The Deputy Head of Agitprop, Alfred Kurella, was a German writer and former member of the Communist Youth who settled permanently in the USSR. A number of documents written by Agitprop members and quoted in this book are in languages other than Russian, for example French.

Although a department of the Comintern, Agitprop was also subordinate to the Central Committee of the Russian (Bolshevik) Communist Party or RKP(b).[10] The Politburo of the Central Committee of the RKP(b) directly supervised Agitprop's policies and operations, and Agitprop IKKI reported even seemingly minor decisions to another Agitprop, that of the Central Committee of the RKP(b).[11] It seems that the Agitprop IKKI was meant to develop rather than implement policies, which were then put into action by other organisations.

Unlike TsIK's decision about the role of the Commission for Cultural Relations, Bela Kun and other Agitprop members openly discussed the development of propaganda tactics in correspondence and reports. The Comintern's revolutionary message had to be disguised and it had to reach the Western public without exposing the Comintern as its source. These requirements resulted in the proposal to use culture as a means of propaganda. The programme was to include: publications in the foreign press; translations of Soviet literary fiction; sending Soviet artists and other cultural emissaries abroad; encouraging the creation of nominally non-political Comintern-run organisations (i.e. Communist front organisations); and securing the cooperation of Western intellectuals. Awareness of these discussions within the Comintern is crucial to our understanding of the real inner workings of Soviet 'cultural' organisations.

'Providing services' to the press: publication of Comintern materials in the Communist press

One of the Comintern's principal means of reaching a Western audience was the Western Communist press, which included periodicals such as *l'Humanité* and *Cahier du bolchévisme* in France and *Rote Fahne* in Germany. The Comintern described the process as 'providing a service to the magazines and bulletins of Communist parties' (*obsluzhivaniye zhurnalov i bulleteney kompartiy*);[12] however, the real purpose was to use the foreign press as a platform for the dissemination of Soviet materials.

The centralised discipline of the Communist network ensured that Comintern materials sent to national Communist presses would be published. The Comintern could directly instruct foreign Communist parties to publish its materials. In 1926, for example, when IKKI needed to lend support to the International Organisation of Assistance to Revolutionaries, or MOPR,[13] it issued a resolution that foreign Communist parties instruct their press to allocate sufficient space to MOPR materials, specifically mentioning the German periodical *Rote Fahne* and the French *l'Humanité*.[14] The success rate for publication of such materials was high. As much as 98 per cent of all Comintern material was printed in the foreign Communist press according to the Inprekorr agency (Internationale Press-Korrespondence), the main channel for the distribution abroad of materials on life in the USSR.[15] To provide additional information, Agitprop resolved to have Inprekorr publish its own regular bulletin every two months in three different languages: German, French and English.[16]

Agitprop aimed to publish two main types of material on the USSR: materials to combat so-called 'bourgeois lies', damaging to the USSR, and materials extolling Soviet achievements. The first was described as 'counter-material' (*kontrmaterial*),[17] which aimed to counteract hostile information presented in the Western press without appearing to be a direct response to it. 'Agitprop shall not engage in denying every new bourgeois lie but shall publish an article in the press on a given topic, irrespective of the content of the articles in the bourgeois press.'[18] 'Shock campaigns' (*udarnyye kampanii*)[19] were organised around specific topics. One such campaign came in 1929 in response to Western publications on the Soviet penitentiary system, in particular the Solovki prison camp, the first of the camps that would form the Gulag. This campaign illustrates Agitprop's tactics: by producing and sending a series of articles, leaflets and brochures to the West, it made use of a variety of media forms to send a single message to the public. Bela Kun proposed including information about Soviet prisons and the Solovki prison camp obtained from the People's Commissariat of Justice (Narkomyust) in Agitprop's own special edition (the Inprekorr bulletin mentioned above). Next, it was decided to publish a separate brochure on the Soviet prison system and the Solovki camp, for which Agitprop made an urgent request to the Joint State Political Department (OGPU) to provide visual materials that would inspire the readers: photographs of prison cells, reading halls and libraries 'suitable for propaganda'.[20] The leading figure of the Soviet literary establishment, Maxim Gorky, was taken on a tour of the Solovki camp in 1929, and filmed. One of the Solovki inmates later recalled white tablecloths and flowers being put on the tables in the dining room for the great writer's visit, and prisoners, even the illiterate, being given newspapers to read as Gorky toured the camp.[21] In 1933, Gorky was also taken to the site of the construction of the White Sea Canal (Belomorkanal): this work was carried out by prisoners on starvation rations and in Arctic conditions. Both of Gorky's trips were widely publicised in the USSR and abroad. It was no coincidence that the French Communist press also published Gorky's accounts of the re-educational, if not redeeming, force of literacy and hard labour on criminals.[22] This was also echoed by the French Communist poet Louis Aragon, who welcomed the re-educative role of the Belomorkanal construction labour camp.

The second type of material published by Agitprop, that of Soviet achievements, was seen as having excellent 'agitation value' among the Western masses; in fact, a positive attitude towards the USSR was considered decisive in the formation of the masses' attitude towards the Communist Party of their own country.[23] However, in 1926, the Agitprop Press Sub-Department found that the current state of its materials was unsatisfactory and amateurish, and that the presentation of Soviet achievements lacked an appropriate form. Its report on changes to propaganda materials on the USSR (*agitmaterial ob SSSR*)[24] marks the start of the creation of a systematic picture of Soviet success in the construction of socialism. Agitprop's Report on the Provision of Information about the USSR to the Foreign Communist Parties[25] proposed selecting materials with the interests of specific target groups in mind: male and female workers and peasants, the intelligentsia, young people, mothers and children and ethnic minorities. The material was meant to paint a favourable contrast between conditions in the USSR and those to which its readers were exposed in the West.

> Presenting Soviet achievements in a concrete way by using examples of various population groups and areas of [socialist] construction will have first-class agitation value, as this is what will make it possible for an ordinary working person to compare a small corner of capitalist society known to him with conditions under the dictatorship of the proletariat.[26]

However, as long as the Comintern relied solely on publication in the Communist press, it was merely preaching to the converted.

Attracting a broader audience

Before the party reverted to a harsher line in 1927–28, the Comintern considered it to be important to target wider segments of the population: the social democrats, trade unionists, workers, and the left-wing bourgeoisie.[27] This required less conspicuous forms of propaganda that could be circulated through non-Communist publications, which is where cultural discourse began to play an important role.

Culture as propaganda

Art and culture had already been an integral form of propaganda within the Soviet Union from the early post-revolutionary days. Street theatre performances, songs and music, Agitprop trains and street posters targeted the mainly illiterate Russian crowds, and were created by artists and poets who supported the October Revolution, for example Mayakovsky, Rodchenko and El Lissitsky. Similar artistic and cultural propaganda was thought by many to be an effective means of creating a favourable picture of the USSR abroad, without making it too obvious. In its 1926 draft resolution on systematic propaganda through art (*khudozhestvennaya agitrabota*, 'artistic agitation work'),[28] the IKKI Orgbureau prescribed the maximum use of literary fiction (*belletristika*) and visual media, including films, slides and exhibitions.[29] Indeed, Agitprop had already been sending slides and revolutionary songs to France and other countries.[30]

The choice of materials was very specific. Bela Kun set up a commission to select feature films of potential value to be screened abroad on a regular basis.[31] Political principles prevailed in the selection of literary works that might be suitable for propaganda. 'Agitprop of the IKKI considers it of utmost importance to publish abroad the best works of Russian fiction,'[32] wrote Bela Kun. This was later amended by hand to 'Russian revolutionary fiction'. Agitprop delegated this task to other organisations, the Moscow Association of Proletarian Writers (MAPP)[33] and the State Publishers (Gosizdat).[34] These organisations also received Agitprop's instructions for the careful selection and preparation of works of fiction, which included distinguishing between those that could be sent abroad in their original form and those that required thorough preliminary editing.[35] The selections had to be based on a critical assessment of the artistic and political nature of each work.[36]

In the 1920s, the Comintern was only just developing its practices for selecting effective propaganda materials and Soviet literature suitable for Western audiences. The aim was to target specific socio-economic groups, and it therefore had to try and address the particular interests of Western audiences. Only non-Russian Comintern members could advise on the selection of materials to be made with a view to Western tastes and the psychology of the European masses.[37] For example, Lentsner, a co-editor of Trotsky's work, pointed out that sending a brochure on the revolutionary poet Demian Bedny, whose poetry was initially intended for the Russian peasant army, to the West was inappropriate and ineffective.[38] Later, the Soviet literary and cultural organisations, MORP and VOKS, would base their choice of Soviet literature on these earlier Comintern guidelines.

Personal contacts: sending Soviet cultural emissaries abroad

In addition to the written word, Comintern began to use personal interactions to spread Soviet art and culture. One of the first steps was to send Soviet artists and performers abroad. Agitprop discussed these visits, during which artists assumed the role of cultural emissaries, exclusively in terms of achieving 'desirable political results' (*zhelatel'nyye politicheskiye rezul'taty*).[39]

As with the dissemination of Soviet literature, Agitprop essentially delegated the task of organising tours to another agency, the Commissariat of Labour (Narkomtrud), but it issued precise instructions for these tours. According to Alfred Kurella, tours abroad needed to present 'the true face of Soviet art' (*nastoyascheye litso iskusstva v SSSR*),[40] and he instructed Narkomtrud to make a strict ideological selection of both repertoire and performers. He also stressed the need for this art to represent the USSR, not Russia;[41] this was a clear attempt to make art and culture work towards the creation of a new image of the post-revolutionary Soviet nation. In 1927, the network of Cultural Rapprochement Societies in a number of countries acquired the title of 'New Russia'; the Association of Friends of the USSR, created in 1927–28, also promoted the use of the name 'USSR'.

Agitprop's instructions regarding foreign tours contained conflicting messages. On the one hand, Agitprop encouraged a broad exposure of Soviet artists abroad and specified clauses to be used in the contracts with foreign agents including: to carry out performances in a number of cities; not to limit performances to large halls attended only by bourgeois audiences; and to organise performances in workers' districts at affordable prices.[42] On the other hand, Agitprop was suspicious of both Soviet actors and foreign agents; it recommended that Narkomtrud have its own representative abroad to control tours and actors, so that Soviet performers could be prevented from 'falling into the hands of blackmailers or obvious enemies of the USSR'.[43]

These instructions for promoting Soviet art and culture were implemented by other Soviet organisations. VOKS also discussed policies for sending artists and writers abroad. Tours by the theatres of Stanislavsky, Meyerhold and Tairov, and the Jewish Chamber Theatre, did take place, mainly before the 1930s. However, this form of cultural influence, where groups and individuals were sent abroad as cultural emissaries, was of limited scope compared with other practices, particularly after 1930.

Comintern's cultural front organisations

The idea of Comintern auxiliary (*podsobnyye*) organisations in the West, commonly known as 'front organisations' or 'fronts', originated under Lenin[44] with the Third Comintern Congress resolution to extend Comintern's influence to the non-Communist masses through non-Communist associations and groups.[45] The nature of auxiliary organisations is best expressed by Comintern's own term, 'camouflage organisations' (*maskiruyuschiye organizatsii*).[46] This term indicated that these nominally non-Communist organisations, for example cooperatives, disabled veterans' organisations, educational and study groups, sports associations and theatre groups, disguised their Comintern or Communist leadership and goals. These fronts were styled as 'cultural and enlightening' institutions (*kul'turno-prosvetitel'nyye uchrezhdeniya*), schools and self-education groups (*kruzhki po samoobrazovaniyu*).[47] The Agitprop Propaganda Sub-Department (*podotdel agitatsii*) of IKKI was responsible for the creation and supervision of these organisations as well as for associated cultural matters.[48] Among the most prominent auxiliary organisations was Workers' International Relief or Mezhrabpom, which was founded by Willi Münzenberg in 1921 on Lenin's request, initially to assist Russia in combating famine. Another was the network of Associations of Friends of the USSR, created in 1927–28 and extended to a number of Western countries. These organisations were meant to increase Comintern (and Communist) influence in non-Communist circles and to assist Comintern branches (that is, national Communist parties, *sektsii*) in acquiring legal status.[49] The Comintern referred to them cynically as 'our "neutral" auxiliary organisations', putting 'neutral' in inverted commas.[50]

The Comintern directive, *Directives pour le travail dans les organisations sympathisantes de masse, à but spéciaux*, spells out two principles of the operation of auxiliary organisations.[51] One was that they should be tightly controlled by the local Communist Party and the Comintern leadership, including approval of their general ideological line and working plans, to guarantee the moral and political influence of the Communists.[52] However, the other was that the Communist leadership of these organisations should take on only a 'camouflaged' or hidden role. Agitprop warned against the mechanical running of non-Communist organisations by Communists.[53] The organisations thus had to avoid having memberships that were composed mainly of party functionaries, and those in the party's trust (*les hommes de confiance du parti*) had to remain in the background as much as possible. As organisations had to appear to be spontaneous, initiated by the public and autonomous, Agitprop recommended a particularly unobtrusive link with national Communist parties, especially for the Association of Friends of the USSR. 'These organisations have to be established in a prudent manner in order to avoid the accusation of being Communist organisations.'[54] To achieve the illusion that auxiliary organisations were distinct from the Communist Party, it was suggested that their leadership consist of non-party members such as social democrats or members of the bourgeois left.[55]

These 'neutral' auxiliary organisations had the following roles: to conduct propaganda among the broad, working non-Communist and neutral masses, establish relations with intellectual and petit bourgeois circles, and organise them into groups.[56] Women, young people and children were listed as important targets.[57] As well as using organisations that were founded earlier – International Red Aid (MOPR), the Workers' International Relief (Willi Münzenberg's organisation) and the Pacifist Leagues – Agitprop planned to increase the number of Societies of Friends of the USSR in countries such as Germany and England.[58] Organisations of this last kind, in particular, were meant to involve the professional intelligentsia, for example doctors, teachers, artists, scholars and economists, and 'men and women from the petite bourgeoisie sympathetic to Soviet Russia'.[59] Cultural organisations also featured among the targeted groups.[60]

Each auxiliary organisation had its areas of responsibility that were specified by Agitprop. International Red Aid was to organise political campaigns and mobilise public opinion against the White Terror.[61] Pacifist Leagues would lead work with anti-war movements,[62] and Friends of the USSR were to inspire sympathy for the Soviet Union in broader circles. The 'neutral' organisations, Mezhrabpom and the Association of Friends of the USSR, were instructed to try and create what the Comintern called 'USSR clubs or "corners"'; they were to be located in the major cities of Europe and the USA, beginning with Paris and Berlin.[63] These clubs would form 'physical centres for agitation in favour of the USSR and Communism'. They would provide open access to Russian books, writings, drawings and exhibitions of Russian posters and craft.[64] The Associations of Friends of the USSR could use conferences and talks, the screening of Soviet films, artistic and theatrical evenings, and the promotion of tours by Russian artists. Personal contacts were recommended; societies were to engage in correspondence with Soviet schools, universities and factory committees. To encourage a broader circle of people to join these organisations, Agitprop recommended that members' financial contributions be nil or reduced to a minimum.[65]

Agitprop listed repeatedly and at length the activities that were recommended for these cultural clubs and 'corners'. It spoke over and over again about permanent exhibitions and displays of photos and Soviet banners; the creation of libraries and reading halls; the broadcasting of speeches by Russian leaders; obtaining portraits, photos and literature directly from the USSR; and evenings of Russian song or dance and talks on Russian literature.[66] All of these activities served one purpose – to gain a legitimate status in reaching the public, under the façade of predominantly artistic centres, which was 'totally independent from both Soviet representation and the Communist Party'.

Aims and expectations

Despite the Comintern's wish for national Communist parties to gain legitimacy and for cultural organisations to appear to be 'neutral', its aim of operating as a platform in political campaigns in defence of the USSR was of the utmost importance. Failure to provide the desired support brought them reprimands. Less than six months after the Bureau of Friends of the USSR was created in Cologne, it was criticised for the passive behaviour of its members and the inactivity of other branches of the Association of Friends of the USSR during a recent anti-Soviet campaign.[67] An older section of the Association in France, with 30,000 members, was also considered to be too passive. The anonymous author of this document criticised visitors to the USSR who came via the Association of Friends of the USSR for not showing enough support for the USSR on their return. They were reported to be not spreading sufficient information about the USSR, and not spending enough time in this work on returning home. Perceived failures of this sort led to a decision to widen the focus to broader circles of sympathising organisations, and to expand access to information by creating additional libraries with information on the USSR in different languages.[68] Even in the mid-1930s, when there were a large number of them in the West, the Comintern continued to send concrete instructions for branch (that is, national party) activities. In 1936, the topics to be diffused in the Western press included socialist construction and achievements, the new Soviet Constitution and, especially, popularising the peaceful, anti-Fascist policy of the USSR. National branches of the Association of Friends were instructed to respond immediately to any adverse statement by producing leaflets and conducting public meetings with workers and delegates who had visited the USSR. New members had to be attracted on as broad a basis as possible – that of sympathy for the USSR, regardless of their other political convictions.[69]

Despite such detailed planning for the organisations, there is no indication of whether the plans came to fruition or of how the Comintern influenced the behaviour of individual members. However, in later discussions of the operations of MORP, VOKS and the Foreign Commission of the Soviet Writers' Union, it will be possible to recognise the same pattern, to identify some of the Western organisations as 'auxiliary organisations' affiliated to Soviet organisations, and to examine the techniques that led to activities in support of the USSR.

Involving intellectuals: an ambivalent partnership

Western intellectuals had been drawn to the USSR since the 1917 Revolution and the Comintern soon began to display a distinct interest in individual intellectuals, particularly those who were influential or eminent. Their enthusiasm for the USSR would certainly be heard in the West and influence public opinion. Ironically, though, the Comintern had an ambivalent attitude towards intellectuals. Its anti-intellectual stance (despite the high number of intellectuals in its ranks) can appear at times to stem from its systematic cult of the proletariat, especially following Lenin's death,[70] although some sources indicate that Lenin was equally dismissive of intellectuals himself.[71] However, throughout the 1920s and 1930s, despite swings in official Soviet policies regarding cooperation with the West, the Comintern tried to engage foreign intellectuals; it was the first Soviet organisation to undertake such efforts in the early 1920s. While the Comintern interacted with certain eminent intellectuals directly, it delegated the reception of foreign visitors to other agencies that were considered to be best suited to dealing with them.[72] Thus, the responsibility for the reception of visiting intellectuals was allocated to VOKS, the subject of Chapters 5–7.[73] There was a distinct anti-intellectual turn in Comintern attitudes in the years 1927–29 that persisted until 1932–33 but, eventually, a new wave of interest in fostering intellectuals as allies arrived. This followed Hitler's ascent to power in 1933 and the subsequent change in Stalin's support for the Popular Front; he became more tolerant of non-Communist supporters and of intellectuals in particular.

The Comintern's most obvious goal in wooing illustrious foreign intellectuals was to gain their expressions of public support for the USSR. In 1922, Grigory Zinov'yev, then the Head of the Comintern, wrote personal letters to the eminent French writers Anatole France and Henri Barbusse to solicit written statements of support for the USSR.[74] The Comintern clearly considered their statements to be very important; they were intended for publication in the same volume as contributions by leading figures of the party and the Soviet state including Lenin, Trotsky, Zinov'yev, Radek, Lozowsky, Chitcherin, Preobrazhensky, Lunacharsky and others.

Henri Barbusse, the author of *Under Fire*, was famous in his day for being a pacifist writer, a Communist and a leader of the pro-Communist ex-servicemen's association, ARAC (Association républicaine des anciens combattants), and the pacifist Amsterdam–Pleyel movement. Barbusse played a major role in the support of the USSR, often on the Comintern's request. During the 1927 Comintern-run celebrations of the October Revolution in Moscow, Barbusse delivered speeches in defence of the USSR to foreign delegations[75] and later addressed foreign visitors attending the Congress of Friends of the USSR ('the Congress of Witnesses') in Moscow.[76] His activities at the request of other Soviet organisations, and his complex rapport with these organisations, will be discussed in later chapters.

Another prominent figure was Willi Münzenberg. He was a writer but above all he was a political activist and an 'organiser of genius',[77] an example of a leader who managed to mobilise intellectuals around their sympathies for Soviet Russia through thematic committees and organisations. During the post-revolutionary famine, he gathered a committee which included intellectuals such as Albert Einstein, the artists Käte Kollwitz and Georg Grosz, and the writers Anatole France and Henri Barbusse, and managed to promptly send boatloads of food to famished Russia. His *Illustrierte Arbeiter Zeitung* ran a special issue, 'Sowjet Russland im Wort und Bild', that encouraged sympathy for Russia and attracted avant-garde artists.[78]

In addition to attracting individual eminent intellectuals, the Comintern aimed to organise rank-and-file intelligentsia into groups and societies. In 1926, IKKI decreed the creation of such committees of intelligentsia in various countries, for example Barbusse's committee and the Committee For the Protection of the Victims of Terror.[79] In a resolution, IKKI declared the need to strengthen the existing committees of intelligentsia and to broaden the circle of intellectuals to be engaged, as they were believed to be the best bridges connecting revolutionary organisations with other potential sympathisers: the petite bourgeoisie and the non-Communist intelligentsia.[80] Münzenberg's International Workers' Aid, which had branches in different countries, was one such organisation that attracted writers and artists. To quote Fritz Adler, International Workers' Aid, which initially received its mandate from Lenin and later from the Comintern, was a 'true diplomatic instrument at the service of the USSR'.[81] When the German Communist Party (KPD) was banned, the 'neutral' International Workers' Aid was still allowed to operate. Manès Sperber later recalled[82] that the 'caravans of intellectuals' he managed to involve created photos, reports and literary sketches dedicated to the USSR. At his 'production factory', he published accounts of German workers' visits to the USSR, aroused sympathy for Russia among the intelligentsia by screening the films of Eisenstein and Pudovkin, and produced his own films about the USSR.[83]

The Comintern and writers

The Comintern displayed a special interest in mobilising literary supporters. 'We would really like to attract, as much as possible, all the healthy elements of the anti-capitalist and anti-bourgeois "literary Left"', Alfred Kurella wrote to Henri Barbusse in 1926.[84] As the Comintern had delegated the task of looking after intellectuals to VOKS, the project of involving writers led to the creation of MORP, a body created and supervised by Agitprop IKKI. As a means of attracting more writers sympathetic to the USSR, Agitprop founded a special literary periodical, the *Herald of International Literature (Vestnik inostrannoy literatury)*,[85] which it considered crucial to the process of engaging foreign writers. Putting one of its members on the editorial board of the magazine would allow Agitprop to keep its hand on the pulse of the *Herald*.[86] How MORP operated and how it was involved with foreign writers and used its periodical is discussed in Chapter 3.

The Comintern was therefore the key player in devising the initial tactics of cultural propaganda, and defined the framework of Soviet relations with Western intellectuals. Its euphemism of 'providing a service' to the foreign Communist press attempted to create the impression of a genuine exchange and not a command, and to disguise its dissemination of propaganda materials as merely the 'supply of information'. To understand the Comintern's thorough manipulation of this relationship and its attempts to exploit the individuals and media available to it is to unveil Soviet intentions in the courting of Western intellectuals. Publishing materials in a national Communist newspaper deflected suspicion away from the Comintern but not from the Communist Party; however, the creation of 'camouflage' or front organisations could deflect attention from Communist circles altogether. Similarly, cultivating individual intellectuals and engaging their actions on the Comintern's behalf was another technique that would point to a seemingly independent author as the source of the message.

However, how these proposed tactics were implemented has not been described. After all, the Comintern delegated its tasks to other cultural and literary organisations. Did these organisations all act in the same way? Did they adopt the Comintern's methods point by point? How successful were they in engaging Western intellectuals? All that has been known to date is that Soviet interactions with Western intellectuals reached their peak in the mid-1930s before beginning to decline. By analysing the operations of other Soviet organisations, one by one, it will be possible to gain an insight into the realisation of some of the Comintern's goals and to observe the successes and failures of Soviet cultural organisations.

3 MORP

Propaganda through coercion

In November and December 1930, a major writers' congress took place in the Ukrainian city of Kharkov – the Second International Conference of Revolutionary Writers. It later became known as the Kharkov Congress and was attended by 134 delegates from thirty-five countries,[1] 85 per cent of all the literary figures being Communists. The largest delegation, the German, included the revolutionary writers Johannes Becher, Ludwig Renn and the Czech-born writer and journalist Erwin Egon Kisch; America was represented by the young Communists Mike Gold and Joshua Kunitz, and France by the surrealists Louis Aragon and Georges Sadoul. The Congress was convened by the International Bureau of Revolutionary Literature with the support of the Comintern Executive Committee (IKKI); during the Congress, the Bureau was renamed the International Association of Revolutionary Writers or MORP. The Congress is primarily remembered for its ideologically harsh resolutions directed at Western writers and press. It criticised the Bureau's national branches (*sektsii*), its directives put the imperatives of Soviet policy above issues of importance to particular countries, and the Congress members almost unanimously stigmatised Barbusse, who was conspicuously absent. After the Congress closed, Aragon and Sadoul publicly renounced their association with the surrealists.

Some of these revealing events will be discussed in detail in the following pages, which will examine what MORP did to engage and influence foreign writers, and how these writers responded to MORP's tactics. This account begins with MORP's origins and its place in the Soviet hierarchy.[2]

The idea of creating the Litintern[3] – a literary equivalent of the Comintern that would unite proletarian writers throughout the world – originated 'from below', from revolutionary writers themselves. The idea was supported by the Russian Communist Party, RKP(b), and the leading revolutionary writers' organisations.[4] Following the 1925 RKP(b) resolution 'On Party Policy in the Area of Literary Fiction', the Liaison Bureau of Relations of Proletarian Literature was created.[5] The Bureau later evolved into the International Bureau of Revolutionary Literature (1926), which was again renamed in 1930 during the Second International Conference of Revolutionary Writers,[6] finally emerging as the International Association of Revolutionary Writers or MORP. This association was Comintern's auxiliary organisation (*podsobnaya organizatsiya*) and had a task that was at once literary and revolutionary – assisting Comintern with the printed word.[7] The Bureau was to translate Soviet materials into foreign languages and to take part in every major political campaign or event. Agitprop suggested that it should publish short articles (*fel'yetony*) covering the new life in the USSR, focusing on areas of interest to foreign workers; it would also provide the works of approved Soviet writers for publication. However, there was a lot more to its operations than this.

MORP shared the Comintern's view that art and literature were powerful ideological weapons that could be used to influence the working class and youth. It called for a united effort in creating proletarian literature worldwide, under the concerted action of foreign Communist parties and the Comintern.

> It is the direct responsibility of all of the [Communist] parties of the Comintern to watch vigilantly over the activity of proletarian literary associations, to assist them in ridding themselves of harmful influences of the decadent individualistic, mystical, reactionary art of the degenerate bourgeoisie, and to assist them in their organisational strengthening.[8]

In order to achieve this, MORP encouraged the creation of associations of revolutionary writers in various countries, under the umbrella organisation set up in Moscow, which should become centres of attraction for all writers sympathising with the ideas of Communism.

However, MORP was hostile towards sympathetic but non-revolutionary and non-proletarian writers. This was especially true between 1928 and 1932–33, following the harsh ideological line taken by the Comintern and the Russian Association of Proletarian Writers (RAPP), MORP's ideological and literary model. MORP's attempted domination of individual writers created complex and conflicting relations between them and MORP, which were described by Jean-Paul Morel as '*le roman insupportable*'.[9] Even Soviet critics described MORP's treatment of foreign writers as intolerant and dogmatic.[10]

Created under the auspices of the Comintern and responsible for implementing the policies of Agitprop IKKI, MORP was accountable to both IKKI and Kul'tprop of the VKP(b).[11] By 1932, MORP seemed to have an established structure and extensive international contacts. Its headquarters in Moscow consisted of the Secretariat, with secretaries in charge of country-specific commissions (*lenderkomissii*) that were also located in Moscow; by 1932, these included German, French, Eastern, Balkan, Anglo-American, Hungarian and Polish/Baltic commissions.[12] MORP's foreign branches (*sektsii*) included the German League of Proletarian Revolutionary Writers (Bund proletarisch-revolutionärer Schriftsteller Deutschlands, or BPRS), created in 1928, the American John Reed Clubs, and the French Association of Revolutionary Writers and Artists, or AEAR, created in 1932. With the exception of the Russian Leopold Averbach, members of the MORP Secretariat in Moscow were foreign *emigré* or refugee Communists, writers who were devoted and dogmatic. Following the defeat of the Hungarian Revolution, Hungarian writers such as Bela Illes, the Chairman of MORP's Secretariat, and Antal

Hidas arrived.[13] Bruno Yasensky[14] was invited by MORP to come to the USSR; he had undertaken revolutionary activities in Poland, then emigrated to France and was expelled twice. Another Polish émigré was Stanislaw Ludkiewicz, appointed as MORP's Executive Secretary (*otvetstvennyy sekretar'*).[15] After 1933, a flood of German and Austrian exiled writers arrived; Johannes Becher,[16] the founder of the German MORP section, represented them in Moscow. Having a membership with this background affected MORP's identity and operations, and was, in part, responsible for its harsh ideological platform and the intransigent treatment of its members and audience. In 1932, MORP gained a number of Soviet writers, some of whom were to be members of the Organising Bureau of the future Soviet Writers' Union; among them were Sergey Tret'yakov, Ivan Anisimov and Yakov Metallov. Another Russian writer, Mikhail Apletin, became MORP's leader in 1935.[17]

Despite MORP's affiliation to the Comintern, it suffered from ongoing organisational and financial difficulties.[18] In 1925, its first Head, the Commissar of the People's Enlightenment, Anatoly Lunacharsky, highlighted the Bureau's unclear status and 'meagre resources' (*skudost' sredstv*). He failed to draw the support of the party or the Soviet government.[19] Five years later, on the eve of the Kharkov Congress, the International Bureau of Revolutionary Literature was still reporting on the lack of staff and structure and its dependence on occasional subsidies from other organisations such as the state publishers (Gosizdat).[20] It was only in around mid-1932 that paid officers-in-charge were introduced as commission secretaries (*sekretari-referenty*).[21]

By 1932–33, having neglected MORP for years, the Comintern had virtually abandoned it.[22] Describing itself as an 'orphan organisation' (*besprizornaya organizatsiya*),[23] MORP vainly appealed to the Comintern for both financial support and leadership. These appeals included requests to finance MORP's support of foreign magazines and newspapers[24] and pleas for the Comintern to review its attitude to MORP in general.[25] MORP needed to find a new patron.

The Soviet Writers' Union, a powerful organisation created in 1932 to unite all of the writers' groups, became MORP's new governing organisation.[26] There was hope that MORP would be strengthened when its membership expanded with the arrival of Soviet writers;[27] that it would gain more influence once it was joined by more established Soviet writers (Fadeyev, Panferov);[28] and that there would be joint meetings with the Organising Committee of the Soviet Writers' Union and representatives of IKKI and the Central Committee of the Communist Party. However, none of this happened. In its letters to the Writers' Union, MORP again and again addressed principally financial issues: unpaid staff ('not only have our staff not been paid their salary for the first half of January, but we don't even have money for current expenditures'),[29] unresolved budget arrangements[30] and mundane difficulties such as the lack of a Russian typewriter.

MORP's ideological rigidity had now become another source of problems. MORP had always expected of its members and affiliates a compliance of the type exercised within the Communist Party; this damaged MORP's relations with foreign writers, thus antagonising its closest supporters. MORP made no effort to encourage them or to attract new members. When the Soviet literary climate gave the impression of having greater tolerance towards the intelligentsia and, in particular, writers,[31] MORP tried to change its tactics and broaden its influence abroad to include 'left-bourgeois writers'. Nonetheless, old habits clearly died hard and, amidst MORP's discussions of greater tolerance, it continued to pursue its familiar ideological hard line towards the West.

> We have to attract left-bourgeois writers who would work under our leadership. We have to widen our ranks by attracting sympathetic writers without, of course, in the least stepping back from our position of principle.[32]

After Hitler's assumption of power, the Comintern attempted to broaden the circles of MORP's European intellectual supporters and reported success; however, by 1934–35, its days were numbered and, at the end of 1935, it was disbanded, having, to quote a Soviet author, 'exhausted its possibilities'.[33] MORP's tasks were taken over by the Foreign Commission of the Soviet Writers' Union.

MORP's operations

The main avenues by which MORP engaged with Western writers were by adopting the Comintern's tactics of influence through three means of communication. These were the press, in which cultural materials and Soviet fiction were published; writers' 'auxiliary' organisations, whose creation MORP encouraged and whose activities it supervised; and individual writers, on whose support MORP relied.

MORP and the press

'Our main task,' wrote the MORP Secretariat leaders Ludkewicz and Illes in 1933, 'is the promotion of Soviet literature, achievements and culture, and of Marxist–Leninist critical thought.'[34] Understandably, the press had a complex role in MORP's operations; it served to publish Soviet work and to engage foreign writers as both readers and contributors. One way of doing this was to publish Soviet materials in the existing foreign Communist and near-Communist press. Another was to create a journal for distribution abroad. MORP's journal, *The Herald of International Literature* (*Vestnik inostrannoy literatury*), appeared in Russian and three foreign languages (French, German and English) with the contents adapted to the different countries.[35]

Producing MORP's own magazine was always seen as a top priority.[36] As its title suggests, MORP's aims were to publish foreign literature in the magazine, to use it to 'guide the Soviet reader's reading of translated fiction',[37] and to control the flow of foreign literature onto the Soviet market.

The magazine was also expected to play an international role by reaching Western writers and involving them in cooperation with Soviet production. It would target the interests of foreign readers of Soviet literature and engage them by publishing book reviews in Russian, German, French or English.[38] It would attract contributions from foreign writers as local correspondents, who would write reviews of literature from their countries.[39] *The Herald* would invite them to talk about their own work, a supposedly successful custom borrowed from Germany and known as *Selbstanzeige.*[40]

The Comintern 'welcomed and approved' the proposed magazine as an instrument of great usefulness.[41] However, it saw the magazine primarily as a means of attracting foreign support, and the Deputy Head of Agitprop, Alfred Kurella, implied that the act of agitating foreign writers and involving them in cooperation (*privlekaya ikh k sotrudnichestvu*) was more important than the original goal. 'We find the publication of such a magazine imperative as, above and beyond the tasks listed in the draft, it could play a major role in the cause of broadening the circle of writers sympathetic to the USSR and to Communism.'[42] Moreover, at this stage, Agitprop reaffirmed its own leading role in the creation of the International Bureau of Revolutionary Literature (*sozdannoy i rukovodimoy APO IKKI*), indicating to the RKP(b) its intention to remain in control of its journal. 'By sending its representative to the Editorial Board, Agitprop of the IKKI will be able to exercise a certain permanent influence over the magazine and to ensure that the desired goal is reached.'[43] Comintern's assumption of control of the magazine had a major effect on the way it would exert influence outside the USSR.

Taken at face value, MORP's optimistic reports in the 1930s on the development of the magazine, renamed *Internatsional'naya literatura (International Literature)* in 1933, show that it had indeed developed in accordance with these plans. 'Widely representing the vanguard of international literature'[44] and published in four languages, it was said to focus on editions for other countries and to attract contributions from foreign writers. About 40 per cent of each foreign issue contained translated Soviet literature and cultural materials, 'tied in with the requests of foreign readers in the various countries'.[45] In fulfilment of the 1927 plan, each issue had different contents depending on the language, the interests of foreign readers having been examined and taken into account.

MORP followed several tactics to involve foreign writers in cooperation. One effective way of obtaining praising publications for the magazine, explained Illes and Ludkiewicz, was to ask foreign writers to provide short replies to, or comments on, specific questions or questionnaires sent out by MORP, for example asking what writers thought about *International Literature*. According to Illes and Ludkiewicz, one such questionnaire brought responses from as many as forty-five foreign intellectuals, of whom fifteen were French: among them were Romain Rolland, Paul Signac, Luc Durtain, Eugène Dabit, Marcel Prenant, Elie Faure, Francis Jourdain, René Arcos and Paul Gsell.[46] Having obtained these favourable comments about its magazine, MORP then published suitable excerpts. 'The comments on the magazines by R. Rolland, Dreiser, Dos Passos and others were translated separately and published in the magazines.'[47] In a similar way, MORP obtained statements from foreign writers containing praise for the USSR.

A special issue of the magazine will appear for the Writers' Congress. It will include numerous replies we received from foreign writers on their attitude towards the issues of the new culture in the USSR, on what strikes them in today's capitalist reality and how the existence of the USSR helped their creative work.[48]

However, a journal printed in the USSR could have only limited distribution in the West, even in foreign languages, so MORP adopted the Comintern's technique of 'providing services' to the Western Communist press – that is, using the Western press for the publication of Soviet materials. MORP's so-called assistance to approximately forty foreign magazines and newspapers, particularly French, consisted of generating and supplying translations, articles and fiction.[49] Bruno Yasensky, the Polish member of the MORP Secretariat and an editor of the magazine *Literature of the World Revolution*, described the agreement that existed with the major Communist newspapers *l'Humanité*, *Rote Fahne* and *Daily Worker*. The agreement involved 'a systematic compilation of weekly literary pages' and 'supplying these newspapers with short articles (*fel'yetony*) and novels by proletarian writers' that would reflect the virtues of socialist construction and the opposition to war.[50]

MORP's achievements included the growing dissemination of a variety of materials: Soviet and foreign fiction; articles by Soviet and foreign critics relevant to a given country; and special sets of information, for example information on the Belomorkanal, children's literature and Soviet drama and poetry. However, keeping these magazines supplied placed an unsustainable burden on MORP. Following the emergence of MORP's national branches, the number of foreign magazines was growing; yet, MORP was driven to deplore the state of its resources, describing them as inadequate to its growing workload and as preventing it from further enlarging its operations. 'In view of the great expense of translations into a number of languages, and a lack of equipment, this funding is clearly insufficient.'[51] MORP's difficulties with the direct financing of 'needy' magazines and branches (*nuzhdayuschiyesya*) shed light on its operations in general. Thus, some operations failed without MORP's support; the Spanish periodical *Octobre*, initially closed as a result of repression, was subsequently unable to resume publication 'as a result of the lack of funds' and MORP's inability to assist it.[52]

Jean Fréville and l'Humanité

MORP's success in getting its materials published in the foreign Communist press clearly depended on the local individuals in charge. One remarkable example of the role an individual could play was the case of Jean Fréville, who replaced Barbusse as literary director of *l'Humanité*, the FCP's official organ. Fréville was a Marxist intellectual, passionate about the creation of revolutionary and proletarian literature in France. A journalist who was fluent in Russian, he wrote on a vast range of topics, from literature and history to politics and economics, and was the right-hand man of the leader of the FCP, Maurice Thorez.[53] The pages of *l'Humanité* abounded with Soviet cultural and literary materials, which Fréville obligingly published; his correspondence with MORP highlights his personal role and motivation in assisting this process.

Fréville consistently welcomed all Soviet materials and reported back to MORP on its success in reaching the pages of *l'Humanité*. He reported, for example, about the plans for a regular Tuesday page, dedicated to materials on the USSR or the publication of stories by Soviet writers.[54] Even when materials were not published, Fréville justified their omission. 'As you must have seen, only a few items were used. Last month's Communist Party Congress and the election campaign have nowadays limited our chances in *l'Humanité*, where space for us is rather strictly limited.'[55]

Fréville was more than a compliant conveyor belt; he actively encouraged MORP to supply him with Soviet literary work for *l'Humanité*, preferably in French.[56] Fréville was personally committed to publishing anything supplied to him from Moscow, either in its original form or by adapting it into an article that he himself would author.

> It will be my great pleasure to use anything you send me on Soviet literature, whether as short literary articles in which I will examine certain issues or certain writers, or by publishing 'as is' articles of particular interest to the French proletariat.[57]

In addition to placing MORP's materials in *l'Humanité*, Fréville helped implement MORP's plan of selecting materials for specific readerships. He offered to indicate areas of readers' interests, based on the regions where they lived, or on specific topics within the theme of socialist construction, so that MORP could send the appropriate materials. 'Thus none of your work will be wasted and everything will be used.'[58]

Fréville was endlessly helpful. When he expressed interest in receiving the magazine *La Littérature internationale* (the French version of *International Literature*), he also volunteered to publicise it: 'We shall do all we can to circulate it as widely as possible.'[59] Another favour was to offer a book exchange, with a limitless supply of works by French writers of interest to MORP. 'Just let me know [what you need] and I'll do my best to help you.' But Fréville was more than a receiver of Soviet materials; he had his own professional interest in them, in adapting them in his own work for the cause. Thus, when he was working on a brochure of proletarian literature, he urged MORP to send him specific works. 'I need a series of Soviet works. I am taking the liberty of sending you a list, asking you to send them to me as soon as possible.' To write a book on proletarian literature, he asked Bruno Yasensky to supply him with Soviet books on the subject, 'to enlighten our comrades and make our work easier'.[60]

Fréville's adaptation of Soviet materials also served another purpose: by processing them and attributing them to a native French source it helped to conceal their origin. This technique of dressing up a Soviet message as coming from a 'native' source, either a newspaper or an individual, lent it more credibility and distanced it from the USSR. Finally, it corroborated the original message that openly originated from acknowledged Soviet publications. Fréville's desire to play a role in the creation of proletarian literature in France was fundamental to MORP's smooth relations with *l'Humanité* and its ability to achieve its propaganda objectives.

'We have to save Barbusse'

Not all of the men in charge of the Western Communist press were as compliant as Fréville. The 'Barbusse affair', revolving around the newspaper *Monde*, reveals MORP's powerlessness when faced with the resistance of a foreign supporter, even a Communist.

The weekly newspaper *Monde* was founded in 1928 by Henri Barbusse as an alternative to the mainstream Communist press.[61] MORP expected that *Monde* would be a channel of distribution for the Soviet message and, quite possibly, MORP's official organ in France.[62] But *Monde* became a thorn in the flesh of MORP and the Comintern virtually from the time of its foundation. Barbusse's idea of attracting broader, non-Communist elements through his weekly meant that *Monde* had to present a range of opinions.[63] MORP, its branches, the Comintern and the FCP all rejected this 'apolitical' position.[64] They maintained that no one could call himself a Communist writer while heading a newspaper that claimed to have no connection with the party.[65] MORP condemned both Barbusse's choice of materials – by *personae non gratae* like Panaït Istrati, Augustin Habaru and Emmanuel Berl – and his reluctance to publish Soviet-supplied materials covering events that MORP intended to promote abroad. (Thus, Bruno Yasensky complained to Serafima Gopner of IKKI about Barbusse's reluctance to publish reports of the Prompartiya [Industrial Party] trials.[66]) These disagreements evolved into a conflict over MORP's attempts to dominate Barbusse.

How was it possible to pressure a high-profile public figure and a leader of international movements into submission? Nothing was achieved either before or during the 1930 Kharkov Congress, which Barbusse did not attend and during which his 'case' was heard *in absentia*. The Congress was torn between condemning Barbusse in the resolution quoted below and attempting to maintain the alliance with him.[67] The struggle continued after the Congress and MORP's archival documents reveal the behind-the-scenes machinations of the Communist circles which attempted to coerce Barbusse into running *Monde* in accordance with MORP's ideas. MORP's correspondence with Barbusse over a period of some years, its discussions of and resolutions about *Monde*, Barbusse's correspondence with Paul Vaillant-Couturier and MORP's letters of complaint to the Comintern all illustrate the persistent, concerted efforts to make Barbusse submit and his resistance.

Between 1929 and 1932, MORP tried various ways of putting pressure on Barbusse directly. At first, it tried to ostracise him. In 1929, an open letter was signed by a number of writers, all members of MORP, including the Westerners Becher, Illes and Yasensky, the Soviet writers Libedinsky, Serafimovich and Mikitenko, and even the former Commissar for Enlightenment, Lunacharsky; the letter attempts to shame Barbusse for lending his good name to the slanderers of the USSR and demands that he either change the nature of his periodical or dissociate himself from it.

> In a time of the intensification of our struggle, you, comrade Barbusse, edit and sign a periodical by means of which you spread, among the masses who trust you, the opportunistic doctrine of the slanderers and enemies of the USSR. The International Bureau of Revolutionary Literature, in its central organ *The Herald of Foreign Literature* and in the organs of its international sections, has several times subjected the line of your periodical to severe criticism, pointed out its main errors and drawn your attention to the necessity of either changing the nature of your periodical radically or removing your name as Chief Editor of *Monde*. You did not consider it necessary or appropriate to do either one or the other. You continue to edit, and sign your name to, the slander of the embittered enemies of the USSR. With whom do you stand, with us in our struggle or against us?[68]

The 1930 Kharkov Congress acted even more brutally by presenting Barbusse with an ultimatum 'either to turn his periodical *Monde* into a revolutionary organ or to stop lending his name to this social-fascist enterprise'.[69]

At the same time, MORP went behind Barbusse's back, with Yasensky reporting the matter to the Comintern and requesting 'the appropriate guidance' (*sootvet-stvuyuschiye direktivy*) from Agitprop.[70] MORP reasserted the position of Soviet organisations as the only sources of information on the USSR and interpretation of Soviet events. 'MORP, as well as other Soviet organisations (VOKS), tried at that time, by means of materials sent from the USSR, to neutralise this harmful and confusing material (*vrednyy i putannyy material*) published on the pages of *Monde*.'[71] *Monde* resisted this pressure by not publishing this 'counter-material', with two or three exceptions. *Monde*'s rate of publication of Soviet materials was unsatisfactory, claimed MORP. Only twelve articles on the USSR were published in the third quarter of 1928, and only one in the third quarter of 1929;[72] in 1931, *Monde* allegedly refused to publish literature sent by MORP.

> In the past year, material on the USSR accounted for only 5 per cent of the entire space in *Monde* (literally 5 per cent). Stalin's 'six conditions'[73] are described by *Monde* as a return to the NEP [New Economic Policy]. The literary material is poor and selected in a crude and tendentious way.[74]

MORP blamed Barbusse for having turned *Monde* 'into an openly social-fascist magazine' staffed by 'renegades expelled from the ranks of the Communist Party'.[75] Not even the FCP was said to be capable of getting through to Barbusse; to quote a MORP letter addressed to Bela Kun, *Monde* had 'fenced itself off thoroughly' (*otgorodil sebya tschatel'no*)[76] from any influence of the FCP.

This assumption about Barbusse's invulnerability to pressure was only partly correct; Barbusse was resistant but not insensitive to attacks. He denied having received a list of Soviet authors and an article on the Saboteurs' trial that MORP claimed to have sent on the Comintern's instructions. As for a report by a Communist insider that, at *Monde*, 'Soviet materials are thrown into the waste basket' (*sovetskiye materialy brosayutsya v korzinu*),[77] Barbusse claimed that all MORP sent were 'unreadable exercises' (*nechitabel'nyye uprazhneniya*).[78] Direct confrontation through an open letter addressed to Barbusse by MORP's Secretariat received a 'very irritated letter of reply from Barbusse' (*'Barbus otvetil ochen' razdrazhennym pis'mom'*).[79]

However, MORP remembered that Barbusse's name carried enormous international weight, which made it difficult for MORP to pressure him indefinitely without the risk of alienating him. Acting in a conciliatory manner, and to compensate for the criticism to which he'd been subjected at the Kharkov Congress, MORP still re-elected Barbusse, at the end of the Congress, to its presidium.[80] Sergey Dinamov of the MORP Secretariat and the editor of *Literature of the World Revolution* took the credit as peace-maker.

> The [Communist] fraction of the MORP Secretariat had great difficulties in overcoming the resistance of the majority of the foreign delegates, who demanded the immediate expulsion of Barbusse from MORP, and in re-electing him, despite everything, to the MORP presidium.[81]

MORP also suggested making a distinction between Barbusse and *Monde*'s editorial board,[82] and continuing to persuade him by whatever means they could devise. When Dinamov suggested efforts to 'save Barbusse' (*spasti Barbussa*), it was really a plan to save MORP's good relations with him.

> Barbusse has worldwide importance. There is no need to rush ahead. One has to try every means of influencing Barbusse – *l'Humanité*, the magazine *Komintern*, Gorky, Lunacharsky. One needs to make one last effort to save Barbusse.[83]

One of the ways of 'tearing Barbusse away from *Monde*' was to resort to the personal influence of other opinion leaders, for example Gorky. Similar steps were undertaken by the FCP Politburo, which asked Gorky and Karoly to remove their names from the editorial board of *Monde*.[84]

But some MORP members took a different stand. *Monde*'s publication of 'slanderous attacks against the USSR by the renegade Panaït Istrati'[85] resulted in a highly critical open letter to Barbusse from the MORP Secretariat. It was published by Inprekorr and signed by the writers Averbach, Becher, Illes, Libedinsky, Lunacharsky, Mikitenko, Serafimovich and Yasensky. Bruno Yasensky, as a member of the Communist fraction of the MORP Secretariat, continually called for the expulsion of Barbusse from the MORP Secretariat and the condemnation of his errors. Other members supported Yasensky's position: Baklanov accused Barbusse of being an unreliable fellow-traveller rather than a Communist and Stande called on MORP to intensify its criticism of Barbusse. As a result, in early 1932, the MORP Secretariat decided to remove Barbusse from the editorial board of *Literature of the World Revolution*. It instructed Yasensky to undertake widespread criticism of Barbusse and *Monde* in the press, including *l'Humanité*, *Literature of the World Revolution*, *Literary Gazette*, *Linkskurve* and others. These decisions were indeed carried out.

Barbusse was hurt, later alluding to the constant attacks of 'certain individuals who call themselves party members'[86] and their 'totally inadmissible, sectarian and unclean' attitude.[87] He expressed his hurt regarding the participants of the Kharkov Congress, who 'have revealed only too openly their ignorance both of revolutionary literature in France and of what literature in general is'.[88]

Attempts to pressure Barbusse came not only from Soviet Communist bodies but also from MORP's French branch, l'Association des Ecrivains et Artistes Révolutionnaires (AEAR), and the FCP. Uncoordinated and contradictory at times, their actions were nonetheless united in their determination to force *Monde* to submit.

FCP and AEAR avoided resolutions, open letters of denunciation and reports to the Comintern that vexed and alienated Barbusse. They resorted to personal diplomacy to manipulate him. In March 1931, after a failed attempt to create a Communist faction within *Monde*, they made more persistent attempts through the influence of Barbusse's old friend, the French Communist writer Paul Vaillant-Couturier. In February 1932, the Secretariat of the Comintern instructed him 'to try to undertake, once more, a series of measures regarding Barbusse in order to try to bring him closer to the party'.[89] The documents relating to this affair, though originally written by the participants in French, are accessible only in Russian translation at RGASPI with the caution 'Not to be divulged' (*Ne podlezhit oglasheniyu*). These documents include the correspondence between Vaillant-Couturier and Barbusse, and a concluding report to the FCP Politburo by AEAR, which was just being formed.[90] They reveal how the FCP, AEAR and MORP tried jointly to resolve the *Monde* affair by bringing Barbusse under the control of the FCP, and how they discussed the issue of those French proletarian writers who were not members of the Soviet-oriented inner circle of AEAR or who were clearly resisting joining it.

Barbusse's friend Vaillant-Couturier acted as the FCP's go-between. His job was to find a gap in the fence Barbusse had built around himself in order to engage him in discussion with the party leadership. The correspondence, initiated by Vaillant-Couturier, reveals Barbusse's trust in his friend but also his Achilles' heel – *Monde*'s disastrous financial situation – and the hurt Barbusse felt at the attacks by Communist literary circles.[91]

> Here are the bare facts: the question is whether the next issue of *Monde* or the following one will appear. The wave of debts swamps us. The situation is not just critical but desperate.[92]

Vaillant-Couturier responded to Barbusse's frankness with an offer of reconciliation with the party, clearly an important issue for Barbusse. 'You will be able to reinstate your contact with the party (about which you rightly complain that it has been too weak) either now, at the present moment, or never.'[93] The price of this normalisation of relations, though, would be the closure of *Monde*, the source of discord between Barbusse and the Communist organisations. 'The party and the Comintern will find it difficult to understand the delays in the liquidation of the enterprise, the continuation of which is of no advantage to anyone.'[94] Vaillant-Couturier then tried to arrange a meeting between Barbusse and the party leaders, making it sound like advice given purely out of friendship yet leading Barbusse to make decisions that were contrary to his interests.

> I hope that you will change your mind regarding Monday. In any case, I could not tell the Secretariat that the meeting is postponed indefinitely; it could give rise to the worst interpretations. [. . .] Being firmly convinced that you have not changed your intentions in the meantime, I urge you as a friend to think of the perilous consequences of this new delay in the matter of ending a situation that has in any case persisted all too long.[95]

But Barbusse refused to commit himself to the measures suggested by Vaillant-Couturier ('Monday impossible letter follows'),[96] and so the latter changed his strategy to one of shaming Barbusse for having published a Trotskyite (Madeleine Paz) and a renegade (Victor Serge),[97] and of describing *Monde* as 'representing a growing scandal'.[98] From friendly persuasion, Vaillant-Couturier moved to emotional blackmail by threatening Barbusse with a break with the Communist Party and by appealing to his sense of honour.

> For months I have been doing all I could in order to avoid the break and to reinstate normal literary relations, but I cannot achieve the impossible. I implore you to think it over. . . . This is now a question of your revolutionary dignity.[99]

While Barbusse was being importuned to meet the leader of the FCP, Maurice Thorez (a meeting which he clearly avoided), he did agree to meet two MORP members, the Soviet writers Afinogenov and Kirshon, who were then in Paris. The French side was represented by Vaillant-Couturier, the Communist film critic Léon Moussinac (at whose place the meeting took place) and the Russian-born Communist writer Vladimir Pozner, who acted as interpreter. The meeting was conducted according to MORP's instructions. It may appear from Vaillant-Couturier's report that the discussion with the Soviet writers was successful. Barbusse was said to have acted in a conciliatory way, accepting the imminent end of *Monde* and suggesting the creation of a *Nouveau Monde*, which would be an organ of AEAR; in the event that *Monde* survived, Barbusse agreed to hand it over to the control of the party.

> In the event *Monde* continues to exist, it was decided that a number of comrades – party – would be nominated to infiltrate it and to redress its line, on the condition that certain members of *Monde* (Rossi in particular) would be removed, either immediately or gradually.[100]

The meeting was said to have resolved another problematic issue, Barbusse's alliance with the politically suspect proletarian writers who were not members of AEAR. (At the time when Vaillant-Couturier and other French Communist writers were working towards the creation of the MORP branch, the Association of Proletarian Writers was acting as an independent association and had a good rapport with Barbusse.[101]) Barbusse was expected 'to select among them the least politically compromised elements and shift them to the AEAR platform'.[102] This supposedly successful meeting thus led to a 'very moderate'[103] written agreement, prepared by Vaillant-Couturier in Barbusse's name and for his signature. In it, Barbusse was to commit himself to cooperate with AEAR, to 'liquidate *Monde*'s heavy past' (*likvidiroval by tyazheloye proshloye Monda*)[104] and publicly denounce the Trotskyite line of the proletarian writers who did not belong to AEAR.

Just when victory seemed near, Barbusse once again stalled by avoiding the meeting where the document was to be signed. Vaillant-Couturier implored, 'I am in a state of total despair, as I didn't see you yesterday, on Saturday. . . . I waited in vain for your telephone call.'[105] The letter of repentance and submission that Barbusse was supposed to sign had been drafted by Vaillant-Couturier; in the Russian translation it is entitled 'A letter in which Barbusse was supposed to break with his muddled past, on the basis of his discussions with Kirshon, Afinogenov and Moussinac'.[106] For years, this letter was attributed to Barbusse and published on the assumption that he had written it.[107] However, in a separate note, Vaillant-Couturier explains that it was he, Vaillant-Couturier, who wrote this letter, in Barbusse's name, to be signed by Barbusse. This note also explains why Barbusse was reluctant to sign it; by signing it, he would have declared his unconditional joining of AEAR. His signature would have excused the 'unjust polemic bluntness'[108] to which he had been subjected by national and international bodies (i.e. the FCP and the Comintern) as being directed merely against *Monde*. By signing the letter, Barbusse would have blamed *Monde*'s policy on 'non-party members, those expelled from the party, Trotskyite elements, social democrats and liberals' who misled the newspaper into becoming counter-revolutionary.[109] Finally, by signing this letter, Barbusse would have given up his connection with the Association of Proletarian Writers, an organisation which AEAR had criticised for its 'petit bourgeois confusion and Trotskyite influence' (*melkoburzhuaznaya putanitsa i trotskistskiye vliyaniya*)[110] and to which *Monde* had opened its pages. Barbusse would have been committed to handing his newspaper over to the control of the 'comrades' of AEAR.

> Following this, I put my periodical *Monde* at the disposal of AEAR, and of no other cultural organisation, and ask the Bureau to nominate a group of comrades who would be instructed to maintain contact with me to develop the conditions of collaborative work.[111]

Barbusse was uncompromising in his reaction to this text. In an indignant reply, he refused to sign this 'total and blunt renunciation' (*polnoye i ploskoye otrecheniye*),[112] categorically denying that it reflected his discussion with the

Soviet representatives. 'I was stunned as I read this text; it has nothing in common with what we discussed with Kirshon at Moussinac's.'[113] Barbusse's understanding of the meeting was that they had agreed on the need to broaden the revolutionary writers' circle by including 'revolutionary writers who are politically less developed, namely a whole range of "proletarian writers" '.[114] He refused to compromise on issues left out of the draft letter: an insulting polemic conducted by *l'Humanité* against him and the boycotting of his recent literary publications (presumably by Communist bodies). Barbusse reaffirmed his devotion to the direction of *Monde* and refused to strike the final blow against the periodical that was 'currently suffering its near-death agony' (*perezhivayuschemu v nastoyaschiy moment svoyu predsmertnuyu agoniyu*).[115] Barbusse even stood up for articles written by Trotskyites and published in *Monde*.

> I think that in Madeleine Paz' article on proletarian literature – quite a realistic and sensible one – there is nothing 'scandalous', just as there wasn't in all the statements by Victor Serge (and just as I don't consider scandalous, from the revolutionary point of view, what was written in *Monde* on the issue of elections, on the issue of the USSR, and on the issue of Doumer's assassination).[116]

Barbusse refused to sign a letter that he considered false and unjustly accusatory. 'This is a document in which I [am supposed to] declare my repentance and remorse towards people who behaved towards me in an unacceptable way.'[117] The draft, according to Barbusse, attempted to make him betray everything he stood for, justifying 'all the absurd attacks of the Kharkov Congress and those of *l'Humanité*'.[118]

The report that AEAR wrote on the 'Barbusse affair' to the Politburo of the FCP[119] presented Barbusse's resistance as a 'treacherous manoeuvre' (*predatel'skiy manyovr*).[120] Of even more concern was his leadership at the forthcoming Geneva Peace Congress, an international forum initiated by Barbusse and Romain Rolland, and which AEAR was also going to join. While AEAR claimed, in a contradictory statement, that 'Barbusse's name has been losing more and more of the respect it enjoyed in worldwide revolutionary circles',[121] it feared in fact that Barbusse's international prestige might lead to a climate that was contrary to the aims of the FCP and AEAR.

> If the preparation of the Congress is really to be entrusted to Barbusse, then there is a danger that the very spirit of the Congress will be distorted and used for the advantage of political groups for which Barbusse's name is currently used as a screen.[122]

AEAR believed that it alone was going to legitimately defend the USSR; it denied this right to anyone who disagreed with the Communist Party, and feared that Barbusse might gain additional prestige from the Congress that would allow him to monopolise it and take the initiative in defending the USSR. 'The struggle for the defence of the USSR and against imperialist war cannot co-exist with a hostile attitude towards the Communist Party.'[123] The organisation that once sought Barbusse's involvement because of his influence and prestige now saw itself as being in competition with him. In order to protect its sphere of influence, AEAR appealed to the FCP to assist it in its involvement in the preparation for the Congress.

MORP steps in

The conflict came to a sudden end following the Decree of the Central Committee of the VKP(b) of 23 April 1932, which led to the disbanding of RAPP and marked the start of conciliatory treatment of intellectuals by the VKP(b).[124] MORP's policy suddenly came to coincide with Barbusse's line: a greater tolerance of political views, and an opening of the ranks of revolutionary writers to broader circles.[125] Comintern, and consequently MORP, now aimed to attract a broader circle of sympathisers and public supporters of the USSR. This change had its effects on *l'affaire Barbusse*.

In May 1932, the MORP Secretariat retracted its members' previous statements against Barbusse. Formally, the writer's 'rehabilitation' was once again based on dissociating him from *Monde*. '*Monde* is a share-holding company, and in fact Barbusse does not govern it.'[126] MORP also recalled previous attempts to protect Barbusse. In 1929, MORP had instigated an article by Yasensky, published in *The Herald of Foreign Literature,* which criticised *Monde* without attacking Barbusse,[127] and MORP's German journal *Linkskurve* had been reprimanded for a blunt article directed personally against Barbusse.[128] The attacks on Barbusse by MORP were now blamed essentially on one member, Yasensky, who had allegedly misled other members.

> The resolution on France was produced by Yasensky and, according to him, approved by the Comintern Executive Committee. Later it emerged that the resolution had not been agreed upon with IKKI, and the [Communist] fraction approved it on the basis of false information.[129]

MORP members retrospectively singled out Yasensky as a scapegoat for leading them to take a decision they had all voted for. 'We voted against Barbusse because Yasensky told us that Barbusse would be expelled from the FCP. This is why I and other comrades were in favour of expelling Barbusse from the MORP Presidium' is the way a Russian MORP member, Yakov Metallov, justified himself.[130]

MORP now concentrated on mending the damage done to its relations with Barbusse. 'Barbusse is hurt by the blunt attack of *Linkskurve* against him; he even wrote that whenever Romain Rolland writes something, we are full of admiration, and when Barbusse writes, we criticise,'[131] explained Illes. MORP also recognised that *Monde* would attract young people who were interested in the USSR.

Yet this reconciliation did not mean that MORP gave up its struggle to take over *Monde*; rather it resorted to a change of tactics, a move away from its methods of obvious pressure. It now returned to its earlier proposal to redress *Monde*'s political line by infiltrating the editorial board with Communist members. Late in 1932, Agitprop's Alfred Kurella, a writer whose 'personal qualities' Barbusse respected, established his presence on *Monde*'s editorial board.[132] According to decisions made in Moscow prior to his departure for France, Kurella's task was to change MORP's approach towards the periodical and to reinforce Barbusse's position at *Monde*. His presence on the board obviously led to a different style of *Monde*, and at the meeting of the MORP Secretariat on 26 November 1933, Léon Moussinac reported that Alfred Kurella had indeed succeeded in clearing *Monde* of the Trotskyite elements and in becoming its virtual head.[133] According to Moussinac, Kurella planned to establish contacts with all the MORP sections and with revolutionary writers, and asked the MORP office to supply him with Soviet materials. The meeting decided to approach the relevant echelons of the hierarchy with a proposal to supply *Monde* with literature once more.[134]

The change at *Monde* was not a brutal takeover but rather an adaptation of Comintern's and MORP's previous methods of exerting influence over it. Kurella impressed upon MORP that the final say in whether to accept materials for publication should lie with the periodical. The way to improve the quality of materials published would be for MORP to move away from what was known as 'programmatic literature' and to choose topics on art and literature that were of actual interest to French readers.[135] Kurella wanted to have greater subtlety in the materials, to avoid the language of overt propaganda and, without abandoning MORP's pet topics (e.g. socialist construction), to add diversity through literary and cultural materials.

> As for the topics, it was agreed in Moscow that the following themes are of particular interest to *Monde*: lively reports on important events of social and political life (socialist construction in the USSR can provide quite a few topics of this kind, but it should not be the only subject!); unpublished documents of Russian and world literature (for example, letters and other documents by Pushkin, Dostoyevsky or Tolstoy that have been recently found; the rediscovered letter by Engels on Balzac); historical and literary commentaries by well-known art critics on matters of particular interest to the French reader; analysis and critical polemic concerning the bourgeois point of view, particularly French, on art and culture; novellas and short stories by Soviet writers who are known in France from their published works. (...) Programmatic articles that only repeat stereotypical formulae stand no chance of being printed.[136]

Kurella's letter suggesting a takeover of *Monde* also indicates the need to acknowledge Barbusse's requests for better quality materials and to refine propaganda with more subtle techniques to reach non-mainstream Communist circles in a new political climate.

Comintern's wish to control, through MORP, the flow of information on the USSR, and MORP's attempts to subdue Barbusse into obedience, created nothing but conflict. Barbusse's refusal to turn *Monde* into an uncritical channel of dissemination of MORP-generated messages, to which Barbusse was expected to lend extra weight, resulted in concerted action by MORP, the FCP and AEAR, which was led by the Comintern. Despite their campaign of at least three or four years, ranging from subtle pressure to outright manipulation, the writer – a figure of international stature and firm principles – managed to resist this antagonistic treatment while at the same time maintaining his commitment to the USSR.

'According to rumours, the money came from Moscow': MORP's auxiliary organisations

On 21–25 June 1935, as if to echo the 1930 Kharkov Congress, another major writers' event took place – the International Writers' Congress for the Defence of Culture. Even though some of its participants had attended the Kharkov Congress, this Congress was quite different. Hosted in Paris by a group of eminent French writers – André Gide, André Malraux, Jean-Richard Bloch and Louis Aragon, with Soviet writers present as guests and not hosts – it was an enthusiastic gathering of pre-eminent international literary figures, who met to discuss the future of culture represented, at that time, by the USSR. This was no Comintern- and MORP-supervised gathering of young revolutionary and proletarian writers; it was attended by authors of different political persuasions, inspired by the idea of the international writers' united front. Some of the many attending included: Barbusse, Aragon, Bloch, Malraux, Géhenno, Benda and Nizan from France; H. Mann, Seghers, Feuchtwanger and Brecht from Germany; Forster and Huxley from England; and Gold and Frank from the USA. The Soviet writer Il'ya Ehrenburg was one of the organisers of the Congress, and included among the large Soviet delegation were writers who were highly respected in the West, such as Boris Pasternak, Isaak Babel and Alexey Tolstoy (even though the Soviet authorities initially did not include Babel and Pasternak in the delegation). During the Congress, the International Writers' Association for the Defence of Culture was born. Although the Communist influence was felt, it is doubtful that the participants were fully aware of the extent of Soviet influence in the creation of this new international writers' movement. And yet, MORP's documents unmistakably confirm that the impetus behind these developments originated in Moscow. Indeed, they point to the role that the Soviet side played in the planning and preparation of this writers' association, which was in fact designed to be a Soviet auxiliary organisation. The events leading up to the Congress are very revealing about the mentality and methods of operation in play at MORP.

One of the early ideas about MORP's operations, proposed by Lunacharsky and the Comintern, was that MORP would be aided by auxiliary organisations in Western countries; these organisations would be constituted as branches (*sektsii*) within MORP and would have revolutionary writers as their members. MORP instigated the creation of some of these branches through its own members, for example the German BPRS, which was formed in 1928; in other cases, it simply affiliated groups that already existed, for example the American John Reed Clubs. Governed from Moscow by MORP along the lines of the Comintern model, the branches published journals, for example *Linkskurve* by the BPRS, *The New Masses* by the John Reed Clubs (replaced in 1934 by *Partisan Review*), and *Commune* by the French AEAR. MORP expected these organisations to be obedient and, in giving them directions, put Soviet political imperatives above the needs of member countries.

Britain did not have a MORP section.[137] MORP's attempts to engage in discussion with the PEN Club failed because its president, John Galsworthy, refused to receive the MORP delegation.[138] Despite its strong revolutionary movement, France was not at the forefront of the creation of MORP sections either. By 1930, there were branches in eight countries,[139] but the French AEAR was officially founded as late as the spring of 1932, the time when MORP's conflict with Barbusse was apparently settled. The remarkable feature of the relationship between MORP and its branches was the amount of disagreement and friction, especially in MORP's relations with the German BPRS and the French AEAR;[140] the latter will be the focus here.

The creation of AEAR

In October 1931, 'despite its insufficiencies and lacunae', Fréville reprinted in *l'Humanité* the part of the Kharkov resolution that dealt with proletarian and revolutionary literature in France. Fréville proposed to enact MORP's directives by rapidly creating the French branch of MORP.[141] MORP had been working for four years prior to that on the creation of the French MORP branch.[142] The main creators of AEAR, according to the Russian version of its periodical *Literature of the World Revolution*, were said to be Vaillant-Couturier (Executive Secretary), Fréville (Deputy) and Moussinac (one of the three treasurers).[143] Fréville was the first to announce the creation of AEAR in a letter to the MORP Secretariat, describing its opening session of 17 March 1932 and listing the membership of the honorary presidium ('as you asked us to do').[144] He went on to request that MORP send a welcoming letter to mark the inauguration of the new organisation.

> Could you please urgently ask the Secretariat of the International Union of Revolutionary Writers to send us, as soon as possible, addressed to me at *l'Humanité*, a letter of welcome to the French branch. This letter will be read out from the podium during the Inaugural Assembly.[145]

As he did with *l'Humanité*, Fréville encouraged MORP's involvement by requesting supplies of Soviet literature for the emerging AEAR. 'We shall need to receive regularly the most important literary and cultural magazines that appear in the USSR.'[146] Fréville was concerned at AEAR's lack of its own journal and again asked MORP for assistance; he felt that MORP's French issue of *Literature of the World Revolution* could be a substitute.

> Unfortunately, we do not yet have a review of proletarian literature in France, but the French version of your magazine published in Moscow can partly make up for it. Would you like me to send you a few names of French contributors? Could you please also indicate the space you can allocate us in your magazine.[147]

A handwritten resolution by a MORP official in the margin of the letter shows that the request was met; instructions were given to send AEAR the magazine *Na literaturnom postu* and several books.

MORP's correspondence with AEAR shows that there was a certain unease among MORP officials and a critical appraisal of AEAR. In claiming that the French section's links with MORP were unsatisfactory, did MORP mean that AEAR was not sufficiently subordinated to it? When it criticised AEAR in September 1932 for 'lacking major creative forces' (*tvorcheskikh sil malo*), having members who were mainly petit bourgeois and being 'ideologically rather weak',[148] MORP was seemingly putting its own revolutionary agenda ahead of attracting broader circles of sympathetic writers. However, Morel argues that, on the contrary, whereas MORP advocated a camouflaged form of political propaganda through art and literature, AEAR members encouraged the development of openly tendentious and polemical literature in France.[149]

AEAR rejected MORP's criticisms, which confirms that its members were not wholly dominated by MORP. AEAR's activities report, requested by MORP, was written by the Frenchman Léon Moussinac,[150] an otherwise disciplined Communist film critic. He had been an FCP member since 1924, a delegate at the 1927 First Conference of Proletarian and Revolutionary Writers in Moscow, and an active contributor to contacts with Soviet organisations. However, he rejected MORP's criticisms at the 10 March 1933 meeting of the MORP Secretariat.[151] Moussinac believed that AEAR had exceeded MORP's expectations; it was not merely a literary auxiliary organisation but was broadly involved in other areas of art and culture. AEAR had demonstrated a great deal of independent activity and initiative, not envisaged by MORP. He pointed out that architect members were working in consultation with Communist municipalities; other divisions were taking part in militant actions: artists made posters and brochures for meetings and rallies and the film division discredited bourgeois propaganda through film. AEAR's literary division, numerically the largest with 137 members, did not seem to rely on MORP for its literature either; it had conducted, through *l'Humanité*, a successful literary competition, and had extensive publishing plans. (Moussinac's report was 'taken into consideration' by the MORP Secretariat, and AEAR's activities were approved.[152])

Later in 1933, MORP acknowledged AEAR's achievements. The sudden increase in its membership brought France to the forefront of MORP's activities and made AEAR the number one on MORP's list of foreign sections.[153] AEAR rapidly grew to some 800 members; it created new branches in the provinces and was involved in extensive political activity through lectures, discussions and numerous rallies. MORP noted the participation of 'big names' (*imena*) at the head of AEAR, such as Rolland, Barbusse, Vaillant-Couturier, Nizan and Aragon, and those who joined AEAR in 1933 alone, including Gide, Malraux, Cassou, Giono and some former surrealists. Beginning in 1933, AEAR realised another one of the Comintern's and MORP's major objectives, the creation of new magazines and newspapers. The monthly *Commune*, the journal of AEAR, was seen by MORP as being another success in France.[154] MORP acknowledged that the French section had succeeded in developing its 'extensive operations' without Soviet financial assistance.[155]

'For the defence of culture': towards an international writers' organisation

In 1932–33, Soviet policy shifted to one of working to attract broader circles of intellectuals on the basis of anti-Fascism. MORP now began to think of replacing its old branches, which until then were limited to revolutionary and proletarian writers, with a new type of united auxiliary organisation that would attract a wider range of Western writers; this was not dissimilar to the way that RAPP and other Soviet writers' associations had been replaced by the all-encompassing, broadly based Soviet Writers' Union. Therefore, in 1935, MORP ordered the American John Reed Clubs to disband, to the shock of their many members, and be replaced with a League of American Writers affiliated to MORP.[156]

The emergence of France as a new stronghold for the Left in Europe gave MORP the idea of creating a new international writers' organisation in Paris; this would still be under the auspices of MORP but less obviously subordinated to Moscow. In yet another 'top secret' (*sovershenno sekretno*) proposal to the Central Committee of the VKP(b) and IKKI on 27 October 1933, the MORP Secretariat proposed to organise a League of anti-Fascist or left-wing writers in Paris. The League would have major world writers at its head who were already involved with MORP.[157] Clearly a front, the League would be 'MORP's auxiliary organisation, which would operate from a place other than Moscow' (*podsobnoy MORPu organizatsiyey, deystvuyuschey ne iz Moskvy*), and was openly referred to as 'our Parisian bureau' (*nashe parizhskoye byuro*).[158] MORP seemingly accepted what it called the 'unavoidable widening of the circle of writers who [would] join' this left-wing League, to enable MORP to move away from its previous revolutionary image in line with the goals of the new policy. Support for the USSR would now take priority over previous ideological considerations about proletarian orientation and obedience to national Communist parties. 'In the current conditions, we fight for anyone who is prepared to fight for the USSR, even if he has had some friction with the Communist Party of his own country.'[159]

Like Comintern's 'camouflage' organisations, the League would make use of culture as a cover for political activities. While the proposal made it sound like a centre of a worldwide literary movement, the organisation would counteract the activities of the PEN clubs,[160] support pro-Soviet political causes by participating in international political campaigns and protests, and set up branches of the League in countries where revolutionary movements were illegal. Another 'camouflage' principle consisted of well-disguised but firm Communist leadership.

> The main precondition for the League must be strong Communist leadership (probably unofficial) and a thorough selection for League membership of all the supposed anti-Fascist writers from the camp of the Trotskyites, Brandlerians and other renegades.[161]

MORP proposed to keep control over the League in several ways. One would be to give the League MORP's own journal, *International Literature*, which could be published in Paris ('there is a perfect opportunity for it that we have already worked out').[162] MORP hoped that another form of control would be for the Comintern to finance the League. 'As for the financial side of the matter, initially it would consist only of setting up the League, to the sum of approximately 1,500 roubles, with a monthly subsidy of 400–500 roubles.'[163]

MORP's proposal for a new international writers' organisation, auxiliary to MORP and with its centre in Paris, was accepted in 1934; ironically, the creation of the Association Internationale des Ecrivains pour la Défense de la Culture would be followed by the dissolution of MORP.

Ideas for the future organisation came from both France and the USSR. The French proposal, *Note au sujet d'une organisation internationale nouvelle d'écrivains*,[164] elaborated on MORP's idea of an auxiliary organisation centred in Paris. This unsigned letter is in French and, although its authorship is uncertain, the evidence points to it having been produced at Barbusse's initiative; he also possibly wrote it.[165] This proposal also envisaged the creation of a literary camouflage organisation with a broad membership. Its leadership would be provided by Soviet political organisations, with guidance through Comintern directives or a 'designated comrade' (*camarade désigné par lui [le Komintern]*) as well as a caucus of members with good political sense. This guidance should be disguised by a façade of eminent names.

> However, the central body and the central apparatus in Paris must be run, so far as the public is concerned, by a Patrons' or Directors' Committee – a kind of very numerous Praesidium which will include all the major world literary names who are neither conservative nor reactionary.[166]

Although this proposal, even more than MORP's before it, wanted to avoid any typically Communist slogans, it could not avoid sending the same political message. Thus, the proposal suggested that the organisation address the struggle not only against war and Fascism but also against capitalism.

> It will be indicated that we are appealing to all writers from the different left-wing tendencies in order to create a united front against war and Fascism among writers. It will be specified that in order to be effective, this struggle

against war and Fascism must also include the struggle against capitalism, which is the cause of war and Fascism.[167]

To further avoid a Communist image, the organisation would need to publish either in the nominally non-Communist *Monde* or in a large publishing house, which should be supposedly apolitical. 'We should consider the possibility of a large company, based on the model of large bourgeois companies, and otherwise totally neutral in appearance and entirely independent.'[168] Similarly, the proposal suggested getting away from an explicitly Communist-inspired name for the organisation; it should have no suggestion of anti-war or anti-Fascist tendencies, and possibly be as broad as *Union universelle des écrivains sociaux.*

The author of the proposal suggested that internationally known opinion leaders would attract other participants and lend respectability to the organisation. 'All the major names of left-wing literature' would have to sign the inaugural manifesto: Gorky, Ehrenburg, Dos Passos, Dreiser, Waldo Frank, Sinclair Lewis, Joe Freeman, Rolland, Gide, Bloch, Vildrac, Thomas Mann, Heinrich Mann, Bertrand Russell, etc. The author of the proposal believed that if French writers could be persuaded to sign the manifesto first, their international prestige would encourage the others and avert possible debates about the manifesto's phrasing.

However, the unexpected twist in this French proposal was that the new organisation, instead of being an auxiliary body to MORP, implied MORP's dissolution.

> First of all, MORP, whose liquidation this new organisation implies (and I know that it has been discussed), may disband itself spontaneously by declaring that it is necessary to establish a broadly based International Writers' Union.

Moreover, the author proposed removing MORP from any obvious participation in its setting up, so that it not be seen as MORP's creature.

> It would be harmful for this major development if MORP itself were to take the initiative in formulating its programme. That would only assist the scheming of all our enemies, who would claim that MORP simply wanted to change its name.

Ironically, the proposal advocated using the same Communist members for the infrastructure – good administrators like Johannes Becher, Léon Moussinac or Georges Friedmann – and making use of the existing MORP infrastructure, as MORP itself would be disbanded.[169] The controlling role of Soviet members is also apparent in the discussion of the prospective budget. It was suggested that, following the appointment of secretaries and in the face of additional running costs, members' fees would have to be supplemented by direct assistance (e.g. for travel costs) or indirect encouragement of members (e.g. in benefits offered by the Soviet government).

This figure does not include the expenses for special Soviet representatives who are likely to come [to France] in order to supervise or act as liaison [to Moscow]. Neither does it include travel expenses required for the implementation of a very interesting project about which he spoke to me. This project would consist of enabling some European writers to stay in Soviet resorts.[170]

As late as May 1935, the MORP Secretariat was still debating this proposal and working out additional tactics. Johannes Becher contested the idea of a manifesto and collecting signatures. Reading his comments during the MORP meeting, one realises the extent of his contribution to the 1935 International Conference for the Defence of Culture; it was he who proposed gathering writers into an organisation by holding a conference.[171] He opposed the use of openly Communist slogans such as 'the defence of the USSR' and 'the struggle against imperialist war and against Fascism'; instead he proposed the slogan 'For the Defence of Culture' and suggested introducing essential issues in the form of a discussion. In the event, this is the course that was taken; in the summer of 1935, the International Writers' Conference for the Defence of Culture was held in Paris and the International Writers' Association for the Defence of Culture created.

Unlike other foreign MORP Secretariat members, Becher recognised the sophistication and diversity of the foreign writers who were to be engaged and, for the first time in MORP's existence, provision was made for a divergence of views. Becher drew the Secretariat's attention to 'nuances of a spiritual nature' (*dukhovnyye nyuansy*) that interested French and German writers and which could not be resolved by the arguments of historical materialism – matters such as death, humanism, heritage and human dignity. He also foreshadowed the difficulties of working with individual writers, mainly French. This included the volatile nature of their alliance with Communism (e.g. André Gide, Victor Margueritte) and the complexity of the ideas they habitually engaged with (Malraux). He admitted the weaknesses in the theory of members of both MORP proper and AEAR, for example their fixation with the notion of socialist realism, which left them unable to defend their positions. Becher said that dealing with complex issues became particularly difficult in discussion with more sophisticated adversaries, such as surrealists, or other philosophically advanced members such as Malraux.

Becher's views were far from signalling ideological openness. In fact, he warned against ideological heterodoxy because it would make it hard to maintain Communist leadership at the Congress and within the organisation.[172] He claimed that maintaining Communist leadership and control would be possible only if the political and ideological base of the organisation were sufficiently narrow.

> If we succeed in keeping the leadership of a broadly-based organisation in our hands, then well and good. But if that is impossible, then we must narrow this base but maintain the management, come what may.[173]

Yet Becher pointed to the need for more subtle methods of influence.

These writers have to be governed in such a way that they don't feel that

directives may be coming from Moscow. In other words, they have to be influenced in such a way that <u>they</u> say what we want to hear.[174]

Apart from reflecting the changes that were occurring in MORP's management and policies in 1935, Becher articulated the development of a less visible influence on the writers who needed to be won over. For the results to be effective, the writers should not only not suspect the controlling influence of Moscow but also remain unaware of the role they were playing.

The International Writers' Association for the Defence of Culture, created shortly after these discussions, did indeed appear to have been founded on the initiative of Western writers who supported the USSR, most of them French. But in truth, MORP was deeply involved behind the scenes. And even though MORP was disbanded in December 1935, Becher's ideas about the best ways to approach Western writers provided the groundwork for the leaders of the organisation that replaced MORP, the Foreign Commission of the Soviet Writers' Union, discussed in Chapter 8.

4 MORP

The closing years

So far I have focused on the operations of MORP that involved the press and writers' organisations. However, all of its operations were largely dependent on the support of individual writers. Until the policy shift of 1932–33, MORP had relied on their uncritical obedience and made no attempt to attract, interest or reward Western writers. After 1932–33, MORP began to change its tactics, moving away from repressive measures and the pursuit of short-term pragmatic imperatives to the cultivation of durable long-term relationships. These changes did not come naturally, partly because they went against MORP's original spirit and partly because MORP's less than satisfactory financial resources were inadequate for its new goals.

Reaching Western writers

Obtaining favours: Romain Rolland

Romain Rolland (1866–1944), winner of the 1915 Nobel Prize for literature, was one of the most influential and respected French writers, an intellectual renowned for having stayed above the battle (*au-dessus de la mêlée*) during World War I. His vast novel *Jean-Christophe* (1904–12) was commonly interpreted as expressing a desire for harmony between nations. He was an unusual case: although he accepted the Soviet Revolution, he condemned violence, and yet he became involved with MORP and other Soviet organisations. These relationships did not begin until around 1930, at a time when he grew close to the Russian Maria Kudasheva, his future wife. After years of an epistolary romance, Kudasheva joined Rolland in Switzerland, initially staying with him as his secretary and assistant. It is unclear to what degree Kudasheva, who had been infatuated with Duhamel in the 1920s and visited him in France, was acting on behalf of Soviet organisations. Neither a Communist nor a member of MORP, Rolland nonetheless became associated with MORP through personal relationships with its leading officials, both Soviet and foreign; these included Alfred Kurella, Léon Moussinac and Sergey Dinamov.[1] He joined the newly created AEAR and agreed to be on the editorial board of its journal, *Commune*, when Aragon asked him to take on the job. Rolland was responsible for a number of appeals, loaded with emotion, for the defence of 'our international motherland . . . the USSR'. He wrote to the MORP leadership offering unsolicited advice about practical activities for MORP and suggestions for useful strategies. For example, he provided advice on the content of *Littérature Internationale* and other projected publications on the USSR so that they might most effectively engage the Western intelligentsia,[2] and suggested ways of improving the standard of French in the weekly *Monde*.[3]

Rolland's numerous appeals and rallying cries in defence of the USSR, widely publicised both there and in France, appear to be spontaneous. However, both sides of the correspondence between Rolland and MORP show that these appeals were written at MORP's request. Thus, Rolland's 1933 publications in *Monde* (e.g. appeals on behalf of the accused in the case of the Reichstag fire) were written at the request of Kurella.[4] Some of the open letters that had a political message, such as Rolland's letter to the American writer Upton Sinclair, were also prompted by MORP's request that Rolland exercise his international influence.[5]

Compliant as Rolland was in responding to MORP's requests for articles or statements, he found it difficult to write on demand or without sufficient reflection; he said he could not write without an inner impetus.[6] These scruples caused some refusals or delays, especially at the earlier stages of his involvement.[7] Given this, it may not be surprising that MORP resorted to manipulation to extract statements from Rolland. In March 1932, Illes sent him a telegram with the request for an appeal 'to all humankind' against the war in China and its immediate threat to the USSR. Following the model of Comintern's letters in the 1920s, which had appealed to a writer's sense of leadership on the international scene, Illes spared neither pathos nor flattery, invoking Rolland's international prestige that would allow him to reach the broad popular masses and ignite an international peace movement.

> Workers of the whole world, who see you as a spokesman for the conscience of the better part of humankind, are awaiting your word. I beg you to join the ranks of the vanguard fighters against imperialism, for peace, for the workers of China and for the USSR. Appeal to all humanity, mobilise in this decisive moment the forces of all those who refuse to derive gold from their brothers' blood.[8]

Rolland agreed, sending copies of his appeal to *l'Humanité*, *Lumière*, *Monde*, French public figures and Gorky for publication;[9] the Russian version was published in *Pravda*. MORP treated this episode as a victory. At a meeting, the MORP Secretariat openly stated that Rolland's protest against the war in China had been used as a vehicle for a statement in defence of the USSR, and Rolland's compliance with MORP's request was claimed as a success by MORP. 'Romain Rolland was mobilised to perform an important task, and we managed to achieve what we wished,'[10] concluded Bela Illes. Encouraged, MORP reaffirmed the need to make optimum use of Rolland in the future ('It is very important for us to have his friendship')[11] and to use personal relations with the writer as an effective tactical move. 'Only personal negotiations with Romain Rolland can contribute to the establishment of close contact with him and make efficient use of him in campaigns for the defence of the USSR.'[12]

The power of money . . .

While cooperation with major established writers depended on their solidarity, MORP's involvement with revolutionary writers often depended on adequate financing. Though MORP was acting on the Comintern's instructions, it was the Comintern that habitually left MORP short of money to carry out those instructions. Appeals to the Comintern and, to a lesser degree, state organisations were in vain. Those of MORP's operations that depended on money reveal the difficulties it faced.

One of MORP's more costly operations was bringing its foreign members to the USSR,[13] for example to attend the 1930 Congress. There were other operations: on Comintern's instructions, MORP brought ten foreign delegates to Moscow to attend and report on the Prompartiya (Industrial Party) trials, a worthwhile publicity exercise according to Illes and Yasensky.

> There were a number of major foreign revolutionary writers at the saboteurs' trial, who, through their articles and notes, informed the proletariat of their countries about the revealed preparations of the imperialist powers to invade the USSR. The writers' presence has had a major international impact and has already given tangible results – e.g. Gleser's article in the *Frankfurter Zeitung* and many others.[14]

Whether they were later paid for by Comintern or not, MORP's invitations to foreign writers clearly had important results in the international writers' community and in generating publicity for Soviet policy abroad. This issue became more important around 1933, when bringing foreign writers to the USSR became an essential MORP operation. The MORP Secretariat was concerned about managing the arrangements, and appealed to the Comintern for:

> permission to expand visits by foreign writers to the USSR and to provide them with some material assistance during their stay in the USSR – particularly before the Congress of the Soviet Writers' Union – so we may convene, following the Writers' Congress, a MORP conference.[15]

Without financial assistance, MORP was unable to bring foreign writers to Russia on its own initiative and to look after them during their stay. Thus, the invitation to Léon Moussinac, who was supposed to replace Aragon, and the Chinese writer Lu-Xiun required the cooperation of the newly created Soviet Writers' Union. 'We cannot do it without your agreement, as we cannot undertake the material responsibility even for their short stay in Moscow.'[16]

. . . and other benefits

Once foreign writers had actually reached the USSR, MORP needed to create a favourable impression. Following collectivisation and the years of the Great Famine of 1930–33, MORP was keen to provide adequate food of good quality for its guests. However, getting food was more than a matter of money; one needed access to special stores for privileged employees of certain departments and for foreigners. MORP was keen to use food as a reward and to prevent even poor visitors from thinking that Russia was struggling. After all, it was the West that was supposed to be suffering under the Depression, while evidence of famine in the Ukraine was carefully hidden. At the same time, MORP employees were also trying to receive some benefits for themselves.

The problem was how to find the right way of asking for that level of funding and related privileges. In the summer of 1932, Antal Hidas of the MORP Secretariat asked the Comintern for help in providing more food for foreign writers who were working in or visiting the USSR.[17] Hidas was asking that the writers be given access to the privileged 'closed distribution store of the Foreigners' Supplies Administration' (*zakrytyy raspredelitel' Insnaba dlya inostrantsev*).[18] While there was no mention in Hidas' euphemistic letter of the food shortages and ration cards in the USSR, he explained his request by reference to 'certain problems' (*zatrudneniya* – a distinctly milder word than *trudnosti*, or difficulties) peculiar to, and to be expected from, foreign revolutionary (and therefore poor) writers. In the same letter, Hidas asked that permanent access to the special store be given to the MORP staff and leadership including Bela Illes, Bruno Yasensky, Aragon, Hidas himself and others. The letter reminded the Comintern of the importance of these visits to the USSR. After all, the invitations had come from MORP and had been agreed upon by the decision-making authorities (*direktivnyye organy*), that is, the Comintern and the Central Committee of the VKP(b).

It is of particular interest that Hidas' request was the first instance of a MORP official departing from the practice of open and unembarrassed discussion of propaganda techniques in internal documents. In fact, Hidas dressed up MORP's attempts to mislead visitors about Soviet reality as a necessary aid to their accurate study of socialist construction and to create 'the propaganda of truth' about the USSR to be told abroad. Hidas wrote that the visiting writers 'study areas of socialist construction, write literary works dedicated to the Soviet Union and, upon their return home, conduct extensive work in disseminating the truth about Socialist construction in the USSR'.[19] While Hidas' request avoided mentioning the gravity of the food situation in the USSR, it made it clear that the writers' reports could be affected if visits were 'unassisted'. Such beggarly trips might reveal to the visitors the true nature of daily life in the Soviet Union and the reality (especially the famine) behind their impressions of socialist construction. 'This is why it is important that the question of their supplies be resolved in a satisfactory manner, as complications of this nature may negatively reflect upon the quality of their creative work.'[20]

There is no doubt that providing special conditions for resident and visiting foreign writers did significantly affect their perception of the USSR. Jean-Richard and Marguerite Blochs' impressions of supplies in Soviet food stores were largely based on the banquets and endless meals available to writers during the First Soviet Writers' Congress and on the Blochs' special privileges. Elsa Triolet also commented on the contrast between the USSR in 1934 ('shops full of goods') and her recollections from earlier visits of the queues for bread and the lack of clothing or ornamental items. It's a matter of speculation how much her impressions were affected by the abundance of food and other privileges available to foreigners.[21]

Writing for payment

One of the items in MORP's expenditure was the payment of foreign writers for commissioned work, mainly articles. One of its requests to the Comintern was to pay writers in foreign currency for their contributions:

> at least some minimal amount of [foreign] currency to cover the needs of foreign magazines and sections (4,400 golden roubles) and, at the same time, to help pay foreign revolutionary writers part of their authors' fees in [foreign] currency.[22]

Reports from MORP on the difficulties of paying foreign writers for their literary contributions reveal how much MORP's operations depended on adequate financing and how much writers' cooperation depended on being paid. MORP noted the loss of literary contributions from writers; for example, Oscar Maria Graf refused to send further articles to MORP as he was owed several tens of roubles.[23] For months, Walter Benjamin, growing increasingly impatient, reminded *Das Wort*, the organ of MORP's German section (which still existed after MORP had closed), about unpaid fees for articles he had sent for publication long before.[24] In some cases, MORP staff members were stranded abroad, unpaid; MORP could not send Ernst Ottwald his monthly salary in Prague, despite the fact that his trip had been approved by a higher authority.[25] Senior, loyal members of MORP could also be alienated as a result of desperate financial need, even to the point of turning away from the cause. In the autumn of 1935, the Secretary of MORP, Mikhail Apletin, drew the attention of the Head of the Department of Culture and Enlightenment (*Kul'prosvetotdel*) of VKP(b) to the financially desperate situation of Johannes Becher, a leading German member of the MORP Secretariat. Apletin quoted a letter from Sonia Hartwig of Harvard University, which recounted Becher's complaints about not being paid. This, according to Sonia Hartwig, had led Becher to the verge of breaking away from the revolution and approaching bourgeois editors. According to her, Becher had grown so desperate that he was prepared to join the enemy camp and his state of mind was having a damaging effect on his friends.[26]

MORP's numerous requests for money and other material support reveal its difficulties and its low status. Much more importantly, these requests destroy the myth that the USSR showed disinterested support for revolutionary authors. MORP was part of an industry that produced propaganda in one form or another. Authors were paid for their services (e.g. in fees for literary contributions), and 'sausage propaganda' (*kolbasnaya propaganda*), through access to food supplies and special shops, swayed them towards a favourable perception of Soviet conditions. While it is understandable that financial difficulties constrained the achievements of MORP, it is surprising to discover how severely the loyalty of some Western supporters was put to the test when the money ran out.

From harsh measures to a change of tactics

As it continuously stressed, MORP saw its role as the exercise of ideological influence over Western writers. Soviet literary organisations – first RAPP and later the Soviet Writers' Union – held immense power over Soviet writers, controlling individual careers and lives with the carrot and the stick. It might seem impossible to us today that MORP, by using the stick, could exact obedience from Western fellow-travellers or even from Communist writers like Barbusse. And yet, writers had differing reactions to pressure, depending on their status and circumstances. Barbusse was capable of accepting, quite humbly, MORP's 'advice' on his literary work. Sergey Dinamov, the editor-in-chief of *International Literature*, once suggested that Barbusse make additions to the already published biography of Stalin. 'Please find attached an excerpt from a book by Frankfurt, the head of Kuznetzstroy. This excerpt is dedicated to comrade Stalin. If you republish your beautiful book on the best man on our planet, this text will be useful to you.'[27] 'I will immediately ask to have it translated for me,'[28] Barbusse replied gratefully.

A beginner in the Communist literary world like Louis Aragon showed himself to be malleable under ideological pressure, but a much older, major non-Communist like Romain Rolland needed to be treated with kid gloves.

Aragon: how to pressure a writer into submission

Louis Aragon, an active and provocative member of the surrealist group, began to gravitate towards Communism in the mid-1920s. Although he participated in the magazine *Surréalisme au service de la Révolution*, his relations with institutional Communism remained unorthodox and his actions unpredictable. In the late 1920s, Aragon became involved with his future wife, Elsa Triolet, a Russian émigré and a writer working in French. When they met, one of Triolet's attractions was that she was Mayakovsky's friend and the sister of his muse, Lili Brik. Triolet introduced Aragon to Mayakovsky, whom Aragon greatly admired, at a time when Aragon was renewing his ties with the FCP and the USSR.[29] In November 1930, with the writer and film critic Georges Sadoul, he attended the Kharkov Congress of Revolutionary Writers and, although he was not an official participant, he stated that he was attending the Congress not as a surrealist but as a Communist. The Congress condemned the surrealist and other non-revolutionary proletarian literary movements. Immediately afterwards, in circumstances which remain unclear, Aragon and Sadoul signed a confession-like document in which they dissociated themselves from the Second Surrealist Manifesto and submitted themselves to the control of the party. 'We consider it necessary to recognise certain errors that we committed previously in our literary activities, errors that we undertake not to repeat in future.' By 1933, Aragon would be considered by MORP to be one of the major French authors; he was translated and published in the USSR, and later became a hero of the Resistance and the leading French Communist writer. But in 1930, his status was very different from that of a writer like Barbusse. The 1930 Kharkov Congress was the turning point for Aragon; it led to his irrevocable submission to the discipline and control of the FCP.[30]

However, after the Congress, Aragon continued to associate with the surrealist group and write articles that ran counter to the party's (and MORP's) ideology. Like Barbusse, who would later be pressured into giving up his association with proletarian writers who were not members of AEAR, Aragon was required to clarify his position in relation to the surrealists. He was used as a pawn in MORP's struggle against the surrealists, and was singled out to make a second public statement of his break from them and denounce his recent articles. If he did not, threatened Jean Fréville in a letter to Bruno Yasensky, AEAR would ask MORP to take 'due measures' (*les mesures qui s'imposent*), in short, expel Aragon from MORP.[31]

Thus, in 1932, during Aragon's stay in Moscow as an official representative of the French branch of MORP (i.e. AEAR), AEAR itself forced him to make a written statement to MORP and AEAR of his ideological position.[32] Barbusse had rebutted every accusatory statement, including those of the 1930 Kharkov Congress, and defended his decisions; not so Aragon. In his letter of self-criticism, Aragon fully submitted himself to the line of the FCP and the Comintern, reaffirmed his allegiance to the decisions of the Kharkov Congress and made a commitment to 'work without reservation towards the creation of agitation literature that will illustrate and support the policies of the FCP and the Communist International'.[33] While Barbusse reaffirmed his association with proletarian writers instead of condemning his allegiance to them, Aragon concentrated on his public disavowal of his former allies, the surrealists. He retracted his previously expressed hopes about the surrealists' participation in the revolutionary movement through AEAR, and regretted having published an article 'next to other articles whose contents were directed towards the distortion of Marxism; thus I could have been seen as being in sympathy with them'.[34] Aragon pointed to an action that he regarded as being indicative of his final break with this group – an article in *l'Humanité*, in which he publicly dissociated himself from a brochure published by the surrealists. Ironically, Aragon did not even take credit for his earlier accurate prediction that the so-called 'better part of the surrealists' (Maxime Alexandre, Luis Buñuel, Alberto Giacometti, Georges Sadoul and Pierre Unik) would break with surrealist circles – a wish that had been expressed by the Kharkov conference.[35]

Unlike Barbusse, who proceeded with the anti-war movement independently of AEAR, Aragon reaffirmed his acceptance of AEAR's prerogative to control the anti-war stance in defence of the USSR.[36] Aragon saw his task as preventing such a war by fighting, on the 'cultural front', those elements that split and slandered the party, 'the only party that prepares for the advent of proletarian culture by means of revolution'.[37]

The joint efforts of two literary organisations, MORP and AEAR, successfully blackmailed Aragon into making a definite break from fellow surrealists, thus ensuring his undivided loyalty to Communist circles and, importantly, establishing the pattern of all his future relationships with organisations of the Communist system.

Repairing the damage: 'Both R. Rolland and Barbusse are absolutely necessary'

While coercion worked successfully with Aragon, who was eager to remain part of the Communist literary world, such treatment was out of the question for Romain Rolland, whose services were solicited by MORP. It was easy to alienate the great writer when he felt undervalued or that he was being treated with insufficient respect; it was then up to MORP to change its behaviour to win back his cooperation. The episode in which Rolland was manipulated into making a statement that was supportive of the USSR has already been described; MORP considered this to have been a success. Nevertheless, the gloss was taken off this apparent achievement by the lack of coordination between MORP and French Communist organisations; when *l'Humanité* published Rolland's statement, it was prefaced with an introduction that presented Rolland as an outsider.

> The great writer Romain Rolland does not belong to the circle of 'our' writers. Known above all as a pacifist who has stayed 'above the struggle', as was the case during the 1914–1917 war, he has subsequently, especially in recent months, become significantly closer to Communist ideas. In any case, he has become a passionate defender of the USSR, the torch-bearer of the new world, against the capitalist conspiracy.[38]

Rolland took serious offence. He considered this introduction to be counter-productive and hurtful, believing it subverted the effect of his appeal. As he wrote to Bela Illes, 'instead of stressing its importance, *l'Humanité* did everything it could to deaden its impact!'[39] MORP could only agree[40] and took the matter up the party hierarchical ladder, appealing to the Comintern and the Central Committee of the VKP(b) against AEAR and *l'Humanité*. In letters to Serafima Gopner and Comintern leaders that were marked 'secret',[41] and to the Kul'tprop of the VKP(b) Central Committee,[42] Bela Illes sketched the story of how MORP, on the Comintern's instructions, had solicited Rolland to write the appeal and how *l'Humanité* had prefaced it with an unflattering introduction that was 'inappropriate, considering the clear revolutionary position he has now taken'.[43] Illes feared that the incident was likely to alienate Rolland rather than attract him to 'our camp'. Illes asked the Comintern to 'give appropriate instructions to *l'Humanité*' and to ensure that the positions of all the national Communist parties accorded better with the position taken by MORP. 'All our work in attracting left-bourgeois writers will go to waste if the local party organs alienate these writers instead of attracting them.'[44]

This episode occurred at the time when Soviet policy towards intellectuals was changing. Comintern's reply went beyond the issue of reconciliation with Rolland and provided more general instructions, including how to redress the treatment of Barbusse over *Monde*, which was still unresolved at that time. In September 1932, at a meeting of the MORP Secretariat, the Comintern representative Dietrich repeatedly insisted on the need to maintain good relations with both Barbusse and Rolland.[45] Dietrich and the MORP leadership outlined an official policy towards the two French writers, emphasising that they should be encouraged rather than re-educated and, as Illes put it, not be criticised from the party perspective.[46] Comintern's new instructions to MORP were to attract a broader range of writers and to try and transform the French section into a truly mass organisation. As Dietrich put it, 'One needs to be critical of their work not by pushing them away, but by explaining their errors to them in great detail.'[47] Comintern's position towards Barbusse became thoroughly conciliatory in recognition of the 'enormous responsible work' he had conducted at the anti-war congress; for similar reasons, the importance of keeping Rolland as a friend was stressed.[48] 'Both R. Rolland and Barbusse are absolutely necessary' to the cause, concluded Dietrich,[49] requesting a retraction of the criticism of both writers by *Linkskurve* and *l'Humanité*. The actions of AEAR and *l'Humanité* were now described as 'the crudest sectarian errors' (*grubeyshiye sektantskiye oshibki*).[50] In May 1932, MORP invited Rolland to visit the USSR to try and repair relations with him. (Rolland replied that at the moment it would be difficult and time-consuming, yet he sent his regards to Soviet writers and hoped to meet them.[51])

As MORP's approach was becoming more conciliatory following the Comintern's policy changes, the question was whether MORP could reinvent itself in ways that were suitable for its new role.

Rethinking tactics

It would require new, more flexible tactics to attract writers who were not politically committed, the 'urban petite bourgeoisie', as a 'possible and partially necessary ally'.[52] Concerned for its present and future, MORP's Secretariat bombarded the Comintern and the Soviet Writers' Union with proposals reporting the ineffective approach taken by other existing Soviet cultural organisations, including its major rival, the All-Russian Society for Cultural Relations with Foreign Countries or VOKS.

> As for us . . ., even here in Moscow we do everything to scare them [foreign writers] away. We can quote you a whole range of facts regarding the unacceptable treatment of foreign writers by Intourist, VOKS and other organisations, and the fact that neither we nor you take proper care of them.[53]

Soviet writers who had only recently joined the newly created Soviet Writers' Union[54] and, later, MORP's new leadership[55] proposed improved methods for contact with Western writers. Characteristically for MORP, these proposals were interspersed with the usual pleas for organisational and financial support.

MORP was now seeking a broader audience and further cooperation from the 'big names'; however, this did not mean an automatic change of identity or attitude among MORP's old guard, the foreign Communist writers who made up its core. For them, MORP would continue to be the organisation to exercise ideological influence abroad and its branches 'the only organisations working with the intelligentsia on the ideological front that have had a significant influence in a number of countries'.[56]

Whenever proposals originated from this group, it was clear that their hearts were not in shifting the spotlight away from proletarian writers towards well-known writers, who were needed for their ability to sway public opinion. 'The publicity and propaganda activity of some of our organisation's members, particularly those "with a name", frequently exceeds the effect of their creative achievements (Gide, Dreiser, Barbusse and others).'[57] MORP still thought of 'aligning' their supporters' creative work ideologically. 'We don't just need these writers' signatures on yet another appeal; they need ... to strive for political changes in their own creative work.'[58] This pressure would be exercised on those writers who had already joined MORP (Gide, Malraux, Cassou), and on left-wing bourgeois writers 'who joined us not as a result of their political crisis but, so they think, as a result of their own creative crisis'.[59] Proposals for genuine innovation and new tactics came from the Russian members of MORP and, for the first time, techniques to attract new adherents were discussed.

'Winning over new allies'

Sergey Tret'yakov was formerly an avant-garde writer, the author of *Roar, China*, which was successfully staged by Vsevolod Meyerhold. Tret'yakov had maintained genuine friendships with a number of foreign writers; in the early 1920s, he had lived in Berlin and later translated some of Brecht's plays into Russian. One of MORP's enthusiastic members, in 1932 he raised the issue of MORP's ineffective approach to its task[60] and later developed his ideas for the First Congress of the Soviet Writers' Union.[61] Unlike the foreign writers in MORP, he had a genuine interest in developing collegial relations with writers in other countries; he spoke enthusiastically about different ways of winning over Western intellectuals, rather than demanding expressions of support from them. For the first time, a MORP member outlined techniques for the long-term cultivation of Western writers. Tret'yakov suggested that, in the context of the anti-Fascist struggle and the need to win over the petit bourgeois intelligentsia, it was essential to get away from MORP's harsh style of interactions and to develop a greater flexibility of outlook.[62]

Tret'yakov proposed the development of a personal approach in dealings with foreign writers. The way to establish and develop personal connections between

MORP and foreign writers (i.e. as individuals and not through their membership of groups) was to capitalise on contacts between individual Soviet writers who belonged to MORP and individual foreign artists and writers. MORP would thus become 'not only an association of writers' organisations represented by their sections, but an association of individuals – a creative and productive association'. MORP would need to change its old ideological orientation, which prevented it from dealing with bourgeois writers, prejudiced it against their views and made it cautious about compromising itself – a process which lost these writers to other Soviet organisations such as VOKS.[63]

> We used to have some kind of fear of compromising ourselves later if we were to communicate with these writers. It is true, it is possible that isolated writers who visit us subsequently turn out to be renegades and slanderers, but we are better off preferring that type of risk to our previous isolation.

This statement was not intended to suggest abandoning an ideological agenda; rather it aimed to introduce more effective techniques so that MORP could be 'much more successful in the struggle to win over the intermediate layers of the petite bourgeoisie and the intelligentsia'. Tret'yakov even proposed that MORP's country-specific *lenderkomissii* undertake a study of alien (e.g. Fascist and social-fascist) aesthetics, and that MORP should evolve into centres that would unite 'theoreticians, Soviet and foreign writers, foreign workers who are in Moscow, etc.' and form part of the strategy of winning over new allies.[64]

Tret'yakov assigned an important role to individual Soviet writers. They could write for the foreign press, both Communist and bourgeois left, and reach an audience more effectively than the dry impersonal style of a newspaper.

> It is known that . . . even the Communist foreign press prefers lively essays, signed by an individual Soviet writer with the imprint of his personality, to Inprekorr's dry and impersonal material.[65]

Another way of using Soviet writers as spokesmen would be to arrange their trips abroad. 'It is known that even the incidental talks by writers who come from the USSR are enormously important for our foreign sections.' Tret'yakov proposed reviving an old technique used by the Comintern and MORP – to develop contacts with individual writers by bringing them to the USSR and making their social and artistic life pleasant and productive. Again, Soviet writers, both individuals and groups, would play an essential role; international writers' brigades also had the potential to make a 'colossal' impact. (Such brigades had already been created during the first Five-Year Plan, following the 1930 Kharkov Congress. Soviet and Western writers, among them Paul Vaillant-Couturier, Joshua Kunitz and Erwin Egon Kisch, visited the North Caucasus, collecting literary material about industrialisation and socialist construction.[66]) For Tret'yakov, the brigades were like the first explorers of the USSR and socialist construction, who would encourage further interest and tourism from the West.

International writers' brigades represent a kind of pioneer along the tracks of getting to know our country and our construction – the ways along which new waves of foreign tourism will rush.[67]

Tret'yakov also raised the question of improving the treatment of foreign writers in the USSR by taking better care of their interests, for example in dealing with publishing houses. He described this assistance as 'a task of a purely managerial, economic nature, but in essence it has a major political significance, as its successful performance will greatly assist in strengthening our links with foreign writers'.[68] In aiming for better working practices, Tret'yakov was, in fact, proposing an alternative to MORP's practice of operating in isolation. He saw great benefits in developing 'true working relations' with other Soviet artistic organisations that were already dealing with foreign countries (e.g. the International Workers' Theatre Association and the International Bureau of Revolutionary Artists) and with those providing hospitality to foreign writers and intelligentsia (e.g. Intourist and VOKS).

Tret'yakov's focus on personal influence was a response to the mistakes of organisations such as Intourist; he concluded that their service was too formal and failed to meet tourists' needs, and so prevented them from appreciating the extent of socialist construction. Tret'yakov proposed a potentially more persuasive, personal service from Soviet writers with first-hand experience of the subject. 'The involvement of Soviet writers (most of whom are currently familiar with our construction) in the work of Intourist would have a most positive political significance.'[69] His idea was to prove highly effective when Tret'yakov personally looked after Jean-Richard Bloch in 1934. Bloch recalled his contacts with Tret'yakov as genuine, spontaneous and highly informative, especially those regarding the Five-Year Plan and the development of Soviet industry.[70]

Tretyakov's proposal was a change in direction for MORP. Until then, it had relied on foreign writers who were already committed to the Soviet Union and it expected instant results. Tret'yakov proposed reaching out to other writers, specifically those whom MORP ideology had regarded as being beyond the pale; in doing so, MORP's traditional hectoring and standover tactics would be abandoned for a more respectful, more inclusive and much more personal approach.

Implementing new techniques

MORP indeed put Tret'yakov's ideas into practice. It established relations with 'fraternal [Soviet] international artistic organisations' and Soviet organisations dealing with foreigners,[71] and appointed representatives to VOKS, Intourist and the Soviet Writers' Union.[72] At a further meeting, it was decreed that Bela Illes should organise and guide cooperation with VOKS, radio, cinema, Mezhrabpom (Workers' International Relief) and the Writers' Union Organisation Committee.[73] The presence of MORP members would give it influence in other organisations and, as will be noted later, lead to a cross-institutional sharing of tactics.

Tret'yakov's suggestions for involving individual writers were also carried out.

He wanted to bring MORP and the Soviet Writers' Union closer together and to involve Soviet writers in MORP's activities; this was implemented in 1933 when more Soviet writers (Inber, Isbakh and Nikulin) were invited to join MORP's French commission and Inber became its Deputy Chair.[74] The idea of writers' brigades also led to the creation of a team that functioned as both a Soviet MORP section and an international writers' brigade. (The brigade, founded in 1933, included the Soviet writers and critics, Dinamov, Anisimov, Mirsky, Serebriakova and Nikulin; it was later complemented by Pavlenko, Vishnevsky, Mstislavsky, Zalinsky, Inber, Lidin and Leonov – writers who already had friendly relations with European writers.)[75] International writers' brigades, consisting of both Soviet and foreign writers, took foreign writers across the USSR. Elsa Triolet, who along with Aragon was part of such a brigade, enthusiastically recalled the trip that they took after the 1934 Writers' Congress, in the company of the French-speaking Isaak Babel and Boris Pasternak. Paul Nizan, who went to Central Asia on a similar trip with his wife Henriette, Isaak Babel and Irina Ehrenburg, came back with material for his book *Sindobod Tocikiston*.

Tret'yakov had been keen to promote correspondence between Soviet and foreign writers, and the MORP papers contain numerous letters from Romain Rolland, Andre Gide, Theodore Dreiser, John Dos Passos, Michael Gold, Martin Andersen Nexø, Carin Michaelis and others. In commenting on the success of this individual correspondence between Soviet and Western writers, MORP made sure that it took the credit for its own role as an intermediary. 'Many Soviet writers correspond directly, with our assistance and following agreement with us (Yermilov, Anisimov, Pil'nyak, Tarasov-Rodionov and others).'[76] This novel use of writers, with their warmth, enthusiasm and uncritical acceptance of their correspondents' political orientation, was a productive move away from the rule of the old guard, consisting of MORP officials and foreign Communist writers, who were often judgemental of their Western colleagues.

Further proposals from above

MORP had been badly neglected by its superior organisations and was wound up in 1935. Despite these difficulties, its activities in its last year hardly suggest an organisation that was merely marking time; on the contrary, it was a period of significant innovation regarding its methods of action. The innovations came from MORP's new Secretary, Mikhail Apletin, the former Executive Secretary of VOKS. After MORP's closure, the Foreign Commission of the Soviet Writers' Union began to operate under the same leadership, with Apletin playing a major role; it seems therefore that, although appearing to give MORP a new lease of life, Apletin was, in fact, preparing the way for a successor institution that was about to take over its members and its tasks. The way in which this Russian literary functionary addressed a superior organisation (and he wrote only to the Soviet Writers' Union) differed radically from the style and approach of Bela Illes and other, mainly foreign, members of the MORP Secretariat. Apletin's correspondence contains concrete proposals that are more like plans than requests; his initiatives and personal leadership style marked a new level of development in the task of influencing Western sympathisers.

The birth of hospitality tactics: how to host a visit

The major change implemented by Apletin, following Tret'yakov's suggestions, related to the way in which foreigners were provided with hospitality. Previously, MORP had peppered the Comintern with requests for money and decent food for its visitors. Apletin did not complain of his financial problems, but focused on ways in which the style of reception provided to Western visitors could win their goodwill and create an initial favourable response. Their perception of the USSR was, understandably, affected by the people around them and the environments in which they moved. Like any visitor anywhere, the visiting intellectual wanted basic comforts and interesting things to do and see. Under Apletin, MORP attempted to meet those needs. An interesting example of his approach can be seen in his proposal for the forthcoming visit by the French writer Victor Margueritte, addressed to the Chairman of the Foreign Commission of the Soviet Writers' Union, Mikhail Kol'tsov.[77]

Well before the visit, Apletin gave careful thought to a number of different aspects, beginning with the visitor's public persona and political orientation. He knew Margueritte to be 'a very "difficult" writer, who has made rather abrupt and sometimes quite unexpected turns on his literary and political path'.[78] But Apletin recognised Margueritte's recent openly pro-Soviet sympathies: his joining of MORP and his signing of anti-Fascist and anti-imperialist statements. The apparent purpose of Margueritte's visit was to 'obtain inspiration' (*poluchit' vdokhnoveniye*) and gather materials for his planned series of novels *The New World*. Knowing this allowed Apletin to develop the idea of managing the visit by building it around his assumed interests. The connotations of the Russian word *obstavit'* ('arrange', 'set up') used by Apletin are 'to handle, to stage-manage', with a strong suggestion of theatricality.

> The purpose of his trip obliges MORP, the Soviet Writers' Union and VOKS to make every effort to set up (*obstavit'*) the work with Margueritte in such a fashion that he really will 'obtain inspiration' and gather the material that will be helpful for his work.[79]

To this end, Apletin developed a programme that took care of every aspect of the writer's visit. In Chapter 1, a programme of this sort, namely that of J.-R. Bloch, was presented from the visitor's viewpoint; Apletin's proposal shows how a typical visit was prepared, and thus sheds light on what really lay behind the experiences that made such a strong impression on visitors.

An examination of the planning process shows why writers came away feeling that their work was widely appreciated in the USSR. Margueritte's visit was meticulously prepared: Apletin planned a publicity campaign for Margueritte during his visit; he arranged for the writer's arrival and stay to be announced by the Soviet news agency TASS; central newspapers such as *Pravda* and *Izvestia*, and literary papers such as *Literaturnaya gazeta*, were to publish short articles on Margueritte; and literary journals would write about his work. Apletin not only specified which newspapers would feature these articles but also proposed the authors who would write them. Parts of Margueritte's stay in Moscow would be filmed. An exhibition would be set up in the foyer of the Writers' Club displaying his books that had been translated and published in the USSR. On the day of his arrival, a meeting would be held on the premises of the Soviet Writers' Union Foreign Commission with the participation of writers, including members of MORP and VOKS. From the start, a great deal of personal attention would be paid to the visitor and his work; an evening at the Writers' Club would be dedicated to Margueritte's work, with a specified number of Soviet writers in attendance. Margueritte could not help but be swayed by such systematic flattery. Writers' tours today are arranged on exactly these same lines.

Also echoing Tret'yakov's suggestions, Apletin assigned a major role to individual Soviet writers who would surround Margueritte during his stay. In fact, people were the most important factor in hospitality tactics. It was planned that Margueritte would be constantly escorted by representatives of cultural organisations, starting from the day of his arrival when he should be met at the station by representatives from MORP, the Soviet Writers' Union and VOKS, and also by 'the comrade who will be assigned to work with V. Margueritte'. For this role, Apletin selected Soviet writers with a special interest in France (Nikulin, Pavlenko, Lidin, Inber, Shaginian, Tret'yakov, Anisimov and Nusinov). During his stay in Moscow and his subsequent tour, the writer would be accompanied not only by a 'politically prepared interpreter' but by a fellow writer who could speak French.[80] In addition to fellow writers and representatives of cultural organisations, Margueritte would have to meet some 'comrades in charge' (*otvetstvennyye tovarischi*), conversation with whom Apletin considered obligatory.

> After V. Margueritte has spent approximately a fortnight in Moscow, a reception is to be held at the VOKS premises. Apart from writers and representatives of publishing houses and the press, one should invite comrades in charge with whom the writer <u>will have to converse</u> during his stay in Moscow in connection with the theme of his series of novels.

While there would be no obvious pressure, and Margueritte would be made to feel that the programme for his visit aimed to satisfy his interests, it is clear that he would be given no choice about the programme. Once his literary plans emerged in conversation, he would visit a list of sites that it was considered he ought to get to know and a number of individuals he ought to talk to. MORP officials would establish the route of his tour and list the kind of documents, photos and other materials and information he would need to gather. At this stage in the creation of his visitor's programme, Apletin did not know what Margueritte's interests actually were, but this was no impediment; he had devised a model to be used in discovering those interests, in shaping them and making the most efficient use of them.

As was discussed in Chapter 1, visitors like Bloch were greatly impressed by their experiences of Soviet cinema and theatre, and these experiences also had an impact on their overall impressions of the USSR. Apletin's plan demonstrates that he placed particular importance on the timing and impact of attendances at films and plays, including their inspirational effect on the visitor's frame of mind.

> During the very first days of the writer's stay in Moscow it is to be made sure that he views a series of Soviet films and plays that could give him an appropriate impetus for his work (for example the films *The Mother*, *Maxim's Youth*, *Love and Hate*, *The Peasants*, *Chapayev*, *Avia-March*, *The Pilots*, *A Golden Lake etc.*) and the plays *The Aristocrats*, *An Optimistic Tragedy* etc.[81]

Apletin's final touch was the statement that all of the expenses generated by Margueritte's visit to Moscow would be paid for by VOKS. The document bears Apletin's handwritten addition confirming that, during a personal meeting with Kol'tsov, verbal approval was given for the plan.

While Margueritte's trip never took place, and there is no evidence how MORP's plan operated with other visitors, much of the material in the chapters on VOKS and the Foreign Commission will show how plans of this sort were implemented by other organisations and what effect they had on visitors.

Monitoring success

MORP had now moved from the single-minded pursuit of its own ideological goals to a new attempt at building a rapport with sympathetic non-Communist artists. The question was whether it would pursue these new relations for its own benefit as resolutely as ever, or whether it now had different expectations.

In 1934, MORP decided to review its relations with French writers. Since 1933, France had held a prominent position on MORP's world map of foreign relations, with a significant number of eminent French non-Communist writers either joining MORP or supporting the USSR. MORP established a close rapport with some of these writers. In the MORP archive there is a document entitled *Biographical information on French writers* that contains sketches evaluating the writers Paul Valéry, Roger Martin du Gard, André Gide, Jean Giono, Victor Margueritte and Romain Rolland.[82] The catalogue, which has the heading 'Not to be disclosed' (*Oglasheniyu ne podlezhit*), contains biographical information about each writer, including notes on their work and their status on the French literary scene; it focuses particularly on the writers' political views, their attitude towards the USSR and their relations with MORP and AEAR. Whether the document was compiled for internal use, or for passing on to another agency or a higher echelon such as the Comintern, it is a clear statement of MORP's achievements. It indicates MORP's criteria for the selection of friendly writers in the period when MORP was helping the USSR work towards the creation of the united front. It is clearly important for MORP to note that most of the writers are 'major' (*krupnyy*), yet the writers' literary value is outlined only fleetingly – for example, there is a brief summary of Roger Martin du Gard's *Les Thibault*. The main emphasis is on the writers' status and influence in intellectual circles: Paul Valéry is described as a member of the French Academy and the successor to Anatole France; Romain Rolland, that old friend of the USSR, is described as 'a major representative of the contemporary Western intelligentsia'; and Gide is described as someone who 'enjoys enormous prestige among the French intelligentsia. . . . He exercises a major influence on contemporary radical writers.'

In the document, MORP had definitely shifted to an acceptance of these writers' non-proletarian origins and of their political orientation. They are described either as bourgeois (Valéry and Martin du Gard) or as left-bourgeois (Victor Margue-ritte), and are redeemed by their willingness to criticise bourgeois society. Martin du Gard is described as a 'vacillating intellectual' and Gide as being conscious of the negative sides of capitalism. Some of their ideas are criticised, as in the case of Rolland's *penchant* for Gandhi, 'the weakest point of his ideological credo'.

MORP had replaced its former requirement for revolutionary allegiance with one of allegiance to the USSR and MORP. The writers on the list are all proven sympathisers and, possibly, people who publicly state their support for the USSR. The document quotes Gide's regular public expressions of sympathy for the USSR and communism, Margueritte's expressed desire to visit the USSR and Rolland's marriage to a Soviet citizen and his reputation as 'the oldest friend of the USSR, who has written a book about Lenin'. The proof of their involvement is found in their relations with MORP or AEAR: Gide and Rolland were both on the editorial board of *Commune*, AEAR's journal; Gide participated in anti-Fascist rallies run by AEAR; and Giono and Margueritte joined AEAR in 1934.

Information about these writers' views and plans is also derived from their letters to Soviet writers. The report lists MORP's successful correspondence with Martin du Gard, Gide, Giono and Rolland. In some cases, the correspondance was conducted personally with individual Soviet writers: Martin du Gard with Yermilov, and Rolland with Fedin, Amaglobeli and Illes. It is from this personal correspondence that MORP followed the French writers' moods, such as the ac-count of Martin du Gard's 'intellectual vacillations' and his growing expression of interest in the USSR, or Giono's expressed wish to visit the USSR. Finally, the document mentions that all of these writers either have been, or are being, translated into Russian and published in the USSR (works by Martin du Gard, Gide and Margueritte are said to be already translated, and a collection of Valery's poems is said to be in the process of preparation).

Thus, MORP's previously expressed ideas about establishing relations with foreign writers were indeed being implemented. Less cautious in the selection of contacts and less openly preoccupied with the writers' ideologies, MORP now mon-itored their activities in support of the USSR and other militant actions. MORP's policy of establishing personal relationships through private correspondence with

Soviet writers aimed to cultivate positive long-term relationships but also, possibly, to gather information on the French writers' positions. However, the catalogue does not state what practical purpose these relations served, and it may be merely a background document. However, other documents confirm that MORP still had practical purposes in mind in cultivating relationships with Western writers.

Making use of writers

Mikhail Apletin's scheme went beyond softening up writers during their visits to the Soviet Union; his proposals also suggest how these writers could be used to promote the USSR once they had returned home to the West. His plan for MORP's contribution to the twentieth anniversary celebrations of the October Revolution is revealing.[83]

Apletin proposed to involve foreign writers in compiling a volume of original works on the Five-Year Plans, and a collection entitled *Foreign Writers on the USSR*. Apletin's ideas were more ambitious and complex than those of his predecessors; foreign authors were to write revolutionary fiction and dedicate it to the twentieth anniversary of the Soviet regime. A volume was to be produced that included portraits of foreign writers and their statements on the USSR; special anniversary issues of *International Literature* were also to be published. The plan included the promotion of Soviet literature abroad: the compilation of a reference book, *Sovietika*, listing all of the translated works of Soviet fiction; the creation of an exhibition of all of the works by Soviet writers that had been translated and published outside of the USSR; and the dedication of part of an exhibition in Paris to the international importance of Soviet literature.[84] Apletin particularly stressed the importance of obtaining contributions from Western writers 'with a major name', so that they would be read both in their countries and in others.[85] The best foreign works would be published in French, German, English, Spanish, Japanese, Chinese, Polish and Russian so that readers in every country could take in the thoughts of left-wing intellectuals from around the world on the glories of the Soviet Union.

To put these plans into effect, Apletin suggested approaching individual writers with the question, 'What has the USSR contributed to your country?'; in return, the writers would be expected to give the reasons for their support of the USSR. However, Apletin wanted not to send out questionnaires to writers but to inspire them. To achieve this, MORP could bring in groups of two or three writers from major countries, or from countries the USSR considered important. They would come to Russia for a few months, with the visits planned to coincide with either the October or the May Day celebrations. Apletin added prudently, 'In some cases, individual visits not linked to festivals are desirable.'[86]

Although Apletin made these proposals during his time with MORP, they would be worked out in more detail and put into practice a few years later, when he was the Secretary of the Foreign Commission of the Soviet Writers' Union. His experience at VOKS influenced his plans for cultivating these writers as future spokesmen. He accepted that there would be preliminary stages in which hospitality was used to gain influence, but without revealing the true long-term intentions. Later proposals considered the specific topics that writers might address, and suggested that these pro-Soviet writings would emerge as a direct result of their carefully manipulated visits to the USSR. The question of how these visits would 'provide inspiration' and induce foreign writers to address the desired topics will be discussed in Chapter 8.

Much has been said in the last chapter, and by earlier scholars, about MORP's awkward organisational and interpersonal methods and its heavy hand in dealing with foreign writers. It preached to the converted, alienated old supporters and failed to attract new members. MORP was in thrall to the Communist agenda, which it put far ahead of harmonious relations with Western fellow-travellers. Even though, in its last two years, MORP dropped its earlier tactics of 'war against its members' for more peaceable ones, there is no evidence that the new tactics were ever put into effect during MORP's lifetime; however, the planning for them shows an approach that developed in several agencies through the 1930s and even beyond World War II.

As MORP's life had been closely linked with the Comintern, so was its death, in December 1935. The softer Soviet policy of 1932–33, followed by support for the united front in 1935, led, that summer, to the creation of the International Writers Association for the Defence of Culture in Paris. From August to December, there was a series of IKKI meetings at which the closure of MORP was discussed. However, the decision was also made by other parties. On 10 December 1935, the Politburo[87] of the Central Committee of VKP(b) adopted the proposal by Mikhail Kol'tsov to close the MORP headquarters in Moscow and its foreign branches, with the exception of the viable ones in France and the USA.

There was no public announcement about its demise; private correspondence among writers associated with MORP confirms that it was disbanded.[88] *International Literature* simply dropped its subtitle 'Organ of the International League of Revolutionary Writers'; the editorial board of the magazine remained at the same address, and MORP's staff and sections moved to the Foreign Commission of the Soviet Writers' Union. MORP, to quote one historian, had become 'invisible'.[89]

However, the closure of MORP did not signal an end to relations with foreign writers. After all, MORP wasn't the only body responsible for Soviet relations with Western intellectuals or the only organisation preoccupied with influencing them. In fact, the examination of MORP's actions and policies in this chapter might create the impression that it either alienated writers through coercive treatment or developed more lenient policies that were never implemented. Parallel to MORP, another organisation operated under the cumbersome name of the All-Union Society for Cultural Relations with Foreign Countries or VOKS. It was a competitor to MORP, operated under a different patronage and had a very different history from MORP's. VOKS had a very different working method and a different record of relations with foreign intellectuals. The next three chapters are devoted to VOKS's extensive activities and its involvement with the West.

5 Laying the foundations of relations with Western intellectuals

VOKS in the 1920s

Whereas the aims and the political goals of our work are no different from those of the Comintern and Profintern, our work is noticeably more complex in its form.

F.N. Petrov, Chairman of VOKS, 1931[1]

While MORP was drumming up Western Communist and pro-Communist support, another organisation, the All-Union Society of Cultural Relations with Foreign Countries (*Vsesoyuznoye obschestvo kul'turnykh svyazey s zagranitsey*), or VOKS, was conducting a more discreet campaign in the West. VOKS did not convene international congresses or encourage its supporters to launch manifestos addressed to all humanity. VOKS was responsible for bringing hundreds of Western intellectuals and writers to the USSR, both eminent and rank-and-file, Communist and non-Communist, and maintaining relations with them in their own countries. Throughout its history, the operations of VOKS were continually shaped by the process of engaging with the non-Communist West, which, as we shall see, brought with it particular difficulties and provides early evidence of the fearful conformity that became increasingly characteristic of life under Stalinism.

Before the opening of the Soviet archives, VOKS was a mystery. Calling itself a cultural society, to imply independence from the party and the state, it denied any political, let alone revolutionary, motivation.[2] Diaries, letters and memoirs, written by those it brought in as visitors, fail to explain its actions outside the Soviet Union; these visitors recalled both VOKS's helpfulness and its controlling, even invasive service within the USSR.[3] Was it an instrument of Soviet indoctrination, as Western authors claimed,[4] or was it simply a cultural organisation which arranged translations, exhibitions and visits by and correspondence with foreign writers – services for which Soviet official scholars praised it?[5]

Gaining access to VOKS documents, kept in the State Archive of the Russian Federation (GARF), overturned the received wisdom that the Western intelligentsia's involvement with the USSR in the post-revolutionary years was an independent, spontaneous response driven solely by their enthusiasm for the Revolution and the new society. We can now unravel the story of how VOKS established its presence on the Western cultural scene and how it attempted to assert its influence over Western intellectuals.

The origins and structure of VOKS

Created in 1925 by the Central Committee of the RKP(b) and TsIK, VOKS was given the mission of establishing and maintaining relations 'between [Soviet] institutions, public organisations, individual Soviet scholars and cultural workers – and those in other countries'.[6] It is clear that VOKS was meant to work towards the same goals as the Commissariat of Foreign Affairs (NKID), namely the promotion of coexistence and trade with the West; however, its foundation documents neither instruct it to conduct foreign propaganda nor subordinate it to NKID or the Comintern. VOKS was accountable to the Department of Culture and Propaganda of VKP(b).[7]

In the 1920s, VOKS's operations were relatively independent and generated by its own leadership – effectively, by its first Chair, Olga Kameneva, who was discussed in the Introduction.[8] Instructions and reports relating to foreigners make it possible to reconstruct the working methods of VOKS staff: the heads of department, the officers-in-charge, known as *referenty*, and the casually employed interpreter/guides. These documents also illustrate the way that ideas were generated and tried out.

For many foreigners, VOKS's headquarters in Moscow was the first port of call, a place where the 'cultural programme' for their stay in the Soviet Union was put together. Visitors found the headquarters building to be ugly and tasteless; still, this was where receptions, celebrations and screenings of the latest films by Eisenstein and Pudovkin were held. This building was also where special guests, such as Barbusse and Feuchtwanger, and foreigners who worked in Russia, such as Armand Hammer or Eugene Lyons, were invited for tea, official evenings and informal concerts. There, visitors would meet 'Madame Kameneva', as she was known, and her staff; they were likely to see highly placed officials, such as the People's Commissars Anatoly Lunacharsky and Maxim Litvinov, and the Soviet cultural elite – people such as Sergey Tret'yakov, Boris Pasternak and Alexey Tolstoy. VOKS's *apparat* consisted of a Secretariat and departments and sectors, for example the Romance Sector, the Anglo-American Sector, the Press Bureau and the Bureau for the Reception of Foreigners. Instead of maintaining branches in other countries, VOKS had foreign plenipotentiary representatives (*upolnomochennyy*) who were usually diplomats of the Soviet embassy and thus employees of NKID.[9] They carried out VOKS's duties as a nominally voluntary task (*obshchestvennaya nagruzka*), such tasks being expected of all Soviet employees. Maxim Litvinov, the Deputy Commissar and later Commissar of NKID, supported and valued VOKS's activities.

The first steps (1925–29)

When VOKS was created, cultural relations between the USSR and most Western countries, including France, were just beginning. VOKS's internal documents show no evidence of a political agenda behind its first contacts with foreigners visiting the USSR; however, other activities put a different light on this picture. In France, VOKS tried first to seduce the Western intelligentsia with an idealised view of the Soviet Union, and then to lead them to act in support of the USSR.

This goal dominated VOKS's activities and tactics and was, in fact, more central to its purposes than were cultural relations.

Like the Comintern and MORP, VOKS used three avenues of influence: the foreign press to disseminate Soviet materials abroad; cultural societies to group and guide Soviet supporters; and personal, face-to-face interactions to influence individual eminent intellectuals. As VOKS targeted non-Communist circles, its approach was radically different from MORP's.

'Assistance to the foreign press'

One of the tasks outlined in VOKS's *Regulations* was to try and get Soviet materials published in the West: this included periodic bulletins on Soviet culture, science and daily life (known as *byt*), guidebooks, reference books and monographs on the USSR and its cultural and scientific life.[10] VOKS also had to supply the foreign press and individuals with photographs.[11] Although VOKS had its own organ, *The Information Bulletin of the All-Union Society of Cultural Relations with Foreign Countries*,[12] its discussions mainly revolve around the process of getting Soviet materials published in the French periodic press. One of VOKS's earlier practices was 'the supply of article material' (*snabzheniye stateynym materialom*) to the press and, as was the practice at MORP, VOKS called this 'assistance to the foreign press'.

MORP dealt with the Western Communist press, which gave it an assurance, if not quite a guarantee, that its materials would be published; VOKS, dealing with the non-Communist press, had no such assurances. Initially, in 1925–26, the VOKS Press Bureau in Moscow sent articles for distribution to the staff of the Soviet embassy in Paris;[13] later they were sent to the VOKS representative. As the VOKS correspondence shows, its representative could do no more than attempt to establish contacts with the French press and offer them Soviet materials.

These materials did not contain overt revolutionary or ideological messages, but purported to inform the reader of Soviet social achievements – from law, education and childhood protection[14] to the development of Soviet trade and industry.[15] Many articles, some translated into French, covered innovations in literature, theatre and cinema, the development of film production and science.[16] With titles ranging from 'Social and legal protection of minors in the USSR' and 'Inventions and improvements in transport' to 'The path of development in Soviet cinema' and 'The main achievements of anthropology since the Revolution', these articles painted a complimentary and encouraging picture of an enlightened, developing society; they avoided polemics or critical materials.

In 1926–27, VOKS sent materials directly to the French periodicals, the Communist *l'Humanité* and the non-Communist *Les nouvelles littéraires*, *L'amour de l'art* and *Le monde slave*. The same articles were sent simultaneously to more than one publisher and, just in case, to the VOKS representative. The selection of topics again favoured the successes of the Soviet period including science;[17] the preservation of museums and exhibitions of Soviet art,[18] and official Soviet views on art;[19] medical, educational and other socio-economic improvements in the USSR;[20] and information on the Soviet republics.[21] The emphasis on achievements since the October Revolution was even more pronounced in films from the Sovkino studio, which VOKS began sending to France from 1926 onwards.[22] These newsreel materials, intended to provide facts about the USSR, presented information on political and social changes tasked with combating the remnants of the old regime and caring for the population. The stories focused on caring for homeless children (schooling, learning a trade: before and after); fighting prostitution (dormitories for the unemployed, workshops, dispensaries); caring for women and children in the new society (the Society for the Protection of Motherhood and Childhood, women and social work, the elimination of illiteracy, free libraries, the workers' university); and other positive images such as the Soviet village, new tractors, hydroelectric stations, Moscow and Lenin.

To find out what literature would be well received in France, the VOKS Press Bureau sent Soviet poetry in translation to the VOKS representative in Paris, asking for his opinion on the likelihood of publishing it in France and the possible demand for such translations.[23] But even when publishers themselves requested materials, VOKS was unable to predict whether they would appear in print. It is uncertain what happened to the materials on Soviet film provided by VOKS in December 1926 at the request of *Cahiers d'arts*. In contrast to MORP's demands to see its materials published by *l'Humanité* and *Monde*, officials from VOKS could express no more than hope, when writing to their representative, that 'The path of development in Soviet cinema' and some of the photos would indeed be published. VOKS reports do not make it clear whether any of these articles ever saw the light of day.

VOKS's materials were of poor quality and outdated and the Soviet Trade representation in Paris complained to VOKS about it. Zamenhof, the manager of the economic sector, cited *La vie économique des Soviets* as an example; this was the magazine of the trade representation and the only Soviet organ published abroad in French, 'which plays the most important role of acquainting the Romance countries with the USSR and bringing these countries closer to the USSR'.[24] VOKS's materials, insisted Zamenhof, had to show evidence of the growth of Soviet industry by sending photos of the openings of large plants, electric stations and grain elevators and by giving attention to trade and a growing cultural sector of society.[25]

VOKS was an obliging supplier when its materials were requested. For example, its staff wrote to Soviet individuals and organisations, looking for articles by Soviet scholars and other materials on Prokofiev and Stravinsky that had been requested by Barbusse's *Monde*.[26] These requests were quite explicit: 'The All-Union Society for Cultural Relations with Foreign Countries requests that you do not decline this task, considering the role of the magazine.'[27] When Victor Margueritte expressed his intention to publish a special issue on the USSR in *Evolution*,[28] VOKS sent him a list of twenty-five items on the same array of topics: education and art, Soviet artistic policy and avant-garde theatre (Meyerhold, the Vakhtangov Theatre, the Kamerny Theatre, the Jewish theatre and ballet) and the emergence of culture in the national republics. VOKS sent *Evolution* additional materials: articles by eminent Soviet scholars of art and literature, and selected stories and excerpts by Soviet writers such as Gladkov, Leonov and Babel.[29]

Although slow to begin with, VOKS succeeded in placing a number of publications in the non-Communist press. In a report on VOKS's activities in France in the mid- to late 1920s, Tsetsiliya Rabinovich, the *referent* for the Romance countries, summarised the major publications on the USSR that had appeared in France.[30] They included Margueritte's special double issue on Soviet art, culture and social life in *Evolution*; Soviet literary works sent to the publishers Montaigne for translation and publication; and the publication, by the Lyons Institute of Comparative Law, of the text of the Soviet Constitution. All these publications were based exclusively on materials supplied by VOKS.

What were the real objectives of VOKS in disseminating these materials abroad? Was it to use cultural information to create a positive image of the USSR and to boost its reputation? Was the picture of industrial growth and social development meant to widen the circle of diplomatic and trading partners? Documents from Kameneva's time leave the real motivation of VOKS unclear.

However, when Professor F.N. Petrov was appointed as VOKS's second Chair in the summer of 1929, he received an oral briefing on VOKS's experience with the foreign press. The briefing came from the editor of the VOKS information bulletin, Aleksandr Dikgof-Derental'. Dikgof-Derental' explained that VOKS's purpose in sending articles to the French press was to counteract anti-Soviet information that had appeared in France. Examples of this unfavourable publicity included the destruction of public education; the looting of art works in former palaces and museums and their sale abroad to obtain hard currency; the decline of Soviet foreign trade; the hardship of travel in the USSR because of filth and the lack of normal living conditions; the destruction of the non-party intelligentsia; the increase in the number of homeless children; and depravity and alcoholism among Comsomol organisations.[31] Dikgof-Derental' believed that VOKS had to continue to combat these defamatory assertions in the same way that Comintern and MORP did, by neutralising the negative information in the Western press with positive 'counter-information'. The most recent accusations about the destruction of the old Russian culture could be counteracted by writing non-stereotypical articles that would show how the Russian cultural heritage was being used. In addition, VOKS needed to highlight new Soviet cultural and economic achievements by showing the achievements of the first year of the Five-Year Plan, including the difficulties that were being encountered.[32]

Dikgof-Derental' spoke critically about some of VOKS's previous activities. Was he, perhaps, indirectly blaming Kameneva? VOKS, he believed, had overestimated the effectiveness of Barbusse's *Monde* and had missed the chance to finance a periodical, *Cri du Peuple*, which had earlier had a brief period of success before collapsing.[33]

(It is noteworthy that Dikgof-Derental' had left Russia after the Revolution to join Boris Savinkov's anti-Soviet organisation abroad. A personal friend of Savinkov, Dikgof-Derental' illegally crossed the border into the Soviet Union in 1924 together with his wife Lubov', who was Savinkov's mistress, and Savinkov.

Arrested and jailed, Dikgof-Derental' was released in 1924. He then became VOKS's official proponent of Soviet propaganda abroad.)

However, publications were only part of VOKS's activities. Its real success lay elsewhere.

Cultural relations society or front? Cercle de la Russie Neuve

One of VOKS's most important tasks was the creation and maintenance of an organised network of Soviet supporters in the West. VOKS's *Regulations* stipulate that, in establishing cultural relations with other countries, it should build relations with Societies of Friends of Soviet Russia and, in countries where Societies of Friends did not yet exist, create Societies for Rapprochement with the USSR. VOKS was to maintain their activities by supplying them with printed materials, speakers and so forth.[34]

These societies indeed originated in the 1920s. The first was formed in Britain before the creation of VOKS,[35] the German society was founded in 1924[36] and the American, known as the American–Russian Institutes, in 1926. Other societies existed in Czechoslovakia,[37] Bulgaria,[38] Japan,[39] Latvia[40] and France;[41] by 1927, there were nineteen such societies in eleven countries.[42] It is striking that different countries had similar associations of intelligentsia sympathetic towards the USSR, created at the same time, conducting virtually identical activities and bearing similar generic names such as 'society for cultural relations', 'cultural rapprochement society' or 'society of friends of the USSR', with the frequently added proper name, New Russia. (These societies of Western intellectuals are not to be confused with the mass workers' Associations of Friends of the USSR, created in 1928 in a number of countries.) The French society categorically denied any involvement with the Soviet embassy or the FCP, let alone receiving any subsidy from these sources.[43] However it did recognise assistance in the form of contacts with VOKS, 'the organisation empowered to disseminate Soviet culture'.[44]

To VOKS, Cultural Rapprochement Societies were a means of gathering together sympathetic Western intellectuals who could exercise public and personal influence and who might become political spokesmen for the USSR in the West. VOKS's relations with these organisations were not intrusive enough to warrant them being called 'fronts'; however, VOKS was involved with their operations, tried to influence them and, in some cases, did indeed fund them. The archival documents reveal the role that VOKS played in the creation of the French, German and American societies, its subsequent influence on members and its interference with their activities (for example, in the UK and France). These societies were VOKS's auxiliary organisations, to use Comintern's terminology.

Olga Kameneva personally fostered Western intellectuals around the New Russia societies.[45] As early as 1924, before the creation of VOKS, she corresponded with an old acquaintance in the Soviet Trade representation in Berlin to discuss ways of establishing Soviet cultural representation in Germany;[46] in 1926, she had a similar discussion with the VOKS representative in Washington about establishing cultural representation in the USA.[47] She travelled to Berlin to personally set up two sections (the literary and the legal) of the Society of Friends of the New Russia, and later went to Cologne to create a branch within a similar organisation, Ost-Europa.[48] Fearing confusion between the already established VOKS-supervised Societies of Friends of the New Russia (*Obschestva druzey Novoy Rossii*), which in some senses she regarded as hers, and the planned Comintern-supervised, mass-oriented Societies of Friends of Soviet Russia (*Obschestva druzey Sovetskoy Rossii*), Kameneva appealed to the Communist Party to dissociate the two societies as much as possible.[49] 'One should not ruin the already smoothly running operations of the Societies of Friends of the New Russia, which conduct their activities among circles that are outside the sphere of influence of . . . workers' associations.'[50] The 'Kameneva societies' targeted the bourgeois intelligentsia: scholars, artists, writers, lawyers and others.[51] Keeping these societies limited to a professional and intellectual audience made them, Kameneva claimed, more attractive to new members. 'It is a proven fact that foreigners get in touch more willingly with us than with the workers' organisations of their own country.'[52]

The creation of the French Cultural Rapprochement Society was one of Kameneva's strongest aspirations. She had been closely following the mood of French intellectual circles and did not consider it possible to establish a society in France until 1927. Reports by the Romance sector outlining the strengths (but mainly the weaknesses) of the various earlier French–Russian friendship societies give an indication of VOKS's expectations. For example, a short-lived French–Russian friendship society created by the French intelligentsia in 1924 (Nouvelles activités franco-russes) was appreciated for its political involvement and its influence in 'the pre-election campaign of the then opposition (Herriot, de Monzie, Painlevé) since it included recognition of the USSR among its pre-election slogans'. VOKS also noted the role of eminent scholars and artists in the functioning of this society, and their interest in cultural exchange with the USSR.[53] However, the Society barely survived a year because, from VOKS's point of view, it lacked sufficient public support and resources. Another society, the Scientific Rapprochement Committee, created in 1925 and linked to the All-Russian Academy of Sciences, earned VOKS's disparaging comments, mainly for its organisational and financial independence from VOKS; it existed on its membership fees, under the auspices of the French Ministry of Public Education.[54] VOKS also commented that the Committee's conservative members were insufficiently interested in the October Revolution celebrations to visit the USSR. Such observations hinted at the criteria that VOKS used to identify sympathisers and potential allies.

VOKS believed that, in any given country, public sympathy towards the USSR depended on the efforts of Soviet diplomatic staff to promote Soviet culture and press. In this context, VOKS maintained that the warming of French public opinion towards the USSR in 1927 was due not only to the establishment of diplomatic relations in 1924 – a major event for both countries – but also to the arrival of Soviet culture in France during the 1925 World Exposition and other cultural initiatives.

> [Our] participation at the Paris Exposition not only contributed to our cultural rapprochement with France, but also contributed to correct information about

our country. And third, . . . it was the 200th anniversary of the Academy of Sciences [of the USSR], which brought scholars from all over the world, including France.[55]

In early 1927, Tikhomenev, a Soviet diplomat in Paris, signalled to Kameneva that some members of the French intelligentsia were trying to create a French–Russian Cultural Rapprochement Society; he gave her the names of the people involved in the early planning. Kameneva replied enthusiastically. She approved of the members of the founding group (*initsiativnaya gruppa*) and believed that the creation of this society would make 'real work' in France possible.

At last the moment has come when France may be included in the circle of true cultural rapprochement. This seems like a promising start, which is confirmed by the names you list. If this founding group really does work, then one could expect that a real society will be formed soon.[56]

Kameneva had no objection to having 'semi-migrants' – known Russian writers who lived abroad – as members. 'Please write to tell me exactly who joined this Committee. Did Ehrenburg, Annenkov and Orlova also join?'[57] Tikhomenev replied without delay that Ehrenburg and Annenkov had been of considerable assistance to the group.[58]

Both Kameneva and Tikhomenev became involved in setting up the society, Kameneva by encouraging its creation from Moscow, and Tikhomenev by keeping in touch with the group and keeping Kameneva up to date. Tikhomenev's letters show that he was well informed of the plans of the founding group, including preparations for the inaugural meeting and its agenda, down to the most minute detail; preparations for the election of a secretary to conduct correspondence and other work; discussion regarding the location and office hours of the Secretariat; and the need to finance the Secretariat and publish a newsletter to maintain contact with members. He concluded that the necessary funds would have to be provided by VOKS.[59]

When a new Soviet diplomat, Divil'kovsky, was appointed to Paris in mid-1927, to act as VOKS's representative (*upolnomochennyy*), Kameneva saw a chance to establish direct links with French intellectual circles. She wrote to the Soviet ambassador, Christian Rakovsky, an old Bolshevik (and a fellow-Trotskyite) and one of the many Soviet officials whom she knew personally.

Unfortunately, I didn't see com. Divil'kovsky, as you suggested, before his departure for Paris, so I was unable to talk to him in more or less concrete terms about the work of VOKS in Paris. And yet, this work is now at such an important stage of development that it is now that one should apply the maximum effort to take it past its initial, organisational stage.[60]

Kameneva threw herself into the creation of the society. First, she sent letters to members of the founding group, urging them to establish the society and anticipating its close cooperation with VOKS. 'I hope it won't be too long before this group becomes active, and that our two organisations will be linked in the united goal of developing cultural relations between our two countries.'[61] Kameneva then travelled to Paris for the inaugural meeting on 5 May 1927, organised by the French founding group, responding to an invitation signed by the leading French writers Jules Romain, Jean-Richard Bloch, Georges Duhamel, Georges Colin, Luc Durtain, Charles Vildrac and Léon Moussinac.[62] She was clearly recognised by this group as the patron of the planned society, and the inaugural meeting was timed to fit in with her stay in Paris.

Kameneva was pleased with the initial course of events. At the inaugural meeting, approximately 150 members of the cultural elite attended: writers, journalists, musicians and film directors. Eminent intellectuals who were present included the composer Darius Milhaud, who had visited the USSR the year before; the artists Fernand Léger, Frans Masereel and Jules Grandjouan; the writer Paul Vaillant-Couturier; and the newly elected Chairman, writer and future Nobel Prize winner, Georges Duhamel, who had also visited the USSR earlier that year. The meeting elected a provisional Committee and outlined a working plan – the creation of theatrical, literary, artistic and other sections, and proposals for exhibitions and translations. Among the issues of particular interest, Duhamel suggested that individual trips to the USSR and an exchange of scholars or ideas be one of the initial projects of the society. The provisional Committee agreed to convene the next meeting and to prepare working plans.

Following her return to Moscow, Kameneva was eager to speed up the development of the French society rather than allowing it to evolve at a natural pace. Through the VOKS representative, she suggested possible events that might encourage the society to be active. She proposed that Divil'kovsky invite Professor Boleslav Yavorsky and the composer Protopopov during their visit to Paris. 'It would be desirable to use them in the interests of cultural relations.' As she explained,

> It would make a lot of sense to arrange, under the banner of the rapprochement committee and away from the embassy, of course, a talk by Prof. Yavorsky, who is perfectly fluent in French, about Soviet music, and to invite representatives of musical Paris, for example Darius Milhaud, 10 Boulevard de Clichy, and his friend Wiener with whom VOKS maintains a certain contact. Maybe they, or other musicians whom they might suggest, would agree to accompany this talk with a concert of Soviet music. If this did not succeed, because of the summer holidays, one could organise tea and invite the French intelligentsia: in a nutshell, one has to try to use them one way or another.[63]

Kameneva's emphasis on conducting the meeting 'away from the embassy, of course' is the first indication of wanting to camouflage the Soviet initiative behind the French Cultural Rapprochement Society, and wanting it to appear independent.

Only a month after the inaugural meeting, Kameneva was growing impatient at the Committee's inactivity. Her relatively subtle suggestions gave way to interference as she wrote letters to French members of the Committee – the Slavist scholar André Mazon and the Communist film critic Léon Moussinac – to try and find out the reasons for the lack of action. She wrote to the Soviet writer Olga Forsh, the then well-known author of historical novels who was in France at the time, calling on her to support the society by joining it.[64] Bypassing the VOKS representative in Paris, Kameneva sent a telegram directly to the embassy: 'To plenipotentiary Tikhomenev Paris Concerned about the lack of information on the rapprochement activities Kameneva 6 June 1927'.[65]

Kameneva received conflicting replies. The eminent Slavist scholar, André Mazon, rebuffed her attempts to hurry him along. In his letter of 15 July, he reminded her that scholarly exchange was going well and that there had been a significant increase in the number of Soviet scholars visiting France, such as the linguist Professor Shcherba and the director of the Moscow Physics Institute, Lazarev. As for the rapprochement society, Mazon assured Kameneva that the Chairman, Georges Duhamel, was working on establishing the committee of literary and artistic rapprochement. Mazon denied any cause for concern and put the lull down to the summer holidays, which had taken prospective members out of Paris.[66]

Unlike Mazon, the VOKS representative Divil'kovsky shared Kameneva's concern and presented a different picture. Did he perhaps feel that he was being held responsible for the inactivity? He blamed the delays on the effect of an unspecified crisis on the spineless French intelligentsia, who were intimidated by anti-Soviet stirrings in the press.[67]

> As you know, as a result of the campaign in the French press, almost all the instigators of the French-Soviet rapprochement society have buried their heads, settled prudently behind fences, and it has been pointless even to think of meeting them. It is only now, after a certain (very minor) decrease in the crisis that one can hope to revive some of them (although, unfortunately, holidays continue). [. . .] We would have been most happy to use O. Forsh's presence in Paris, but . . . she is also away on holidays at the coast.[68]

The definitive reply to Kameneva came from Léon Moussinac, the Communist film critic. A note from Moussinac revealed the reasons for the society's delay, and his own future role as VOKS's covert emissary within it. His note makes clear his close contacts with Moscow and his role as the bearer of VOKS's 'special task'. 'Dear comrade, Please trust that I will do my best to succeed in the task with which I have been personally charged, but do not be too impatient.'[69]

We would be left guessing what was the significance of Moussinac's 'special task' had there not been another very similar document in the VOKS archives. In it, Ellen Crawford, a member of the Central Committee of the British Communist Party, reveals that, during a visit to Moscow in 1927, she received 'a special task' from Kameneva. Crawford's task was to clarify the situation within the British Society for Cultural Relations, find ways in which VOKS could finance it to ensure its viability, and explore the possibilities of setting up new branches in the provinces.[70] Crawford played the same role in relation to the British cultural society as Moussinac did in relation to Russie Neuve. As Crawford states, she was the insider who informed VOKS about the dynamics of relationships within the British Society. Eager to enhance its activities, she speaks openly about having been entrusted by 'the Soviet comrades' to persuade the leadership of the Society to accept VOKS's subsidy, and about having done all she could to fulfil the tasks she had been assigned.

Moussinac also informed Kameneva about the situation within the French society, and raised the question of financing. He confirmed Kameneva's suspicion that the delays in getting the society operational arose from internal, rather than external, causes. He then attempted to discredit the Chairman, Duhamel, whose desire for the society to be financially independent Moussinac saw as the main obstacle to its establishment. At the same time, Moussinac wished to promote his own efforts at speeding up the process. Duhamel, he wrote, regarded as premature his steps to find premises for the Secretariat and the secretary. Duhamel based his position on the lack of finance and his reluctance to accept a subsidy from the source suggested by Moussinac. This was most likely to be the VOKS subsidy already mentioned by the embassy official Tikhomenev, similar to the financial arrangement referred to in Crawford's letter.

> He [Duhamel] argued that there was no need to hasten anything, that he was determined to carry this matter to a successful end, that he had been greatly concerned about it; that he had spoken to Mazon and Langevin about it, that he would convene the provisional committee at the end of June and that he would like, first of all, to ask the [French] Ministry of Foreign Affairs for a subsidy. I was surprised, and he replied, still in his charming way, that he cared about ensuring, above all, total financial independence – in other words, if he were to accept the immediate practical solutions we were offering him he was simply afraid of compromising himself![71]

Moussinac criticised Duhamel's cautious and slow style of working, his tendency to discuss issues with too many parties, and his refusal to give in to pressure and manipulation; these led Moussinac to conclude that Duhamel was an unsuitable chairman.

> Duhamel wants to surround himself with all possible 'guarantees'. He wants to speak at the same time to the left and to the right, ahead of and behind him. I think he will be a difficult chairman. Anxious, suspicious, deep down a schemer, he can only be manoeuvred with caution.[72]

In relating his own attempts to speed things up, and contrasting Duhamel's interests with his own, Moussinac pointed to the existence of two opposing groups within the society, one of which clearly shared his intention to set up the society quickly.

> On the basis of what he says everywhere, he [Duhamel] wants to succeed in shaping, in a useful and interesting way, a group of French intellectuals [who

are] friends of the USSR; but for the reasons that I have already outlined to you and which are peculiar to Duhamel, this shaping will be slow, which is the opposite of what we wish. For the time being, Vaillant-Couturier and I can do only little, except pressure Duhamel without making it obvious. Some of the members of the provisional Committee that I have seen would, like us, have liked the group to show some effective signs of life before the holidays (a literary or critical conference, a Soviet film screening etc.) in order to show our desire for some practical action on the part of members of the group who are upset by Duhamel's precautions, which delay everything.[73]

It seems Moussinac's concerns may have been well founded. From a report by the *referent* of the Romance sector, Tsetsilia Rabinovich, it is known that 'apart from that first, organisational meeting, the society never met'.[74] Acknowledging this failure, VOKS rethought its approach for any future friendship society, and decided that it had to target a different membership and to increase VOKS's own leadership.

> This society wasn't viable, as it aimed at only a narrow circle of intelligentsia – writers, journalists and some of the scholars from the Scientific Rapprochement Committee. 'It was a basic mistake,' writes comrade Divil'kovsky, 'to try to achieve an autonomous unification from disjointed and hostile Parisian circles.'[75]

VOKS realised that leaders chosen from among the French elite were intractable and unlikely to take direction from VOKS; an elite leadership would be incapable of taking positive action and would prevent active members from taking the reins into their own hands. VOKS now concluded that (outside the ranks of the proletariat) the foundation of what it described as 'friendship with the USSR' had to be sought among intellectuals who were, above all, already demonstrably and reliably on the Left. 'It [the left-wing intelligentsia] should therefore be the basis of the society.'[76]

> Well before com. Divil'kovsky's letter, we stated the unviability of this society because, among other things, it was headed by representatives of the intelligentsia who were too eminent and who, in fact, could only play the part of honorary members, and not of worker bees.[77]

The 1927 celebrations of the October Revolution in Moscow became the litmus test that confirmed VOKS's new decision to seek out potential allies among politically loyal circles. 'The arrival of the representatives of the left-wing intelligentsia for the October Revolution celebrations convinced many of us that in France as well we should aim at left-wing circles.'[78] As for the eminent representatives ironically described as 'noble pacifist intelligentsia' (*blagorodno-patsifistskaya intellighentsiya*), who held differing political views, they would now be allocated only 'the ornamental part, that is the presidium and the periphery'. VOKS also found Duhamel to be 'too eminent' and easily deterred by political events. The

VOKS report scornfully described him as being '"too sensitive" to the fact of the execution of twenty White Army officers' – a reference to an incident that must have further cooled both Duhamel's eagerness, as his diaries suggest, and VOKS's sympathies towards him.[79]

This discussion bluntly brought up the issue of control by VOKS, the Soviet embassy and the FCP, even though VOKS spoke of the need to disguise these links.

> This society must be directly linked with VOKS, and behind the scenes with the [Soviet] embassy and, depending on the political situation, [the society must] maintain conspiratorial links with the Communist Party, through the Secretariat.[80]

The emphasis on disguising the Soviet/Communist leadership of the nominally non-political Cultural Rapprochement Society, and the camouflaged nature of its relations with the Communist Party, reiterated Comintern's and MORP's wish to give any future cultural society respectability. Later, in 1929, in his briefing to Petrov, Dikgof-Derental' would openly restate that VOKS's foreign representation 'must not have anything to do with official Soviet foreign institutions, and must be located away from them'.[81]

This development also uncovers the role of Western Communist intellectuals. Léon Moussinac, who was tasked to act covertly on VOKS's behalf, represented Soviet interests within the provisional Committee and leaked information about the Society to the Soviet embassy. Paul Vaillant-Couturier played a less clear role in this episode, but Moussinac mentions him as an ally. Finally, in order to resolve the problem of establishing the French society, and having given up on Duhamel, VOKS gave a 'special task' to another Communist, the caricaturist Jules Grandjouan, who was in Moscow for the October celebrations. 'This is the arrangement we have reached with comrade Grandjouan – a Communist who is not known as a Communist or a Communist Party member.'[82] Grandjouan's task included absorbing Duhamel's committee into the one to which Grandjouan belonged, a more mass-oriented and revolutionary committee that had been generated by Willi Münzenberg. 'Upon his return to Paris, he [Grandjouan] has to work on the merging of "his" committee that originated in summer 1927, with Duhamel's society, assisted by International Workers' Aid.'[83] Finally, this contact through Grandjouan allowed VOKS to use the Cultural Rapprochement Society as a point of reception and dissemination of Soviet materials. 'Grandjouan took away materials given to him by VOKS (diagrams, posters, publications) and, with VOKS's assistance, obtained a film compilation covering a number of issues in Soviet life.'[84]

The Cultural Rapprochement Society Russie Neuve was finally created in January 1928 and functioned until 1939. It is hard to ignore VOKS's interference in its creation. Rather than generating cultural rapprochement, which, to a degree, had already been taking place, VOKS aimed to create a compliant, VOKS-supervised and VOKS-dependent body. Yet, while VOKS had an open understanding with

Western Communist members, eminent intellectuals were resistant to pressure from VOKS and had to be influenced indirectly. As a result, VOKS changed its tactics in late 1927, now placing its bets on the left-wing intelligentsia and using them as the nucleus of an association that was designed according to Comintern's model of auxiliary, camouflage societies.

'Conduits of our cultural influence': establishing links with individual intellectuals

Establishing and fostering relations with individual Western intellectuals was central to VOKS. Its Bureau for the Reception of Foreigners had been created to take care of them during their visits, to meet foreign delegations and individuals, to arrange excursions for them and 'assist in acquainting them with [Soviet] cultural life'. Working with the *referenty* in a given country, the Bureau would arrange the programme for foreigners,[85] which had to include 'excursions to factories and plants, to workers' clubs, educational institutions, research institutes, museums, fine arts galleries, as well as organising scholarly conversations with Soviet scientists'.[86] Indeed, hosting foreign visitors became VOKS's central technique for establishing durable contacts with their targets. Kameneva personally encouraged foreign visits.[87]

The first visitors

Leading intellectuals began to visit the USSR through the services of VOKS in 1926–27, and VOKS's initial handling of them showed no political motives. The Professor of Slavonic Studies André Mazon, who was mentioned earlier, came from January to February of 1927.[88] He was followed by Georges Duhamel, the future member of the Académie française, and his friend, the doctor and writer Luc Durtain (in April 1927), who were both involved in the subsequent failed attempt to establish the French–Soviet Cultural Rapprochement Society. A number of famous guests came for the tenth anniversary of the October celebrations: Henri Barbusse from France, Theodore Dreiser from the USA and Stefan Zweig from Austria.

These visitors were received with traditional Russian hospitality, backed by careful organisation and planning. VOKS's internal correspondence regarding the visit of Duhamel and Durtain shows how much care VOKS took over their visit. VOKS covered all their arrangements, from sightseeing to finance, and arranged an intensive cultural programme with traditional sights that would meet the interests of intellectuals. The visitors were taken to the Hermitage, the Russian Museum and Public Library, Peter and Paul's Cathedral and Academician Pavlov's Laboratory in Leningrad, and the Kremlin in Moscow. Some excursions focused on post-revolutionary landmarks like Lenin's Mausoleum, and on recent cultural achievements. At the Gosizdat publishing house, the authors were presented with their own works translated into Russian, and sound and film recordings of their visit were made; the authors were also filmed at the film factory *Kinofabrika*.

Meetings with groups of Soviet scholars and authors were arranged. In one of the reports, VOKS specifically mentioned the input of Victor Serge (Kibalchich), who would later be prosecuted for his Trotskyite beliefs and stranded for years in internal exile.[89] At the time of these visits, Serge was among those who met the visitors at the station and accompanied Duhamel and his party; VOKS praised his contribution as 'being of the greatest assistance in informing our guests about contemporary Soviet literature, art and culture'.[90]

The care that VOKS took to cosset its French visitors set a precedent for the kind of generosity that many subsequent eminent visitors would find striking. During Duhamel's visit to Leningrad, the Bureau for the Reception of Foreigners gave instructions to the VOKS representative in Leningrad, Derzhavin, to pay his expenses wherever possible.

> First, they have to be met at the station and provided with the most gener- ous service, and second, opportunities must be sought for doing it free of charge in order to reduce their expenses to a minimum during their stay in Leningrad.[91]

In his account of his visit to Russia, *Le voyage de Moscou*, Duhamel later spoke with gratitude of the hospitality and what he called little privileges offered by his hosts in times of hardship.[92]

Such care and generosity were not at first extended to Theodore Dreiser, who suffered on account of poor communication between his hosts. Mezhrabpom, the organisation that originally invited him, failed to inform VOKS that it was sup- posed to look after him in Moscow. A week had passed before VOKS provided Dreiser with an interpreter and organised his sightseeing programme, receptions, meetings with Soviet intellectuals and members of the government and an exten- sive trip across Russia.[93] Although a Mezhrabpom representative in New York had assured Dreiser that all his expenses would be covered, Dreiser had to make several claims to the reluctant VOKS to be reimbursed for expenses already in- curred. In fact, VOKS refused to pay for Dreiser's private secretary in Moscow. Dreiser's financial disputes with Kameneva erupted at least twice into vehement arguments, during which he threatened to cut short his stay and return to America. While trying to placate Dreiser, Kameneva blamed the disorganisation on the confusion between VOKS and Mezhrabpom, and on VOKS's limited resources.[94] There was another reason why Dreiser did not benefit from the generosity shown to Duhamel: from the outset, Dreiser had insisted on being independent and had refused to join the October celebrations. During his trip, he realised that not being part of the official programme had its negative side: wasted time, being left out of activities and misunderstandings about money.[95]

The most lavish of all the visits seems to be the one enjoyed by Henri Barbusse in October 1927. Organised jointly by the Comintern, Krestintern, MORP, the Moscow Committee of VKP(b), Mossovet, VOKS, the Soviet Writers' Federa- tion, tertiary institutions and countless other organisations, it was coordinated and supervised by VOKS. The Communist writer Barbusse was not only given a more luxurious reception but also allocated a suite at a hotel as grand as the Metropol (unlike Durtain and Duhamel, who shared a room at the Tsekubu hostel),[96] with secretary and interpreter supplied, and was treated to trips across the USSR and to endless banquets. It was also as if his more publicised visit was a rehearsal for the receptions of the most eminent French guests in the 1930s: Rolland, Gide and Bloch. Barbusse's visit was the first example of public involvement in what would become a celebration of foreign visitors. From the start, the meeting at the railway station by representatives of all the host organisations turned into a public rally, with welcoming speeches, a response by Barbusse and ovations. The traditional cultural programme (Lenin's Mausoleum during the day, the opera *Yevgeniy On-egin* at the Bolshoi Theatre at night) was supplemented with literary evenings in the writer's honour and meetings with university students. The high official status given to the visiting writer took him away from the literary and cultural sphere and involved him in activities far removed from writing. Barbusse met Civil War heroes and the Army commanders Budyonny and Kuybyshev during the Red Cavalry Parade, and Georgy Chicherin, the People's Commissar of Foreign Affairs, organised an official banquet in his honour. As well as post-revolutionary sites, Duhamel was also shown a demonstration of achievements in the area of 'social-ist construction', something that visitors would see a great deal of in future. To mark the contrast with the appalling shacks of pre-revolutionary Russian workers, Barbusse was taken to a residential construction site for the workers at the Mos-sukno factory. The interpreter/guide quoted Barbusse as having commented, 'This construction is the best propaganda for the worldwide October [Revolution].'[97] Today, we can only speculate on the importance that the interpreter/guide may have attached to Barbusse's comment; however, it came from a writer of inter-national standing who was about to address a crowd of international visitors, all guests of Comintern gathered in Moscow for the tenth anniversary of the October Revolution. Barbusse's praise, quoted in the interpreter's report, is significant; it is the first open reference to the effect that VOKS hoped to achieve through show-ing foreign visitors carefully selected achievements of the Soviet regime.

However, not all visitors were enthusiastic about such sights. Theodore Dreiser remained unimpressed by the new workers' apartments; he found them too small and lacking facilities for basic hygiene.[98] He thought no better of the rooms of the critic Sergey Dinamov, which had neither toilet nor bath, nor of the apartment of film director Sergey Eisenstein, big by Soviet standards but small by American.[99]

Establishing contact

VOKS made contact with the wide range of foreign authors in different ways. Some, such as the German philosopher Walter Benjamin, had travelled to Russia for personal reasons rather than on VOKS's invitation. In 1926–27, he visited Asja Lacis, a Communist theatre director who inspired Benjamin's confessional *One Way Street*. His other desire was to explore Marxism and Communism by experiencing life as it was lived in Moscow. The German avant-garde theatre director Erwin Piscator was invited by the Association of Young Russian Theatre Directors, which then offered VOKS the chance to join forces in looking after him.[100]

However, most of these visits were initiated by VOKS. Its *Regulations Regarding VOKS Staff* (*Ustav* and *Polozheniye o shtate*) instructed *referenty* to identify, in the countries for which they were responsible, 'individuals and organisations capable of serving as conduits of our cultural influence' (*otdel'nykh lits, organizatsii, uchrezhdeniya, moguschiye yavit'sya provodnikami nashego kul'turnogo vliyaniya*).[101] Accordingly, VOKS made an approach to certain intellectuals, for example Duhamel and Dreiser, either directly or via organisations such as Mezhrabpom. Some guests, like Duhamel, took pride in being invited to the USSR.[102] Others, like Dreiser, waited to be persuaded of the interest and value of the trip, and demanded assurances such as having all their costs met.

The VOKS archives leave us guessing about the reasons behind the choice of these first visitors; the recommendations of the VOKS representatives abroad do not make this clear. Divil'kovsky informed the Moscow office about forthcoming visitors but, while he praised them as writers and journalists, he made no mention of their political orientation. The author Alfred Fabre-Luce was presented as a well-known political writer, and André Beucler as 'a beginner, yet already a rather well-known poet and fiction writer'.[103] The introductory letter for Géo London described him as a member of the editorial board of the newspaper *Le Journal* and contained a highly flattering recommendation of the author as 'one of the most outstanding representatives of contemporary French journalism'.[104] Divil'kovsky also indicated the visitors' areas of interest – in the case of London, this was school education, social and daily living conditions and the women's movement.

Divil'kovsky advised VOKS to treat these visitors with openness and to give them the opportunity to see as much as possible, with no pressure. As London was planning to write about the USSR in the French press, Divil'kovsky hoped that VOKS would allow him experiences that would give the French public 'a detailed and colourful report on Soviet reality'.[105] He stressed that the visitor had to be treated with subtlety and without force-feeding: 'Do not impose anything upon him' (*nichego yemu ne navyazyvat'*). Similarly, before the visit to Russia of Lucien Vogel, a major French publisher who intended to publish a special issue of *Life* magazine entitled *A new smiling Russia* and also the father-in-law of Vaillant-Couturier, Lunacharsky requested that Kameneva provide the visitor with hospitality and extensive opportunities to see the USSR. 'It will be most advantageous for us if he receives the broadest information possible.'[106]

In this spirit, writers such as Dreiser and Benjamin were allowed the opportunity to wander freely around Moscow. Dreiser was escorted by his secretary, the American Ruth Kennell, who lived in the Lux Hotel, a residence for foreign Comintern members; Benjamin went in the company of his friends, mainly Communists, and on his own. Whether or not Dreiser was pleased with the sights chosen by the official guides and by his American compatriots who lived in Moscow (Scott Nearing, Anna-Louise Strong and Louis Fischer) and the British Walter

Duranty (who worked for an American magazine), there is no evidence of official control over him. His criticisms did not attract any attempt to rein in his freedom, and VOKS excused them by reference to his age, physical ailments and inflexible individualism. 'Dreiser is too old and sick to enter into the essence of phenomena which he has come across for the first time', commented VOKS officials.[107]

The first evidence that VOKS was beginning to select prospective French contacts appears around 1927–28. An unsigned and undated inventory, 'Palmarès anthologique (de la guerre à nos jours)', clearly compiled by a French 'friend' around this time, lists members of the French intellectual elite, mostly authors.[108] Its title, 'Poètes (et critiques artistiques), Communistes, socialistes, révolutionnaires, sociaux, pacifistes internationaux, évolutionnistes, sympathisants etc. susceptibles de collaboration, évolution "à gauche" etc.' shows that the inventory was politically motivated. While the French word 'collaboration' can mean any form of cooperation, 'susceptibles de . . . évolution "à gauche"' (liable to develop towards the left) unmistakably indicates the desirability of political conversion. It is now possible to see that most of the people on this list can be identified as being affiliated, at one time or another, to the USSR. First, there are the actual supporters: the Trotskyites Victor Serge and Maurice Parijanine (a Russian pseudonym meaning 'The Parisian'), a writer and journalist at *l'Humanité*; the loyal Communists Barbusse, Moussinac and Grandjouan; and some of the sympathising visitors such as Duhamel and Durtain. Second come the hoped for, rather than actual, supporters. Some of the intellectuals whose names appear would indeed become involved with the USSR a few years later: among them are Aragon, still described as a surrealist and not a Communist,[109] and André Gide, whose active interest in the USSR would not begin until the early 1930s. Such identifiers or tags do not always provide an explanation for the appearance of a particular name on this politically motivated list. André Breton is described as a surrealist and the author of the Surrealist Manifesto, Picabia as a 'literary cubist and artist', and Picasso attracts no comment. It is only possible to speculate about the reasons for their inclusion. A number of surrealists had joined the Communist Party in 1927, and many were associated with the journal *Révolution surréaliste* (later renamed *Surréalisme au service de la Révolution*). The likely explanation is that listing the literary activities of people who were principally writers (Aragon, Barbusse, Bloch, Crémieux, Duhamel, Durtain, Eluard, Fabre-Luce, Gide, Grandjouan, Margueritte, Moussinac, Parijanine, Rolland, Serge, Vaillant-Couturier and Vildrac), and supplying the titles of their newspapers or magazines, made sense in the context of VOKS's operations. VOKS was concurrently involved in efforts to establish a friendly relationship with the left-wing intelligentsia and to get Soviet materials published in the Western press or disseminated abroad in other ways. The list describes Jean-Richard Bloch as being attached to the magazines *Clarté* and *Europe*, and as a founder of a number of reviews. Max Jacob is listed as a founder of the cubist literary movement and a participant in the magazines *Europe*, *Clarté* and *NRF*. Victor Margueritte is described as belonging to *Evolution*, and Madeleine Marx to feminist newspapers and magazines. The name of Léon Moussinac is associated with *l'Humanité* and *Clarté*, and Maurice Parijanine,

besides publishing in *Clarté* and *l'Humanité*, is said to be linked to Russian literature and proletarian criticism.[110]

The list is consistent with VOKS's *Regulations*, which instruct VOKS to
befriend intellectuals who could become potential conduits of Soviet influence
abroad. VOKS seems to have chosen wisely because, in the 1930s, Aragon,
Bloch, Rolland, Gide and other writers on this list indeed became devoted Soviet
supporters, and the pages of the magazines listed in the inventory became a forum
for their support.

The proof of the pudding: VOKS follows up its portrayal in the West

The proof that the visitors' trips had produced the hoped for pro-Soviet response
frequently came in the form of travel writings and in the visitors' on-going public
support of the USSR. Although Duhamel's book was less conclusive and lent
itself to conflicting interpretations, he clearly stated that the way he was received
had allowed him to see the real Russia.[111] Duhamel believed that visiting a variety
of institutions and meeting a wide variety of Russian people had allowed him to
understand the country; he enjoyed being recognised by those who had seen his
portrait in the Soviet press and appreciated his generous reception. He particularly
valued VOKS's helpfulness and tried to counter the already circulating rumours
suggesting that VOKS was really designed as an agency to control foreign visitors. Similarly, Dreiser's statement before leaving the USSR contained numerous
criticisms of the country, as did his book *Dreiser Looks at Russia*, but once at
home, he acted as a supporter of the USSR, especially during the Depression.

Almost from its foundation, VOKS showed a preoccupation with the way that
the Soviet Union was seen in the West, especially as it was portrayed by visitors.
This made VOKS watchful of or even apprehensive about the impressions its visitors would take home with them. From 1925, VOKS kept letters of thanks written
by foreigners after their visits,[112] and their travel articles, which were published
in either the Soviet or foreign press.[113] After Dreiser's departure, the Soviet critic
Sergey Dinamov, who had helped to look after him, wrote to Kameneva, 'Please
find attached Dreiser's article and letter regarding his general impressions of the
USSR, for you to use as you see fit.'[114]

VOKS wanted to be informed about both its visitors' publications and the re-
sponses these generated abroad. This information was gathered by reading and
analysing foreign reviews of its visitors' writings. From 1927, VOKS subscribed
to an increasing number of French newspapers and magazines,[115] requesting that
Divil'kovsky send regular press surveys, compiled by the Embassy Press Bureau
(*Buro pechati polpredstva*), of what the French press wrote about the USSR.[116]
On the request of Tsetsilia Rabinovich, *referent* for the Romance countries,
Divil'kovsky purchased and sent Andrée Viollis' *Seule en Russie*, Duhamel's *Le
voyage de Moscou*, Miglioli's *The Soviet Village* and Géo London's *Elle a dix ans,
la Russie rouge*.[117] He was then asked to send not only books but also articles and
press reviews.[118]

The Romance sector in Moscow soon began to compile its own reports of books written by visiting authors. It is important to recall that the *Staff Regulations* envisaged that the *referenty*'s primary task was 'to follow the cultural life of the countries it [VOKS] is providing service to, taking into consideration their political and economic peculiarities'.[119] French publications on the USSR were thus of interest to Rabinovich, who made written assessments of them. She often disagreed with Western opinions, contrasting her own views with the reception the USSR received in France.

> Andrée Viollis, the *Petit Parisien* journalist, visited the USSR and was looked after by VOKS. She has written a book, *Seule en Russie*. In this book she talks about all aspects of life in the USSR in a fairly objective and well-wishing manner, as much as her bourgeois essence permits. The book is written in lively and engaging language, and many French people say that this book has made the best impression of all the books that have been written in French on the USSR.
>
> Duhamel's book on the USSR, which is not considered here to be an entirely friendly one, is perceived quite differently by the French intelligentsia.
>
> Luc Durtain's book *Moscou – la capitale de l'URSS* is written in an enthusiastic tone.[120]

It is apparent that Rabinovich makes no critical remarks about Durtain's book, while she treats Duhamel's book with reserve. Was it because Durtain's naïve observations provided unambiguous support for the new society, while Duhamel's book contained too many inconclusive reflections? Furthermore, in spite of the very positive reception of Viollis' book (possibly the best-received book in France, as Rabinovich herself acknowledges), Rabinovich makes clear her suspicion of non-Communist, bourgeois visitors. It is noteworthy that the purpose of this internal report seems to be a critique of these French authors rather than a reflection of how their books were received. Rabinovich's language is full of what, by this time, were common (but not yet compulsory) class-conscious *clichés*, notably, 'as much as her bourgeois essence permits'. It is hard to miss the contradiction in the report, which simultaneously describes Viollis' account of Russia as 'lively and engaging' and 'fairly objective'. A report on the Communist Grandjouan's book expressed no such reservations and only stressed its positive effect on the French public.

> By the way, Grandjouan published, in the name of his Committee, his book entitled *Living Russia*, provided with beautiful illustrations. The book, which is written in an enthusiastic tone, made a strong impression on the broad democratic circles in France, and particularly on the working masses.[121]

By voicing its very first concerns over the portrayal of the USSR in France, VOKS was trying to establish its own authority over what it considered an acceptable representation of the USSR. But Rabinovich's reports also showed concerns about the political orientation of visitors, and thus revealed the first signs of a changing attitude towards them. Viollis's book may have been sympathetic and well received, but misgivings caused by her bourgeois origins were of more concern to Rabinovich than the success of the book.

All the same, Rabinovich's suspicious assessment of the writings of foreigners had not yet become the norm. In contrast, the Anglo-American sector treated its visitors' opinions with more tolerance. True, those who escorted Dreiser also used similar language to Rabinovich, calling Dreiser 'typically bourgeois' and saying he had the 'petit bourgeois individualist ideology' and was thus unable to appreciate Soviet reality.[122] 'Dreiser . . . is a typical bourgeois writer with a specific petit bourgeois individualist ideology.'[123] Nonetheless, his interpreter, Davidovskaya, and the final report on his visit (possibly written by Anglo-American *referent* Sergey Trevis) were optimistic about the long-term outcome of the writer's visit.[124]

> Dreiser will still present the situation in such a way that his readers will understand that under the Soviet regime, the broad working and peasant masses have been given and are enjoying a freedom that never existed before, either under the tsar or elsewhere.[125]

Later, in 1930, the critic Sergey Dinamov, who also looked after Dreiser, described Dreiser's book with similar tolerance.

> After his 1928 trip to the USSR, Dreiser published a book, *Dreiser Looks at Russia*. It contains, alongside some erroneous views and a mistaken interpretation of Soviet reality, a number of positive points which have caused a ferocious campaign against the writer in the bourgeois press.[126]

One can't help reflecting on the reasons why Dreiser's writings were treated with far less severity than those by his French counterparts. It is unlikely that it was due to Dreiser's international importance. Perhaps, in what was left of these relatively liberal times, the totalitarian mentality had not yet become all-pervasive, both in the USSR and inside VOKS. VOKS's attitude towards visitors was not as dogmatically monolithic as it would become very shortly after, and there were still opportunities for some differences of opinion between sectors and members within the same organisation.

1928–29: a change

However, these internal differences within VOKS were soon to disappear. The years 1928–29 were particularly significant in Soviet history and in the operations of VOKS. In the course of consolidating his undivided power, Stalin defeated his main opposition – the triumvirate consisting of Trotsky, Zinov'yev and Kamenev

– leading to Trotsky's expulsion. Another important event occurred in 1928; this was the first public show trial, the Shakhty trial, also known as the sabotage trial. In March 1928, Soviet and foreign engineers and technicians were charged with carrying out subversive actions including causing industrial accidents, wrecking machinery and generally sabotaging Soviet industry. During their trials and executions, the myth of 'the foreign conspiracy' and of 'saboteurs in the pay of foreign powers' was created.[127] In an atmosphere in which the country was said to be full of foreign spies, it is not surprising that changes descended upon VOKS, the organisation whose task it was to work with foreigners. This campaign also swept away Olga Kameneva.[128] In February 1928, a Workers and Peasants Commission (*Rabkrin*) conducted an inspection of VOKS and, while rating its achievements highly, found Kameneva's performance as its Chair unsatisfactory. The meeting of the VOKS party organisation decreed the removal of Kameneva from her position.[129] Judging from her VOKS correspondence, she remained in charge, presumably until the beginning of July 1929.[130]

After this date, the VOKS archives show signs of significant change within the organisation. The attitude towards visitors became more suspicious. In the absence of any internal or external directives, it is self-evident that Soviet policies had to be reflected in the operations of Soviet organisations. In 1929, *referent* Tsetsilia Rabinovich became Head of the Romance sector. Without suggesting that changes were limited to the French sector, it is clear that Rabinovich's personal stamp was felt in the introduction of a firmer control over visitors. It was Rabinovich who, in 1927, had produced a report on the French intelligentsia and the Cultural Rapprochement Society, pointing to the need for a left-wing orientation in France, and it was Rabinovich who had written the first critical reviews of the French visitors' publications.

Whether coincidentally or not, a number of critical reports of the USSR were published in France around 1928–29. Written by former visitors, in some cases friends who had turned enemies, these reports must have come to the attention of VOKS. Elsa Triolet would later refer in her memoirs to what she called the treachery of Paul Morand, the author of *Je brûle Moscou*; she called the book 'a libel' on the Moscow literary scene, where he had been welcomed. Another Frenchman, Henri Béraud, wrote what Triolet called a 'repugnant report' (*otvratitel'nyy reportazh*).[131] During his stay in the USSR in 1928, Panaït Istrati, who later wrote *Vers l'autre flamme*, personally informed the GPU (Main Political Directorate) of his intention to publish in France the undisguised truth about the USSR. According to Istrati, this would be the best antidote to the misinformation published about the USSR in the West.[132] Staff at VOKS discussed Istrati's change in attitude and decided that they had overestimated his loyalty.[133]

As well as changing its attitude towards foreigners, VOKS changed the treatment they received; however, suspicion and hostility were not obvious to the visitors and were revealed only in internal reports. The interpreter/guides had been compiling reports in the years from 1927 to 1929,[134] but the degree of detail and the tone differed according to the sector. Thus, the Anglo-American reports were concise, and even the exceptionally detailed ones (for example, those on Dreiser) were written in a tolerant tone.[135] On the other hand, the reports and instructions of the Romance sector reflected a tighter control over visitors, with greater scrutiny of their background, political orientation, impressions of the USSR and anticipated accounts in the West. The cases of the authors Georges Lefebvre and Andrée Viollis serve as a good illustration of these changes.

Georges Lefebvre, a journalist at the newspaper *Le Journal*, arrived in Moscow in October 1929 to study Soviet living conditions and culture.[136] VOKS arranged for him to visit the pretrial detention unit of the Lefortovo prison; it was not an uncommon tourist destination in Moscow in the 1920s, most likely part of the 'counter-information' to dispel the Western myth about the appalling conditions in Soviet prisons.[137] The purpose of Lefebvre's visit, as Rabinovich advised the Leningrad VOKS representative, Derzhavin, was to write a book on the USSR. In contrast with her past instructions, Rabinovich's tone was openly apprehensive and her suspicion and hostility undisguised. She cautioned her staff about Lefebvre. 'Lefebvre works for the French newspaper *Le Journal*, which in itself sufficiently determines his true face. [. . .] This is why one has to be reserved with him, although on the surface remain very polite.'[138] Rabinovich gave another reason for further vigilance: 'Besides, one has to keep in mind that he knows Russian quite well, although he tries to hide it.'[139] Was it the past experience with other visitors who understood Russian, like Panaït Istrati, that made Rabinovich suspicious? Was it an early symptom of the mass hysteria and the fear of spies incited by the Shakhty trials? The letter offers no clues as to whether her caution stemmed from VOKS's past experience or whether, as is more likely, it marked the beginning of the fear induced by the harshening of the political climate – reflected in the story of Andrée Viollis.

'It is impossible to win over the Marquise D'Ardenne de Tizac': an interpreter's response

Suspicion towards visitors was now affecting interpreter/guides' behaviour. The *Staff Regulations* mention this category of VOKS employees only briefly, stating that they were recruited on a casual basis and briefed jointly by the Bureau for the Reception of Foreigners and the Shareholding Tourist Society (*Aktsionernoye obschestvo po turizmu*); these two agencies arranged periodic training courses.[140] Nothing more is said in the *Regulations* about the interpreter/guides, apart from the fact that they were expected to provide a service to foreigners.

The role of interpreter/guides, and the expectations placed upon them, emerge more clearly from VOKS documents. They were required to write reports on their charge's visits, and the signatures of interpreter/guides can be found on many documents; the tone and the amount of detail range from one report to another. The Anglo-American sector made individual lists of the sights to be visited by foreigners. A typical list prepared for a rank-and-file member of the British intelligentsia (a doctor) includes a collective farm, a court of law, an isolation ward for contagious diseases, a factory, the Klara Zetkin Maternity Hospital, a venereal disease clinic, the Institute for the Protection of Mothers and Infants, the House of the Commune, the Tret'yakov Gallery, the Museum of the Revolution and Lefortovo Prison and its pretrial detention unit.[141] The stays of eminent visitors, with their reactions and moods, were described in greater detail. Dreiser's secretary, Ruth Kennell, made a note of the times when he was surly or displeased as a result of his physical ailments, the lack of comforts and his tiredness, while Dreiser's VOKS interpreter, Davidovskaya, noted his pleasure and admiration during their trip to Nizhniy Novgorod.[142] (Dreiser's privately appointed secretary, Ruth Kennell, was part of a small American colony already living in Moscow. During his stay in Russia, they became intimate and her letters reveal that she loved him; nonetheless, she displayed a greater loyalty to the Soviet system than to Dreiser and submitted her copy of his travel diary to VOKS after his departure.)

However, the reactions and behaviour of the French visitors' interpreter/guide, Ludmila Rastigher-Ronskaya, marked a change in outlook and possibly a new direction for VOKS. Andrée Viollis was a French travel writer, the author of the successful book *Seule en Russie*, whose third husband was the Marquis D'Ardenne de Tizac; she visited the USSR for the second time in 1929. Rastigher-Ronskaya was assigned to escort Viollis during her trip to Central Asia.[143]

The first part of the Viollis file contains what was becoming, by then, a standard description of the cultural programme and of Viollis' areas of interest. Perhaps Rastigher-Ronskaya paid particular attention to detail because she listed more thoroughly than other interpreter/guides the places that Viollis had visited; she also described conversations that they had. The visitor, she wrote in her report, responded favourably to the usual cultural programme in Moscow including visiting theatres and museums, and discussing works by Soviet authors with VOKS, displaying familiarity with Soviet literature and volunteering positive responses. It is clear that the programme was a success because it had been carefully arranged around the visitor's interests. Viollis was known to be interested in the condition of women, including interactions between the sexes and the problems of motherhood and childhood, so VOKS organised visits to the Home for Prostitutes, the Homeless Children's Refuge and the Homeless Children's Exemplary Commune. In view of her interest in school education, Viollis was taken to the Decembrists' School, named after the December 1825 insurgents, where she could discuss mixed education and students' self-rule. This part of the report was recorded in the neutral tone that was usual for such an account, and suggested a positive reaction by the visitor to what she was shown and her receptiveness to the different experiences.[144]

Nevertheless, the positive tone of the report changed strikingly when Viollis left for Central Asia, where she travelled from 4 October until 23 November. The file contains Ronskaya's postcard of 5 November 1929 to her superior, Rabinovich, in which she makes painfully clear that, away from Moscow, the trip was not running smoothly:

> Dear Tsetsilia Iosifovna,
>   If you could only imagine the torture your messenger has been subjected

to, you would have taken pity on me. Nothing happened in particular, but I am terribly exhausted from fussing over her, and whatever juices I had in my body have been sucked out.[145]

The card deplores the effects of isolation, which prevent Ronskaya from reporting adequately on her worries and seeking guidance from Rabinovich. It seems that Ronskaya's sole desire, when she gets home, is to report to her superior.

> I insist on convening, upon my return, a meeting at which I will report on what was done, as it would be impossible to convey it in sporadic conversations. . . . I am under the impression that you have lost both of us from your sight. It may be wrong for me to write such personal cards, but it will only become possible to compile an official report in Moscow. . . . Your exhausted Ronskaya.[146]

Ronskaya's official report followed – a report which sheds light on VOKS's intentions towards visitors and provides an insight into what a guided tour of the USSR was expected to achieve.[147] It shows the importance not only of the sites visited but also of the role of interpreters as propagandists in the visitors' programme. Visitors represented more than a tourist audience; Ronskaya saw Viollis a priori as a political opponent whose sympathy must not be trusted, a member of a hostile bourgeois audience who had to be transformed through exposure to what was commonly known as 'the truth about the USSR'.

> There is no doubt that Andrée Viollis should be classified amongst those bourgeois journalists who are organically alien to everything Soviet as a result of their individualist nature. Her sympathy towards everything new happening in the USSR is purely platonic, if not purely hostile.[148]

Viollis, continued Ronskaya, was entirely opportunistic in visiting the USSR, and the ideas of profit (*vygoda*) and sale (*torgovlya*) recur in her report. 'The USSR is a fashionable theme in demand abroad, and Viollis derives profit from her knowledge of Russian life.' On the other hand, Ronskaya remembered that Viollis was a potential source of information on the USSR (a 'conduit of Soviet influence') to a growing audience.

> She probably does a lot of political writing because it is unprofitable for the West to further ignore the results we have achieved in the past eleven years, and they have to take them into account. There is also a trend in France to renew, or rather re-animate, its trade links with the USSR. There are also entire groups of people who, according to Viollis, have not the slightest idea of what the USSR is like, and do not believe in its ability to trade.[149]

It was VOKS's task to expose Viollis to 'counter-information', that is, to the achievements of socialist construction. She was meant to become persuaded of the viability of Soviet society, including its economic viability, and to take home positive messages about this to France. Her impressions of the USSR were supposed to be crucially affected by the places she visited; the intention was to dispel the anti-Soviet myth in her mind and, through her, in the West.

> Perhaps those cotton processing plants that work without interruption day and night, the magnificent bank and committee buildings, cotton fields and trains, hydroelectric power stations etc. that Viollis saw during her trip will convince these factions that Soviet industry really does exist.[150]

However, unlike the period spent in Moscow, the trip to Central Asia was not running according to plan; the effect of the scheduled sights was undermined by an undisguisable and tawdry reality, 'the overcrowded railway stations, the trains and hotels filled with people, and the bureaucratic institutions we had to deal with'.[151] In listing these drawbacks, Ronskaya was careful to attribute the word 'shortcomings' to Viollis ('<u>what she sees as</u> shortcomings'[152]). But Ronskaya was anxious about Viollis' disinclination to be moved by the sights she was meant to admire. Moreover, Ronskaya was worried about her own role; it is clear that as an interpreter/guide she was also required to act as a propagandist and would be held responsible for the visitor forming what was regarded as the correct opinion of the Soviet Union. Ronskaya was expected (and expected herself) in some way to mitigate or sweep away the reality that had obviously made a negative impression on her visitor, and she was to achieve this transformation by placing the so-called shortcomings into historical perspective.

> I did whatever possible to get it through to her that this is a growth-related disease, that you cannot demand Bukhara, where a year ago there was no drinking water and people lived in mud huts, to provide comforts at the level of a London hotel; that the feverish construction of plants and factories has attracted more people to Central Asia than the railway network and the hotels can handle, and that the railways and hotels are being built, which she saw for herself in any case.[153]

However, the visitor was clearly resistant to Ronskaya's persuasion. For Ronskaya, these disagreements meant defeat in a political battle, and her own personal failure.

> But while comprehending the legitimacy of this situation on an intellectual level, Viollis could not come to terms with not having the comforts she is accustomed to. . . . But here any guide becomes helpless, as it is impossible to persuade [*aghitirovat'*] the Marquise D'Ardenne de Tizac. It is against her interests for France to follow in Russia's footsteps, and Viollis could never talk about it without horror.[154]

But the worst was still to come. Viollis was not only Ronskaya's audience but was also likely to be the author of articles which could be full of horror stories, spreading the worst possible publicity in the West – just what Ronskaya was meant to prevent.

> Viollis' hypocrisy will no doubt allow her to tell plenty, in certain circles, about the lack of comfort in the USSR etc, and by using her facts they will be able to distort the true reasons for the difficulties the USSR is undergoing.[155]

However, having anticipated such a pessimistic outcome, Ronskaya admitted that the opposite could also be possible: namely that Viollis' response to positive experiences and Soviet success might after all be stronger than her aversion to discomfort, and that she might communicate a positive message in the West. If that turned out to be the case, Ronskaya wanted to make certain that it was she who got the credit for it.

> In the event the circles sympathising with the USSR begin to take over, Viollis will be at the forefront of the well-wishers, and her agitation may be very effective, as the positive material gathered by her during the trip is enormous.[156]

Ronskaya's fears about Viollis turned out to be unfounded. Years later, Viollis spoke with eagerness about her wish to revisit 'Moscow under its amethyst-coloured skies of angelic softness'.[157]

Ronskaya's report stems from VOKS's store of experience and marks the beginning of a new chapter. It has its roots in VOKS's previous work, its anxiety over the portrayal of the USSR in the West and its *raison d'être* as an organisation that was meant to influence foreigners. Ronskaya's report reflects the growing suspicion towards non-Communist guests and their treatment as potential traitors to the cause with which they had at first seemed to sympathise. With the strictly guided tours, interpreter/guides found themselves in the position of spokesmen – or rather spokeswomen, because they were mostly female – responsible for the opinions their visitors would take home. As long as Viollis remained in Moscow, VOKS had no difficulty in appealing to her interests and maintaining the customary façade built from high culture and its social interactions. It was during Viollis and Ronskaya's lengthy and uncomfortable trip to Central Asia that the mythology, the Potemkin villages erected to delude visitors, collapsed. Now the interpreter found herself cut off from VOKS's reliable sources of support and glamour that would have allowed her to maintain control over the visitor, that is, to impose her opinions on Viollis. What Ronskaya feared most was that instead of acting as a 'conduit of Soviet influence', Viollis would write a 'repugnant report' for which Ronskaya would be held responsible. In self-defence and on her own initiative, Ronskaya produced a document designed to deflect blame away from herself. It is ironic that the report accurately lists all the reasons for foreigners to feel uncomfortable during their trips, describing in detail Viollis' dislikes and objections, quoting her critical remarks, passing on the perceptions of the USSR held in the West – and yet also revealing the interpreter's personal opinion of the USSR. Moreover, in an attempt to protect herself, Ronskaya demonstrates her propagandist's skills by quoting the politically required arguments. What could be seen as a hysterical piece of writing, and a fine example of a letter of denunciation, would soon be transmuted into a standard document – the interpreter/guide's compulsory report – which would methodically address all of the points that Ronskaya had spontaneously incorporated into her account. Ronskaya's report is symptomatic of the beginning of a new era in the life of VOKS, and sets a precedent for the behaviour of the emerging *Homo sovieticus* – a cog in the VOKS, if not the Soviet, machine.

As the Soviet Union entered a new chapter, so did VOKS. Working in a new political climate, under new management, in an atmosphere of suspicion towards those who used to be treated as friends, how would VOKS operate in the 1930s, after the year of the Great Break?

6 Manufacturing support
VOKS in the 1930s

VOKS is capable of influencing circles otherwise inaccessible for indoctrination.
VOKS representative in London, 1930

The years 1928–29 marked the consolidation of the Stalinist state and central-ised power. The new decade began with increasingly disturbing events: the 1930 Prompartiya show trial and the peasant resistance to collectivisation followed by repression, deportation and a massive famine. Cultural revolution, also proclaimed in 1929, meant proletarian antagonism towards the intelligentsia, both Soviet and foreign. After that, it was only a matter of a few years before the beginning of the Great Terror. What seemed to be truly consolidated was the Soviet bureaucratic machinery; VOKS was part of it.

By the early to mid-1930s, VOKS's relations with Western countries were well established. After Hitler's assumption of power, its contacts with Germany and Austria were interrupted; however, those with France and the USA were becom-ing increasingly more active. The VOKS archives document what had become routine activities in the 1930s, that is, hosting foreigners' visits to the USSR. They also document how VOKS acted abroad, namely how it built contacts with Western intellectuals, how it involved itself in Cultural Rapprochement Societies and how it disseminated Soviet materials.

From 1929 to 1930, VOKS's agenda was clearly stated in its internal docu-ments. Chair Petrov's correspondence and protocols of meetings openly state that cultural exchange and friendship with Western intellectuals were a means of gain-ing Soviet political influence. VOKS received orders from the VKP(b) Central Committee to conduct political campaigns abroad, for example to promote the Prompartiya trial. Upon receiving instructions, Petrov would instruct his foreign representatives on the appropriate course of action.[1]

VOKS was associated with the People's Commissariat of Foreign Affairs or NKID. NKID diplomats served as VOKS representatives abroad; their experience of foreign countries made them realistic about the limitations of Soviet influence. However, there was a second organisation with which VOKS was connected:

the ominous People's Commissariat for Internal Affairs or NKVD. From 1936 it was headed by Nikolay Yezhov, whose name came to symbolise the Great Terror and who was replaced, in 1938, by an even more sinister figure, Lavrenty Beria. VOKS's Secret Department (*Sekretnyy otdel*) was clearly a branch of the NKVD, and the two were a hindrance to VOKS's operations, particularly from 1936 onwards.

Hospitality, VOKS style

Hosting foreign intellectuals' visits had become a major part of VOKS's operations. The number of visitors who came to the USSR through VOKS virtually doubled every year after 1929, reaching a peak around 1934–36 during the time of VOKS's third Chair, Aleksandr Arosev. NKID dealt with diplomats, the Comintern with Communist parties, and MORP with writers who were clearly supporters of the Soviet Union. All of the agencies, including those in competition with VOKS, recognised VOKS's exclusive position as the agency responsible for the foreign intelligentsia, and sent their visitors to VOKS.[2] Arosev liked to remind the party leadership of VOKS's unique role.

> Both Intourist and VOKS are dealing with an audience that is not 'processed by' anyone. The enormous vacillating mass, consisting of the petite bourgeoisie and the intelligentsia, which is very influential in Western Europe and America, is left entirely to VOKS and Intourist.[3]

Rank-and-file professional intelligentsia often came to the USSR, via VOKS, in groups. As in the 1920s, VOKS seemed to place no demands on them and acted as an agency that took full care of their stay and gave them practical assistance – helping to extend a visa,[4] providing a letter to the Lenin library,[5] arranging meal passes to the Writers' Club or passes to theatres,[6] establishing contacts between visitors and Soviet writers and organising meetings.[7] Above all, VOKS was there to schedule a sightseeing programme and to provide interpreter/guides to escort them.[8] The 'barrage units leading the army' (*zagraditel'nyye otryady*), as Arosev called interpreter/guides, now had a clear job description: they were officially accountable for their visitors and reported on them in writing.

Little is known about VOKS interpreters except for their names and working languages. Visitors barely ever mention them in their travel accounts, even though their impressions of the USSR were sifted through the interpreters' point of view. Even the Blochs, who had fond memories of their interpreters, wrote nothing about them – Valentina Mil'man, Boleslavskaya (Bolya) and Natalia Kamionskaya. However, Gide leaves the reader with no doubt about how little he trusted 'the charming comrade [Bolya]':

> Nothing indeed ever floors her, and she provides an answer to everything; the more ignorant she is of a subject, the more cocksure she becomes . . . Our

charming guide is as obliging and devoted as it is possible to be. But there is this about her that is rather fatiguing – the information she gives us is never precise except when it is wrong.[9]

The interpreters' reports do, however, tell us a great deal about themselves and VOKS. Initially, these reports contained a list of places they visited, accounts of conversations with visitors and some of their remarks.[10] In 1936, Arosev introduced standard forms with new spaces for noting the visitor's statements, the interpreter's conclusions and a character assessment of the visitor. In a special meeting of 14 May 1937, calling on his staff to increase their vigilance, Arosev instructed interpreters to conduct detailed, revealing conversations with their charges and to expand reports even further. 'I propose that you go beyond the framework of the forms and write more fiction (*belletristika*).'[11]

Interpreter/guides' reports indeed provide fascinating reading about VOKS's role in planning, conducting and monitoring the visits of foreigners. However, the reports have to be read with critical distance because of the known tendency of interpreters to gloss over and exaggerate to suit the expectations of their management.[12] With the heading 'not to be disclosed' (*ne podlezhit oglasheniyu*), and bearing pencil marks and handwritten comments in the margin, these typed reports were clearly passed on to senior members of staff and to Arosev for screening.

From these reports we learn that, although the cultural programme offered an increased number and choice of places to visit, the principle remained the same as before. Visitors were taken to the already familiar socio-cultural (*kul'turno-by-tovyye*) institutions promoting Soviet achievements, rather than to places of traditional Russian cultural and historical heritage. Along with collective farms and the Bolshevo commune for underage criminals, visitors were shown the Central Park of Culture and Rest (the future Gorky Park) and the obligatory Moscow Metro, opened in 1934. Visits to art exhibitions of European and Russian masterpieces were alternated with visits to the Lenin Museum, the Anti-religious Museum and the display of drawings by Soviet children. Other institutions routinely visited included the Mother and Child Rooms (*komnata materi i rebyonka*) at the Kazansky or the Northern railway stations, and the Institute of Child and Adolescent Health (*Institut okhrany zdorov'ya detey i podrostkov*). The most visited high school was the Decembrists' school.

The real change in VOKS's cultural programme in the 1930s was that it became structured and controlled. Deviation from the official list of sites would no longer be tolerated, and visitors could no longer be allowed to wander off unsupervised.

Preconditioned visitors: background

Although visitors shepherded by VOKS were known to have come from a broad political spectrum, most were already well disposed towards the USSR, especially those who came after 1933. As one of the interpreters described a group from the left-wing magazine *Vendredi*, they were 'Communists, socialists, sympathisers and those who, as Chamson put it, sympathise out of fear' (*i kommunisty, i sotsial-*

isty, i sochustvuyuschiye i, kak vyrazilsya Chamson, 'sochustvuyuschiye so stra-kha').[13] VOKS hosted political enemies, too: the writer Pierre Drieu La Rochelle, who at the time was hesitating between Nazi Germany and the USSR, came on Malraux's recommendation in 1935;[14] the virulent anti-Communist writer Louis-Ferdinand Céline came in 1936; the French Parliamentary Deputy Montagnon, who had been received earlier by Mussolini and major German political leaders; and the editor of a financial/industrial paper, Villard.[15] However, all of the visitors seemed to come with some motive or purpose.

Visits were triggered by a chain of personal influences and recommendations. One sympathiser sent another. Some, like Vildrac and Durtain, came for a second time,[16] and some were brought along by other Soviet supporters, such as the group from *Vendredi* organised by the writer André Chamson.[17] Many had been sent by influential intellectuals already familiar with VOKS: Aragon, Barbusse, Malraux, Gide and Rolland. It was to VOKS, and not to Comintern, that Barbusse sent the Communist scholar Georges Friedmann, Secretary of the Scientific Commission of the Cercle de la Russie Neuve,[18] 'a young writer and scholar of the highest quality'.[19] Other visitors were sent by Broun, the VOKS representative in Paris, carrying personal letters to the VOKS Chair.

Sympathisers did more than generate new visits; they provided an audience that was a priori keen, positively disposed towards the USSR and receptive to VOKS's programme. Visitors had already been informed about specific subject areas that VOKS promoted, and they asked to be taken to the appropriate places. A Mme Bagnol wished to see achievements in the area of motherhood and child-hood protection, and women's conditions;[20] teachers asked to be shown schools, crèches, preschools and children's theatre;[21] and doctors wanted to visit the Medical Institute, hospitals and maternity wards.[22]

This way in which visitors channelled their own activities was particularly evident in the arts. Visiting artists sought professional contacts with their Soviet colleagues,[23] and French directors asked to meet the Soviet film and theatre directors Eisenstein, Tairov and Nemirovich-Danchenko.[24] They often already knew what films, plays and exhibitions they wanted VOKS to show them. Pierre Herbart, who later travelled with Gide around the USSR, wanted to see a good ballet at the Bolshoi Theatre and the films *Three Songs about Lenin* by Dziga Vertov and *Aerograd* by Dovzhenko. He knew that Nikolay Pogodin's play *The Aristocrats* was about the re-education of criminals in the Belomorkanal labour camp.[25] Schtamreich, a journalist at *Ce soir*, asked to be shown the 1936 film *We from Kronstadt*, which he knew to be about the plight of Revolutionary sailors and soldiers,[26] and the conductor Désormière and his wife wanted to see the paintings by 'workers' circles', which they had learned about from *Journal de Moscou*.[27] Sculptor Jacques Lipchitz was so eager to see Meyerhold's theatre productions and exhibitions of Soviet artists that he extended his stay.[28]

Some visitors had independently prearranged contacts with individual Soviet artists and writers. Artist Frantz Masereel saw caricaturist Boris Yefimov and then, through Aragon and Elsa Triolet, who were also in Moscow, he met Triolet's sister Lili Brik.[29] The home of Lili Brik, Mayakovsky's muse of the 1920s, was frequented by numerous foreign visitors who enjoyed her renowned hospitality, even after World War II. While VOKS was happy to organise meetings with Eisenstein, Meyerhold and other cultural icons, it was less enthusiastic about foreigners making their own contacts, unsupervised and beyond the aegis of VOKS. We shall see some examples of this in the next chapters.

Overwhelmingly, foreigners requested to see places and people that were already on VOKS's list. This showed that they were well informed, but it also meant that they lacked information in other areas to enable them to make different requests. Interpreters' reports contain no requests for activities or visits to places not included in the VOKS 'set menu'. Former visitors and sympathisers had clearly done a good job of supplying an audience that could fit into the VOKS mould.

What are they thinking? Visitors' reactions

Having a preconditioned audience was a promising start; however, handling this audience was no simple matter. Interpreters' reports are filled with their concerns and fears about visitors' reactions. Interpreters' opinions about their charges were determined by their charges' opinions of the USSR.

Interpreters praised tourists who expressed an interest in the places they were taken to see, and who said positive things about the USSR. Those who, like Lacroix, showed a 'friendly disposition towards the USSR' (*k SSSR nastroyen druzhestvenno*) made 'a most positive impression' (*vpechatleniye o nyom samoye polozhitel'noye*).[30] Equally, Mme Bagnol was said to 'give the impression of a person very well disposed towards the USSR' (*proizvodit vpechatleniye cheloveka, ochen' raspolozhennogo k SSSR*).[31] According to her interpreter, she spoke of Soviet achievements with great pleasure (*s bol'shim udovol'stviuem govorit o nashikh dostizheniyakh*).[32]

Interpreters recorded the positive comments made about Soviet institutions in great detail. They quoted one visitor as saying that the mother and child protection system had made 'a strong impression'.[33] A writer recorded only as Dreyfuss found that the Moscow Metro was incomparable. He loved the Mother and Child room at the Kazansky Railway station, where he spoke to its headmistress and children, inspected bedrooms with pot plants and watched games, dances and gymnastics. 'Dreyfuss kept writing everything down and finally said that it all made a wonderful impression on him.'[34]

Pierre Herbart admired the editing in the Soviet film he saw,[35] and he enjoyed the play *The Aristocrats* and the famed responsiveness of the Soviet audience. So did the composer Roger Désormière.

> Désormière liked the play and the acting very much. Désormière finds that our audience has a very lively response to the action, and it pleases him greatly, as he is terribly bored with overfed audiences.[36]

Interpreters approved of visitors whose overall estimation of the USSR as a superior country was an extrapolation of their liking for one particular aspect of the programme. Mme Bagnol found that the USSR was well ahead of France in the area of motherhood and childhood protection.[37] After a visit to the Institute for the Handicapped (*Institut defektologhii*), the psychologist Pollack is reported as saying

> that in France schools are terribly backward, that schools for [mentally] handicapped children are under the care of nuns, where they [the children] are kept in isolation and are not allowed to talk to each other; discipline is terribly harsh, nothing in common with [Soviet] methods and the skilful approach [here] to children.[38]

Ironically, among those visitors who were not considered 'a success', that is, those who were dissatisfied, the commonest cause of complaint was exactly what all of the satisfied visitors had liked: the cultural programme and the choice of sites. VOKS's assumption that all foreigners shared common interests was clearly misguided, and attempts to do a blanket promotion of what appeared to be a popular site (the Institute of Mother and Child, the All-Union Construction exhibition and the Children's Drawing exhibition) failed to impress every visitor. Dissatisfied visitors complained about being slotted into VOKS's established pattern and not being shown anything outside the programme,[39] and made disparaging remarks about being made to conform. 'Mme Bloch[40] declared that this visit, like her entire stay in the USSR, had given her nothing. She was shown things other than those she wished to see.'[41] Visitors complained of both excessive organisation ('I am used to doing as I please, and here they don't let me')[42] and insufficient organisation: wasted days when they were taken nowhere, the lack of coordination between Intourist and VOKS, and a lack of consideration of visitors' interests. 'When at last things are arranged a bit, the tourists are shown not what they want to see, but what they are indifferent to or what is of no interest to them. They leave dissatisfied.'[43] However, such strong expressions of discontent were rare.

For a time, I believed that interpreters' records were used to assess and improve sites that would make good propaganda, and to improve VOKS's services. However, the opposite became clear: VOKS was reluctant or unable to adjust its programme to those whom it did not suit, and the reactions of its staff were a judgement on the visitors, not on the sites, the classic response of the bureaucrat. Interpreters were inflexible with visitors whose reactions did not live up to VOKS's own expectation of approval and acceptance of everything Soviet. In their anxiety to elicit an unalloyed favourable response from their visitors, the interpreters recorded and grew defensive about even minor criticisms from visitors who were actually sympathetic. Compared with 1929, Professor Tenier of Strasbourg University noted many changes for the better, except in housing;[44] the Ticier couple praised the enviable attitude of the Soviet regime to science ('France ought to learn from the Soviet authorities' attitude towards science') while criticising the hasty and bad implementation of many good and innovative ideas (sealing roads and pavements with asphalt). Interpreters were then quick to accuse their visitors of being ideologically hostile. 'Generally speaking, Mr

Ticier's attitude towards the USSR is fairly positive, although it is impregnated with the psychology of a petit bourgeois intellectual.'[45] Such comments echo the assessment of visitors by the French sector in Kameneva's day, with the exception that, by now, this political language had become a cliché encountered in many interpreters' accounts.

The opinions of more eminent visitors were tolerated better, even when they were ambiguous and swung from one extreme to another. In 1935, René Arcos, the founder and co-editor of the left-wing periodical *Europe*, came to the USSR. Arcos' interpreters recorded every nuance of his reactions to the places he visited and to his own comfort. During his initial visits (free of charge, courtesy of VOKS) to a Leningrad theatre, the Hermitage and the Detskoye Selo (the former summer residence of the Tsars), Arcos was described as left-wing and pleased with everything.[46] In Moscow, he was reported to have complained about his tiny room in the Savoy Hotel with neither a desk nor a lamp, the ugly and tasteless VOKS building, the rude hotel staff and messages that were not delivered. But then, thanks to visits to Zavadsky's theatre and a parade on Red Square, his mood began to improve. The Metro and the women's health clinic particularly impressed him; he finally started to write again and declared that he would convey his positive impressions in France. From that moment, his interpreter, Gladkova, was pleased with Arcos and made no more negative comments about him.[47]

The interpreters' reports took on a negative tone when they could not maintain control over the tourists in their charge. One interpreter was irritated that François Drujon had come to VOKS only on the third day of his stay in Moscow, instead of presenting himself immediately upon arrival.[48] Lack of feedback from visitors was another cause for complaint. Interpreter Ghilyarevskaya was concerned that the lawyer Milhaud did not comment on his trip to the Bolshevo commune. She noted his secretive demeanour (*skrytnost'*) and suspected him of 'sizing things up' (*prismatrivayetsya*).[49] The interpreters grew frustrated when they realised that they were not meeting their visitors' interests, or providing things that they wanted to do. 'So far, we have nothing to offer him, and besides, he shows no interest in anything specific.'[50]

The interpreters' hostility became open when visitors broke the rules that were laid down by VOKS and the interpreter was unable to enforce them. Interpreter Pokhitonov took an instant dislike to Iya Gay (Lady Abdy, first wife of Sir Robert Abdy), the daughter of the Russian artist Grigory Gay. She did not complain or criticise and was happy to be shown institutions, clubs and schools; and yet Pokhitonov wrote, 'As for Gay herself, she makes a very unpleasant impression on me personally: she is no doubt a figure close to the *emigré* circles hostile to us.'[51] Although Gay claimed to be sympathetic to the USSR and complained about the lack of information in the West, Pokhitonov objected to her supposedly importunate and intrusive behaviour (*vela sebya nazoylivo*[52]), conversing in Russian with workers on a factory visit, and making irreverent remarks about the Soviet leadership. 'It is impossible to list all of the ridiculous questions she asked; for example, she believes that "although our leaders are uneducated" they have exceptional intuition, thanks to which they succeed in ruling the masses.'[53] Responses of that sort earned the visitor the withdrawal of VOKS's services. There are inked lines next to reported critical comments by Mme Bloch and by English tourists. In the report on Gay, a pencilled comment says, 'What impudence!' (*naglost'*), followed by instructions to withdraw services to her (*prekratit' obsluzhivaniye*).

There were also limits to VOKS's own ability to maintain control, and unforeseen incidents occurred. Interpreter Ghilyarevskaya was shocked when she brought tourists to a collective farm in Mnevniki village, not far from Moscow. She and her charges discovered it was far from an exemplary place to visit; it was a poor, dried out, desolate, dirty collective farm, with swarms of flies. The childcare centre lacked playground equipment; dirty children slept on camp beds and there were no tables; they saw 'destitution and nothing else' (*i nischeta i bol'she nichego*). A good school building contrasted with the 'sheer hell inside' (*ad kromeshnyy*). 'It would have been better not to show this collective farm at all. . . . Comrade Zalivanov [the collective's agronomist] agreed that one must not show such a collective farm to foreigners, and he had been shocked when we arrived.'[54]

A more serious episode occurred in 1936 during the visit of Gabrielle Duchêne, one of the oldest friends of the USSR, a feminist and, at the time, the Secretary General of the French Cultural Rapprochement Society.[55] What happened to her seriously threatened to destroy the carefully constructed façade of the Soviet version of Potemkin villages. Duchêne and her companion were taken to the Bolshevo commune, one of the most tested destinations, which, as interpreter Ghilyarevskaya noted, Duchêne sincerely admired. However, they were accidentally taken to the dormitory for bachelors, the worst place in the commune. 'We had to think up the excuse that it was a dormitory for inmates who have just arrived and who haven't settled in yet,' Ghilyarevskaya explained in the report. This embarrassment grew distinctly worse when Duchêne was approached by an inmate who introduced himself as the stepson of the French Cubist sculptor Jacques Lipchitz. The youth had disappeared a few years earlier while visiting his father in the USSR, and his mother in France was desperate to find him. The youth gave Mme Duchêne a message for his mother, explaining that he had been travelling in the USSR under a different surname and had been locked up in Bolshevo for six years. 'This conversation with him hit the group like a thunderbolt. There were loud exclamations, conjectures and discussions; we should guard ourselves from such meetings.'[56] This episode was referred to the VOKS Secret Department (*Sekretnyy otdel*).

The only visitors' criticisms that VOKS interpreters were keen to report were those that were directed at other Soviet institutions, such as hotels or VOKS's competitor, Intourist. VOKS passed on tourists' complaints about the inefficiency of services that had a damaging effect on the visitors' impression of the USSR.

> Jacques Meyer reiterated the complaints of many other foreigners regarding poor service in the hotel, endless promises, accompanied by 'in just a minute'

and 'I promise', promises which will only be met in three days. He spoke of the need to improve order within Intourist, as foreigners form a bad and incorrect impression of the USSR.[57]

Other damning comments were directed at Intourist itself. 'Ailborne [the correspondent for *Les nouvelles littéraires*] spoke disapprovingly of the work done by Intourist – he said that everything in the USSR made a good impression on him, except for Intourist.'[58]

Interpreters also took note of the concerns raised about VOKS's own notorious inefficiency when they were expressed by proven and eminent friends. The artist Masereel advised VOKS 'to reply to letters from France as soon as possible, because it has now become a saying that VOKS never responds to letters'.[59] While there is no evidence that VOKS subsequently attempted to improve its general efficiency, it did try to service individual eminent visitors more efficiently. Thus, VOKS Chairman Arosev personally replied to René Arcos' letter announcing his intention to visit the USSR.[60] As we shall see in a later chapter, VOKS made special efforts to arrange the visit of Romain Rolland reliably in an attempt to compensate for the unreliability of other Soviet organisations.

Though visitors' comments had no effect on the programmes run by VOKS, their reactions were taken as an indication of whether they were people who could be counted on, or people who should be shunned.

Spokesmen or slanderers?

Before visitors left, their interpreters tried to find out whether they were leaving as friends or enemies. What would they tell the West about the Soviet Union? Conversations and interviews before their departure provided a good indication of visitors' intentions. Grateful for the hospitality and generous treatment they had received, many visitors made pledges to act as spokesmen for the USSR. Interpreters took these down in writing. A physicist named Basset said that he would publish articles in *Ce soir* and promote the USSR among the petite bourgeoisie.[61] A doctor of psychology named Goldberg said that she would give a series of talks both to her profession and to the Friends of the USSR, and would write a book based on materials supplied by VOKS.[62] A representative of the French Ministry of Justice visited the Institute for the Handicapped to study the legal system as it applied to underage criminals and retarded children.

> Upon her arrival in France, Mme Bardet will present a report of what she saw in the USSR, on the basis of which the Ministry will try to use the experience of the USSR in the forthcoming radical restructuring of French legislation on underage offenders.[63]

It is noteworthy that the sculptor Jacques Lipchitz, who came to the USSR in 1935 and was known to be looking for his stepson, Andrey Skimkevitch, was one of the grateful visitors. As his interpreter wrote, Lipchitz described himself as being energised by Soviet artistic achievements; he said he would work in the artistic section of the Paris Rapprochement Society and give talks and write articles.[64] He even received a commission to make a bust of Felix Dzerzhinsky, the founding father of Cheka – the precursor of NKVD. Without suggesting insincerity on Lipchitz's part, one is left wondering whether his motivation was to keep on the good side of the Soviet authorities as long as his stepson was a hostage. It was not until 1957 that Andrey would be released from the Soviet camps.

Grateful visitors wrote to the VOKS Chair, thanking him for the personal attention they had received. 'Before leaving, I would like to tell you how deeply touched I was by the most kind and cordial attitude you displayed towards all of us, and to me in particular,' Paul Gsell wrote to Arosev in 1934.

> In France, I intend to make public knowledge the exceptional attention with which representatives of the foreign intelligentsia were surrounded here, and the exceptional role VOKS played in its social mission of attracting the sympathies of all thinking people abroad to the new Russia.[65]

But some visitors made interpreters wary. François Drujon's interpreter was dismissive of his plans to write a book about the USSR, even though Drujon had been introduced by Aragon. 'There is hardly any sense in encouraging this desire, although he claims to be an anti-Fascist and the editor of some republican rag in the provinces.'[66] It was even more difficult to deal with sympathetic visitors who were well equipped to argue against the viewpoints they were supposed to be absorbing. During the visit of Georges Friedmann, the Marxist sociologist about whom Barbusse had said that 'all our comrades and friends can have absolute confidence in him', interpreter Gladkova described him as a man of unfriendly disposition. 'Friedmann gives the impression of being a very intelligent man who knows the USSR well, but who is not disposed in a very friendly way to it.'[67] Apparently, Friedmann disapproved of the severe sentences given to the accused in the Trotskyites' trial of August 1936.

> 'After all, they used to be Bolsheviks,' he said. Friedmann was most displeased by my statement that 'they had known very well what kind of abyss they were rolling towards; they were treated with kid gloves (*s nimi slishkom dolgo nyanchilis'*) for too long.' It seems to me that we have to continue to provide service to Friedmann, but to redouble our attention in order to learn in more detail about his meetings outside VOKS.

Visitors assisted VOKS by giving advice on how it could expand its operations and improve its promotion of the USSR. The former minister in the French government, Charles Pomaret, pointed out that any Soviet achievements to do with children – provisions for children's leisure and children's theatre, and the care that the Soviet government took to promote foreign languages among the masses – could attract interest in France and should be displayed at the forthcoming 1937 International Exposition. His interpreter/guide Pokhitonov added that Pomaret considered the promotion of these programmes as particularly important 'because nothing is done in France in this area'.[68]

Pierre Herbart gave Pokhitonov the names of French intellectuals who could be invited to the Soviet Union; perhaps this is the source, or one of the sources, of Pokhitonov's 'memory list' (*Dlya pamati*), which will be discussed later.

> In a conversation, Herbart asked me why VOKS wouldn't invite some of the representatives of the French intelligentsia to visit the USSR, and gave some names as examples. I replied that we had already selected some of them for invitation in 1936, and asked him to give me a list and brief characteristics of those people whose invitation he believed expedient and who could be useful for the cause of French–Soviet cultural rapprochement.[69]

Malraux suggested to Arosev the best way to win over writer Pierre Drieu La Rochelle, whom he was sending to VOKS. 'He is a political adversary but an honest person, and he ought to be shown the best of what could be shown through Intourist.'[70] Familiar with VOKS's techniques, Malraux suggested ways in which VOKS could best deploy the inducements at its disposal: meetings with interesting people, impressive sights and trips, and experienced interpreters.

> I would be happy if you could put him in touch with what interests him here most, that is, with new people. Even better, if you could get hold of an experienced interpreter, I think a meeting with the *Znamya* editors should be organised. If you could do it, and generally help him see Soviet construction in its most significant aspect (for example, one of the construction sites in Stalinogorsk, as he won't have time to go to Siberia) I would be very grateful to you.[71]

'We have to take serious care of him', (*nado im zanyat'sya ser'yozno*) Arosev wrote to his staff.[72]

Once home, supporters of the USSR were eager to promote it; VOKS played a significant part in this process.

Dissemination of materials: new channels

'The supply of articles' (*snabzheniye stateynym materialom*) to foreign countries continued to be one of VOKS's priorities. France was high on its list of recipients of literature, and VOKS spent two or three times more on it than on Italy or South America.[73] As VOKS documents show, former visitors and those influenced by them became a major channel for the dissemination of Soviet materials abroad. Broun, the Soviet representative in Paris, whose name is known only from the signature on his letters, became a major source of such materials. By 1937, he was receiving three to five phone calls or visits a day. They came from French ministries, educational institutions, and literary and artistic circles; some came from the French embassy in Moscow,[74] some from the Association for the Study of Soviet

Culture in Paris, and some from university professors and students at Parisian schools.[75] Broun supplied his callers with articles, translated fiction, newsreels, newspapers and magazines, photographs, slides and gramophone records.

Whether these callers had visited the USSR themselves or had been put in touch with Broun by sympathisers, they were already favourably disposed towards the USSR. They asked for materials on subjects in which VOKS specialised: socialist construction, the planned economy, collective farms, the health system and maternity. They asked about innovative social institutions, sanatoria, summer camps, the construction of the Metro and the new Jewish republic of Birobijan, which had been established in 1928.[76] As Broun wrote to Moscow, his callers wished to use these materials to spread the word to wider circles by organising exhibitions on the USSR at universities and schools, or through the Association for the Study of Soviet Culture.

Broun gave his callers what they had come for, but he also gave them additional materials. It could be a package containing the VOKS series *URSS en construction*, the French version of *International Literature*, works by Soviet writers such as Gorky, Sholokhov, Il'f and Petrov in French translation or, perhaps, Soviet music.[77] The Moscow VOKS office also added materials of its own choice: *Pravda*, the daily paper of the Communist Party, or *Journal de Moscou*, a foreign language invention of Maxim Litvinov, the NKID Commissar.[78]

The irony of the situation is that, although VOKS wished to expand its operations, it could not keep up with the growing number of requests. It did not generate its own materials and had a limited amount of material available for distribution. From France, Broun complained that delays undermined VOKS's operations.[79] Printed materials were constantly in short supply and newsreels were out of date. He insisted to Moscow that they had to be recent, no more than seven to ten days old.[80] Broun knew that Westerners expected services to be on time; he understood how important this was in fostering a rapport with individuals and in assisting them, particularly students and authors. But, although VOKS dealt with foreign countries, it was a typically Soviet institution and so Broun's requests went largely ignored.

Broun's work was also slowed down by VOKS's suspicion of the political background of his callers. Long gone were the times when Kameneva wanted to attract *émigré* writers. In fact, VOKS refused to supply materials to Russian *émigré* circles, even the Union for the Return to the Homeland (*Soyuz vozvrashcheniya na rodinu*), which was essentially pro-Soviet; eventually, it was grudgingly allowed some materials, but only those that were surplus.[81] VOKS refused to supply a Sorbonne academic with a list of Soviet academicians until Broun provided a character reference for him.

Was Broun, who worked outside the USSR, aware of the extent of Soviet paranoia about foreign spying in the mid- to late 1930s? Perhaps only partially, as amidst the Soviet calls for vigilance in 1936–37 he continued to protest against VOKS's inefficient and counterproductive ways. He argued that it was impossible to check the background of all enquirers, especially those from the provinces. As late as 1937, he cautioned VOKS against unjustified suspicion of the Western intelligentsia and students, who were driven by a genuine interest in the USSR and not by a wish to obtain state secrets. Broun reminded VOKS that its aim was to encourage cultural exchange by welcoming these enquiries and informing the French public about the USSR. The current approach, concluded Broun, would inevitably lead to a restriction of VOKS's services to a narrow circle of well-known people from Paris.[82] Surprisingly, on this occasion, VOKS acknowledged Broun's argument and, in future, required him to notify VOKS only when individual visitors and groups intended to travel.[83]

But Broun, like other VOKS representatives in the West, had another important function – to supervise and influence pro-Soviet cultural organisations.

VOKS's auxiliary organisations: cultural fronts?

Pro-Soviet cultural organisations were important to VOKS; it noted that their number rose from one in 1923 to forty-two in seventeen foreign nations in 1931. Bound by interest in and sympathy for the Soviet Union, members of the American–Russian Institute in the USA, the Cultural Rapprochement Societies in Germany and France, and the Society for Cultural Relations (SCR) in Britain exerted a mutual influence. To VOKS, however, these were more than cultural organisations.

> We attach enormous importance to the activities of these organisations as the best conduits of our cultural and political influence on the country's society. We are persuaded that the main task of the VOKS representative is to set up the correct leadership for the Rapprochement Society's activities.[84]

VOKS saw its own role as supplying Cultural Rapprochement Societies with information on Soviet growth and specific topics; they were to absorb and also to distribute it. Their members, the progressive intelligentsia, were expected to engage in political actions through statements, rallies, lectures and publications. These actions could either be timed to support political campaigns, for example the Prompartiya trial, or be linked to the promotion of specific topics, such as the Five-Year Plan or agriculture.[85] The very title of the VOKS document *How foreign friends of the USSR act abroad in its defence (Kak druz'ya SSSR vystupayut zarubezhom v yego zaschitu')* makes VOKS's expectations of these societies clear.[86]

However, because these cultural societies were associations of independent intellectuals, it was difficult for VOKS to manipulate or coerce them. VOKS was as sceptical of intellectuals as the Comintern was, believing that this '[social] stratum located between the classes . . . by its very nature has always been doomed to dual politics'.[87] VOKS believed that these societies could not be relied on to take action and, in consequence, Chair Petrov took a radical and unrealistic line: if cultural societies were ineffective as political tools, VOKS should replace their membership with a more pliable one or create a new society.

> It seems to me that the main reason why our societies are weak is that they are extremely insular – they almost never renew their membership. It is im-

perative, at all costs, to inject new blood into them by involving new, more radical members from the circles of the working intelligentsia. If this meets any resistance from the Society's leadership, we recommend starting the immediate creation of parallel units that would be more energetic and close to us in spirit.[88]

How did interactions with VOKS affect the operations of the Cultural Rapprochement Societies? Were they independent bodies or Soviet fronts? How effective was VOKS in influencing and moulding them to suit its own goals?

VOKS revives the SCR

The Society for Cultural Relations between the Peoples of the British Commonwealth and the USSR (SCR) was founded in Britain in 1923 through the Soviet Commission for the Establishment of Cultural Relations with Other Countries. It is unclear who created the SCR, or how. Was it indeed D.N. Pritt, who would later become a famous barrister and politician and a staunch defender of Soviet policies?[89] Soviet sources trace the SCR's origins back to Gorky, who, following H.G. Wells' 1920 visit to Russia, arranged the first book donation to Soviet scholars from Britain. In 1923, this apparently led to the creation in London of the founding group of the SCR.[90]

With Russia and Britain not having a tradition of close cultural relations, VOKS never became as friendly with the SCR as it would have wished. Ivan Maysky, the Soviet ambassador to the UK, commented on the insurmountable distance between him and the otherwise sympathetic members of British society.[91] As in France, illustrious members on the Society's presidium – Bertrand Russell, G.D.H. Cole, G.B. Shaw, Beatrice Webb, E.M. Forster, Leonard and Virginia Woolf, Aldous and Julian Huxley, Harold Lasky[92] – contributed to the Society's prestige but they did not ensure its malleability as a political body. Even though the SCR showed Soviet films, arranged exhibitions and spread information about Soviet achievements, it refused to play a political role.

In May 1927, Britain had severed diplomatic relations with the USSR following an accusation of spying against the Soviet Trade Representation. Until May 1930, when diplomatic relations were restored, the USSR maintained limited cultural relations with Britain through the SCR.[93] Throughout 1927–30, VOKS had been unable to assert any influence over the SCR, as it had no representative in Britain. Appointing an interim non-Soviet citizen to work for VOKS was rejected because, as VOKS admitted in its internal correspondence, it was sometimes 'forced by circumstances to clothe its activities in semi-conspiratorial forms' (*vynuzhdennaya inogda siloy veschey oblekat' svoyu rabotu v polu-konspirativnyye formy*). The VOKS representative had to be a Soviet insider (*svoy*), competent in assessing the local situation but able to make decisions from the point of view of VOKS and the USSR.[94]

And so, after relations between Britain and the USSR resumed, Ioelson, the Head of the Press Department (*Zaveduyuschiy otdelom pechati*) of the Soviet embassy, was appointed VOKS's representative in London. His primary task was to revive the relationship between VOKS and the SCR; Moscow blamed its desultory condition on the lack of Soviet leadership within the SCR (*net nadlezhaschego sovyetskogo rukovodstva*).[95] At a time when Petrov was issuing instructions for Rapprochement Societies to activate Soviet counter-propaganda in their own countries (March 1930), the SCR was politically inactive. Ioelson blamed this on its Honorary Secretary, Catherine Rabinovich, whom he described as a society lady who used the SCR as a 'letter box' (*pochtovyy yaschik*), replying to enquiries and attending to its business only once a week. All that we know about Rabinovich is based on Ioelson's letters. According to him, she refused to take a political stand and made it impossible for the SCR to operate as VOKS's political springboard. Worst of all, when diplomatic relations between Britain and the USSR were severed in 1927, Rabinovich, who was already Head of the SCR, had wanted to resign and had suggested that the Society be closed.

It is important to acknowledge that, despite VOKS's criticism, the SCR had been promoting Soviet culture. Ioelson confirmed that Soviet films were a huge success in London, and that Eisenstein's *General Line* and Pudovkin's *Mother* and *The End of St Petersburg* were regularly screened by different societies.[96] Catherine Rabinovich had genuinely struggled to rescue the SCR from financial hardship. Despite VOKS's supplies of films and other materials, and membership fees from 319 English and seventy-five Russian members, the SCR had been struggling financially. Rabinovich persistently asked VOKS for money, commenting on the low budget and the inability to deal with enquiries. 'Unless there is an immediate increase in the bank balance, the Society will have to cease its existence,' she wrote to Novomirsky on 7 May 1930.[97] Even though Novomirsky sent £50 to the Society, Rabinovich's days as Honorary Secretary were numbered.[98]

In Moscow, VOKS supported Ioelson against Rabinovich. They regarded as harmful a leader who had previously wanted to 'desert', who did not consider the SCR to be a social and political presence and who discouraged attempts to create SCR branches in other cities. VOKS suggested replacing her with someone more steady, preferably an English person who could both show devotion to cultural rapprochement and appeal to the British audience. But how could a Soviet representative assume control over an independent cultural organisation which had its own leadership?

Ioelson's plan involved removing Rabinovich by broadening and renewing the membership, strengthening the board and gradually increasing Soviet control over her. He thus decided to introduce more Soviet members to the Executive Committee – for example Moisey Ginsburg, the Chair of the London branch of Tsentrosoyuz (Central Union of Consumer Societies, a Soviet organisation), and the journalist Sergey Ingulov, who was the TASS representative in London.[99] Ioelson's proposal echoed the decisions made in the late 1920s regarding the French Cultural Rapprochement Society, giving preference to rank-and-file, democratic members rather than to big names.

> During the creation of the founding group there is no need to chase after just the big names. On the contrary, we consider it imperative, at the moment,

to broaden the membership of the Rapprochement Society by involving the democratic intelligentsia. It is essential to attract and involve in the Society a few local Communists without, understandably, advertising their membership [in the Communist Party]. In those countries where we succeeded in doing so, the results are most positive.[100]

Furthermore, to ensure that the actual work was done regularly, Ioelson proposed introducing a paid position for a secretary, with a salary of £40–50. His proposal reads like a *fait accompli*. 'Rabinovich shall be removed. An English person shall be employed as a secretary to work daily. Plus one or two more staff.'[101] He even considered as a nominee for the position of the next Honorary Secretary Hilda Browning, who, he knew, wanted to democratise the Society and to spread it to the provinces.[102] Moscow welcomed the idea of getting rid of 'her ladyship', referring to Rabinovich's attitude (*barskoye otnosheniye*), and was prepared to consider the question of funding these changes.[103]

In the summer of 1930, while in Moscow, Ioelson became sick and had to stay. The Soviet ambassador in Britain, Sokol'nikov, designated Sergey Ingulov, the TASS representative in England, as the VOKS representative.[104] Ingulov, formerly the first founding editor of *The Teacher's Newspaper (Uchitel'skaya gazeta)*, had previously been the number two in the Agitprop of the Central Committee. A year later, his political text *Politbeseda* would become compulsory for students, and be printed by the hundreds of thousands. He was appointed as VOKS representative against TASS's wishes.

In November, Ingulov still described the SCR as mechanically drifting along with the flow (*mekhanicheski sledovavshego za shedshim samotyokom*). At best, his proposals for change apparently met with a lukewarm, if not a hostile, reaction (*ochen' prokhladnoye i dazhe slegka vrazhdebnoye otnosheniye*) in the Society.[105] Ingulov's task of getting rid of Rabinovich, 'the evil genius' (*zloy geniy*) of many years, turned out to be hard because in addition to Rabinovich's own desperate resistance to being removed, many members of the Executive Committee believed that she would be irreplaceable in the Society. It was no easy task to persuade the British part of the Executive to accept her resignation on the grounds of ill health, and to fill the Society with Soviet members who would outnumber the others.

> As a result of Rabinovich's resistance and agitating (*agitatsia*) against the Society, both inside and outside, she is not leaving alone. The Society's Treasurer is also leaving, as if out of solidarity with her and in protest against the interference of 'external influences'.[106]

How were Soviet representatives expected to influence the Society, direct its course and block any unwanted developments? Partly by getting a Soviet member of the Society elected to a leading position on the Executive Committee.

> In fact, all the financial matters will be decided upon by the permanent Financial commission, which, on our insistence, has been preserved. Ginsburg,

the Chair of the London branch of *Tsentrosoyuz*, is a member and is the real leader of the Commission; it will give us the opportunity not only to influence but to determine the direction of the Society's activities.[107]

An important matter, which VOKS had trouble getting around the English members, was the anticipated nomination of the Executive Secretary.

We attach great importance to the selection of candidates, and because of that we have insisted that this matter be first discussed at a special commission, with Ginsburg, once again, as a member. We have agreed with him that he should not approve of any of the candidates without the agreement of myself and the embassy.

Ingulov scored further victories. Choosing a candidate who was a Russian-speaking English person rather than an English-speaking Russian would provide a clear guarantee that the Executive Secretary would not be a Russian *émigré*; it was likely that a left-wing English sympathiser would be selected. Finally, Ingulov kept in mind the actual activities that he wanted the SCR to conduct.

After these transplantations and restructurings are over (and we are pressing for the creation of branches and the broadening of activities to areas outside London) it will be possible, at last, to start lectures and other informational and cultural work which, up till now, has been absolutely insufficient.

In a letter to Petrov on 24 November 1930, Ingulov summed up the reorganisation of the SCR. Following the resignation of Rabinovich and the former treasurer, a new secretary, Isobel Goddard, was appointed; she was an old member of the Society and was a Labour candidate for Parliament. A series of cultural events was planned, with a photo exhibition to be opened on 5 December by Bernard Shaw and a concert organised for the SCR by the Russian colony; new branches were being created, with plans for lectures by English and Soviet speakers. 'All of this gives a new impulse to our work after a prolonged organisational crisis.'[108]

But, from Moscow, Petrov wanted to use the coup to promote a different agenda. He expected the SCR to start acting as a political tool for the Prompartiya trial campaign.[109] Petrov's list of instructions was hugely ambitious. Get the SCR to publish a bulletin on Prompartiya using VOKS materials, involve the press, and produce a resolution. Make a list of existing SCR members interested in Soviet cultural construction, and regularly send them materials on Prompartiya. Target Soviet sympathisers so that they could be brought closer to the SCR and then used. Be on the lookout for Britons who had visited the USSR, so that VOKS could send them information, write letters to them, etc. Make use of supporters and members in prominent positions: G.B. Shaw, Julian Huxley and John Strachey and his sister Anabel William-Ellis. Finally, if all else fails, create a new, more radical society, for example a Committee for the Defence of Soviet Culture.

Ingulov replied that these proposals were out of the question. After summing up VOKS's (and his own) achievements in influencing the SCR and persuading it to change course, Ingulov argued that there was still a limit to how much VOKS could interfere with the SCR and use it as a political tool. Though he praised Goddard for her initiative, he now blamed other members and the Society as a whole for being exclusively oriented towards culture (*sugubo kul'turnicheskoye napravleniye raboty*).[110] It was true that new activities had taken place: a meeting between the SCR and the Russian colony; a planned meeting with Anna Louise Strong regarding the first Five-Year Plan; and the stunningly successful Soviet photographic exhibition, which Shaw and Sokol'nikov opened. But, at the same time, the Executive Committee was slow and hung on to its old working methods. The Secretariat, on the other hand, was more open to influence, and Ingulov proposed to 'stay closer to the *apparat*' and to introduce changes 'from below' (*yavochnym poryadkom*).

Ingulov argued that it was out of the question to either create a more radical society or, considering the current membership of the SCR, try and involve the society in political actions or even in discussions of the Prompartiya trial. 'Private conversations with those members of the Executive who are the closest to us convinced me that putting this question on the agenda, at either an Executive or a general meeting, would inevitably result in scandal.'[111] Initially optimistic about the prospects for the SCR under its new management, Ingulov now changed his tune: the membership was conservative, the atmosphere anti-Soviet and the poster exhibition in Parliament had been cancelled. It was out of the question to involve G.B. Shaw in the Prompartiya trial campaign.

Had the VOKS coup in the SCR been pointless? After bringing down the old leadership and establishing a new one to suit its own aims, VOKS had clearly failed to create a puppet organisation. However, the coup did lead to changes. Having a greater number of Soviet members on the Executive Committee tipped the balance of power within the SCR. New branches did open, and the membership increased from 600 in 1931 to between 1,100 and 1,200 in 1932. In 1935, there were fifteen branches with a total of 1,500 members, and an additional thirty-five organisational members. In ten months in 1935, VOKS counted forty to forty-five lectures on Soviet culture and economics.[112] The SCR's London section arranged group tours to the USSR, a weekend school, and receptions for Soviet visitors, including the VOKS Chair Arosev and the writers Lidin and Sholokhov.

Even though its political agenda proved to be unrealistic, VOKS acknowledged that the SCR had achieved success in cultural promotion and memberships.[113] It even quoted the SCR as an exemplar of how to conduct wide-ranging activities and manage funds; London's SCR operated on a third of the budget that the US Cultural Rapprochement Societies required.

> There is no doubt that the Society is well-known in London. It has managed to cover and engage in its work fairly wide circles of the intelligentsia and to make contact with scientific, pedagogical and social organisations. Typically,

a concert of Soviet music took place in London recently. It was reviewed in fourteen newspapers, among them *The Times,* the *Manchester Guardian,* the *Morning Post* and the *Daily Telegraph.*

Cercle de la Russie Neuve: VOKS's auxiliary organisation?

While the SCR circulated information on the USSR yet remained politically independent, its French counterpart Russie Neuve was entirely dependent on VOKS for its operations.

Broun, the VOKS representative in Paris, kept a close watch over intellectual societies and organisations that maintained relations of any kind with the USSR. He was particularly involved with Russie Neuve (later renamed Société de l'étude de la culture soviétique). His reports, and those by the Romance sector in Moscow, contain more detailed documentation on Russie Neuve than the society's own published sources.[114] According to him, the society was growing, increasing from 640 members and 120 sympathisers in March 1931[115] to 1,000 members in early 1937.[116] We know from his list that the members were mainly writers, journalists and publishers; but, there were also students, academics and teachers, doctors, artists and actors, with smaller numbers of lawyers, engineers, business people and scientists.[117]

Broun's fortnightly accounts show the extent to which VOKS materials nourished the French society's activities. Even if he was including his own input into the direction of the society, the amount of VOKS-supported activities seems impressive. In 1932, it held regular sessions at which talks and discussions alternated with film screenings, among them Eisenstein's *Battleship Potemkin* and Dziga Vertov's *Man with a Camera, The End of St Petersburg* and *Through Tears.*[118] In 1934, Broun reported on ten screenings of Soviet films and over twenty talks on subjects that, alongside medicine, education, the life of young people and the economic situation, included the penal code, the financial system, ethnographic studies and nationalities, and exploration of the Arctic.[119] In 1936, over twenty talks covered topics such as the new Soviet constitution, the issue of nationalities in the USSR, building the classless society, the theatre, literature, art, cinema, medicine, economics and finance, children, underage offenders, science and religion.[120] Russie Neuve marked official Soviet celebrations – both the cultural, like Gorky's birthday, and the political, such as the fifteenth anniversary of the October Revolution.[121]

Broun's reports show that the society provided a forum for Soviet visitors to France and French intellectuals who had been to Russia. Alongside the writers Vs. Ivanov, Babel and Ehrenburg were official Soviet speakers, for example the embassy official S. Chlenov. As increasing numbers of people travelled to the USSR, more and more eminent French speakers spoke about their impressions: the writers Vaillant-Couturier, Vildrac, Bloch and Vladimir Pozner, Professor Jean Baby, architect André Lurçat, sociologist Georges Friedmann and academician Jean Perrin.[122]

According to Broun, eminent French intellectuals played a prominent role in this society; his 1937 report listed the old friend of the USSR, Gabrielle Duchêne, the film critics Georges Sadoul and Léon Moussinac, physicist Paul Langevin, Marxist sociologist Georges Friedmann, the Communist writers Vladimir Pozner and André Wurmser, sympathisers Vildrac and Durtain, architect Paul Gsell and sculptor Jacques Lipchitz.[123] They now organised themselves into study groups called commissions to generate information on the USSR through their own scholarly research. Commissions were headed by members with expertise in that area: the most active, according to Broun, was the literary commission, headed by Vildrac and Pozner; the economic commission was headed by Roger Francq, the scientific commission by Henri Wallon, the commission for theatre by E. Autant and L. Lara, and the film commission by Léon Moussinac.[124] All of this work was based on materials supplied by VOKS. The research and major lectures of these commissions were published and covered subjects such as mathematics, astronomy, physics, biology, psychology, history, linguistics, technology and philosophy. Their success in disseminating Soviet information through local speakers and authors was the culmination of Kameneva's efforts in the 1920s, and shows why VOKS monitored them so closely.

The peak of their achievement in spreading the word came in July 1937 when the society opened a documentation service to the public; this allowed an even wider audience to gain access to the Soviet sources in its collections.

> Our readers will be able to consult there the entire collection of *Journal de Moscou* and all the VOKS publications. They will also find different studies we have published, classified by topic, and documentary files on the main issues regarding the USSR.[125]

This could be read as a sign of the society's success in disseminating information supplied by VOKS; however, this impression conflicts with other reports from Broun that show the fragility of Russie Neuve. The 1935 report suggests that the society was suffering from stagnation.[126] The report alludes to a split in the society at the beginning of the year, and a disruption of its activities including the publication of *Documents de la Russie Neuve*. This 1935 report undermines the credibility of previous reports by stating that the active nucleus of the society never exceeded fifty members. In this report, Russie Neuve was compared with the mass-oriented Association of Friends of the USSR (whose competition Kameneva feared) and the AEAR; the report claims that it was through these organisations, and not through Russie Neuve, that the main visits to the USSR were undertaken. The report concluded that the society needed support to boost its reputation and broaden its sphere of influence. French artists should become better acquainted with Soviet art, there should be more publications about VOKS and Broun should be allowed more scope for action.

Ironically, VOKS's close involvement with Russie Neuve, and Russie Neuve's role as a branch of VOKS, are best revealed not by the successes but by problems arising from the society's dependence on VOKS. There is no evidence that the society was financially dependent on VOKS or that VOKS directly interfered with it, apart from supplying materials. However, Broun systematically commented on the inability of Russie Neuve's commissions to function because of constant delays in the supply of literature by VOKS; at the end of each report, he stressed that the activities run by Russie Neuve were dependent on materials sent from the USSR. In fact, the Romance sector reported that Russie Neuve did nothing from April to June 1932, mainly because VOKS failed to supply the expected materials, thus paralysing the society.[127] At the end of 1934, Broun warned Moscow that, unless the society received up-to-date materials for the following year, it would be unable to operate in 1935.[128] In his 1937 report, Broun again complained, this time about the shortage of illustrated materials, slides and illustrations for various topics that the Society needed.[129] He insisted that, in order to conduct its activities, the Society needed a permanent and regularly updated collection of literature on all subjects.[130] Clearly, VOKS was the only source of Russie Neuve's supplies.

One area of potential success never came to fruition – visits from Soviet cultural emissaries. Compared with the stream of French visitors to the USSR in the 1930s, Soviet visits to France remained negligible. In 1928–29, Mayakovsky and Babel were refused permission by Soviet authorities to travel to France. Tours by the Meyerhold, Vakhtangov and Jewish theatres, and visits by film-makers such as Eisenstein, stopped in the early 1930s. Pasternak and Babel's late arrival at the 1935 International Writers' Congress in Paris would not have taken place without pressure from French intellectuals. Travel was limited even for the leaders of VOKS. Arosev's visit to France in 1934 appears to be the only trip taken by a VOKS Chairperson after Kameneva's 1927 trip.[131] Even after VOKS asked the Paris representative to assist any visiting Soviet cultural emissaries (for example, the poets Bezymensky and Kirsanov[132]), they were sent to Paris by the powerful Soviet Writers' Union and not by VOKS.[133]

As if out of touch with political realities, Broun continued to urge VOKS to encourage visits to France. Even in 1937, in a political climate that would clearly preclude any suggestion of foreign trips by Soviet citizens, he still emphasised their potential.[134] He described the successful reception held and contacts made during the visits of the poets Bezymensky and Kirsanov, the directors L. Vishnevsky and Dzigan, and the writers Leonov, Tynyanov and A. Tolstoy. He reported on the success of a VOKS-organised concert of Soviet music, with Prokofiev's participation:[135] a full house, the presence of other eminent guests in the audience, an introduction by the sculptor Paul Gsell, the particular success of Prokofiev's *Lieutenant Kijé* and Prokofiev being called to take a bow a number of times.

> I believe that by this concert we have marked the beginning of a serious display of Soviet musical art in Paris. If we succeed in this task, we can be sure that Soviet music will take a solid place as part of major concert performances.

At a time when foreign travel was unthinkable for most Soviet citizens, Broun made long-term plans for bringing Soviet 'cultural resources' to France. But VOKS could not take up his proposals, which were not only unrealistic but dangerous to individuals in the climate of Soviet politics in the 1930s. There might have been much to be gained from such proposals; however, doomed as they were in the interwar period, they would become a major feature of Soviet post-war cultural policy.

7 VOKS and the 'famous foreigners'

The Soviet Union's propaganda apparatus worked assiduously, if not always effectively, at cultivating the loyalty of the Western rank-and-file intelligentsia; it could also call on the support of many of the West's most eminent intellectuals. Fostering friendships with 'famous foreigners' (*znatnyye inostrantsy*), as Arosev called them, was an important goal of the state-run machinery, and VOKS often hosted eminent guests jointly with other organisations. It took care of George Bernard Shaw, invited by the Association of State Publishers (OGIZ), Lion Feuchtwanger, a guest of the Soviet Writers' Union, and Victor Gollancz, who came via the Literary Agency (Litaghentstvo). By maintaining excellent relations with these eminent friends, VOKS did far more to ensure their support of the USSR than MORP had achieved.

Monitoring contacts

Fostering contacts with Western intellectuals was a lot of work. Arosev personally worked on bringing in the writers Margueritte and Rolland, the politician Herriot and the composer Maurice Ravel.[1] His staff closely monitored their activities. The roll-call of VOKS's eminent friends is long and impressive. Pokhitonov, the Head of the First Western Department, kept a 'memory list' (*dlya pamyati*) entitled *Main personal contacts*,[2] which included influential public figures such as Malraux, the scientists Perrin and Nobel laureate Langevin, and the former government minister Pierre Cot. The Anglo-American sector's lists[3] included the Americans Leopold Stokovsky, John Dewey and Paul Robeson, and the British Harold Lasky, John Strachey and Sidney Webb. VOKS reacted anxiously when visitors failed to arrive, particularly because of outright refusals, and it noted when Gide and Ravel became ill, Signac died and Langevin simply cancelled his trip. It followed intellectuals' actions after they returned home, noting what they did to benefit the USSR. VOKS kept records of those who were members, participants or leaders in cultural organisations, such as Cercle de la Russie Neuve, AEAR, the American–Russian Institute (ARI) and the British SCR; these records include dozens of names. After their visits, VOKS made a note of every single book that was written and lecture delivered by Durtain, Vildrac, Dana, Lenormand and

Andersen Nexø. Sidney and Beatrice Webb were described as being enthusiastic about the USSR upon their return to Britain. They were going to publish articles in American magazines, talk on the BBC, address the SCR (whose Vice-Chair Mrs Webb agreed to become) and write a book describing the Soviet system and democracy. They were particularly grateful to Tsentrosoyuz and VOKS, which had paid so much attention to them, and asked for more materials to be sent to them quickly.[4]

There was no limit to the minutiae of VOKS's notes reporting these details. The French sector's reports were notably more detailed than those of the Anglo-American sector. According to Pokhitonov's list, Prenant was known 'to intervene constantly in the defence of the Soviet Union'; Rolland 'called himself a supporter of the Soviet system in every one of his statements', and André Gide proclaimed on Moscow Radio on 7 November 1936 that the USSR was 'the youth and the future of humankind'. Were French supporters far more numerous and active than other Western intellectuals or are these details a reflection of Pokhitonov's own style?

Reception of eminent foreigners: efforts to impress and commit

The blueprint for Soviet hospitality has been outlined extensively in memoirs and diaries and in historical studies.[5] However, the VOKS archives best illustrate how these trips were put together; they include the hidden motivations and machinations and the personal responses of VOKS staff, themselves highly revealing of the policies and processes of the Soviet state.

VOKS distinguished itself in the reception of 'famous foreigners' by making its services more sophisticated and better tailored to the wishes of celebrity visitors. It genuinely tried to provide a quality of service and pamper its guests – as much as was possible in the USSR in the 1930s. Plans for the reception of Albert Marquet, Henri Barbusse and Victor Gollancz give an idea of the ingenuity and skill with which VOKS received them. VOKS also recorded how visitors responded to its services and their experiences of the USSR.

VOKS went to great lengths to arrange these trips so as to make the visitor's stay in the USSR enjoyable and enticing. The agency provided comfort, prestige, flattery and even money as inducements to travellers. René Arcos was brought to the country free of charge, courtesy of VOKS. Ravel's invitation included several lucrative enticements: a return trip to Russia and travel within the country, hotel accommodation, ten concerts in major cities at 1,000 roubles per concert, and radio broadcasts.[6] The old Soviet supporters Durtain and Vildrac seemed to almost take advantage of the many opportunities offered by VOKS. They themselves asked to visit the USSR at VOKS's expense and to collect fees for their publications, although these payments could not be spent outside the USSR.[7] Arosev agreed, outlining the details of the proposed trip and the conditions of the stay to each writer.

You are therefore invited to come with your spouse by your preferred sea route (London–Antwerp–Leningrad) and once you have arrived in this last city, you need only go to our branch. It is located at 2 Lassale St, and they will be advised by us to follow you to M.

All you will have to pay is your journey from Paris to Leningrad, and from there on you will be our guest for a fortnight. After that, you will certainly be able to use your royalties freely, which you will be able to collect for all your articles in our newspapers and which will cover all the expenses for your forthcoming trip across the USSR.

All that remains for us is to welcome you and your spouse to our country where you may be assured in advance of finding the most friendly welcome everywhere, especially at VOKS and all its branches.[8]

Invitations of this sort were clearly rewards for support that had already been given. In a letter to the VKP(b) Central Committee, VOKS official Chernyavsky requested permission to invite Martin Andersen Nexø, a Danish revolutionary writer, to visit. In support of his request, Chernyavsky wrote that Andersen Nexø was one of the first European writers to speak in defence of the USSR. His *Towards the Dawn*, written after his 1922 visit, was one of the first positive books written about the USSR. Since then, he had visited the USSR several times, including attendance at the First Congress of the Soviet Writers' Union; he had supported the anti-Fascist front and had been very active at the 1935 Paris Congress for the Defence of Culture. His visits had created a response all across Scandinavia; he had helped the SCR in Denmark and toured the country giving talks about the USSR. His financial situation was difficult because of a boycott of his books, and inviting him to the USSR would give him financial and moral support.[9]

Visitors' accommodation and conditions of travel arranged by VOKS had improved since the 1920s. In 1927, Duhamel and Durtain shared a room in a hostel for scholars; in 1935, VOKS placed Vildrac, Durtain and their wives in the Metropol Hotel and offered them 'first-class service, including cultural sightseeing (theatres, museums, etc.) and a car charged to the account of VOKS' (*obsluzhivaniye 1oy kategorii*).[10] The class of service provided by VOKS clearly depended on the visitor's status. Proven supporters were always favoured. The Danish writer Karen Michaelis, whose trip was arranged by Intourist, was given a first-class service, paid for by VOKS. This included a VOKS interpreter and the following trip: Moscow, Kharkov, Dneprostroy, Sevastopol, Yalta, Batum, Tiflis to Ordjonikidze and Moscow, for which VOKS paid 5,000 roubles.[11] VOKS paid for her room in the top Natsional Hotel, including the cost of food and transport. However, when the 'eminent architect' (*vidnyy architector*) Lurça came to the USSR, he was placed in the more modest Novo-Moskovsky Hotel. During his trip to Kharkov and Dneprogess, he was to travel third class, later upgraded to second (that is, from a hard to a soft bunk), with the additional twenty roubles per day paid by VOKS.[12]

Following their practice in the 1920s, VOKS arranged formal celebrations for their eminent visitors, often in collaboration with other organisations. On 26 July

1931, VOKS, OGIZ (or *Ob'yedineniye Gosudarstvennykh Izdatel'stv*) and the Soviet Writers' Federation jointly put on the seventy-fifth birthday celebrations of George Bernard Shaw. The event was staged in the Column Hall of the House of the Unions (*Kolonny Zal Doma Soyuzov*).[13] Emotional speeches were made in his honour. 'Bernard Shaw's visit highlights his friendship for the Soviet Union, his immense and genuine interest in socialist construction, victoriously realised by Soviet workers under the leadership of the Communist Party,' declared the Head of OGIZ, Arkadiy Khalatov, who opened the meeting. Before long, Shaw's birthday party turned into a celebration of his support for the USSR.[14] Shaw and the audience were reminded of his earlier acts of support.

> In the speech he made in Leningrad yesterday, Shaw said that the path that Lenin had shown us is the path we are now following. It is the path that leads humankind to a new, beautiful future. Shaw said yesterday, 'If the future is with Lenin, we can all rejoice. But if the world follows the old road, I will have to leave this world with sadness.' He said in *John Bull* at the end of the year, 'The lazy, drunk, dirty, superstitious, slavish and hopeless Russia – the Russia of repulsive Tsarism – is now becoming an energetic, sober, clean, unshakeable and modern, independent, flourishing and selfless Communist country.'[15]

All of the speakers voiced the same expectations of what Shaw should say to his compatriots about the USSR. 'We hope that on his return home Bernard Shaw will be able to support this by word and deed', Lunacharsky proclaimed.[16] Comrade Kotov, a representative of seventy-one 'shock workers' (*udarnyye rabochiye*), reinforced these expectations: 'We hope that back in England, Bernard Shaw will continue to speak about Soviet achievements in the same way.'[17] Shaw's response to these speeches sounds informal, understated and even ironic. He described setting out for Russia with his companions, Lord and Lady Astor, and how their relatives had come to see them off at the station, bringing them food, pillows and tents to take into the wilds of Russia. Shaw confirmed the assumption that he would tell 'the real truth about Russia' in the West.

> My comrades, I have been telling them the real truth about Russia for the last ten years, I didn't wait for the development of your five year plan. I believe it was somewhere around the year 1918 when Russia was very badly spoken out in the Western Europe that I took the opportunity to send a book to Lenin with a very enthusiastic dedication in the hope that that would get published in our papers in Europe. [. . .] But I want to assure you that even in that time and I knew a good deal of what you were suffering and going through I myself believed from the very beginning that you would go through and whether I believed that or not I knew it was my business to back you for ail (sic. all?) I was worth right through the reason I make this visit to the Soviet Russia is not to be able to tell the English people something I did not know before but in order to be able when they say that ah, you think Russia is a wonderful

place, but you have not been there and you have not seen it. Now I can go back and say I have seen it.[18]

We already know that supporters like Shaw, Arcos and Webb lived up to the pledges that they made on their visits to the USSR, as did many others. But can their positive outlook, their sympathy and their support for the USSR in word and deed be linked to the treatment they received there from VOKS?

An artist in the land of the Soviets: Albert Marquet and Soviet hospitality

The visit of Albert Marquet to the USSR provides a revealing case study. It shows how a visitor could arrive in the Soviet Union in a politically neutral frame of mind but, with a programme carefully planned and carried out by VOKS, be cultivated and turned into an ardent sympathiser.[19]

Marquet, a landscape artist and a former member of the Fauve movement, was never a name that was widely known in the USSR. VOKS first heard about his prospective visit from its Paris representative at the end of July 1934, who urged it to be cautious. Broun wrote that Marquet, an artist of some standing in France, could be difficult to handle. 'I doubt that you will be delighted with him, of all people; but in any case he is something of a leader of an [artistic] movement and he is recommended by Herriot's friends.' 'It would be good if he were received well,' continued the representative, underlining the second part of the sentence.[20]

The Moscow office acknowledged the importance of 'the famous French artist'.[21] 'We must work with him as seriously and in as much depth as possible.' The instructions, most probably Arosev's, said that the chief means of impressing Marquet should be with Soviet art, because 'his reports on our art, upon his return, will carry significant weight and be widely distributed, as he is the head of a particular artistic group'.

The artist's personal sensitivities were included in the preliminary design of the programme. The Moscow office instructed the Leningrad office of VOKS to prepare 'a suitable reception at the railway station' (*prosim Vas organizovat' yemu sootvetstvuyuschuyu vstrechu na vokzale*) and to provide publicity. They had to be careful not to go overboard. 'It is essential . . . to find out how to receive him, that is, whether it is worth while making a lot of noise (*stoit li ochen' shumet'*).' He would be taken to the Tret'yakov Gallery and the Pushkin Museum in Moscow, and he would meet Soviet artists.[22] A group of colleagues, principally artists and art critics, was appointed to accompany Marquet at all times; the artistic life of Leningrad was to be presented to him 'through the company of appropriate experts', and meetings were to be organised with a number of artists from the list suggested in the letter, which included such well-known figures as Kuz'ma Petrov-Vodkin. These careful arrangements make it clear that Marquet, while being attentively looked after and entertained, was going to be tightly controlled.

Today, VOKS's report on Marquet's stay, however biased, remains the main source of information on how he spent his time in the USSR. Against the back-drop of activities in the artist's schedule, the report records the gradual warming of a visitor who was initially reserved and possibly quite unsympathetic.[23] As the interpreter Overko frankly admits, VOKS's initial attempts to impress Marquet in Leningrad did not succeed. Marquet failed to appreciate the traditional Russian paintings he was shown.

> The collection in the Russian Museum failed to interest him. He scrutinised our eighteenth century in a most condescending way. As for our impression-ists, he said *ce n'est pas mal* about Korovin. His praise did not go higher than that.[24]

However, meetings with people produced better results. Meeting Marquet seems to have made an enormous impression on the Leningrad artists, and their enthusiasm and warm reception (and the 'cultural programme') drew a response from Marquet, which contributed, by his own admission, to his overall positive impression of the visit.

> Our artists . . . were left with the most positive impression of the meeting with Marquet. It is true, the conversation wasn't very lively, partly because Marquet is quiet and not a talker, and partly because our artists' knowledge of French is poor. The general impression, as both Marquet and his wife put it, was that the guests remained very pleased with what they saw and the reception they were given by the Leningrad artists.

Flattery, particularly that creating the impression that Marquet was well known and revered in the USSR, proved to be more reliable in suborning the artist's loyalty. Marquet was (understandably) impressed by the display of his own work in the Museum of Contemporary Western Art, making this visit more of a success for all concerned than his earlier one to the Russian Museum. But, in fact, before Marquet's visit, VOKS had instructed the Museum to take Marquet's paintings out of storage where they had been kept and hang them as if they were part of the permanent exhibition. 'The museum was warned well in advance that it was necessary to exhibit the works of Marquet that were held by the Museum, and to allocate them a good location.' This move produced the desired effect: the artist was said to be 'extremely pleased with the way his paintings were hung and the condition of his works in the Museum'. The rest of the collection impressed him, too, and he praised the Museum's display, which included first-class works by Matisse and Cézanne, as 'undoubtedly the best collection of French masters in the world'.[25]

Soviet writers and artists who could speak a common language with visitors were given a special role. VOKS arranged for Marquet to be surrounded by artists and other members of the cultural elite. They acted in a seemingly authentic way and betrayed no signs of stage management in the personal attention they paid to

Marquet. How could he have suspected that he had been set up when the writer Valentin Katayev met him with flowers, escorted him to the Museums and Artists' Club, and invited him home? Other meetings included tea parties at the Soviet Artists' Union and encounters with young people, especially young artists. Such meetings even featured a hero from the crew of the *Chelyuskin*, who had been a member of a polar expedition that was rescued by Soviet pilots from the sea-ice after their vessel had been crushed by ice and sank in the Arctic earlier that year.[26] Reverence and flattery again worked their magic on Marquet, who was pleasantly surprised by the Soviets' admiration for his art. How could he suspect that these enthusiastic exchanges with young Soviet artists who, in all likelihood, had only recently learned about his existence and his art, were stage-managed?

> Marquet was surrounded by young people . . . saying that they were happy to shake the hand of the Master who had painted such wonderful works, that their dream was to learn from him and that his paintings were a constant model to them.

'[He] was moved and said he had not suspected that he had so many friends in the Soviet Union. He was particularly moved by the attitude of the young people, whose exhibition he promised to see the next day.' It clearly left Marquet well disposed to this exhibition, which he found to be 'full of life, hope and health'.[27]

The report reveals that, in between sightseeing, visiting art exhibitions and meeting people, discussions were conducted with Marquet about how Soviet artists lived and worked. Through these personal contacts, Marquet became persuaded that the Soviet government had created excellent working conditions for artists. The message clearly registered because the interpreter wrote, 'Marquet remarked that never had he known a government to take such care of artists as in the USSR.'

As his stay progressed, the interpreter noted Marquet's increasingly positive responses. He was reported as praising the reception he received, because 'in no other city in the world had [he] been welcomed in such a hospitable and cordial way as in Leningrad'.[28] Although instructions had been given not to overdo the publicity around this 'modest, shy and quiet man', Marquet was obviously not insensitive to personal attention and an appreciation of his art. We can only suppose that he was impressed by his celebrity status, as articles on him appeared in *Vechernyaya Moskva* (9 August), *Pravda* (10 and 15 August), *Literaturnaya gazeta* (15 and 19 August), *Journal de Moscou* (18 August) and *Sovetskoye iskusstvo* (17 and 23 August). Before he left the country, Marquet spoke to the Soviet press and gave an interview, saying how charmed he had been by the people and the landscape, and that he would like to come again in order to paint.

VOKS considered Marquet's visit to be a success and summed up the importance of having won over someone whose positive account of the USSR would be heard in the West. The reception techniques used had clearly been well chosen and the operation had run smoothly.

Marquet's importance and place in French contemporary art is known – he is a major master of the realistic landscape, connected with many prominent French artists like Matisse, Rouault and others. The French artistic community will undoubtedly listen to his opinion of the USSR, therefore I regard as most expedient the work that was conducted with him to familiarise him with Soviet art, work and daily conditions.

The Soviet artistic community was widely involved with this work.

The work went according to plan.[29]

The success of Marquet's visit illustrates how a generic, formula-based reception plan was adapted for an individual artist. Every aspect appealed to the cultural interests of the apolitical Marquet. Art and culture were used as a shuttle to transfer Marquet's positive perceptions of the culture to perceptions about the Soviet state. Although Marquet never became an active public promoter of the USSR in France, he made favourable personal comments. This is how Il'ya Ehrenburg related Marquet's return from the USSR.

When he [Marquet] returned to Paris, he was asked whether it was true that the USSR resembled hell. He replied that he understood little of politics and had never voted in his life. 'I did like it in the USSR, though. Just imagine, a large state where money does not determine people's lives. Isn't that wonderful? . . . Besides, I don't think they have an Academy of Arts there, at least no one told me about one.' (The Academy of Arts had been restored shortly before Marquet's visit to Leningrad; but what he noticed there were the Neva river, the workers, the school children – he did not have a chance to notice any academicians.)

Among Communist workers in Paris there were some members of artistic amateur groups who were fond of Marquet's paintings and were devoted to the USSR. They collected money, and when Marquet returned from the USSR they came to see him, saying, 'We will pay for your trip and your stay so you can go back to Leningrad and paint the Neva.'[30]

Communicating with old friends

Looking after Barbusse

VOKS maintained excellent relations with its long-term supporters Barbusse and Rolland. Unlike MORP, it made no demands and put no pressure on them, and their relations with VOKS appeared to be based on mutual assistance.

VOKS unfailingly treated Henri Barbusse as a welcome and celebrated guest.[31] Whenever he came to the Soviet Union, he was placed in the best hotels, the Metropol or the Natsional,[32] and taken across the USSR to see the latest major industrial site, for example the opening of the Dneprostroy hydroelectric station.[33] Just as Marquet's paintings had been urgently put on display in the museum to create a favourable impression on him, so the Lenin Library was requested to assemble all of the books that Barbusse had published in the USSR and to set up an exhibition of his work.[34] VOKS was sensitive to Barbusse's dislike of pompous receptions and overblown publicity. 'I will let you know additionally whether it is necessary to attract wide attention in the press around Barbusse,'[35] Apletin wrote to the Leningrad representative and cautioned further, 'Until Pokhitonov clarifies the question with Barbusse himself, do not inform the press of his arrival.'[36] Upon Barbusse's arrival in Leningrad, VOKS officials instructed Moscow by telegram to keep the level of publicity subdued: 'Inform press less noise' ([*V*] *pressu soob-schite men'she shumu*).[37] VOKS was sure to let it be known how much it esteemed Barbusse – for example, at one of its celebratory public welcomes at the railway station.

> Not only are you our loyal and devoted friend – you remain one of the most tireless and ardent defenders of the USSR.
>
>   You belong to a group of foreign intellectuals who are still relatively few and who long ago linked their destiny to that of the revolutionary working masses.
>
>   From the very first, most difficult years of the establishment of Soviet power, when the most ferocious reaction of international intervention growled and surged around the Soviet state; at the time when the ranks of most intellectuals, as well as their ideas, were dominated by chaos and total confusion – it was you, comrade Barbusse, who firmly and unswervingly placed in the balance all your immense literary talent, all your creative power and all your authoritative influence in order to defend the First Proletarian State and Communism!

It is enlightening to examine the business side of Barsusse's relations with VOKS. They managed a direct interchange of their magazines, *VOKS* and *Monde*.[38] Barbusse clearly encouraged VOKS to send him information on the USSR for publication in *Monde*, in order to reach 'the numerous circles that are not definitively intoxicated by the abundant reactionary propaganda'.[39]

In return, Barbusse advised VOKS about topics that would be useful for publication in France. At the beginning of collectivisation, following the Comintern's and MORP's practice of sending 'counter-material' to combat the Western version of Soviet events, he asked for articles on 'State rural and agricultural collectives', and 'the current anti-religious campaign in the USSR'.[40]

> On these two important questions, the bourgeois newspapers in our countries spread the most fantastic and implausible news items, as is their custom. It would be highly desirable if *Monde* were able to publish the comprehensive clarification which everyone wishes for.[41]

However, Barbusse, being *Monde*'s editor, did not indiscriminately publish whatever VOKS supplied and questioned the suitability of some articles for publication.[42] He refused to give in to VOKS's requests to stop printing French materials that were critical of the Soviet Union – for example, articles by Panaït Istrati. However, he remained conciliatory in his correspondence with VOKS.[43]

> I admit that it is most unfortunate that *Monde* has published Panaït Istrati's interview. Once I had received that issue, I sent a telegram to *Monde* to express my strong objection to it and to give orders no longer to publish anything by Panaït Istrati in *Monde*. . . . I shall introduce rigorous control over the line of the newspaper, in the centre as well as in cities where there are groups of Friends of *Monde*. . . .
>
> However, I recognise that Panaït Istrati has talent and that we are prepared to publish his purely literary pieces in our newspaper.[44]

Barbusse and VOKS also maintained a relationship in matters that did not directly concern either of them. VOKS turned out to be an effective buffer between Barbusse and other Soviet bodies. In February 1930, *Monde* distributed a questionnaire entitled 'Is there a crisis of doctrine in socialism?' (*Y a-t-il une crise doctrinale du socialisme?*) among Soviet Party leaders. When none of the addressees (who included Stalin, Bukharin, Rykov and Lunacharsky) replied, *Monde* attempted to find out why, using VOKS as an intermediary.[45] The answer, which came through VOKS, was that the questions had been inappropriate ('the development of this questionnaire has taken a form which prevents our addressing it to those comrades whose response is of interest to you')[46] and that the very questions and their phrasing could not bring about the desired results: 'It is not only the meaning of the responses which prevents us, but the questions themselves, which were phrased in such a way that the enquiry could not provide the results you wished to obtain.'[47] Barbusse and Desphelippon, *Monde*'s executive director, found it incomprehensible that Soviet agencies were preventing a valued French audience from gaining access to this very important information on the USSR and wrote about it to VOKS.[48]

> We are dealing with a very important audience – an audience that cannot be reached by ordinary Communist propaganda – and which, therefore, has a picture of Russia and the [Communist] International, which has been distorted by its enemies. It was a chance to win a large number of new sympathisers. But alas! there is none so deaf as he who will not hear.[49]

Even though VOKS was not responsible, it gave a sympathetic hearing to Barbusse's frustrations.

> If Communist newspapers like *l'Humanité*, *les Cahiers du Bolchevisme* and others . . . had brought up this major question, they would have had absolutely no impact because these newspapers speak to a limited audience of

the converted and the loyal, and it is important to exercise influence on the broadest layers of readers.

I cannot understand the Moscow comrades being critical of this questionnaire. It follows entirely the spirit and the directives of the newspaper and as I affirm once again, it is capable of helping us significantly with sympathisers or those who are poorly informed or who hesitate.[50]

On another occasion, in August 1930, *Monde* stopped reaching its Soviet subscribers. Barbusse appealed to VOKS, once again, to find an answer.

Whom shall I approach in order to stop this? It seems to me that letters that I send to Moscow are not read by those to whom I have addressed them, and I cannot obtain an answer. I am relying on you to give me a clear explanation of the unacceptable situation in which *Monde* has been currently placed because of the refusal to distribute it in the USSR.[51]

Reinforcing the importance of *Monde*, 'one of the few international papers telling the truth about achievements in the USSR', Barbusse complained that it was 'a ridiculous situation when the newspaper that defends revolutionary goals the best and most clearly, apart from the militant newspapers of the Communist Party, is forbidden in the USSR!'[52] Again, VOKS obtained a reply from Glavlit (the Main Administration for Literary and Publishing Affairs), stating that no resolution to forbid the distribution of *Monde* had been issued and that only individual issues containing anti-Soviet articles by social democrats and the opposition had been intercepted for censorship reasons.[53] In November 1930, VOKS dispatched the next collection of materials to *Monde*.

The fact that, during these disagreements, VOKS remained a bystander rather than a source of pressure and acted as a conciliator and intermediary between Barbusse and those who opposed the policy of his magazine gained it the appreciation of Barbusse, who ranked it above other Soviet organisations. In a letter to Arosev, thanking him for birthday greetings from VOKS, Barbusse expressed his gratitude for a long-standing friendship.

My dear comrade and Chair,

Of all the wishes that my good Soviet comrades have sent me for my birthday, yours and those of VOKS have touched me the most. I am happy to assure you, in my turn, of my loyal friendship and my gratitude for the great and important task of international cultural solidarity that you have been undertaking on behalf of you magnificent new country.[54]

When Barbusse died in the USSR in 1935, his secretary Annette Vidal wrote to acknowledge everything that VOKS had done for the writer.

At the time of leaving the USSR in order to return the body of our great friend and comrade to the French proletariat, I am eager to thank VOKS for the reception it has always given us, as well as for all the attention it gave me personally through S.I. Pokhitonov.[55]

VOKS won Barbusse's gratitude and cooperation by treating him diplomatically and without pressure. Though Barbusse was an ally who required no persuasion to act as a spokesman for the USSR, it took VOKS, rather than any other Soviet agency, to nurture his devotion to the USSR.

Placating Romain Rolland

It is more difficult to interpret Romain Rolland's relationship with VOKS. It started in the early 1930s when VOKS noted Rolland's first statement that was supportive of the USSR in *l'Humanité*. 'I am not a Communist but I hail the heroic struggle for the fulfilment of the Five-Year Plan. Let the conspirators be thrown out. Hands off the Soviet Union.'[56] VOKS clearly became Rolland's main channel of communication with the USSR. It was to VOKS that Rolland sent Rabindranath Tagore, who was about to visit Russia; at the same time, he advised VOKS of Tagore's interests and suggested meetings with leading writers such as Pasternak.[57] It was to VOKS that Rolland wrote to enquire about the new music to which his *Colas Breugnon* was being set.[58] When he suspected that his correspondence with Gorky, then staying in Sorrento, was being intercepted, he wrote to VOKS to request that it alert Gorky verbally.[59]

Rolland's letters to VOKS may create the impression that he used VOKS for his own ends. The letters are filled with complaints, irrespective of whether they relate to VOKS, and VOKS took care of them. However, Rolland's frustration arose from the fact that, although he did his utmost to support the USSR in the West, he was insufficiently assisted by other Soviet agencies. When the distribution of *Monde* and *Europe* in the USSR stopped in 1930, Rolland expressed his indignation to VOKS about the obstruction of media that were carrying the Soviet message in France.

> It is a pity that the French friends of the USSR have no decent journal in which they could write effectively, since *Europe* and *Monde* are now prohibited in the USSR. We'll just have to sit with our arms crossed, as it would be out of the question for us to write in *l'Humanité*, given what it has become.[60]

He complained about other Soviet institutions that failed to assist him. After Professor Kogan's death, Rolland wrote to complain that the Academy of Sciences of the USSR had stopped supplying him with clippings from the Soviet press containing the numerous public addresses he had been requested to write: an appeal against war in *Pravda*, an article on the deaths of Karl Liebknecht and Rosa Luxemburg in *Krasnaya Nov'* and an open letter to Zweig and Shaw in *Literaturnaya gazeta*. He wrote to VOKS saying that he had not been sent a letter informing him that he had been elected as an honorary member of the Academy of Sciences of the USSR. Rolland further complained about the poor supply of materials: he had not received school programmes for the *fabzavuch* – workers' training schools (*fabrichno-zavodskoye uchilische*) – and the *tekhnikum* – vocational technical colleges – which he had requested long before; these were materials that he planned to use as background information in his own articles. When Rolland expressed his irritation at such incidents ('It is somewhat annoying to note such general carelessness'), he deplored the counterproductive nature of Soviet institutions, which were obstructing the ongoing work of a conscientious spokesman.

> This negligent attitude goes against the interests of the Soviet cause. How can one work in a useful way when it is so difficult to have relations that are followed up and to receive basic dispatches, for example of articles that I have sent or those that are addressed to me? I confess that this is discouraging.[61]

As with Barbusse, VOKS acted as an intermediary between Rolland and other organisations. It hurried to placate the 'très cher et honoré maître' by sending instructions to all the appropriate bodies – for example, asking Mosgorspravka (Main Administration for Literary and Publishing Affairs) to send the missing articles to the writer.[62] For its own part, VOKS promptly responded to Rolland's requests, for example when Arosev personally sent him the score of Kabalevsky's music for *Colas Breugnon*.[63]

As it had with Barbusse, VOKS gave Rolland personal treatment. The VOKS Chair Arosev and the Secretary General Apletin wrote to him in person. The many letters that Arosev wrote to Rolland in 1935–36 include one expressing sympathy on the death of Rolland's father and one giving him the news of Gorky's death. Arosev was in charge of Rolland's visit to the USSR; he went to Poland to meet the writer in person and accompanied him to Moscow by train. In Moscow, Arosev insisted that Rolland stay in his apartment in the Kremlin.[64] Mikhail Apletin also maintained a correspondence with Rolland. Knowing Rolland's liking for Russian lacquered Palekh boxes, he would send them to him as presents. He supervised Rolland's correspondence with Soviet writers, and letters from Soviet writers were sent to Rolland via Apletin as intermediary.[65]

Apart from encouraging his intellectual and political connections with the USSR, VOKS helped Rolland in his personal life. He particularly came to rely on VOKS in his relationship with, and later marriage to, the Soviet citizen Maria Kudasheva. In 1930, he asked VOKS to help her obtain permission to extend her stay in Switzerland with him,[66] and in 1933, after their marriage, he again asked for VOKS's intervention so that she could retain her apartment in Moscow.[67] Later, she took over most of Rolland's correspondence with VOKS, writing in Russian, on his behalf, in perfect Soviet style. VOKS's correspondence with Maria Kudasheva-Rolland was frequent and detailed, and is kept in separate files in the archives. It was to her that Apletin wrote to pass on to Rolland various pieces of news relating to his work in the USSR, for example the 1938 broadcast of the radio montage *Jeune Beethoven*, based on Rolland's work and featuring the famous pianist Henrih Neighauz.[68] Chapter 8 will show how Rolland's continued reliance on assistance of this kind lulled him into a dependence on Soviet organisations.

The twilight of VOKS

The Moscow trials of 1936–38, and the massive arrests that took place in those years, caused serious damage to the Soviet Union's relations with its Western allies and dampened the enthusiasm of Soviet supporters. But this was not a one-way process, as the Soviet Union's enthusiasm for its Western 'friends' declined, too. Fear of espionage and calls for vigilance against the Trotskyites, saboteurs and other 'enemies of the people' affected the political atmosphere in the country. As the USSR grew in strength in the mid- to late 1930s, its leadership became less concerned about Western public opinion.[69] These changes significantly affected VOKS.

The anatomy of denunciation

VOKS documents from 1936 reveal the degree to which the fear of spies and saboteurs was artificially induced by the Soviet leadership. In 1936, Arosev received direct party instructions to strengthen vigilance in Soviet cultural relations abroad. He now had to seek approval for VOKS's activities from the Central Committee, NKID and NKVD.[70] Arosev accounted directly to Nikolai Yezhov, the future NKVD boss and former Secretary of the Central Committee. 'It is to you, Nikolay Ivanovich, that I am writing because you are the one who issued me with a number of instructions to increase vigilance because enemies have been trying to use VOKS.'[71] These instructions translated into a suspicion of the visitors managed by VOKS, and even of VOKS staff for each other. From 1936, the number of files in VOKS's own Secret Department grew, and staff wrote letters to the NKVD denouncing colleagues, visitors and strangers.

Interpreters sent reports to Arosev and to the VOKS Secret Department and Arosev, in turn, sent letters to the Central Committee and the NKVD.[72] The Secret Department filed interpreters' reports, for example the one that included the episode with Duchêne and Lipchitz's stepson in Bolshevo. Interpreters also wrote letters to the authorities, denouncing suspicious behaviour. In January 1936, Gladkova, *referent* for Spain and Latin America, reported an incident between herself and a political immigrant from Latin America. A member of the Comintern, he lived in the Soviet Union and gave Gladkova Spanish lessons in exchange for Russian lessons. In a moment of distress, he told Gladkova about his disagreement with his section, his imminent expulsion from the Soviet Union and his fear that he would never be allowed to return to his native land. Noticing a change in expression on Gladkova's face, the man begged her not to denounce him. Terrified, she literally fled from his room and immediately reported the whole episode in minute detail.[73]

Suspicion, disguised as vigilance, began to affect VOKS's operations. In 1936, VOKS was denied a request to organise a number of exhibitions of foreign paintings.[74] Later in the same year, Glavlit searched the VOKS premises for Trotskyite literature, in order to confiscate it.[75] In April 1936, while Arosev was away, Chernyavsky, acting Chair, and Kuresar, the Head of the VOKS Secret Department, requested that the NKVD Special Department (*Spetsotdel GUGB NKVD*) formalise the practice of opening certain categories of letters. These included incoming and outgoing correspondence with foreigners who had been serviced by VOKS, as well as letters sent to the Soviet Union via plenipotentiaries abroad using diplomatic mail, addressed to Soviet writers, artists and scholars.[76]

> Considering the fact that the content of the letters represents a distinct interest for our work, and in order to check whether they have any anti-Soviet and counter-revolutionary content, it is essential for us to open the above letters. . . . We are raising the question of secret coding (*taynopis'*) being present in the abovementioned letters.

Chernyavsky and Kuresar suggested that the NKVD either provide VOKS with instructions so that VOKS could check the letters or arrange for them to be sent directly to the NKVD 'for adequate checking' (*dlya sootvetstvuyuschey proverki*).

The staff at VOKS were under suspicion, too. One evening in March 1936, during Arosev's absence, Chernyavsky and Kuresar waited for the employees to leave work and then searched their desks. They got to the desk of Pokhitonov, the Head of the First Western Department, and, as they later described, discovered his papers in chaos: drafts of letters, lumps of sugar, a jumble of correspondence, folders labelled with the wrong names, etc. They discovered a similar mess in the desks of other staff, including unfinished letters, delayed orders, etc.[77] On 25 March, Pokhitonov was fired 'for violation of the instructions of the VOKS management' (*za narusheniye rasporyazheniy rukovodstva VOKS*).[78] The NKVD was notified about both the search and Pokhitonov's dismissal. In May, Pokhitonov was arrested.[79] Other interpreters were clearly so frightened by this episode that when one of them met Pokhitonov's distressed wife in the street, she felt obliged to report this meeting, including her conversation with Pokhitonov's wife, to the Secret Department.

Arosev's own behaviour clearly reflected the external pressures to which he was subjected. Minor as they may seem now, he wrote to the NKVD to report episodes that he found worrying. On 21 August 1936, he wrote directly to Yagoda, who at the time was both People's Commissar of Internal Affairs and the Commissar-General for State Security, passing on a report from interpreter Shpringer.[80] During a tour of the Palace of the Pioneers, a member of a Czech group 'asked where com. Stalin lives and where he sleeps. I replied, in the Kremlin; but he also wanted to know the specific house, to which I replied that I didn't know.'[81]

From May 1936, Arosev wrote frequent, repetitive letters to such powerful men as Yezhov, Molotov and Stalin. Some trivial, others containing unrealistically grand plans, these letters betray Arosev's anxiety as well as his growing fear. Alongside letters in which he tried to strengthen VOKS by proposing that it be merged with Intourist, he defended himself against allegations that VOKS was allowing enemies into the USSR. He sent Yezhov a list of the people invited to the USSR by VOKS, to prove that there were no hostile or criminal elements among them as the Party Decision of 28 February 1936 had alleged.[82] He claimed that many visitors falsely called themselves VOKS invitees. He defended himself by blaming plenipotentiaries in embassies abroad for sending foreigners to the USSR as if they had been invited by VOKS, but without actually discussing it with VOKS. He accused other Soviet organisations, both political and scholarly, of bringing in visitors who called themselves VOKS invitees. VOKS could not, he asserted, be responsible for those whom it had not invited. 'All the invitations that VOKS has ever issued in the time of my leadership have always been arranged after consultation with the Central Committee, through its Kul'tprosvetotdel, and with NKID.'

After making further proposals to merge VOKS with Intourist,[83] in both November[84] and December 1936,[85] Arosev moved on to suggesting that VOKS should be in charge of the reception of all foreigners. Was he trying to strengthen VOKS or his own position, which was already insecure, by undermining Intourist? He accused Intourist of providing a poor and 'uncultured' service (*yego nedostatki vyrazhayutsya, glavnym obrazom, v plokhom i nekul'turnom obsluzhivanii inostrantsev*)[86] and decried its 'doubtful slant' on the correct way to conduct tours (*chasto pokazy delayutsya s somnitel'nym uklonom*). Arosev also turned against MORP, which he held responsible for the Gide scandal. Claiming to know Gide well, Arosev alleged that he had been opposed to inviting Gide to the USSR – at least, in the way it was organised.

> Invitations to people like Gide have to be prepared with particular care. While preparing [for a visit], one needs to take into consideration the peculiarities of this person. Gide's peculiarity is that he is a man of extremely shaky principles.

Arosev laid the blame for the Gide scandal on individuals, especially Mikhail Kol'tsov, the Chair of the Foreign Commission, who had personally invited Gide,[87] and on the leading Soviet writers Pasternak and Pil'nyak for having a bad influence on Gide.

> In addition, the [Foreign] Commission of the Soviet Writers' Union allowed very close interaction between A. Gide and his companions, on the one hand, and Pasternak and Pil'nyak on the other. I believe that the influence of the latter two was not a very positive one.
>
> The reason I am writing this is that I consider it essential to take this experience that is so full of blunders into account.[88]

In hindsight, it is impossible to ignore the fact that Kol'tsov and Pil'nyak would soon join other victims of Stalin's repressions. Was it jealousy and rivalry or the survival instinct that made Arosev strike against competing organisations and individuals in order to strengthen his own position and that of VOKS?

> On the basis of the above, I consider it essential to propose a stricter control over invitations to 'famous foreigners' (*znatnykh inostrantsev*). For this, it is necessary <u>to consolidate within one organisation both the invitations to and</u>

service of foreigners (not of tourists, of course, but of major individuals). For example, considering that neither of the invitations arranged by VOKS had such a deplorable outcome as the invitation to Gide, the said organisation could be VOKS.[89]

Despite the Gide fiasco, some 'famous foreigners' continued to arrive before the war; in fact, the number of British visits peaked in 1937. Given Arosev's views on the correct way to receive visitors, how were the visitors managed and how did VOKS handle the conflicting responsibilities of hospitality and vigilance?

The publisher of the Left Book Club comes to the Soviet Union: Victor Gollancz

In April 1937, VOKS and the Literary Agency (Litagentstvo) invited the British publisher Victor Gollancz to visit the USSR.[90] An Oxford graduate and a member of the Society for Cultural Relations with the USSR, Gollancz had founded, less than a year earlier, the Left Book Club (LBC), to support, through the distribution of books and pamphlets, the anti-Fascist Popular Front and left-wing causes. For the LBC, the Soviet Union was an alternative to capitalist rule and a force resisting Hitler. As well as international left-wing writers like Malraux, Orwell and Koestler, the LBC published works by Soviet authors and British sympathisers with the USSR. These books included Pat Sloan's *Soviet Democracy*, Sidney and Beatrice Webb's *Soviet Communism: A New Civilisation* and Hewlett Johnson's *The Socialist Sixth of the World*. At the time of the Moscow trials, the LBC refused to publish anything that was critical of Soviet policies, rejecting Orwell's *Homage to Catalonia*, and publishing only party-line material such as Dudley Collard's *Soviet Justice and the Trial of Radek and Others* and J.R. Campbell's *Soviet Policy and its Critics*.

The LBC's popularity was enormous and it grew rapidly. In addition to publishing at least one book per month and recommending it to its subscribers, the LBC developed national and international branches in South Africa, New Zealand and Australia. The orange covers of LBC books found more interested readers than its organisers had expected and, by its first anniversary in May 1937, the LBC had 44,800 members; by World War II, there were 57,000. A key left-wing institution of the late 1930s, it had a network of 1,500 local left-wing discussion groups, produced the monthly periodical *Left News*, and ran a film screening group, *Kino*.[91] Suspicion that the LBC was yet another Soviet auxiliary organisation would be understandable.

Victor Gollancz, as the founder of the LBC, was known for his strong views and has often been assumed to have been a Communist and a Soviet agent of influence; after all, his closest associates – Harold Lasky and John Strachey – were known for their sympathetic view of Communism. At a time when VOKS was hosting only invited visitors, the fact that Arosev chose Gollancz need not necessarily mean anything more than that Arosev believed that Gollancz was a safe bet. After all, publication in Gollancz's LBC would have assured a wide dissemination of Soviet materials throughout the English-speaking world. VOKS's accounts of Gollancz's visit will help us to understand the rapport that existed between him and the Soviet authorities and resolve the misconception about Gollancz and the LBC being in the Soviets' pay.

Gollancz's reception programme followed VOKS's usual *modus operandi* regarding hospitality. While Litagentstvo took care of Gollancz's practical arrangements (*material'naya storona dela*),[92] VOKS played the central role in entertaining him. VOKS kept him on a very tight schedule. Gollancz arrived on 30 April 1937, the day before May Day so, on the first day of his visit, he was shown the military parade on Red Square and the popular march (*demonstratsiya*); on day two, he saw the Archangel'skoye Museum Estate and the play *Interventsia* at the Vakhtangov Theatre. On day three, he had business meetings including a lunch with NKID at the luxurious Natsional restaurant and a discussion with Litagentstvo. Gollancz's professional interests as a publisher took him to the *Pravda* printery on day four and to the Association of State Publishers (OGIZ) on day seven. In between, he visited the Bolshevo commune on day five and inspected the canal between the River Moskva and the Volga canal on day six. On day eight, he visited the Dinamo factory, and he attended two receptions on days four and seven. If VOKS wanted to impress Gollancz with the Soviet intellectuals who were invited to these occasions, they succeeded; invited guests who gathered on 4 May for the reception at VOKS included the writers Tret'yakov, Bonch-Bruyevich, Nikulin and Leonov, the composers Prokofiev and Glière, the film-maker Pudovkin and many others.[93] On 9 May, Gollancz had lunch with Arosev, Kol'tsov, Umansky (an NKID diplomat and a representative of Litagentstvo) and some VOKS staff.[94]

At the same time as entertaining their guest, VOKS and Litagentstvo kept their agenda in mind. Special time had been set aside for a planned conversation with Gollancz, described in a document entitled 'Re conversation with Gollancz' and including a list of items for discussion.[95] The aim of the rather one-sided 'conversation' was to persuade Gollancz to contribute to a series of activities for the celebrations of the twentieth anniversary of the October Revolution in the UK. VOKS's wish list was unusually lengthy and detailed. VOKS wanted the London SCR to prepare for the anniversary by creating a celebration committee that would arrange a concert and a meeting in the Queen's Hall on 6 November, put on talks about Soviet achievements and perform Russian songs. Other celebratory activities were to include another evening event in a theatre where Soviet films could be shown and entertainment provided by Soviet dancers and singers; Gollancz was expected to suggest other topics of great interest for further evening events, and an exhibition for the twentieth anniversary. Perhaps the topic could be industrialisation, collectivisation and culture? Would other topics, such as Soviet politics or science, be of interest? If so, VOKS representatives could give talks. Could VOKS publish something for the twentieth anniversary in the UK; in fact, maybe Gollancz would publish something for the occasion? Which public figures could visit the USSR for 7 November? There is no way of determining whether VOKS managed to convey these and other wishes to Gollancz, or to ask its planned questions on SCR operations, the London SCR journal, the need for printed materials and the possibility of exhibitions on the Soviet Constitution and Mother and Infant Protection (*Okhmatmlad*). Nor is there any record of Gollancz's response at the time of the discussions; however, we will return to the implementation of these plans later.

While the notes recorded by VOKS in Moscow make no comment about Gollancz's responses, those recorded by the Leningrad VOKS official Orlov do.[96] His notes betray a constant frustration with the reactions of Gollancz, who was by now tired. In Leningrad, VOKS found itself in a strange competition with the writer Alexey Tolstoy, the author of the novel *Peter the Great*. Gollancz was met at the station not only by VOKS but also by Tolstoy's secretary and, after a VOKS-ordained visit to the Hermitage, he was whisked away by the secretary to the town of Pushkin (formerly Tsarskoye Selo) to have lunch with Tolstoy.

According to Orlov, Gollancz was not an easy client to entertain. He did not enjoy the ballet premiere *The Partisans' Days* and 'spoke negatively [about it], declaring that he believed that "propaganda in art was superfluous and unclear"'. Rivalry between VOKS and Tolstoy continued and when the Lenfilm screening of *Peter the Great*, which was organised by Tolstoy, had to be cancelled, 'VOKS did not interfere, as Tolstoy was deliberately guarding Gollancz as his own guest'. However, VOKS also encountered further obstacles while entertaining Gollancz. Not many of the writers who were invited for lunch at VOKS actually arrived. Gollancz himself made a bad impression on his hosts: he showed no interest or appreciation, and was unresponsive.

> I have to say that in Leningrad Gollancz's behaviour was only on the border of civility and very pompous. When, following your wishes, I gave him all of the Pushkin anniversary editions, he took them without any interest. If I had not insisted that he should familiarise himself with them, he would have limited himself to ordering them to be taken to his room, without unwrapping them.[97]

While VOKS officials were wishing Gollancz farewell, he 'went beyond any civil behaviour and allowed himself to offer leftover Soviet money to Ada Vasil'yevna'.[98] (As visitors were unable to exchange Soviet roubles for foreign currency, they had to dispose of them in the USSR.) In a disparaging tone, already familiar from reports by other VOKS officials, Orlov summed up Gollancz's character:

> His substance is sufficiently clear. Altogether, while in Leningrad, he did not display any of the qualities of a man who is interested in our life. A 'publisher', he did not ask me a single question about our publishing practices, nor did he show any reaction to the information I provided. As for Moscow, he said that he had had enough, and that he was tired of all the receptions and banquets. To be honest, Gollancz has made a negative impression. One can understand why Tolstoy is courting him, probably being connected through issues of concern to him as a writer.

To take Orlov's report at face value, Gollancz's visit was a total failure. However, subsequent documentation suggests that Orlov was at least partly mistaken. On 1 July 1937, Gollancz sent a grateful, even enthusiastic, letter to Arosev.

> Ever since I got back from Moscow I have been meaning to write in order to thank you and all the other comrades most cordially for the really marvellous time you gave us. I had, in fact, never thought that such hospitality was possible. I now have quite a terrible nostalgia to pay you all a second visit.[99]

Moreover, once he was back, Gollancz encouraged three more parties of British tourists to visit the USSR through his LBC.[100] Further groups, also organised through the LBC, followed in 1938.[101]

Was Gollancz's trip a success after all? Litagentstvo clearly assumed so, as the principal outcome was the plan to use the LBC to publish Soviet literature.[102] In 1937 alone, Gollancz was sent a considerable quantity of literature for publication. The list included Bogolepov's *The Financial System of the USSR*, Joffe's *The Industrial Revolution in the USSR,* Dr Danyushevsky's *The Fight Against Prostitution in the USSR*, the anthology *A Picture Book on the USSR* and Arsen'yev's *Dersu Uzala*. Before the end of the year, Gollancz's staff were to select 200 of the 300 pieces of information contained in *Facts About the USSR* that would be suitable for a British edition. Litagentstvo was ready to compile a book for the twentieth anniversary of the USSR that would cover the progress of industrialisation, collectivisation, the cultural revolution, the life of the national republics, new living standards, children and youth, and art and sport; Gollancz promised to send concrete suggestions for this book. Litagentstvo was preparing English translations of other Soviet books to be sent to Gollancz – *Recollections about Lenin* and *Guide through the Soviet Union* – and he promised that more books would be sent later: *Soviet Youth on Itself, One Hundred Soviet Words* and *A Book on the Red Army*. In 1938, he received *A Short History of the USSR, Economic Survey* and *Moscow Weekly News*.[103] For his part, Gollancz sent *Famous Plays 1938–39* to Rokotov, deputy editor of *International literature*, via VOKS.

However, none of the plans materialised. Gollancz did not publish most of what Litagentstvo sent, and a close relationship was never established with him. When Grinyov, the VOKS representative in London, sent VOKS the LBC's 1937 catalogue of books, from a long list of materials provided to Gollancz, only Bogolepov's *The Financial System of the USSR* featured in a list that was otherwise made up of entirely British authors.[104] VOKS later summed up its impression of him during his visit as 'a "businessman", and not a very pleasant one', and admitted that his 'commitment to publish Soviet books through the Gollancz publishing house was not fulfilled'.[105]

Gollancz's political position following his visit also disappointed VOKS. 'In his political statements about the USSR, he showed himself friendly but reserved.'[106] Initially, he was said to have spoken regularly at LBC-organised rallies and anti-Fascist meetings, although he was also reluctant to open a debate in the LBC about the Moscow trials. However, in 1939–40, VOKS noted that Gollancz had turned away from the USSR. 'After the Soviet–German Pact, and particularly the Finnish events, Gollancz became hostile towards the USSR. In the March issue of *Tribune* he condemns the USSR in relation to Finland, however pointing out that England must not be hostile towards the USSR,' VOKS's 1940 report reads. The file on Gollancz contains a clipping of his article of 12 June 1940, 'Where are you going? An open letter to Communists', and VOKS criticised him for 'showing his true colours' in joining a widely organised campaign by certain 'Socialist intellectuals'. These were said to be trying to confuse members of the British Labour Party by setting them against the Communist Party, the Comintern and the USSR. VOKS also accused Gollancz of allowing anti-Soviet publications in the LBC.

Clearly, VOKS's hospitality failed to influence Gollancz to the extent that he would compromise his principles as a publisher and a public intellectual. Despite his sympathies for the USSR, he did not subjugate his integrity to the demands of Soviet organisations and could not be controlled by them.

Moscow 1937: the interpreter's story

In December 1936, another 'famous foreigner' arrived in Moscow: this time it was Lion Feuchtwanger, an exiled German Jewish writer living in the south of France. Feuchtwanger was internationally known for his historical and anti-Nazi novels, which included *Jew Süss*, *Success* and *The Oppermanns*; he was outspokenly opposed to the policies of Hitler's Third Reich, well before Western nations abandoned their policies of appeasing Hitler. Feuchtwanger had been invited by Mikhail Kol'tsov, Chair of the Foreign Commission of the Soviet Writers' Union and Arosev's rival, who sought special approval for this invitation from the Central Committee and the Politburo. He maintained that the same attention needed to be accorded to Feuchtwanger as to André Gide.[107] Feuchtwanger's visit was very important to his hosts. Perhaps he would write a rebuttal to Andre Gide's *Return from the USSR*? Maybe he could reverse the critical views of the Moscow trials held by other intellectuals in his circle? As it was known that he had been critical of the 1936 trials of Zinov'yev and Kamenev, his visit was timed to coincide with the second trial, that of Pytakov, Radek and others.

A left-bourgeois writer, Feuchtwanger went to Moscow, by his own accounts, as a sympathiser, hoping to confirm that the Great Experiment was a success. He shared Jean-Richard Bloch's doubts about the restrictions to personal freedom in the Soviet Union. For him, André Gide's *Return from the USSR* was a warning and a source for reflection.[108] It is not known what his exact expectations of the USSR were on the eve of his visit. Feuchtwanger, who was looked after jointly by the Foreign Commission and VOKS, was received with the highest honours, including a meeting with Stalin, and sat in on the 1937 trial. Shortly after his return to France in February 1937, he published the notorious *Moscow 1937*, in which he praised Stalin's Soviet Union and justified the trials. Bringing Feuchtwanger to the Soviet Union thus paid off for the Soviet propaganda machine.

However, at the time of his stay, such an outcome was unpredictable. Arosev was quick to relegate responsibility for the visit to the Writers' Union and warned Stalin, Molotov and Yezhov that Feuchtwanger might be another Gide.

> At the moment, Feuchtwanger is in Moscow. He is an important figure in terms of his influence on European minds. His name is known across every continent, plus he speaks the main languages of all the continents. In addition, regardless of his literary talent, this man has great appeal. He has numerous friends and a thick crowd of fans.
>
> As to his character, he is a petty man. His attitude towards us is very uncertain. He is also the responsibility of the Soviet Writers' Union. On the basis of initial reports about conversations with him, his actions on his return from the Soviet Union cannot but inspire our concern.[109]

Arosev's information about Feuchtwanger was based on reports by D. Karavkina, an employee of the VOKS Second Western Department. A future translator of Hoffmann and Hesse into Russian, she was appointed as Feuchtwanger's interpreter and secretary and wrote daily reports about him.[110] Photographs captured them both smiling and looking content; however, Karavkina's reports convey a different picture, in which Feuchtwanger appears as an ironic, sceptical and essentially critical figure. Retyped and bearing handwritten comments, Karavkina's reports were clearly passed on to her superiors. By the time Arosev wrote to Stalin, Molotov and Yezhov, he had received at least four of her reports.

Karavkina's caution was understandable. As an interpreter, she would have been warned to be extra vigilant and would have been on the front line of responsibility for Feuchtwanger. Her negative assessment of Feuchtwanger is understandable given the frequency with which his critical comments appear in her reports. Even accepting that her reports are biased, they nonetheless reflect Feuchtwanger's reactions, his sources of information about the USSR and Karavkina's role as an official propagandist. Seen through his interpreter's eyes, much can be learned about the evolution of his views during his stay.

Feuchtwanger's reactions to his custom-made programme were unpredictable. Though a sympathiser, he often responded as a political adversary and refused to play the game. 'He has shown no interest in Soviet life, our construction and art,' wrote Karavkina. When asked about his impressions of the Metro – the Muscovites' pride and joy – he replied that he could not compare, as he never took the metro and always travelled by car. As in Gollancz's case, his motivation for being in Moscow seemed purely selfish. 'As the basis of his schedule, Feuchtwanger uses his "writer's business", such as negotiations with publishers, editors, authors and directors for stage and screen adaptation of his writings.'[111]

Luxury and comfort – Soviet style, at least – failed to impress Feuchtwanger. The Metropol Hotel, which had so enchanted the Blochs in 1934 with its old-world glamour, was an endless source of grievance to Feuchtwanger. He 'complained about small things going wrong (*nepoladki*): the light, the furniture, etc.' and was worried in case his possessions were stolen from his room. Worse still, he believed that seemingly minor details revealed bad general management. 'He immediately added that such petty details probably had had a significant impact on the mood of Andre Gide, a highly strung person and an artist.'[112]

Small things led Feuchtwanger to generalise about living conditions in the USSR. 'In the morning, Feuchtwanger spoke endlessly about how life in the USSR is full of inconveniences. He complained about service in the hotel, unreliable mail deliveries and a whole range of other faults.'[113] His observations again extended to Soviet life in general. 'He declared that so far, the living standard in the USSR is infinitely lower than in other European countries; when our worker begins to live like a French one, then the Soviets will conquer the entire world.'[114] His criticism of the low living standard was concrete and based on his own observations. 'He was then thinking aloud about the living conditions of the employees at the resort where he had stayed. They earn 70 roubles [per month] while a pair of shoes costs 180 roubles. And so forth, along those lines.'

Having labelled Feuchtwanger as small-minded ('his character seems very petty', a recurring critique in these reports) and observing that 'petty things obscure his view of major ones',[115] Karavkina admitted that he expressed approval, too, however grudgingly. 'You do not have to defend the Soviet Union to me; I do understand perfectly well how grand everything here is (*kak vsyo grandiozno*) and what gigantic work (*gigantskaya rabota*) is being done here,'[116] she quoted him as saying. Towards the end of December and in early January, Karavkina noted that Feuchtwanger was becoming more receptive. He showed an interest in the daily life of the workers, wanting to visit their homes and shops and asking Karavkina about her own living conditions. He even praised the construction of Moscow.

> Despite his scepticism, Feuchtwanger was struck by the grandeur of the Moscow reconstruction plan and spoke about it with admiration, enquiring about every detail of its development and approval, as well as its implementation.

Having earlier commented that Feuchtwanger was very interested in the theatre, Karvkina now reported that

> he liked the performance of [Gozzi's play] *Turandot* a lot, with an excellent cast. During one of the interludes, Goryunov publicly announced that Feuchtwanger was in the audience. He received an ovation and was dragged onto the stage. He was very embarrassed but obviously pleased.[117]

Another source of pleasure for Feuchtwanger was meeting Soviet intellectuals. Having initially asked to meet Alexey Tolstoy, Babel, Pasternak, Il'f, Petrov and Eisenstein,[118] he greatly enjoyed the VOKS party on 21 December at which he met the artists Konchalovsky and Kukryniksy, the writers Afinogenov, Leonov, Serafimovich, Roshal' and Simonov, the actors Giatsintova and Il'insky, and others.

Feuchtwanger was very pleased with the reception at VOKS. He liked the fact that there were representatives from different layers of the Soviet intelligentsia present and that he had the opportunity to talk to them. He found that everything was very much 'in the European style'.

He was very pleased to have attended a private dinner at Il'f and Petrov's, in the company of Babel and Katayev, to which he was invited on 3 January 1937.

Meeting Soviet readers was also a highly stimulating experience – not just because Feuchtwanger was known to the audience, but because it gave him the chance to have a meaningful exchange with a thinking readership that had an excellent and detailed knowledge of his books.

> At first he wasn't pleased that he had been dragged out of the house, but the young people's speeches visibly got to him, and when his turn came to speak, he did it with some force (*pod'yom*) (as much as his temperament allowed him to) and defended his heroes, whom the young people had criticised, quite firmly. In conclusion, he declared that the last part of his trilogy about contemporary Germany, the first part of which was *Success*, would have a positive ending, which he owes to his visit to the USSR and what he saw here. This is what he considers to be the most valuable experience he acquired here. On the way back, Feuchtwanger spoke of the pleasant impression the TsAGI young people had made on him, their intellect, the thoughtful attitude to the books they read and the high level of their knowledge.[119]

This meeting of the literate and the thoughtful was at the Central Aerohydrodynamic Institute or TsAGI. Nonetheless, other meetings had the opposite effect. Being in constant demand, assailed by visitors, invited and solicited to write articles, Feuchtwanger also grew tired and irritable. During a 'friendly meeting' at the *Kino* newspaper, about a dozen staff members 'surrounded him and despite his obvious displeasure made him answer their questions. He was most indignant and cross (*on byl ochen' vozmyschen i zol*) for it was meant to be a "friendly" meeting.' Another meeting, at the Masters' Club (*Klub masterov*), made 'an oppressive impression on him. In fact, apart from Mikhoels and Vishnevsky, there were no major actors or artists. The concert was worse than mediocre. It wasn't worth dragging him out at midnight to a concert like this. He was very displeased and very tired.'

Karavkina's reports reveal that, even in 1937, Soviet organisations did not manage to completely control their visitors' stays. The protective wall erected around Feuchtwanger against undesirable influences was not foolproof. 'Although com. Apletin and I are trying to control visits to Feuchtwanger as much as possible, from time to time some people manage to get through and have a very harmful influence on him,' wrote Karavkina on 3 January 1937. The effect on Feuchtwanger of meeting these unapproved people was to subvert the impression of conditions in the Soviet Union that it was intended he take away with him. On 15 December, Karavkina wrote,

> At this time some woman literally burst into his room. She turned out to be Erich Musam's widow. Feuchtwanger was beside himself, as he does not like it when people burst in so unexpectedly. The next day he told me that he was very unhappy that she was dragging him into her 'ugly stories' (*nekrasivyye dela*), that she had 'done silly things' (*nadelala glupostey*) here, had been

involved in a Trotskyite matter and arrested, and that he had no intentions of getting mixed up – in other words, he was very displeased with her. All the same, he told her to come on 22.12 at 4 pm.[120]

Incidents like this were clearly a jolt to Feuchtwanger and it was feared that they would disillusion him. On 3 January, Karavkina reported that, the previous day, Feuchtwanger had received Piscator's wife, the actress Yanukova. Piscator had lived in the USSR for several years after 1929, and by the time of Feuchtwanger's visit had returned to the West.

> She told him plenty of horror stories (*ona yemu narasskazala vsyakikh uzhasov*) about our accommodation difficulties. In addition, apparently Piscator had paid 200,000 roubles for an apartment which he never got because he had been cheated.
> She made the worst impression on him by telling him that in summer she had to sleep in a park for two weeks as she had no roof over her head. 'What? An actress from a Moscow theatre could find nowhere to sleep?' He became so agitated (*vzvolnovan*) that he could barely wait for my return to tell me about it.

Undesirable information even came from authorised sources – Soviet writers. One of them told Feuchtwanger that 'Russia never had its own [school of] painting, nor does it have one now.' An asterisk in ink on Karavkina's typed report directs the reader to a handwritten footnote: 'Tret'yakov said this (*Eto skazal Tret'yakov*).'[121] On another occasion, Feuchtwanger asked Karavkina if it was true 'that Pasternak is in disgrace (*v opale*) as his work does not coincide with the party's general line'. He had learned this at Il'f and Petrov's dinner with Babel and Katayev. 'Then he told me an anti-Soviet joke. When I asked him in amazement who had been supplying him with such information, he did not say.'[122] It is surprising that, in 1937, Soviet intellectuals still spoke to foreigners and spent time with them relatively freely and openly. However, it is equally surprising to note that, unlike Gide, Feuchtwanger trusted his interpreter and naïvely shared his impressions with her. How was he to know that by quoting his Soviet colleagues he was endangering them, that Karavkina wrote down every word he said and that her denunciatory reports went to the very top of the Soviet hierarchy?

Feuchtwanger's trust went even further: he engaged in frank polemics with Karavkina. He repeatedly questioned the lack of political freedom in the USSR.

> In his opinion, there is no freedom of speech in the USSR. He then added that he is not against dictatorship as 'he understands the need for it' in the current conditions, however he considers 'a bit more tolerance' essential.[123]

He told Karavkina that this awareness, confirmed by his knowledge of Gide's experience, made him cautious about expressing his opinions. 'He was saying, among other things, that it is "dangerous" to express one's opinions here, and that this is what happened to André Gide, and that he had been told that they don't like criticism here, particularly by foreigners, and so forth.'[124]

Soon enough, Feuchtwanger experienced this lack of freedom at first hand. Maria Osten-Gressgener, a German political migrant to the USSR, the author of *Hubert in Wonderland: Days and Deeds of a German Pioneer* (1935) and Kol'tsov's common-law wife, asked Feuchtwanger to write an article for *Pravda*. It was an article about Gide and Osten had supplied him with materials. To Feuchtwanger's surprise, the article did not get published when he expected it to. 'I reassured him that they had simply run out of time,' Karavkina explained.[125] But then *Pravda* contacted him, asking for corrections before they would publish his article. Feuchtwanger was indignant.

> It has been a difficult day today, as Feuchtwanger could not wait to pour onto me all his indignation because *Pravda*, he says, demands that he make corrections in his article on Gide. This, he said, proves that Gide was right about the lack of freedom of opinion and that one cannot express one's opinions, etc.
>
> Mekhlis [the editor] suggested that he change certain parts, namely those relating to Stalin's 'personality cult'. I explained the essence of the Soviet nations' attitude to com. Stalin, where it came from, and that it was totally wrong to call it a 'cult'.
>
> He was fuming for a long time, saying that he was not going to change anything. However, by the time Maria Osten arrived he had cooled down, sat with her in the study meekly and corrected everything she asked except a sentence on 'tolerance' which he would not get rid of under any circumstances.[126]

The trials were another matter of great concern to Feuchtwanger; he had come to Moscow deeply disturbed by the 1936 trials of Kamenev and Zinov'yev. The idea that the old Bolsheviks could be accused of treason and, worse still, would confess to monstrous crimes made no sense to him. Karavkina was quite unable to justify it to him and he impatiently awaited a meeting with Georgy Dimitrov, the Comintern leader and internationally revered Bulgarian hero, who had bravely resisted trumped-up charges at the Reichstag fire trial.

> He said he was looking forward to a meeting with com. Dimitrov. He needed to talk to him about the Trotskyite trial, because it had had a shattering effect in Europe and had cost the Soviet Union two-thirds of its supporters. Because of this it was now important to undertake some explanatory work to correct the situation.[127]

However, Dimitrov also failed to supply Feuchtwanger with convincing arguments.

He told me about his visit to Dimitrov, who received him at home for dinner. He went there especially in order to discuss the Trotskyite trial. He said that Dimitrov was very nervous (*volnovalsya*) in talking about it and took one and a half hours to explain it to him, but 'did not persuade him'. Feuchtwanger then declared to me that abroad this trial is being considered in a very hostile light and that it is seen in the same category as the Reichstag Fire Trial. 'Nobody' can understand that it is possible that fifteen 'committed revolutionaries', who had risked their lives so many times plotting against the lives of the leaders, would suddenly all confess and repent. I explained to him that his entire mistake consisted precisely of considering these Trotskyite counter-revolutionaries as 'committed revolutionaries', when they were in fact totally unscrupulous people who strove to gain power by all means, stopping at nothing.[128]

It seems that, at every turn, his hosts' goal was to try and persuade Feuchtwanger to accept the USSR as it was shown to him. Karavkina either tried to remove the causes of his criticisms, for example by arranging repairs at the hotel, or found endless counter-arguments to his criticisms. According to her, Feuchtwanger did seem to be receptive to persuasion. 'I have been trying to prove to him that this kind of reasoning is false, by using a whole range of examples, with which he agrees.'[129] 'As for Gide, I explained to him why we were indignant. It was because of his hypocrisy and because he was playing into the hands of the Fascists. He quite agreed with the latter.'[130] She corrected minor points that touched upon her national pride.

> Apparently, Ionov told him that books are illustrated badly here because we are short of artists. I assured him that he misunderstood Ionov and that we do have wonderful graphic artists and beautifully published books.[131]

'I listed a number of Soviet artists and suggested he visit the Tretyakov gallery. He said he would definitely go,' she recorded a week later.[132]

Others influenced Feuchtwanger too, for example Maria Osten. 'Feuchtwanger is very good friends with her and trusts her',[133] noted Karavkina approvingly. During his negotiations with publishers about the screen adaptation of his novel *The Oppenheim Family*, Karavkina admitted that Feuchtwanger was receptive to arguments and showed no signs of pettiness.

> When they got on to the contract, although Feuchtwanger defended his author's rights, he did not show, from my point of view, either greed or stubbornness, and easily gave in when com. Usiyevich pointed to the impossibility of this or that requirement he had made. In addition he said that although in America he had been offered much better financial conditions, nonetheless he preferred to have the film made in the USSR.[134]

However, as Dimitrov had discovered, it was hard to persuade Feuchtwanger in political matters. Boris Tal', an editor of the central daily *Izvestia*, to whom Maria Osten took Feuchtwanger, also failed to influence his views about democracy and freedom of speech. 'Today he told me about this conversation, saying that Tal' did not persuade him.'[135] Only four days later, Tal' would act as an interpreter during Feuchtwanger's meeting with Stalin. Stalin would be the figure who influenced Feuchtwanger in the most significant way.

As Feuchtwanger's stay continued, Karavkina predicted that he would return home with a negative attitude.

> He said to me ironically that he would like to see whether they would publish, in the USSR, his work in which he would describe life here as 'uncosy', as it seems to him. That no matter how wonderful it is in the Soviet Union, he still prefers to live in Europe.[136]

Even though she continued to stress her efforts as a propagandist, Karavkina was honest in admitting that her persuasive powers were limited. 'I don't know whether my evidence to the contrary had any effect on him.' Unlike other two-faced Soviet interpreters, who flattered visitors while writing about them disrespectfully, she also recognised Feuchtwanger's positive side ('His comments are always subtle and interesting'[137]) and was direct with him. 'He declared that I was "a local patriot", to which I retorted that I simply understood these matters better than he did and considered it my duty to set him straight.'[138] Unlike Ronskaya, she comes across as a genuine and zealous propagandist rather than a meek and fearful pawn in the system.

Karavkina's reports about Feuchtwanger stop abruptly on 4 January, before his meeting with Stalin on 8 January. The only other record of his stay in Moscow is the recently published record of his three-hour-long conversation with Stalin, based on Tal's notes and containing the gist of their questions and answers.[139] Feuchtwanger's subsequently published *Moscow 1937* is so different in content from Karavkina's reports that it is difficult to understand what his true opinions were.

The book's very opening challenges Karavkina's assessment of Feuchtwanger as a sceptical and disapproving visitor. In it, he forcefully states his obligation to bear witness and defend the USSR.

> The Soviet Union is fighting many enemies, and its allies provide it with only weak support. Stupidity, ill will and stagnation try to discredit, defame and deny everything that is productive in the East. But a writer who has seen its greatness dares not evade bearing witness, even if this greatness is unpopular and many will find his words unpleasant. This is why I am testifying.[140]

Almost nothing in Karavkina's reports prepares the reader for the opinions and tone of the book. The Feuchtwanger in Karavkina's accounts relies on Gide's assessment of the USSR and quotes him to back up his own negative observations. In *Moscow 1937*, Feuchtwanger becomes Gide's opponent. He accuses Gide of what Karavkina had accused Feuchtwanger of in her reports: pettiness, short-sightedness and the inability to see the big picture behind 'the multitude of small inconveniences that complicate daily life in Moscow and prevent one from seeing the important things'. Feuchtwanger, as the author of *Moscow 1937*, claims to rise above the inconvenience of petty problems. 'While in Moscow, I tried hard constantly to control my views and redress them either way, so that momentary impressions, pleasant or unpleasant, would not affect my ultimate judgement.'[141] If we recall Karavkina's reports, there seems to be an inconsistency here, at least with the man as she perceived him.

Unlike the Feuchtwanger in Karavkina's reports, who had no interest in social-ist construction, the Feuchtwanger in his book presents a glowing picture of a de-veloping society, including the reconstruction of Moscow and the Metro. 'The re-construction of Moscow is the most grandiose among this kind of works.' 'Thanks to electrification, Moscow shines like no other city in the world.'[142] 'Their metro . . . is indeed the most beautiful and comfortable in the world.'[143] The writer's imagination of Feuchtwanger allows him to see the glorious future in embryo in the forward planning for Moscow: 'Moscow will be beautiful.'

Feuchtwanger's sceptical calculations in Moscow about workers' low income and the high costs that they faced do not prepare us for his optimistic portrayal of workers' daily life as he presents it in his book. Life is said to be improving, now that the famine is over, with food and goods sold at prices that are accessible to the average citizen. Feuchtwanger now uses counter-arguments to balance the shortcomings of life in the Soviet system. He claims that the crowded living con-ditions and poverty have been compensated for by public spaces: clubs, stadiums and libraries, which he describes as 'rich, beautiful and spacious'.[144]

Feuchtwanger the author rewrites his own original experiences, editing out encounters with critical and unhappy Soviet citizens. In *Moscow 1937*, the Soviet people are almost unanimously happy, criticising only minor details of the world in which they live. There is no mention of the desperate individuals who came to see Feuchtwanger to tell him about their misery and to seek his assistance.

> All the people whom I met in the USSR, including accidental interlocutors who in no way could have been prepared for a conversation with me, al-though occasionally criticising certain shortcomings, were apparently quite in agreement with the existing order as a whole. Indeed, the entire city of Moscow felt satisfied, harmonious and even happy.[145]

Feuchtwanger self-censors, omitting all references to the lack of freedom and tolerance he had complained about previously. 'I stated with satisfaction that my frankness in Moscow did not cause any offence. Newspapers published my com-ments in the most prominent places, although the [Soviet] leaders perhaps did not particularly like it.'[146] He has forgotten the frustration he experienced when he was forced to cut and edit his article. 'Soviet newspapers did not censor my articles, even when I complained about the intolerance in certain areas or the ex-cessive cult of Stalin, or else demanded greater clarity in the conduct of a serious political trial.'[147] Feuchtwanger outdoes even J.-R. Bloch in justifying the lack of democracy. The Soviet Union could have never achieved what it had achieved, he argues, had it allowed parliamentary democracy of the Western European type. Freedom of speech in the USSR would be no more than the freedom to vilify the Soviet regime.

> Never would it have been possible to build socialism with unlimited freedom of vilification. . . . Soviet leaders found themselves facing the alternative of either spending a significant amount of their force to refute senseless and evil attacks, or putting all their efforts into the completion of construction. They have decided in favour of limiting the freedom of vilification.[148]

How is it possible that Feuchtwanger's views changed so much? Could they have evolved so radically by the end of his stay that he accepted the global picture of the USSR presented to him by his hosts? If this was indeed the case, it is surprising that Karavkina's reports do not reflect any of this evolution. Feuchtwanger's change would appear to be inexplicable. If his views had evolved so rapidly and radically, we would surely expect to see signs of this evolution in Karavkina's attentive and detailed reports; but there are none. The influence of external events on Feuchtwanger at this point seems unlikely. Even though the book is filled with criticism of Western society and expresses a repeated fear of Fascism, there was no new development in Europe between Feuchtwanger's recorded arguments with Karavkina in January and the publication of his book a few months later that could plausibly account for him becoming more accepting of the Soviet Union as an alternative to Nazi Germany. The book, positive in argument and tone, does not give us grounds to assume that it was hypocritical or, as some authors have suggested, opportunistic on Feuchtwanger's part, for example that he was keeping on good terms with the Soviet Union in case he needed to flee there. If we are to accept the veracity of Karavkina's reports (and we have no reason to dispute them) and the genuineness of the opinions expressed in *Moscow 1937* only a few months later, something must have happened following the completion of Karavkina's reports to have radically altered Feuchtwanger's views. If this is the case, his meeting with Stalin on 8 January 1937 is the event that is most likely to have changed his opinions.[149]

It appears that meeting Stalin had the most singular impact on Feuchtwanger. He found himself under the spell of the Soviet leader's personality and, as he himself admits, he came to trust Stalin.

> Gradually I felt that I could speak frankly with this man. I spoke frankly, and he repaid me with the same. [. . .] He appeared to me to be an individual. Without always agreeing with me, he remained at all times deep, intelligent and thoughtful.[150]

It is this trust that made Feuchtwanger accept Stalin's answers to the questions that had troubled him, beginning with Stalin's personality cult. In *Moscow*

1937, Feuchtwanger blends the explanations given to him by Stalin into his own narrative, making the two indistinguishable; in this way, he fully accepts Stalin's justification of the adulation, the countless busts and portraits of himself as leader, as the sincere, albeit naïve, expression of people's gratitude for the better life he had given them.

> People need to express their gratitude and their endless admiration. Indeed, they think that everything they have and what they are, they owe to Stalin. . . . This feeling grew organically with the growth of economic construction. People are grateful to Stalin for bread, meat, order, education, the creation of the Army which ensures this new wellbeing. People must have someone to whom they can express their gratitude for an unquestionable improvement in their living conditions, and for this purpose they have chosen not an abstract notion, such as 'Communism', but a specific person, that is, Stalin. . . . When people say 'Stalin' they mean prosperity and the growth in education.

More importantly, meeting Stalin led Feuchtwanger to resolve his doubts concerning the trials; a lengthy chapter in his book fully accepts the official Soviet position. Weaving Stalin's arguments into his book allows him to resolve in his own mind some of the questions that he had unsuccessfully raised with Karavkina, Dimitrov and others. For example, Trotsky, because he was not a Bolshevik, would stop at nothing in his attempt to overthrow Stalin, even if it meant conspiring with the Fascists[151] – this was just as Karavkina had put it to him. Feuchtwanger also explains how it was completely plausible that the accused had committed their crimes and then confessed. All of them, professional revolutionary conspirators inspired by Trotsky, regarded Stalin's state as a distorted image of what they envisaged for the nation. Being Trotskyites, they had been demoted and resented not having positions that were as high as they felt they deserved.[152] Previously, Feuchtwanger had been unsure of the crimes that they had allegedly committed but, from the time of his meeting with Stalin, he clearly felt privy to the secret material containing accusations against Radek and Pyatakov, 'revealed' to him by Stalin. Although he was personally convinced by these arguments, he nevertheless remained concerned by the lack of transparency in their presentation by the prosecution. Crimes, he explains, had been revealed during the investigation and the accused were confronted with them before the trial. In the face of irrefutable accusations, all they could do at the trial was to confess. The lack of a public presentation of the evidence was explained to (and by) Feuchtwanger as a desire not to confuse the Soviet people. Confession was seen as being tantamount to their guilt and considered to be more important than the presentation of that guilt.[153]

By the time that Feuchtwanger attended the trial of Radek and Pyatakov, he was ready to believe what he was about to see.

> In the course of the first trial, I was in the atmosphere of Western Europe, but at the second, in the atmosphere of Moscow. Some of my friends, who are

fairly sensible people, describe these trials as tragicomic, barbaric, lacking in credibility, and monstrous both in form and content. After the trials, a number of people who used to be friends of the Soviet Union became its enemies. While I was in Europe, I also found the charges levelled at the Zinov'yev trial to be groundless. I saw the entire trial as some kind of show, staged with bizarre, blood-curdling skill. Yet at the second trial, when I saw and heard Pyatakov, Radek and their friends, I felt my doubts dissolve like salt in water, under the impact of what the defendants had to say, and how they said it. If all of that had been fabricated and staged, I do not know what the truth is any more.[154]

In the face of such a forceful presentation, Feuchtwanger's previous doubts regarding the transparency of the prosecution totally evaporated. He found that all of the accused made their confessions in a convincing, genuine manner. He detected no signs of malnutrition or torture, and the individual manner in which they confessed left him in no doubt that the confessions were freely given and the accused were, in fact, guilty as charged.

The contradictions between Feuchtwanger's critical, even hostile, responses during his visit and the unexpected praise that filled the book that followed can be compared to the development of Gide's views. Gide's outspoken praise throughout his trip misled his hosts and did not prepare them for his book criticising the USSR. The main recorded difference between Feuchtwanger's and Gide's visits was that Feuchtwanger was received by Stalin. It is unlikely that Stalin agreed to see him because he was considered to be a more important writer than Gide. Was it in an attempt to prevent another Gide fiasco that Feuchtwanger was exposed to the influence of the great man himself? Was Feuchtwanger granted the interview because of Stalin's ability to influence Western intellectuals – Barbusse, G.B. Shaw, Emil Ludwig and Romain Rolland? Gide's book appeared in November 1936 and Feuchtwanger met Stalin in January 1937. Stalin was clearly prepared for his conversation with Feuchtwanger. His previous experiences of other Western intellectuals would have prepared him for the type of conversation that he would be likely to have with Feuchtwanger. He had been clearly informed about his visitor, his queries and frame of mind: Karavkina's reports, which reached Stalin via Arosev, provided ample material on Feuchtwanger. Feuchtwanger was swayed by Stalin's charisma and was persuaded by his slow but weighty and consistent arguments, which alleviated his previous doubts and which he reproduced in his book. As a theatre lover, Feuchtwanger fell under the spell of Stalin's spectacle, and later the spectacle of the trial. The persuasive tone of Feuchtwanger's book, and its explicit intention to defend the Soviet Union, appears to be genuine and seemingly indicates that, at some point, Feuchtwanger had dismissed his previous doubts and accepted the views of those who had tried to convince him.

Feuchtwanger was the last eminent Western intellectual supportive of the USSR whose visit received major publicity. As VOKS admitted, 'In 1938, following the trials of the anti-Soviet centres in Moscow, the greater part of the Western intelligentsia turned away from the USSR.'[155] Despite the orders given to VOKS to improve and increase its political propaganda abroad, VOKS found it impossible to sustain its activities because of the loss of the support of its former allies within the Soviet administrative system. At this point, it might have seemed that Stalin's government could no longer rely on Western intellectuals or that it had simply lost interest in attracting them. The pre-war history of the Foreign Commission of the Soviet Writers' Union contradicts both these suppositions and demonstrates that, in fact, there were alternative tactics that would allow the USSR to maintain foreign cultural contacts even when other forms of communication had failed.

8 The bond of friendship

Foreign Commission of the Soviet Writers' Union and French writers

The Foreign Commission of the Board of the Soviet Writers' Union (*Inostrannaya Komissiya Pravleniya Soyuza Sovetskikh Pisateley*, or *Inkomissiya*) emerged after the closure of MORP in December 1935.[1] Unlike MORP, the Soviet Writers' Union was a powerful organisation, tightly connected with the Central Committee of the VKP(b) and with Stalin personally.[2]

After MORP was closed, the Foreign Commission took over its headquarters, its journal *International Literature* and some of its staff. Its first Chair, Mikhail Kol'tsov, was a well-known political journalist, an energetic leader and popular with Western writers. His Deputy, and later Chair of the Commission, the writer Mikhail Apletin, was a capable bureaucrat who had mastered the art of looking after foreign intellectuals while working at VOKS and MORP. He was in charge of maintaining relations with foreign writers and further developing the practice of diplomatic, non-aggressive and seemingly non-political rapport. Most of the work was conducted by *referenty* in charge of one or more countries; however, unlike VOKS, the Foreign Commission also relied on the assistance of Soviet writers.[3]

The Foreign Commission was established during the peak of Soviet relations with the West and it began by operating like VOKS, even interacting with the same authors. The Foreign Commission handled foreign writers' translations and publications in the Soviet Union, sent Soviet materials to foreign writers and took care of their requests for assistance. Initially, it brought in foreign visitors, but later it relied on correspondence as its main channel of contact. When I consulted the Commission's documents, kept in the Moscow Russian Archive of Literature and Art (RGALI), I was able to reconstruct the ways in which it had maintained foreign relations: first, after visits by foreign writers had decreased in 1937–39; second, after 1939–40, when the USSR was left with very few loyal supporters; and, third, during World War II, when all cultural relations were disrupted.[4]

The major interest of the Commission's archival documents is its correspondence with French intellectuals, mainly writers and all supporters of the Soviet Union: Romain Rolland, Jean-Richard Bloch, André Malraux, Paul Vaillant-Couturier, Louis Aragon, Elsa Triolet, Luc Durtain, Jean Cassou, Frants Masereel, Paul Nizan, Victor Margueritte, Marcel Cohen, André Chamson, Andrée Viollis and others. There is also correspondence with literary groups and representatives of left-wing magazines, such as *Europe* and *Vendredi*.[5] I found other, complementary correspondence in the archives of individual French writers: Fonds Jean-Richard Bloch and Fonds Romain Rolland in the Bibliothèque Nationale, and Fonds Elsa Triolet in the Centre Louis Aragon–Elsa Triolet, CNRS, in Paris.

This correspondence reveals that the secret of the Commission's successful relations with these writers was that it reached a greater degree of sophistication than other organisations in its personalised, friendly tactics and covert means of influence. Apletin's own personal style of letter writing – friendly and helpful, caring and even intimate – was undoubtedly a legacy of his cooperation with Arosev.

It is enlightening to see how the Foreign Commission adjusted to changing political and international conditions by refining methods of interaction that had been developed earlier by other organisations, and what benefits it managed to gain by these means. A fascinating pattern in the relations between the Commission and French writers appears upon examination of the correspondence between them.

Manufacturing rapport in the early days: 1935–36

At the beginning of its operations, the Foreign Commission worked in ways that were similar to those of VOKS. It invited foreign intellectuals to visit and tried to cement their relations through a direct, face-to-face exchange. In fact, the Soviet Writers' Union had been doing this, and taking care of their visitors' stay, even before the Commission's formal establishment. Its Organising Committee, headed by Mikhail Kol'tsov, had prepared the First Congress of the Soviet Writers' Union and was in charge of bringing foreign writers to the USSR. After the Commission was created, it often looked after foreign writers jointly with other organisations, such as Intourist and VOKS. Its distinct role was to acquaint visitors with Soviet literature and institutions.[6] At this stage, the Commission was conducting its seduction of foreign writers in the same way as other Soviet organisations: by presenting the USSR from an attractive angle. 'The Foreign Commission of the Soviet Writers' Union, Intourist and Soviet reality create all the necessary conditions for these invited writers,' commented Kol'tsov during a May 1936 meeting with Soviet writers.[7] The Commission created individual reception plans *à la* VOKS, which Apletin considered decisive in shaping foreigners' perceptions and ensuring their support for the USSR.

> It is expected that a large number of foreign writers, including major ones, will come to visit this summer. Their stay in the USSR poses a very responsible task for us in terms of working with them. It has to be prepared properly and in advance, because the result of their stay here will have a great impact on their further work in relation to the popularisation of the Soviet Union.[8]

Apletin was conscious of having to accommodate certain visitors, especially the difficult ones. He took particular care of what he described as the set-up for each visit. In the case of Gide who, according to Apletin, 'wasn't a Rolland, but a writer who was less accessible to the Soviet reader', the set-up included planning meetings that would demonstrate to Gide his popularity with Soviet readers. This meant drawing in responsive audiences and preparing conferences attended by scholars, students and the book lovers' circle of the Chemical Faculty, holding literary evenings where writers recited their works, and organising a musical performance.[9] Knowing that 'Gide is the kind of person who dislikes prearranged plans' meant that it was necessary to maintain the illusion of spontaneity. The programme had to avoid the appearance of being staged and yet remain stimulating. 'At the same time, we took Gide's interests into consideration, namely, that he is interested in the issue of the new man and the national republics. It will all be foreseen in our plan.'

As we know, despite the preparations and the fact that Gide responded enthusiastically to what he was shown, this carefully thought-out plan failed. Gide's *Return from the USSR* appeared to be an act of treason to the USSR and the Western Left.[10] Nonetheless, during his stay, Gide had made countless enthusiastic statements and political proclamations,[11] demonstrating, without any doubt, that he was genuinely responding in the way that had been planned and predicted by the Commission.

A significant change in the Commission's approach, compared with that used by VOKS, was that, instead of using interpreters, Soviet writers looked after visitors, making them vital participants in the hosting. Being a writer, Kol'tsov knew that foreign writers had to be treated differently from regular tourists and Foreign Affairs bureaucrats. 'One thing only is lacking, which we have to remind ourselves of all the time: we provide very little personal hospitality by individual Soviet writers,'[12] he said at the Commission's meeting in late May 1936. Tret'yakov, Babel and Pil'nyak were quoted as examples of those who personally welcomed foreigners and invited them to their homes, despite their modest living conditions. Indeed, as related in previous chapters and in memoirs, Dreiser was looked after by Dinamov, and Ehrenburg and Babel played host to Aragon, Bloch and Malraux. Gide spent time with Babel, Pil'nyak and Eisenstein, and was particularly moved by his meeting with Pasternak.

The Commission competed with VOKS over access to foreign writers, and Soviet writers commented on the firm grip held by the VOKS interpreters over their visitors. As Boris Pil'nyak noted, 'they [foreign writers] lately have been "fixed up" (*obstavlyayutsya*) by VOKS in such a way that they have no time to spare. They have an interpreter who makes all the decisions for them.'[13] Neither Kol'tsov nor these Soviet writers were to know that, at this very time, VOKS was accusing them of exerting a negative influence on foreign visitors and that, before long, many of them, including Kol'tsov, would pay dearly for their involvement with foreigners.

But Kol'tsov's reason for encouraging individual Soviet writers to show 'personal initiative' was solely for the benefit of the Soviet Writers' Union. He tried to arrange official assistance, through food parcels, for needy writers in France and

Czechoslovakia and make it look as if it had come spontaneously from individual Soviet writers and not been organised by the Writers' Union. Wary that this 'sausage propaganda' (*kolbasnaya propaganda*) would be too transparent, Kol'tsov proposed ways to make it less obvious:

> It is necessary that specific individuals send it all to other specific individuals, and not by the Soviet Writers' Union, or the Soviet Composers' Union, or the Soviet Architects' Union . . . . The Union will only benefit because the sum of its individual members' noble behaviour serves its general reputation.[14]

This unofficial form of contact had already proven successful, in some important cases, in interactions between Western visitors and individual Soviet intellectuals. Where do we draw the line between Soviet writers' genuine enthusiasm about meeting their Western counterparts and the official tasks imposed upon them by their organisations? In what capacity did Tret'yakov, the former Futurist and MORP member, relate to Jean-Richard Bloch; or Babel to Malraux; or Il'f and Petrov to Feuchtwanger? Indeed, French and Soviet writers sought these contacts and sustained their friendships because they themselves wanted to, regardless of whether the meetings had been arranged by VOKS, the Foreign Commissions or the writers themselves. However, we also know that Bloch never suspected that the intriguing and mysterious Lev El'bert, who accompanied him to the Caucasus and was an endless source of information, was a 'special designation' NKVD official.[15]

In the footsteps of VOKS: the Foreign Commission in 1935–39

The Foreign Commission initially acquired its visitors in the same way as VOKS and, in the main, they were already sympathisers. They were introduced by their French colleagues: for example, Romain Rolland sent Georges Friedmann, his former student and 'a very good and honest person',[16] and Friedmann, in turn, recommended Gabrielle Duchêne, 'one of the oldest and most loyal fighters (*militantes*) and friends of the USSR'.[17] Most of these people were already sympathetic to the USSR before their contact with Soviet agencies.

Correspondence provides solid evidence that the enthusiasm and support of the visitors often grew while they were in the Soviet Union and that they committed themselves to promoting the USSR on their return to France. Their letters to the Foreign Commission provide more reliable evidence of this than the self-interested, second-hand reports of the VOKS guides. In a thank-you letter sent at the end of his trip, André Chamson expressed his admiration for 'the Republic of Equality and Labour' which had embarked on 'the great road of building Socialism and broadening culture'.[18] 'Thank you for everything. I will write to you from Paris, where I will be very busy informing as many people as possible about everything good, beautiful and great I have seen,' wrote Marcel Cohen after his visit in 1938.[19]

But the Foreign Commission's correspondence was more than a polite exchange of thank-you notes. In the late 1930s, it became the main working channel through which the Commission assisted French writers and maintained a close rapport with them. Apletin's personal efforts were central to this. Barghoorn states that, in the post-war period, 'this affable man probably did all that was possible to put foreign writers and literary scholars in touch with Soviet colleagues'. The same was true in the Commission's early days. Even though, unlike Arosev, Apletin spoke no foreign languages and had not been friends with Western writers, his letters, translated into French and possibly drafted by a *referent* on his instructions, have an undeniable personal style. Apletin began by picking up MORP's old contacts. In a letter to Jean Cassou, he introduced the Commission as MORP's heir and assured Cassou that the books that he had sent to MORP for Bela Illes and Sergey Dinamov would reach them through the assistance of the Foreign Commission.[20] (Indeed, Dinamov remained the editor of *International Literature*, which had become the Foreign Commission's journal.) Apletin then invited Cassou to cooperate with the Commission and encouraged him to send his new works and offered to send him Soviet literature.

Apletin's letters show little evidence of attempts to influence or manipulate French writers. There seemed to be no apparent motivation or obvious benefits; Apletin seldom requested anything and, above all, he presented the Commission as a generous, altruistic body, which makes it difficult to unravel the mechanism of influence. It involves a feat of detection to demonstrate that such exchanges represented a subtle and almost imperceptible form of propaganda. At a time when the Writers' Union treated Soviet writers with an unpredictable mixture of rewards and repression, its treatment of foreign supporters relied only on encouragement and rewards.

Like VOKS, the Commission took care of the writers' concerns and business affairs by providing an array of services. Apletin represented the writers to other institutions and individuals, and helped them with various requests. He wrote to the International Organisation of Assistance to Revolutionaries (MOPR)[21] on behalf of Gabrielle Duchêne, 'one of the leaders of the women's anti-Fascist committee', and intervened on J.-R. Bloch's behalf when his daughter was refused an entry visa to the USSR. It was Apletin who sent Rolland's writings to various publishers: an article on the French Revolution to *The Marxist Historian* (*Istorik marksist*)[22] and a translation of his letter to Erlich, editor of the *SSSR na stroyke*.[23]

Apletin tried to be dependable in his dealings with foreigners, possibly a lesson learned from VOKS. He singled out Romain Rolland as being a writer who especially needed regular supplies of printed materials. 'As a very first thing, it is necessary to collect every book of Romain Rolland's you have published [and send them] to him.'[24] In fact, Apletin believed that sending foreign writers every piece of information about them that appeared in the USSR, or copies of their published and translated works, was of major importance 'in the establishment and strengthening of cultural relations between foreign writers and the Soviet Writers' Union'.[25] He thus asked the Soviet Writers' Union to obtain all of the available translations of foreign writers from all of the relevant publishing houses for shipment to France.

At the same time, it is hard not to notice the distinctly artificial side of Apletin's correspondence, which, to begin with, he generated. After initially asking Rolland to send birthday greetings to an old Kazakh poet, Dzhambul, Apletin acted as if their exchange had been spontaneous and the relations genuine. 'Thank you very much for your greetings to Dzhambul. They made a very strong impression [on him],'[26] he wrote to Rolland. He then informed Rolland about the publicity these greetings were given in the USSR: 'The original was reprinted in the *Literary Gazette* as a facsimile on 25 May.'

Apletin tried to create publicity around the French–Soviet exchange, in both France and the USSR. When he sent 139 Soviet cuttings on Balzac and twenty-six on Beaumarchais to René Blech for the International Writers' Association, he suggested that Blech mention it in the press. 'Perhaps it would be good if you could mention this fact, even in a few lines, to demonstrate these cultural ties.'[27] Was this simply to create a picture of the friendship between the USSR and eminent Western figures and show their support for the USSR? After all, these letters were also sent to the Soviet press for domestic propaganda. Kol'tsov asked J.-R. Bloch to write a six- to eight-page article for *Pravda*,[28] and a handwritten note on Chamson's letter of thanks for his visit says, 'To be published in the *Literaturnaya gazeta*.'[29]

Finally, it is evident that Apletin wanted to remain in charge of the contacts that he had generated. When asking Aragon to respond to a Soviet student who wished to research his work, Apletin instructed him to correspond through the Commission. 'If you can possibly answer him, could you please do it through us as intermediaries.'[30] The purpose of using French writers' letters sometimes remains unclear. For example, one can only guess why, and on whose request, Apletin sent the letters of Rolland and his wife to the Agitprop of the Communist Party Central Committee, requesting them to be returned 'after use'.[31]

Friendship by correspondence

Apletin's letters make the reader believe that perhaps his main purpose was the long-term building of a rapport with individual writers. As I have noted, his approach to letter writing was similar to that of Arosev's, and his letters sounded personal in style and content. He often sent greetings that made French writers' birthdays and literary successes sound as if they were the cause of national celebrations in the USSR. That old friend of the Soviet Writers' Union, Romain Rolland, received countless greetings for his seventieth birthday from the Writers' Union, the Composers' Union, the Academy of Science, workers in politico-cultural institutions and individuals, for example Nikolay Ostrovsky, Stanislavsky, Meyerhold and Nemirovich-Danchenko.[32] On 29 January 1936, the Foreign Commission really did put on a celebration of Rolland's seventieth birthday, and an official evening was broadcast on radio.[33] In fact, an entire file of the Foreign Commission contains materials from the Soviet press about the celebration of Rolland's seventieth birthday.[34]

Apletin's letters are striking for their undisguised flattery. He flattered French writers by following their literary success in France. 'Warm congratulations great success well deserved Thank you for book Regards to Elsa Apletin,' reads Apletin's telegram to Aragon.[35] In many letters, Apletin posed as a personal fan. 'I found your articles about Spain in the recent editions of *Europe* extremely interesting. I impatiently await your book *Espagne, Espagne* and will be very grateful if you would send it to me, as well as *Birth of a Culture*,'[36] he wrote to Bloch. Had he really read and admired Bloch's book, or was it a rapport-building tactic based on giving a writer the recognition that all writers crave?

Many of Apletin's letters were dedicated to the celebration of French writing in the USSR. VOKS manufactured Western artists' fame in the Soviet press, museums, the artistic and literary community and with the public; in the same way, the Commission boosted publicity, and Soviet newspapers and magazines, including the Commission's journal *International Literature*, praised French writers' work and published translations of them. Apletin congratulated Vaillant-Couturier on the success of his book *The Misfortune of Being Young* in the USSR, listing reviews in the newspapers *Omskaya Pravda, Severnyy komsomolets, Rabochaya Moskva* and *Sovetskoye metro*.[37] Apletin's letters read as if they represented the entire Soviet readership.

> Your book has had an enormous success in our country. The men and events described in it, as well as the author's ardent appeals, make a strong impression on the readers. Please allow me to congratulate you once again on your book's huge success in our country,[38]

he wrote to J.-R. Bloch on the success of *Espagne, Espagne*. Messages that he passed on from Soviet readers, often workers and peasants, created the impression that the popularity of French writers in the USSR was spontaneous. Even less well-known writers, like Francis Jourdain, would be made to think that their lives and works were widely known in the USSR when Apletin wrote, 'Please allow me to add to it here the warm and sincere voices of the numerous Soviet friends who have long been yours in every artistic and literary circle of the USSR.'[39] The Dnepropetrovsk railway workers were said to send Malraux, 'the outstanding writer of the French people and its revolutionary traditions', their 'warm proletarian greetings'. The message that Malraux had a massive audience in the USSR was reinforced by their request for his new books. However, it was also made to sound as if Malraux's literary value resided in his books being a powerful weapon in the anti-Fascist struggle.

> We await new books – missiles in the struggle against the Fascist reactionaries – from André Malraux, passionate fighter against Fascist barbarity, a major, honest and truthful artist who donated his talent and his ardent heart to the service of the revolutionary working masses, who are struggling for new conditions of human existence. We ask our comrade André Malraux, comrade-in-arms to Henri Barbusse and Romain Rolland, to send from us, the workers – readers of his work – greetings to all the workers in art and culture

in the western countries, who are aligning in a united anti-Fascist front for peace, labour, freedom and the defence of the Soviet Union.[40]

In addition to sending the traditional Russian wishes ('please accept our heartiest wishes for long life and good health'), Apletin's letters also sounded as if they were showing appreciation for political support in the anti-Fascist struggle.

> Your unyielding avant-garde actions, both in the arts and in the political arena, including your tireless and continual statements in defence of all the victims of the sinister Fascist henchmen in all the countries that have fallen under their savage domination, your unyielding loyalty to all humanitarian causes, primarily those of the exploited and persecuted proletariat, have also earned you numerous warm friendships in our country. We are happy to be their most cordial spokesmen.[41]

To add weight to his congratulations, Apletin sent numerous clippings from the Soviet press praising foreign authors. To Aragon, he sent a copy of *Literary Review* (*Literaturnoye obozreniye*), which included his portrait and an article on his work,[42] and to Jean Cassou, a Soviet edition of *Romancero de la guerre civile*.[43] To Nizan, he sent a Ukrainian translation of his *Antoine Bloyer*[44] (a text that Nizan and his wife had arranged to be translated for the Soviet magazine *Our Achievements*[45]) and a special 1937 issue of *International Literature*, which included his literary portrait and a photo.[46] All available media were used to promote the work of foreign writers in the USSR. Apletin informed Bloch about one of his stories being broadcast on the radio[47] and Rolland about a radio broadcast of the adaptation of his *Jeune Beethoven*.[48]

When French writers' works were published in the Soviet Union, making them famous, this fame was fed back into the loop to make sure that contact with the writers continued. 'In view of [our] great interest in your work, we would like to ask you to remember the Foreign Commission of the Soviet Writers' Union, especially when your new works appear,' read the letter to Jean Cassou.[49] When the French writers returned home, the Foreign Commission intensified its efforts, using publicity as encouragement and reward. Following Chamson's trip, Apletin sent him a newspaper cutting of a speech he had made, a *Pravda* article on his work by Anisimov[50] and, later, a Russian issue of *International Literature* containing his novellas ('which were of great interest to Soviet writers').[51] Following his 1936 visit, Malraux was sent forty-six newspaper cuttings from twenty-eight different newspapers (including factory, village, district, republican and Moscow papers) that documented his stay in the USSR. These cuttings dealt with, for example, meetings with his readers at a plant, with students of the Institute of Philosophy and with representatives of the Komsomol, and visits to the offices of *Pravda*, to Maxim Gorky and to the Soviet Writers' Union. Included in the packet were greetings from readers and fans (among them, *udarnye rabochiye*, 'shock workers' on the Stalin Railway).[52]

Financial incentives, on the other hand, were difficult to provide because roubles could not be taken outside the USSR; however, the Commission and *Inter-*

national Literature used royalties to entice foreign writers to come back to the USSR so that they could spend their royalties there. 'The author's rights for your novellas have been deposited in your name in the Moscow bank and are awaiting you.'[53] Indeed, Jean-Richard Bloch was delighted to discover, upon his arrival in the USSR, that he had at his disposal 'a tidy little sum' from his previous publications in the USSR,[54] and Durtain and Vildrac were reminded, before their arrival in 1935, that their royalties were waiting for them.[55]

From today's perspective, these clippings may seem to be no more than mementos; however, they were clearly important to their addressees and provided the recognition that every artist craves. Who could resist the seduction of fame when it was of a magnitude that only the USSR could offer? We can recall that Rolland complained when VOKS failed to send him his clippings. Among the pages of their *Journal du voyage en URSS*, the Blochs carefully preserved clippings that documented their 1934 visit: photographs of Jean-Richard, and statements and articles by him.

The fact that French writers were receptive to this recognition and publicity is reflected in the language of their replies, which often mirrored the language of the Soviet newspaper articles, the letters from the Commission and the fervour of the greetings. Even a writer of international importance like Rolland responded by acknowledging his devotion to the Soviet state.

> Do not doubt my fraternal devotion to the USSR. The fact that I witnessed the victory of the USSR and the creation of a new world makes me happy in my old age (my heart is [still] young). (…) I am sure that we are about to enter a great era for arts nourished by the living juices of the profound folk art of the various nations of your Union. Music and poetry will advance. They are ready to spring up everywhere in your country, and all the other arts will soon follow suit.[56]

Supplying materials to writers

The Foreign Commission took care to hide its true intentions in its personal dealings with writers; this was also true of the supply of Soviet literature sent to French writers. What was intended to pass as genuine assistance, offered in an impartial spirit of learning, also had a strong undercurrent of refined propaganda.

Apletin typically made it sound as if he were sending material to French writers to inform them individually about Soviet literary events, such as the 750th anniversary of the Georgian poet Rustaveli[57] or the forthcoming seventy-fifth anniversary of the work of the Kazakh poet Dzhambul (with his poems attached).[58] Georges Friedmann regularly received *Journal de Moscou*, and Dinamov and Chamson conducted an exchange of *International Literature* and *Vendredi*.[59] Publications were sent to those French writers who were expected to be interested in them: to Friedmann, who had asked for specific philosophical and sociological works; to Nizan, who received a new edition of Marx;[60] and to Romain Rolland, who was sent a copy of *Suliko*, Stalin's favourite song.[61]

From around 1937 onwards, these materials became distinctly political. Apletin sent Stalin's speeches and his *Brief Course of the History of the VKP(b)*,[62] and Molotov's report, *The Third Five-Year Plan and the Soviet National Economy (1939–1942)*, translated into French. Apletin explained to Julien Benda that Stalin's *Brief History* was 'an important event in the spiritual life of our country';[63] it should interest any writer with profound judgement, Apletin noted, as it helped one to understand the USSR better.[64] Identical personalised letters with the same message were addressed to a group of other 'writers with profound judgement': Romain Rolland, Francis Jourdain, Charles Vildrac, Pierre Unik, Martin-Chauffier, Claude Aveline, Paul Nizan and possibly some others.[65]

Some writers responded with enthusiasm to the Soviet literature they had been sent. 'I am reading with great interest and admiration Yu. Krymov's remarkable novel *Derbent the Tanker* published by your magazine *International Literature*,' wrote Georges Friedmann to Apletin.[66] It is possible that Apletin knew that he would strike a responsive chord in Friedmann with the doubtless riveting tale of an oil tanker; on the other hand, perhaps he was just plugging away at the same old song.

Even if that were the case, there was another motivation. Like VOKS, the Commission was looking for opportunities to get Soviet materials published in the West. When asking the Academy of Sciences of the USSR to assist André Ribard, Apletin reminded them that Ribard, an active member of the Popular Front and a supporter of the USSR, would be able to publish Soviet historians' works in his magazine.[67] However, Apletin was more subtle when using French writers directly for this purpose.

The last paragraph of Apletin's letters routinely contained a subtle suggestion that French writers should use the enclosed materials to write a review or as the basis for some other publication, either in France or in the USSR. At the end of his letter to Aragon about Dzhambul's anniversary, which included a copy of Dzhambul's poems, Apletin made a request. 'Perhaps your or some other French newspapers could publish an account of this book. We shall be happy to pass your birthday greetings to the poet if you could kindly send them to us.'[68] Marcel Cohen,[69] Jean Cassou[70] and Aragon[71] all received identical letters asking them to publicise Molotov's speech on the Third Five-Year Plan. These oblique requests came with promises to have their reviews published in the Soviet press. 'If you happen to make some observations about this document in a French magazine or newspaper, and if you could kindly send us a copy, it will be our pleasure to publish it in our press.' Without appearing to pressure French writers, these letters appealed to their desire to be part of the communal cause by showing assistance and good will. 'If you consider it useful to express your opinion about the issues touched upon here, we will be happy to pass it on to our readers,' Apletin suggested to Nizan.[72]

For the twentieth anniversary of the October Revolution, Apletin made a whole series of requests. In 1935, while serving as the Secretary of MORP, he had planned to prepare a collection of articles by eminent foreign writers that were dedicated to the anniversary. These plans were now realised through the Commission's special publication *Les écrivains du monde sur l'URSS*.[73] Apletin had asked Malraux, Bloch, Nizan and other French writers for contributions in the form of a four- or five-page article.[74] He and Dinamov, as the editor-in-chief of *International Literature*, made it sound as if these French writers – 'the best representatives of foreign literature' – were being given the honour of being chosen; their publications, they were told, would attract the attention of the better part of humanity.[75]

Though he was using flattery to appeal to foreign writers to act as spokesmen for the Commission, Apletin wished, at the same time, to control the process and the result. He appeared to be undemanding, allowing the writer a certain freedom; if time did not permit, the author was free to limit himself to a brief comment or an essay – 'perhaps you could send us some reflections?'[76] So that this did not appear to be an order, writers were free to chose their preferred genre.

> However, we would ask you not to consider these questions as a schematic plan or a questionnaire but only as a draft of points, according to which the articles will appear in the volume. (...) The choice of genre and the form of your article is naturally yours to choose,

he wrote to Jean-Richard Bloch.[77] But flexible as these requests sounded, the subject matter was, in fact, closely restricted, ranging from socialist construction to Stalin's constitution, with a compulsory glorifying slant.

> Perhaps, if it is not too difficult, you could express your opinion on Soviet economic and cultural construction, especially on those aspects that interest you in a concrete way, that is the Soviet people and the solution of the national question. We will be happy to publish your opinion on the effect the USSR has had on culture and on the cause of the defence of peace, as well as your opinion on Stalin's Soviet Constitution.[78]

The Commission and *International Literature* were, in fact, asking French writers to publish ready-made Soviet messages as their own. In some cases, Apletin and Dinamov asked them to reprint ready-made texts in the French press. They were quite direct with proven supporters. 'I am sending you the intellectuals' appeal. I think it would be useful to publish it in the press,'[79] Apletin wrote to Aragon. Dinamov sent texts to Chamson for publication in *Vendredi*.[80] Vaillant-Couturier was sent Marshak's fables in translation, to be published on the 'Page d'enfants' in *l'Humanité* or *Mon camarade*.[81] Nizan, who had been sent Vishnevsky's *Nous tous, peuple russe*, V. Katanyan's biography of Mayakovsky and documentation on proletarian literature, was asked to provide a review.[82] French writers wrote to confirm their acceptance; witness Friedmann in his letter to Apletin, addressing him with the familiar 'tu', 'I hope you have received my article for the volume on the twentieth anniversary.'[83]

Confirmations of this sort are really superfluous given that so much of this material did actually appear in the French press. Accompanying these materials are the newly uncovered dispatches and personal requests addressed to the French intelligentsia; it is these that provide an insight into how the materials managed to achieve publication in France. One of the goals of Soviet cultural organisations in the 1920s was to find 'conduits of Soviet influence' in the French media; the archives of the Commission reveal how artfully its staff maintained an array of personal relationships with French intellectuals to achieve that end.

Emissaries, advisers and informants

French writers were more than Soviet spokesmen in cultural and political matters – they acted as the Foreign Commission's emissaries, advisers and sources of valuable information. As sources of information, they sometimes acted on requests from the Commission and sometimes on their own initiative. Dinamov did ask Aragon to send him talks given by Malraux, Nizan and Moussinac at the Maison de la Culture, possibly for publication in *International Literature*.[84] On the other hand, it is unclear whether Friedmann had been asked to inform the Commission about presentations by l'Association pour l'étude de la culture soviétique (formerly Russie Neuve) or whether he had been asked about issues debated in *Europe*, the contents of some forthcoming articles, including his own, and the creation of a new society, l'Union des intellectuels français pour la justice, la paix et la liberté.[85] It seems possible that Friedmann was acting voluntarily, while being aware that Apletin would be interested in this information.

Some French writers acted as, and were considered to be, Soviet emissaries in the West. When the USSR did not reply to the organisers' invitation to participate in the International Folklore Congress, Friedmann alerted Apletin. In fact, he wrote to Apletin at the organisers' request, describing as deplorable the possible absence of the Soviet delegation in view of the importance of Soviet contributions to the subject. '[Your] absence will be even less comprehensible considering that the richness of Soviet folklore is well known, as well as your scholarly research in this area.'[86] He urged Apletin to make sure that a Soviet delegation was sent 'for the benefit of Soviet cultural and other interests'.

Supporters gave constructive comments and advice when they felt that the USSR needed help. The protocols of the Commission's meetings with Soviet writers and foreign visitors provide fascinating evidence of this. During a meeting in 1936, Malraux gave a detailed critique of Soviet cinema and art, speaking about its reception by audiences in France and suggesting how to improve Soviet cultural propaganda targeted at French audiences. His remarks echo the disappointment in the French press at the lack of new, revolutionary art, and his own comments at the First Congress of the Soviet Writers' Union in 1934. Malraux compared *We of Kronstadt*, a film he considered to be talented but uneven, having no style of its own and unconvincing passages, with earlier Soviet classics.[87] He accused *Chapayev*, another film that was popular in France, of having the same lack of style. 'One shot has been taken from Eisenstein, another one from Pudovkin, the third one is simply mediocre, and it [the film] fails to achieve artistic unity.'[88] He believed that oversimplification in Soviet literature and art had led to 'a mixture of Pasternak with Panferov'; he objected to the glossing over of difficulties, believing that a work of art could only be engaging and convincing by honest confrontation, as was Sholokhov's *Virgin Soil Upturned*. 'The moment Sholokhov shows a fraction of the difficulties, his work comes to life and becomes interesting and involving.' Malraux was in favour of showing Soviet theatre and cinema in France and believed that bringing the four or five best Soviet films, and Meyerhold's theatre, for a tour would make the work of the International Writers' Association for the Defence of Culture interesting and useful. As for *We of Kronstad*, he believed that it 'would make a great impression but it won't be the same triumph of Soviet cinematography that some of Eisenstein's and Pudovkin's films were'. Malraux also knew that Eisenstein was filming a new feature, *The Bezhin Meadow*. 'Babel told me that Eisenstein is making a wonderful film. Perhaps, thanks to this film, Soviet cinema will become, once again, number one in the world.'[89] However, *The Bezhin Meadow* would never be completed – it was banned because of its 'erroneous viewpoint'.

Malraux clearly had Soviet interests at heart but there was little chance that his advice could be taken because it contradicted the ideological rigidity of the Soviet arts in the 1930s. Socialist realism had already taken over as the only creative method, and going against it was unthinkable.

There were also political reasons why the Foreign Commission was unable to follow its sympathisers' advice. Like Malraux, Louis Aragon tried to help resolve the critical situation of the French version of *International Literature*. In June 1938, its French distributors, the left-wing Editions sociales internationales, brought the fall in popularity and sales of the magazine in France to the attention of the Soviet publishing house Mezhdunarodnaya kniga (International Books).[90] The magazine, the distributor said, was being sent irregularly, was insufficiently lively and did not provide an adequate reflection of Soviet intellectual life.

A Soviet official, R. Maghidov, Chairman of the Central Committee of the Polygraphic Industry Workers, consulted Louis Aragon in Paris; in January 1939, Maghidov reported Aragon's views on the problems and the ways of overcoming them to Rokotov, the magazine's new editor-in-chief, having replaced Dinamov.[91] In Aragon's opinion, the magazine suffered from being seen as an overt propaganda medium, which was apparent in both its marketing and its content. Part of each issue was distributed gratis and the French translations it contained were of poor quality; both of these factors lowered its status and alienated French writers who, once they had published in it, forfeited the opportunity for further publication in France. To solve this array of problems, Aragon proposed making Jean Fouquet, Head of the literary section of *Ce soir*, the French representative of *International Literature*. He would assist the magazine with practical issues, ensure adequate contacts with French writers, select books to be sent to Moscow and keep the editors aware of creative trends in France. Aragon also offered to provide his own help to the representative.

Aragon was frank in pointing out that overt propaganda was inefficient: French authors did not relate to *International Literature* because it had stopped being a literary magazine and turned into a monthly version of *Journal de Moscou*, 'celebrating political occasions and allowing its content to be dominated by these political dates and other purely political considerations'.[92] Like Malraux, Aragon provided constructive ideas, suggesting that novels, stories, plays and articles on literature and the arts be selected for publication. Like Malraux, he called for a discussion of more complex issues, such as writers' creativity (both successes and failures), and for more information to be given on writers from countries such as the USA and Britain. Old and once reliable methods would not engage the cooperation of French writers any more.

> Until then, French writers will not reply willingly to the editors' questions and requests to express their opinion on such and such topic. In this order of things, Aragon does not find it sensible to discuss general issues, which are, by the way, almost always political issues. He insists that *Littérature internationale* must be, above all, a literary magazine.[93]

It is hardly surprising, though, that the Commission disregarded Aragon's judgement. Instead of acting on his advice, Apletin reported on the 'inadmissible state of distribution of the French version of *International Literature* abroad' to A. Fadeev, the Head of the Board of the Soviet Writers' Union.[94] Apletin wrote that, since 1937, 50–60 per cent of the copies had failed to sell. Ignoring the problems identified by the distributors and Aragon, Apletin put all of the blame onto the distributor. 'The distribution is in the hands of Hachette, who is a Fascist and who, of course, deliberately keeps Soviet magazines in basements and returns such a striking percentage of them.'[95] There is no evidence that any further attempts were made to change the content of the magazine, publication of which ended in 1943. VOKS's attempts of 1939 to take over *International Literature* and make it its own journal did not succeed.[96]

Apletin's response to Aragon's suggestions, and his blatant shifting of blame, may come as a surprise. Strikingly different from his usual obliging tone found in correspondence with foreign writers, it also differs from his chatty cynical tone which is often found in VOKS's internal correspondence. When it comes to his report about *International Literature*, Apletin's style fits in with F. Barghoorn's characterisation of him as the author of 'conventionally chauvinistic work' reserved for domestic consumption and internal correspondence.

> Apletin, like many other Soviet cultural functionaries, is a charming and gracious person. It was, therefore, disconcerting to find, in the Moscow Library of Foreign Literature, a conventionally chauvinistic work by him on *The World Role of Soviet Literature*. The contrast between what Soviet intellectuals, officials, and party leaders are likely to say in conversation with non-communist foreigners and what they say and write for domestic consumption is one of the most discouraging aspects of their behaviour.[97]

Apletin's 'triplespeak' cannot be attributed exclusively to his chameleon-like personality; he was helpless against the current political conditions. The issue of *International Literature* was raised in January 1939, a year after Dinamov, the magazine's editor-in-chief, had been removed from his position and arrested. He shared the fate of other Soviet writers and of MORP, VOKS and Comintern staff who disappeared during the purges. In this climate of suspicion and mass accusations, how could the Foreign Commission expose itself by accepting any blame for problems associated with the magazine? Blaming a foreign, 'Fascist' publisher for the problem was the only way that the Commission could justify its behaviour without directly endangering any participants.

Malraux and Aragon's assistance could not change either the course of Soviet politics or that of the Foreign Commission; nor did the advice of Broun, the VOKS representative in Paris, carry any weight. This closed mentality meant that a number of potential avenues of Soviet cultural propaganda in the West were left unexplored. In fact, in 1937, the Foreign Commission returned to using more overt tactics of political propaganda. It was not in the power of either Apletin or the staff of *International Literature* to refine the tactics that had clearly become ineffective in reaching French educated and literary circles.

French writers as a source of unofficial information

Among the favours that French supporters performed for the Commission was being a source of information that the Commission could not obtain in other ways. Monitoring only the mainstream and left-wing French press, the Commission obtained limited information. To whom could it turn when it suspected that adverse information was being circulated about the USSR and Soviet culture? When André Mazon claimed that *Slovo o polku Igoreve* (*Song of Igor's Campaign*), an epic about the unsuccessful campaign mounted by Prince Igor, did not date from the late twelfth century but was an eighteenth-century fake, Apletin asked Aragon to report on any opinions that would not otherwise come to the attention of the Foreign Commission.

> We would be very happy to learn what the French magazines and newspapers say about our literature. We are not referring to newspapers and magazines known to everyone. The lack of this kind of information, even if we were to receive it [only] through letters, sometimes leads to very unpleasant occurrences.[98]

In some instances, friends of the Commission informed it about attacks against the USSR and what they had done to defend it – an initiative reminiscent of that described in VOKS's report of the early 1930s, 'How friends of the USSR act abroad in its defence'.[99] Following the publication of André Gide's *Retour de l'URSS*, Georges Friedmann described to Apletin how he had participated in debates by writing an article, 'stern in content', addressed to Gide and published in *Europe*.[100] He also claimed that this article had an impact on Gide. 'I only know that my article in *Europe* made a strong impression on him and that apparently I made him think about several points.'[101] While many other supporters also wrote anti-Gide articles, Friedmann reported his actions to the Commission. Whether or not this report had been requested by the Foreign Commission, there is no doubt that Friedmann wanted the Commission to know about his efforts.

Other writers ingratiated themselves with their Soviet friends even at the cost of being indiscreet and disloyal towards their French colleagues. In 1939, *Vendredi*, the Commission's important left-wing channel, which had flourished at the time of the Popular Front, closed. Georges Friedmann was unwilling to reveal, in a letter, complex issues about its closure, which Apletin, unable to obtain information, had asked him to do.[102] Yet René Blech readily revealed the internal details that he knew. 'I know its [*Vendredi*'s] former editors very well and am well aware of both the details of its existence and those of its so-called death.'[103] Having outlined the precarious financial circumstances of magazines in France and the recent withdrawal of support for *Vendredi* by Daladier, Blech proceeded to give a biting characterisation of two other *Vendredi* members and friends of the Commission, Jean Guéhenno and André Chamson. Blech described Chamson as an amoral individual.

> This man has absolutely no principles and is amoral; he is the type of political writer who ingratiates himself to the strong of this world and who has no convictions whatsoever, except that he must derive the maximum benefit possible.

Guéhenno, according to Blech, was 'even worse' (*tut delo obstoit yescho khuzhe*) – 'a self-satisfied, narrow, [but] personally honest and convinced "bleating pacifist" who is assured that he knows [God's] truth'.[104] While Moussinac had acted on VOKS's instructions and Friedmann genuinely volunteered in defence of the USSR, it is unclear what motivated Blech's venom, apart from personal animosity.

Apletin's cultivation of friendly relations between the Foreign Commission and French writers, bestowing favours upon them and encouraging gratitude on their part, led to a dynamic in which these writers, prompted or not, displayed a greater loyalty to the Commission than to their own country and colleagues. Some provided advice to improve Soviet propaganda techniques in the West (Malraux and Aragon) while others participated in orchestrated campaigns against opponents of the Soviet Union (Friedmann) or revealed internal information and reported on colleagues (Blech). Whatever prompted these actions, and regardless of whether their personal motivation was selfless or selfish (e.g. a desire to gain the Commission's approval or to inflict personal revenge), the Commission clearly encouraged this behaviour, even when it could derive no tangible benefit from the information offered.

Adjusting to new conditions: 1939–45

The 1939 Molotov–Ribbentrop Pact and the 1940 Soviet invasion of Finland resulted in vehement public protests and left the USSR with virtually no supporters. The Commission's relations with its very few remaining friends became further

complicated because a large number of Soviet writers, major figures in its relations with Western writers, were no longer there. Of the 101 writers elected as
Board members at the First Soviet Writers' Union Congress, thirty-three were
found to be 'enemies of the people'. Out of 597 delegates attending this Congress,
180 suffered from Stalinist repression.[105] Nonetheless, the Foreign Commission
managed to maintain its French contacts after 1939, even though they became
very limited. Who were the French writers who remained loyal to the USSR, and
how did the Commission continue to interact with them in these difficult times?

Monitoring the French allies

Until 1939, the Commission followed its supporters' actions by surveying the left-
wing French periodicals. Its archives contain summary reports, *svodki*, routinely
compiled by, for example, Natalia Kamionskaya, a *referent* and former translator
at MORP.[106] These reports, written in Russian, contain a record of all of the articles about the USSR that were published in the left-wing French (and occasional-
ly other non-Soviet) newspapers and magazines: *Lu, Vu, Europe, Cahier de l'art,
l'Humanité, Est, NRF, Commune, L'Art vivant, Mercure de France, Les nouvelles
littéraires, Vendredi* and *Marianne*.[107] *Svodki* listed the Soviet works and authors
reviewed and promoted by these magazines; it is easy to recognise those 'export-
ed' by MORP and recommended by the Comintern. The authors of *svodki* kept
watch on Western writers and recorded their actions as spokesmen for the Soviet
Union. The list of names, almost identical to the VOKS list of potential sympathisers of the 1920s, includes all of the major figures of the French literary Left. A
significant part of the *svodki* was to note the political support that was offered by
these figures, including that offered to causes adopted by the USSR, mainly protests against Fascism and against war waged on the USSR.[108] The Commission's
political interests in *svodki* were as undisguised as those of MORP.

With the banning of the Communist and pro-Communist press in France in
1939, the Commission lost both its forum in France and its source of information
about French intellectual circles. It now had to rely on non-French newspapers
– the German *Parizer Tageszeitung*, the *New York Times*, the British and American
Daily Worker – to enable it to monitor supporters and compile summary reports.
Although entitled 'Reviews of French literary life', these new reports focus on
the public response to Soviet policies and on the mood and activities of Soviet
supporters.[109]

The reports do not attempt to embellish the image of the USSR that prevailed
in France. They reflect the severing of most of the Commission's links with the
French literary scene and its attempts to continue receiving this information in any
way it could. Alongside a report about the publication of Elsa Triolet's *Memoirs of
the 1939 War*[110] are reports that monitor the involvement of French writers in the
war: for example, Malraux's volunteering,[111] and the call-up of Chamson, Eluard
and Friedmann.[112]

In 1939–40, summaries of non-French newspapers reported censorship and
repression by Daladier's government, with attacks on culture and on the French

Left: the confiscation of thousands of books from private libraries by the French police; the confiscation of the writings of Communist and socialist writers, including Gorky, from the Editions Sociales Internationales; the burning of Maurice Thorez' library, kept in the Ivry Municipality, by the Prefecture; and the raid on the premises of the International Writers' Association for the Defence of Culture, followed by the confiscation of all of its documents and the closure of the Association.[113] Testimonies of support for the USSR now almost completely ceased. The exception was Maurice Thorez' discrediting of Nizan, who had publicly condemned the Molotov–Ribbentrop Agreement and left the FCP. In an article entitled 'Maurice Thorez unmasks Nizan', Nizan was accused of being a police agent and a traitor.[114] From 1939 to 1940, the rest of the former supporters were reported as having distanced themselves and being disapproving of Soviet policies. In fact, protests against the assault on Finland were reported in the French press, with Paul Valery, Georges Duhamel, Jean Perrin, Victor Basch and other French intellectuals who were formerly sympathetic to the USSR signing an open letter against the Soviet offensive.[115] Negative statements about the USSR were also made by Duhamel[116] and Chamson.[117]

In the Commission's reports, critical statements by former allies were often underlined or included handwritten comments; these critical statements include accounts of the appeal against the Finnish war that were signed by Duhamel, Perrin and Basch.[118] Handwritten comments in the margin of one report note Chamson's depression, low spirits and anti-pacifist attitude. The comment 'Summary report is not to be released' was added to virtually anything else that was written by former allies in protest against the Finnish war, for example next to a report about a protest against the Finnish war that was published in *Parizer Zeitung* on 1 February 1940.

It is probable that the Commission monitored French public opinion through the foreign press so that it could provide information to other Soviet agencies at a stage when other legitimate channels were cut off. One area of focus was the attitude of French writers towards their country's war against Hitler, which France declared on 3 September 1939. In accordance with Stalin's instructions, the Comintern leadership had sent directives to Communist parties on 8–9 September 1939; the comrades were to make statements against the war, to discredit its imperialist nature, to vote (wherever there were Communist deputies) against military appropriations and to tell the masses that the war would bring them nothing but hardship and devastation. Most French writers, however, did not follow this directive.[119] Information on French opinion leaders' responses to the war supplied by the Commission showed that no one was taking the anti-war line. In a letter of 30 December 1939, an official who called himself 'Friedrich' explained why information on the political positions of foreign writers was limited.

> Unfortunately, we are unable to provide a report on all the writers whose names are given in the list you sent us. The majority of the writers named have refrained, since the beginning of the war, from any political position, and it is extremely difficult to obtain precise information on their attitude towards the war and the USSR.[120]

Friedrich supplied information only on Rolland and Margueritte, neither of whom condemned the war. From the beginning, Rolland had sent Daladier a statement of support for the war, and Margueritte took his signature off a leaflet demanding instant peace. Friedrich ended by saying that he would keep the writers on the list in mind and provide immediate information on them as soon as it became available. It is noteworthy that, although Rolland had distanced himself from the USSR by 1938 and Margueritte had never become an active supporter, Soviet organisations had not stopped monitoring their opinions and stressing the importance of their position.

The bonds of friendship

Although the Commission made no attempts to reclaim the loyalty of French writers who had definitely distanced themselves from 1938 to 1939, it continued to correspond with supporters and former supporters who agreed to carry on relations. The basis for maintaining the correspondence was that the Foreign Commission handled these writers' personal and family affairs. Apletin's letters to them could be mistaken for letters to close friends. He used the familiar 'tu' (*ty*) form of address with the Communists Aragon and Friedmann. In his letters to Rolland, Bloch and Aragon, he unfailingly asked about their wives and sent them his greetings. Dispatches of literature and sheet music alternated with souvenirs, presented as gifts rather than as propaganda materials. Although Apletin appeared to undertake his correspondence personally, groups of French writers were sent identical letters written in his personalised style. Letters written by other Soviet staff were identical to Apletin's in style, content and even structure. Dinamov, the editor of *International Literature*, used the same technique in his letter to Nizan in 1937. While sending a Soviet article, he referred to mutual friends and showed personal interest in Nizan's life and work. Sending a Soviet article was made to sound incidental to the letter.

> As Moussinac tells [us] that you have not forgotten your Russian and can easily read newspapers and magazines, I am sending this [article] to you without a translation. It has been a long time since we received anything from you. On which book are you working now? Please write to us.[121]

When several months later, after Dinamov's arrest, the deputy editor of *International Literature*, Rokotov, sent Nizan another article, he copied Dinamov's style, that of a personal friend, and concluded with a paragraph that was virtually identical to the one in Dinamov's letter: 'On which book are you working now? It has been a long time since our publishing house has received anything from you.'

The replies from French writers are the best evidence that they were successfully engaged in this exchange. 'Our friend Moussinac recently gave me your news,' replied George Friedmann to Apletin, again using the familiar 'tu' (*ty*), 'and I am taking the opportunity of a day off to write to you directly with my news and to assure you that I do not forget my Soviet friends'.[122]

But nothing cemented relations with the Foreign Commission better than familial and personal ties. They guaranteed the Commission its hold on French writers, even in times of doubt and disillusionment with the USSR.

Romain Rolland

The Foreign Commission was also involved with Romain Rolland in the mid- to late 1930s. Although Rolland did not make any further supportive statements from 1938 onwards, he also didn't make any statements that condemned the USSR. He maintained his relations with the Foreign Commission and, after he stopped corresponding with Soviet organisations, relations were kept alive through his Russian wife Maria Kudasheva, who took over all of his correspondence with people in the USSR. Files containing the Russian correspondence between Maria Kudasheva and Apletin show how active this link was. A large part of this correspondence was concerned with the translations and publications of Rolland's literary work in the USSR.

Rolland's involvement with the Foreign Commission had an additional impetus – Maria Kudasheva's son, Sergey, who lived in Leningrad and whom Rolland had met during his 1935 trip to the USSR. At this meeting, Rolland heard Sergey's critical reports about life in the USSR and later reflected on them in his diary *Voyage à Moscou*, which he banned from publication for fifty years. The Foreign Commission virtually took over the supervision of Rolland's stepson, and the writer's contact with him appears to have been in its hands. In May 1939, Romain Rolland personally asked Apletin to intervene on his and his wife's behalf, and ask for permission for Sergey to visit them.[123]

> My wife recently wrote to you about her son Sergey Kudashev, whom we would be very eager to see again this summer. I support her request, in as much as the general conditions in Europe make it possible for him to leave the USSR for two months. It is understood that at the first call he will return to his post, and I take responsibility for that.[124]

Apletin's reply suggested that he and the Foreign Commission had a crucial role to play in this process: he reported to Rolland that his letter of request had been read out at a meeting of the Bureau of the Foreign Commission and that he had been instructed to support Rolland's request. Indeed, he then approached Sheverdin, an official of OVIR, the office issuing foreign visas, for permission. On another occasion, in June 1940, it was Apletin who announced to Rolland that Sergey had been admitted to postgraduate studies in mathematics.[125]

There were a number of reasons why Rolland and Kudasheva continued to have relations with the USSR, even after 1938. There was the enormous industry that translated and published Rolland's work in the Soviet Union. One has to wonder to what degree family connections were a contributing factor in Maria Kudasheva taking over the correspondence with the Foreign Commission, despite Rolland's disillusionment with the USSR and even after his death in 1944. One wonders as well whether the presence of a hostage had any part in Rolland's own cautious silence on the events of the 1930s. He may have condemned them in private but, in public, he kept silent, neither attacking nor defending them.

Louis Aragon and Elsa Triolet

The Aragon and Triolet couple were loyal supporters who had numerous literary and personal connections to the USSR. Aragon had come a long way since his political submission to MORP in 1929–30, becoming widely known and published in both France and the USSR. Co-editor with Jean-Richard Bloch of the pro-Communist newspaper *Ce soir*, Aragon used its pages to defend the Molotov–Ribbentrop Pact. He and his non-Communist wife Elsa were actively involved with the USSR and had a distinct influence on other visitors' perceptions of it. Aragon and Triolet's relations with the USSR were mutually beneficial; the benefits derived by the Commission have been discussed but the benefits for the couple deserve separate attention. Both corresponded with Soviet writers, many of whom they knew personally from Elsa's earlier days in Russia, and they visited the USSR whenever they could. The couple's main personal link to the USSR was Triolet's sister, Lili Brik, Mayakovsky's muse and, later, his literary heiress.

Triolet and Aragon's official relations with the USSR were conducted through Communist and Soviet organisations – the Comintern, FCP, AEAR, MORP and VOKS – but most of their correspondence with Soviet organisations and individuals is concerned with their literary self-promotion. Translations and publications of their work in the USSR were the subject of an ongoing correspondence with Gosizdat[126] and *International Literature*.[127] Triolet's own correspondence with Soviet authors and artists, including Yasensky,[128] Kuleshov, Tikhonov[129] and Vishnevsky,[130] was a mixture of personal matters and issues relating to her and Aragon's work, in particular in dealings with the Writers' Union. Through Yasensky, MORP sent Soviet materials (*Literaturnaya gazeta*, *Krasnaya Nov'*, *30 dney* and books) to Triolet; and it was in private correspondence that Yasensky made requests to receive Triolet's Russian translations of speeches made during the 1935 International Writers' Congress for the Defence of Culture in Paris and to assist with their publication in the USSR.[131] This combination of mutual requests and favours, and the mixture of official and private relations, was the basis of Triolet's connections with the USSR. Triolet also resorted to personal contact with such Soviet literary officials as Aleksandr Fadeev and Vs. Vishnevsky to discuss Aragon's and her publications in the USSR.[132] In these letters, she displayed impatience and discontent about the fate of their publications or delays in publication;[133] she complained if Aragon's new book had not been mentioned in the Soviet press[134] or if her own work had not received sufficient notice.[135] Her sister Lili was a willing and confident go-between in dealing with the Soviet literary authorities in Moscow.[136]

The Foreign Commission played a particularly visible role in these contacts, through Aragon's correspondence with Apletin. But it was Lili Brik who sought the assistance of the Foreign Commission as a go-between. When World War

II broke out and correspondence with France was disrupted, Brik used the Foreign Commission as the only channel of contact between France and the USSR. Through Apletin, she tried to reach the otherwise uncontactable Aragon and Triolet in German-occupied France. It was to Apletin that Lili Brik sent her letter addressed to Aragon and Triolet in 1942 with the news of their mother's death and the reassurance that she was safe. Brik relied on Apletin again later, hoping that he would act as a connecting link: 'Do please, if you receive any news of them or their books, to send either over to me without delay.'

Triolet and Aragon were among the first French writers with whom the Commission renewed contact immediately after the Liberation in 1944. Aragon's leading role in the renewal of support for the USSR by the French intelligentsia immediately following the Liberation will be discussed in the following section. The couple's friendly relations with the Foreign Commission, which provided many mutual advantages and which were encouraged and facilitated by family ties, lasted until Elsa's death in 1970. Only then did Aragon speak frankly about their life of convenient blindness and the lies that he told during the many years of his Communist involvement. He died in 1982.

Jean-Richard Bloch

In the mid- to late-1930s and throughout the war, the Foreign Commission maintained a uniquely personal relationship with Jean-Richard Bloch. As I have argued elsewhere, his involvement with the Soviet Union began during his 1934 trip to the First Congress of the Soviet Writers' Union, and that allegiance determined his subsequent choices and actions.[137] Bloch became one of the most loyal Soviet supporters, despite his concern about the Moscow trials and the shock of the Molotov–Ribbentrop agreement. Marguerite Bloch later told their daughter Claude that, on the day of the Pact, when the postman with whom Bloch was friendly announced that the Germans and the Russians had struck a deal, Bloch was surprised that the postman could believe such stupidity.[138] The Pact came as a terrible shock to him and he had great difficulty accepting it; with Aragon in the army, Bloch remained the only French intellectual who could bring himself to support the Pact.[139]

Although there is no official evidence of his membership of the Communist Party, a Comintern document confirms that, in April 1938, after the Munich Agreement, he joined the Communist Party 'having written a very good letter to the leadership of the party asking it to allow him to join its ranks'.[140] Bloch was the only French writer who spent World War II in the USSR and, because of this, his relations with the Commission remained immediate and uninterrupted.

Bloch had developed many close professional relationships and personal friendships in the USSR. Ehrenburg's assistance was more effective in persuading Bloch to come to the Writers' Congress than the inefficient Soviet Writers' Union's Organising Committee.[141] After the Congress, Bloch continued to correspond with the interpreters Mil'man[142] and Boleslavskaya,[143] the writers Kol'tsov,[144] Tret'yakov,[145] Lidin[146] and Vishnevsky,[147] and Bloch's escort during his trip to the

Caucasus, Lev El'bert.[148] His relations with the USSR were at their closest during World War II when, as a Jew and a Communist, he fled Nazi-occupied Paris to find refuge in the Soviet Union. He was allowed to enter the USSR in April 1941 at the special request of the FCP, supported by the Comintern.[149] His emotional letter to Stalin says it all: how grateful he felt and how much he admired the USSR and the Soviet leaders.

> I have always been receptive to the lessons of Marxism–Leninsm and of the high political philosophy to which you, comrade Stalin, have erected a monument at once theoretical and practical. You did this by leading the Soviet peoples to prosperity, independence, dignity and peace.[150]

From the beginning of his stay in the USSR, Bloch, the writer, launched himself into promoting the Soviet wartime experience. He made this commitment with enthusiasm and emotion.

> How can we not follow the example of this experience, so unique in the history of humankind? How can I not redouble my zeal and my efforts as a writer to contribute to the spread of the benefits of this wisdom and this magnificent learning to my French homeland, which is now paying so dearly for the collapse of its ruling class and the treason of its capitalist cadres?[151]

Bloch's reactions to being in the USSR during wartime run counter to the common experience that positive views of the USSR were the result of short-term visits only, which included a limited exposure to the reality of life in the USSR. The Blochs did experience privations and hardship, evacuation and sickness, which they endured as part of the Soviet wartime experience. Like other Soviet writers, Bloch was issued with a document called *liter* which, in times of rationing, allowed writers to obtain food from special distributors. Bloch had to share his *liter* with the Soviet writer Andrey Uspensky. Uspensky's son Vladimir, now a Professor of Mathematics at the Moscow State University, recalls that, as a ten-year-old, he was sent to take his father's *liter* to Bloch.[152] Bloch was staying in the Metropol Hotel, where he had stayed in 1934, and Uspensky recalls being offered a chocolate from an unimaginably beautiful, large chocolate box, which he was too shy to accept. He also recalls that some writers were issued with a Category A *liter* and some with a lower Category B one, while others, like Uspensky's father and Bloch, had to share a Category A *liter* between them. To Uspensky, the irony of the situation was that, even though, as a foreigner and member of a privileged group, Bloch was placed in the deluxe Metropol hotel, he had to share the A *liter*, which placed him in the lowest category, even below that of the B *liter*.

The Foreign Commission was in charge of Bloch during his stay in the USSR. Apletin's correspondence with Bloch shows that their relationship was warm, friendly and very close. As before the war, Apletin wrote personal cards and birthday greetings. 'Dear Margarita Ernestovna, I wish you a happy birthday with all my heart,' he wrote in Russian to Bloch's wife in 1943, addressing her in the

Russian manner by first name and patronymic and wishing her happiness and an eventual return to liberated France.[153] On Bloch's sixtieth birthday, Apletin sent him more greetings in Russian summing up his literary and lifelong achievements.

> Dear friend, On the day of your sixtieth birthday please accept your true friend's warmest greetings and sincere wishes for you to live and work for many, many years as beautifully and with as much dignity as you have so far. (...) A big hug and kiss (Mikh. Apletin).[154]

Apletin's attentions continued in 1944. He sent Bloch wishes for a speedy recovery after surgery. 'My dear friend, I give you a hug and a kiss. I am happy that the operation was successful. I will be still happier when you have completely recovered and returned to your [battle] post.' Grateful for this treatment, at the end of his sojourn in the USSR, Bloch wrote to the Soviet Writers' Union and the Foreign Commission 'of which dear comrade Apletin is such an excellent secretary', thanking them for trying their best 'to make our life here as gentle and easy as the circumstances permitted'.[155] Again, he spoke of his desire to repay what he saw as his debt by bearing witness in the West to the Soviet wartime experience.

> During these forty-four months, I have been trying to bear witness about France to the USSR, and about the USSR to my French readers and listeners. I will continue this task in my country.[156]

Informing the Western world about Soviet heroism during the war was a price he considered to be too modest to repay his own debt. Gratitude, admiration and a sense of obligation fill Bloch's letters.

> I am proud to have spent the war years among the admirable Soviet people. I shall bear witness of what I have seen and thus shall play my humble part in making known the unparalleled Russian and Soviet epic of these years.[157]

Indeed, after Bloch had returned to liberated France, he helped to rebuild the French–Soviet cultural, literary and political network. Apletin promptly asked Bloch to fill him in on the events of the French literary scene from which he had been cut off. 'All we learn about French literature lately has reached us through the British and Latin American press,' complained Apletin shortly after Bloch returned to France. 'From France, whose literature interests us so much, we have received next to nothing.'[158] As in pre-war days, Apletin asked Bloch to supply information, using Soviet readers' hunger for news from France and publishers' eagerness to print French books as arguments.

> Dear friend, we are counting on you in this respect. [. . .] We are hoping that there will be a change which will translate into letters, magazines and newspapers being sent out. We dare to count on your help and that of your wife.

Similar to letters sent before the war, this one gave encouragement to Bloch. Bloch's play, he said, had been very successful in the Soviet Union and an article from the local newspaper supported this news.

> I will now stop complaining in order to give you some good news. In the Far East, beyond Lake Baikal, there is a city called Chita, and your play *Toulon* has been staged there, and it has been a great success. Please find attached an article from *Zabaikal'sky rabochy.*

As before, Apletin concluded his request with a warm farewell, explaining that his impatience arose only from the lack of personal news from J.-R. Bloch rather than the lack of news of the French scene. 'I am sending you a great big hug, and I am anxious to receive your first letter.'

Bloch's reply followed, revealing tragic details: while he was away, his eighty-six-year-old mother had been deported to Auschwitz, and Bloch found her home abandoned and looted. He had learned about the deportation of his daughter, France, to Germany; she had not been found, and her husband had been executed by the Germans. (He would later find out that his daughter France had been hanged by the Gestapo.) He listed those of his family members who remained alive. Despite his grief, he covered most of the areas about which Apletin had enquired: he had discovered a network of Soviet supporters including sympathetic media, individual writers and even societies of friends of the USSR. It appears from Bloch's letter that the old network, destroyed by the war, was coming back to life. In place of the pre-war left-wing press, new periodicals, dedicated to the USSR or published by the FCP, were emerging. And although their presentation could not compete with 'capitalist' magazines ('The British and the Americans are making significant propaganda efforts by publishing weeklies with many illustrations, on beautiful paper'), Bloch praised their content.

> *Les Nouvelles Soviétiques*, which is very well edited, is very interesting and is very much appreciated by the public, looks dull. *France–URSS* publishes an illustrated monthly, and only the paper shortage prevents it from being published at a significant print run; it sells no less than 175,000 copies. The party publishes an illustrated newspaper, *Regards*, which currently, because of the paper shortage, comes out twice a month; it is very well done and sells very well.[159]

Bloch outlined the re-emergence of old supporters and correspondents. Elsa Triolet had received the Goncourt prize, André Chamson had come to make peace with Bloch and had written a good war book ('which I haven't read yet, but about which I have heard good reports') and Jean Cassou was recovering after being tortured by the SS ('fractured skull and spine').

Finally, Bloch announced the resurrection of a society of left-wing French intellectuals, initiated and presided over by another old friend, Aragon, with the assistance of other pre-war Soviet sympathisers, even those who had distanced themselves on the eve of World War II.

> And finally, Aragon has devoted himself to the creation of a Federation of all the intellectuals' associations of the National Front and the Resistance. It has been recently founded under the title of The Union of French Intellectuals (*Union des intellectuels français*) with Aragon as its Deputy Chair and Duhamel as Chair. Joliot-Curie is its Secretary General.[160]

Bloch lived up to another promise he had made – he remained a spokesman for the Soviet Union and took upon himself new requests from the Writers' Union. He was well placed for this, having resumed his position as the editor of *Ce soir*. He was indeed asked to contribute to the collection *Les écrivains du monde entier à Maxime Gorki*, commemorating the tenth anniversary of the writer's death. The request followed the pattern established before the war, with the book's content predetermined and an appeal to the international importance of the subject matter and the task itself.

> We would like to ask you to contribute your memories about Gorky and to give your views about the importance his work has had for literature in your country and for the literature of the whole world.
>   Gorky worked hard to unite anti-Fascist writers, and fought against Fascism himself. It would be good if you could speak about the writer's struggle in this area.[161]

Bloch's assistance was not limited to supplying information on request. His very last act as a spokesman for and defender of the USSR was dedicated to the glorification of Stalin. It came in the form of a speech for l'Association France–URSS in 1946 was published posthumously as a brochure by *Europe* and Les Editions Sociales for Stalin's seventieth birthday: *Staline. L'Homme du Communisme*.[162] Jean-Richard Bloch died unexpectedly in March 1947.

The Foreign Commission of the Soviet Writers' Union achieved more complex results than other organisations and led French writers to act in many different ways for the benefit of the USSR. Early on, writers were seduced by images of the USSR but, later, the main attractions became the achievement of literary fame and the personal bonds created by the Commission. It is impossible to deny that French writers were motivated to assist the USSR by a genuine desire to do so, mixed with gratitude, recognition and their obligation to the Commission. For Aragon, Triolet and Bloch, assisting the Commission caused no obvious conflict between their actions and their political beliefs. For Aragon and Triolet, the rewards for their assistance were literary and other opportunities. Bloch's actions that benefited the USSR, particularly during and after the war, were his way of repaying the debt for what he saw as saving his life. Just as he had been an ideal visitor during his trip to the USSR, receptive to Soviet messages and eager to disseminate them, so, after the war, he continued to be an ideal spokesman and source of information for the Foreign Commission.

However, Rolland represents an exception. After his disaffection, the Commission continued to treat him as if he had remained an active supporter, publishing his work on the huge Soviet market and assisting him in his personal requests. Was this made possible because Rolland had withdrawn his political support in a private, non-confrontational way? Or was it because a mixture of favours and potential blackmail by the Commission made it difficult for the writer and his wife to disengage themselves from the pretended alliance? Did Rolland remain silent partly because the Commission had a tight grip over Sergey's life?

Whatever the reasons, those few French writers who remained loyal to the USSR provided a bridge to post-war Europe and made it possible to restore relations with the intellectual Left. With very few old staff and Western friends left in the late 1930s, the Foreign Commission managed to rapidly recover its French support network by using the same channels as before – sympathetic writers, left-wing magazines and an intellectual friendship society.

Epilogue

In November 1997, I attended an international conference, 'Jean-Richard Bloch ou l'écriture et l'action', held in Paris. It was organised jointly by the late historian Michel Trebitsch and the Bibliothèque nationale de France, where Bloch's archives have been kept thanks to a gift from his daughter, Claude Bloch. I had already discovered Marguerite and J.-R. Bloch's *Journal du voyage en URSS* and was fascinated by the way that Bloch had turned into a life-long supporter of the Soviet Union during his trip in 1934. The letters that form their journal clearly show the process of the seduction of Western writers by their Soviet hosts. I hesitated before presenting publicly my paper at this conference – after all, it was being held to commemorate the fiftieth anniversary of J.-R. Bloch's death. Above all, I did not want to offend Claude Bloch, who had been extremely kind and helpful to me and other researchers. In my talk, I skipped quotations that showed the Blochs' trusting acceptance of Soviet hospitality, such as, 'One is never treated so well as when one pays nothing.' However, my message was clear: the Blochs' reactions were representative of the Western intellectual Left who were seduced and duped by the Soviets; they closed their eyes to the nature of the Soviet system.

My presentation was met with thin applause, followed by a vehement response from a member of the audience. Bloch's archivist jumped off her seat and exploded in invective expressing her outrage at my paper and accusing me of misusing the Blochs' letters. The audience applauded, confirming that Bloch's admirers and colleagues – former and current Communists – were also outraged by my disrespect for Bloch's memory. Some historians later expressed their solidarity with me but they did so privately, after the session. Although I had been anxious about presenting my paper, I was completely unprepared for this vitriolic response.

The next day I received a phone call from Odette Hollander, my cousin, who worked for the Communist review *Regards*. Years ago she had worked with Francis Cohen, the son of Bloch's friend Marcel Cohen and himself an eminent intellectual. A founder of a major 1960s Communist review *La nouvelle critique*, Cohen had employed Odette, then a young Communist, and taken her under his wing. When he went to Moscow in the 1960s and 1970s, he visited my grandparents. I had met Francis Cohen in Paris and interviewed him for my research.

Through Odette, he now summoned me. Knowing that he had been in the audience when I gave my paper on Bloch, I went to see him with trepidation.

Well into his eighties, he was sick and had recently lost both his wife and son. However, old age, grief and frailty did not detract from his message to me. He wanted me to understand that, in the 1920s and 1930s, people like Bloch and himself had been sincere and idealistic in their commitment to the USSR. That Hitler's threat had left them with no political alternative. That for my generation it was easy to misinterpret the past and misunderstand their actions. That my paper had hurt people like him, old fighters and believers. I replied that I was, in fact, well aware of this: arguments explaining and justifying the position of left-wing intellectuals had been used in the debate for a long time and were widely known. My task was different – to show an unknown side of the Western Left's attraction to the Soviet Union, by exposing the Soviet role in it. I don't think he wanted to hear this.

These two episodes made me realise that, even after the collapse of the USSR, support for the Soviet Union was still strong in certain intellectual circles. Bloch had died in 1947, Malraux became a follower of de Gaulle and Feuchtwanger never reprinted *Moscow 1937*; but many others – Aragon and Pozner, Georges Sadoul and Howard Fast – remained at the forefront of Communist parties. Johannes Becher became Minister for Culture in the new German Democratic Republic, in which Alfred Kurella and Willi Bredel also had important government positions. Fellow-travellers Cassou, Vercors and Martin-Chauffier took turns in heading the French Comité national des écrivains (CNE). Vindicated by the Soviet triumph over Hitler and assisted by the emergence of People's Democracies, Western Communist parties and the Left gained many new members.

It is clear that the USSR had used many post-war initiatives to influence the international political climate. It backed countless friendship and rapprochement associations, such as France–URSS and the National Council of American–Soviet Friendship. Having switched its slogan from 'anti-Fascism' to 'world peace', the Soviet Union now stood behind the World Peace Congress[1] and the Cultural and Scientific Conference for World Peace. As before the war, it generously rewarded those who accepted the Soviet line. Between 1950 and 1953, a number of Communist and left-wing intellectuals and artists were awarded the Stalin Peace Prize: Pablo Picasso, Frédéric Joliot-Curie, Anna Seghers, Hewlett Johnson, Martin Andersen Nexø, Johannes Becher, Pablo Neruda and Paul Robeson.

Culture was a powerful Soviet weapon in the Cold War, affirming Soviet superiority over the West. Despite the Iron Curtain, the USSR built on the strategy of cultural export that had been blocked in the late 1930s. Stars of music and ballet such as Sviatoslav Richter, Maya Plisetskaya and Mstislav Rostropovich were sent all over the world as cultural representatives; the Bolshoi Ballet and the Moscow Symphony Orchestra filled the best international concert halls. The writers Ehrenburg and Fadeev represented the USSR abroad as peace emissaries, and Yevtushenko flew as far as Australia to recite his poetry to large audiences. The Soviet Union continued its other pre-war practice, that of luring, deceiving and influencing supporters, old and new: Fernand Léger, John Steinbeck, Rafael Alberti and Pablo Neruda, Jean-Paul Sartre and Simone de Beauvoir, Yves Montand and Simone Signoret, and Arthur Miller and James Aldridge were welcomed with open arms, promoted and celebrated. These new loyalties were often short-lived and many intellectuals later moved away from the USSR, repelled by the invasions of Hungary, Czechoslovakia and Afghanistan; but nothing made some of the old faithfuls, like Vladimir Pozner and Francis Cohen, reconsider their positions. The Soviet myth survived for many years. At the 1949 Kravchenko trial, French intellectuals rejected revelations about the 1930s Great Terror, collectivisation and concentration camps. Later, the West appeared to be blind to the blatant lack of political and artistic freedoms, even in the face of defections by artists such as Nureyev and Baryshnikov, and the prosecutions and expulsions of Brodsky and Solzhenitsyn.

It is important to return to the origins of Soviet cultural propaganda and to reflect on how it developed between the wars and what effects it had. In this book, I have shown that the Soviet cultural myth was a major contributing factor to the enticement of many Western supporters. This myth consisted of the present achievements and, even more so, the future visions of the Soviet Union and it appealed to Western intellectuals with pre-existing political sympathies and predictable interests. Post-revolutionary political propaganda, undisguised and crude, had little effect on the unconverted and, over the years, the tactics used earlier by Soviet organisations became refined and more sophisticated. Cultural discourse made political influence more palatable; it camouflaged political intentions and obscured the aims and even the source of it.

Soviet organisations hesitated between pursuing the big international names and accepting the less prominent but more numerous and cooperative left-wing intellectuals. Whatever target audience they focused on at a particular time, they had to adapt their approach to suit these distinct audiences. Even a political organisation like the Comintern insisted on moving away from mass-oriented revolutionary agitation that targeted impersonal audiences and periodicals. Following the Comintern's model, other organisations also began to focus on cultural or political groups (auxiliary organisations) and on individuals. From the start, VOKS concentrated on influencing potentially sympathetic groups of intelligentsia and eminent artistic and literary figures through a more personal, preferably face-to-face, approach. The Foreign Commission went further, focusing exclusively on individual writers. However, the best efforts of these organisations were frustrated in 1928–32 and from 1936 onwards by the imperatives of Soviet policies, which hopelessly undermined the tasks that these organisations had been given to perform.

Converting Western intellectuals by showing them Soviet achievements was only the first step; Soviet organisations needed the intellectuals to exercise influence in their own circles. Of course, these organisations operated through their own staff, from chairpersons to *referenty* and interpreter/guides, but without the active participation of Western intelligentsia their influence was limited. Leading foreign intellectuals into action by using coercive measures in the Communist style, as MORP had done until 1933, was limiting and often unrealistic. From the mid- to late 1920s, VOKS relied on more subtle tactics. Even though Kameneva was impatient to see immediate results with the auxiliary society Russie Neuve at times, VOKS was more successful with individuals, establishing a proper long-term rapport with them before using them; this approach was developed into a fine art by the Foreign Commission when it was adopted in the mid- to late 1930s. Soviet organisations resorted to different incentives to build such a rapport: personal attention, assistance and services, and encouragement and flattery as well as physical comforts and privileges, and financial assistance. Both VOKS under Arosev and, later, the Foreign Commission under Apletin built durable long-term relationships and reinforced ongoing ones in ways that made these Soviet organisations look disinterested and even altruistic, as though they were acting in the interests of cultural exchange and for the benefit of their Western friends. Soviet writers and artists were brought in to make these relations stimulating and authentic, even though the kind of influence and information they provided did not fully comply with the expectations of Soviet organisations. This type of seemingly genuine relationship, based on friendship, indeed made Western intellectuals effective 'conduits of Soviet influence'. As Becher had hoped, through the influence of and manipulation by Soviet organisations, Western intellectuals were saying what Moscow wanted them to say, without them realising it. They became the best promulgators of Soviet propaganda, both through their ideas and through their personal influence on fellow writers and audiences. The impressive number of left-wing societies and periodicals in which they collaborated, and the quantity of their publications and statements, speak for themselves. They were able to touch audiences and readerships that were far beyond Soviet reach. By putting their own names to articles, statements and reviews sent to them by the USSR, they disguised the original source of the propaganda and legitimised it by giving it their authority and prestige. Even if readers suspected the influence of Moscow behind Romain Rolland's support of the Soviet Union, it is unlikely that they were aware that his appeals had been prompted and words had been put into the great artist's mouth. As a result, with the support of leading intellectuals, the interwar intellectual scene was characterised by the acceptance and veneration of the USSR.

In many instances, Western intellectuals acted beyond the call of duty, displaying great loyalty to their Soviet friends. They influenced and manipulated each other, both voluntarily and on request from these friends. They acted as representatives and defenders of the Soviet Union abroad. They leaked information from Western organisations and passed it to the Soviets. They behaved in a sycophantic and subservient way towards Soviet leaders and bureaucrats to whom they were indebted for services and favours, real or perceived. In fact, their loyalty towards the USSR led them to indiscretions and disloyalty towards their own countries and colleagues, but they did not consider such actions amoral because they believed they were acting in a noble and higher cause. I am persuaded that the train of thought that led my grandmother to act as a courier for an espionage organisation was the same as that which led Ethel and Julius Rosenberg to participate in the atomic spy ring and the Cambridge Five to use their high positions in the British government to pass top secrets to the USSR.

I do not maintain that this book primarily demonstrates the petty and venal nature of Western supporters. I do not doubt that at the time they were sincere in their vision. It is true, though, that this book contains revelations about the conduct of the intellectual, artistic and literary Left between the wars that puts them to shame. Many of them were indeed misled by their own vanity, believing the totally implausible assertions about their loyal readers and admirers in the Soviet Union and about their own importance. They were seduced by luxuries, free meals and banquets, holidays and royalties, and they were flattered by the attention of the powerful. Their regal treatment and the glamour of their fame in the USSR became part of the Soviet myth and a major determinant of their loyalty to the USSR. One cannot ignore the fact that, in the process of being seduced in such a way, they turned their backs on people they had personally seen to be in misery, and painted as a future Communist paradise a country that was starving and suffering under increasing repression. They found excuses for remaining silent about what they had learned. Worse still, they perpetuated the lies that they had swallowed in the West.

But there were things that would have been very difficult to ignore. I wonder what Western intellectuals thought about the disappearance of the pre-war Soviet officials and artistic elite. Didn't they want to know what had become of those who had invited them to visit and shepherded them from city to city? It is known that Rolland wrote to Stalin begging him to spare Bukharin's life and that Malraux kept asking about the fate of Kol'tsov. But did the others ever enquire about the disappearance of Kameneva and Arosev? Didn't they want to know what had happened to Meyerhold, at whose dinner table they had sat, and Babel, with whom they had travelled the country? Weren't they surprised that, without explanation, correspondence that had long been conducted with Dinamov and Tret'yakov was suddenly being signed by other people?

Soviet organisations that dealt with foreigners were probably the most affected by the purges. The Comintern lost at least a third of its staff, as did the Board of the Soviet Writers' Union. The editorial team of *International Literature* lost half of its members. VOKS lost two Chairs, and information about the fate of the rest of its staff, *referenty* and interpreter/guides is unavailable. What became of Tsetsilia Rabinovich and Ludmila Rastigher-Ronskaya? Was Pokhitonov ever released after his arrest in 1936? We know that, after arrest, many died, either in prison or in camp, from torture, shooting, starvation or disease, but we do not have exact details about how, where and when. Soviet sources have long been euphemistic, saying 'victim of Stalin's repression'; for years NKVD deliberately misinformed the victims' families about the circumstances and dates of their executions. So even now the circumstances and dates of death of those who promoted the very system that killed them are often incomplete and unreliable.

Grigory Zinov'yev (b. 1883), one of the leaders of the October Revolution, Chairman of IKKI (1919–26). Victim of the first Moscow trial in August 1936.

Found guilty of forming a terrorist organisation to assassinate Soviet leaders. Shot on 25 August 1936.

Karl Radek (b. 1885), a Bolshevik journalist and leading 1920s IKKI official. Victim of the second Moscow trial in January 1937. Found guilty of treason, espionage and terrorism. Sentenced to ten years in prison. By some accounts, murdered by common-law inmates in May 1939.[2]

Nikolay Bukharin (b. 1888), political leader and theoretician, member of IKKI (1919–29). Victim of the third Moscow trial in March 1938. Found guilty as a member of a conspiratorial 'bloc of Rights and Trotskyites'. Shot at Moscow Lubyanka prison on 14 or 15 March 1938.

Bela Kun (b. 1886), Head of Agitprop of the Comintern. Circumstances and date of death (1938 or 1939) unclear.

Olga Kameneva (b.1881), the first Chair of VOKS, dismissed in 1929. Banned from Moscow and Leningrad in 1935. Imprisoned in August 1936 after Lev Kamenev's trial. Shot on 11 September 1941. Her younger son, Yu. Kamenev, aged 17, shot on 30 January 1938. Her older son, A. Kamenev, aged 33, shot on 15 July 1939.[3]

Christian Rakovsky (b. 1873), Soviet Ambassador to France from 1925 to 1927. Shot with Olga Kameneva on 11 September 1941.

Aleksandr Arosev (b. 1890), diplomat, writer and the third Chair of VOKS. Dismissed and arrested in 1937. Shot on 10 February 1938.

Aleksandr Dikgof-Derental' (b. 1885), journalist and editor of the VOKS bulletin. Arrested and shot in 1937.

Sergey Ingulov (b. 1893), journalist, VOKS representative in London in 1930. Arrested on 17 December 1937. Shot as a member of a counter-revolutionary terrorist organisation in 1938.[4]

Vladimir Kirshon (b. 1902), playwright, member of RAPP and MORP. Expelled from the Communist Party and arrested in 1937. Shot for Trotskyite activities on 28 July 1938.

Stanislaw Ludkiewicz, Polish Communist, emigrated to the USSR in 1931. MORP's Executive Secretary (1932–35). Expelled from the party and dismissed from his position. Circumstances and dates of arrest and death unknown.

Sergey Tret'yakov (b.1892), writer, member of MORP and the Foreign Commission. Shot as a Japanese spy on 10 September 1937.[5]

Bruno Yasensky (b. 1901), Polish writer, MORP Secretariat member. Shot in 1942.

Boris Pil'nyak (b.1894), writer, member of the Foreign Commission. Arrested on 28 October 1937. Shot for crimes against the state on 21 April 1938.[6]

Boris Tal' (b. 1898), journalist, member of the *Izvestia* editorial board. Arrested on 2 December 1937. Shot on 17 September 1938.

Sergey Dinamov (b. 1901), journalist, member of MORP Secretariat and of the editorial board of *International Literature*. Arrested in 1938. Died, probably executed, on 20 November 1939.

Isaak Babel (b. 1894), writer, member of the Foreign Commission. Arrested on 16 May 1939. Shot for espionage on 27 January 1940. Stalin personally signed the order for his execution.[7]

Vsevolod Meyerhold (b. 1874), theatre director. Arrested on 20 June 1939. Having been forced to make admissions under brutal torture, he withdrew his confession in court. Sentenced to death as a member of a Trotskyite organisation and a British and Japanese spy on 1 February 1940; shot on 2 February 1940.[8]

Mikhail Kol'tsov (b.1898), writer and journalist, first Chair of the Soviet Writers' Foreign Commission. Arrested on 12 December 1938. Shot as a member of a Trotskyite organisation and a German spy on 2 February 1940.

Maria Osten-Gressgener (b. 1908), German writer and journalist. Returned to Moscow from Paris in 1939 to assist the arrested Kol'tsov. Arrested on 24 June 1941 and transported to a prison in Saratov. Shot as a French and German spy on 8 August 1942.[9]

'Bolya' Boleslavskaya-Wolfson (year of birth unknown), interpreter/guide, employee of the Foreign Commission of the Soviet Writers' Union. Arrested in 1940. Shot as a spy on 14 July 1941.[10]

My grandparents were lucky to have survived. Unlike many of their friends, Western and Soviet, they lost their faith, became very critical of the Soviet system and found it almost impossible to remain silent while living in the USSR. The thin veneer of Soviet propaganda was much harder to maintain within the Soviet Union than outside. What they could not accept was the blindness of those who continued to believe a lie, and the silence of those who had the opportunity to express themselves freely in the West and chose not to do so. This was what I did not tell Francis Cohen. In the light of this, how moved I was by the wisdom of Claude Bloch who, after I had presented my paper, said to me, 'These things did happen. They have to be told.'

Notes

Introduction

1 RGASPI, Comintern, Fond 495.
2 GARF, TsIK, VOKS, f. 5283, op. 1a, d. 8.
3 RGASPI, MORP, f. 541. The original organisation was first renamed the International Bureau of Relations of Proletarian Literature before becoming MORP.
4 Originally called *The Herald of International Literature* (*Vestnik inostrannoy literatury*), it was renamed twice: first as *Literature of the World Revolution* (*Literatura mirovoy revolyutsii*) and second as *International Literature* (*Internatsional'naya literatura*).
5 GARF, VOKS, f. 5283.
6 It was created as the Commission for the Establishment of Cultural Relations with Other Countries (Komissiya po organizatsii kul'turnoy svyazi s drugimi stranami), which in turn had replaced the Permanent Commission of Foreign Aid of the Presidium of TsIK of the USSR (postoyannaya komissiya zagranichnoy pomoschi pri Prezidiume TsIK Soyuza SSR), created by TsIK in September 1923.
7 A. Chernobayev. *V vikhre veka* (*In the Whirlwind of the Century*). Moscow: Moskovskiy Rabochiy, 1987, p. 148. Also see O. Aroseva, V. Maksimova. *Bez grima* (*Without Makeup*). Moscow: Tsentrpoligraf, 1998.
8 Chernobayev, ibid., p. 167.
9 A. Golubev, V. Nevezhin. 'VOKS v 1930e–1940e gg' ('VOKS in the 1930s–40s'). *Minuvsheye. Istoricheskiy al'manakh* 14, Antheneum-Fenix, Moscow, 1993, p. 316.
10 S. Dullin. *Des hommes d'influence: les ambassadeurs de Staline en Europe, 1930–1939*. Paris: Payot, 2001.
11 RGALI, The Foreign Commission of the Praesidium of the Soviet Writers' Union, Fond 631.

1 The Soviet myth and Western intellectuals: from attraction to action

1 B. Russell. *The Autobiography of Bertrand Russell*. London: George Allen and Unwin, 1967, p. 102.
2 'Ce que nous avons vu en Russie'. *L'Humanité*, 24 August–September 1920.
3 *C'est la lutte finale (six mois en Russie soviétique)* (French original).
4 Meeting organised on 20 June 1922 by the Committee of Assistance to the Russian People (Comité d'assistance au peuple russe) at 103, rue d'Arcueil, Malakoff, Comités et organisations pour l'Aide à la Russie (1921–1923), CARAN, Fonds 7 Police Générale, Inventaire 13942.
5 Ibid.; also see 'La Conférence Nansen' in *Clarté*, 15 February 1922.
6 Comités et organisations pour l'Aide à la Russie (1921–1923), CARAN, op. cit.

7   See A. France. 'Au secours des enfants russes!'.

8   H. Barbusse. 'Le devoir socialiste'. *L'Humanité*, 24 October 1920.

9   'Ce que j'ai vu en Russie'. *Petit Parisien*, October 1922. CARAN, Fonds 7 Police Générale, Inventaire 13491 (URSS).

10 *Paul Nizan, intellectuel communiste (1926–1940)*, articles and unpublished correspondence. Paris: Maspéro, 1967, p. 104.

11 S. Spender. *World Within World: The Autobiography of Stephen Spender.* London: Hamish Hamilton, 1951, p. 132.

12 B. de Schloetzer. 'Le théâtre artistique de Moscou'. *NRF*, December 1923, p. 763.

13 P. Abraham. *Vendredi*, November 1935.

14 R. Maurer. *André Gide et l'URSS*. Bern: Editions Tillier, 1983.

15 Jean-Richard et Marguerite Bloch. *Journal du voyage en URSS* (unpublished). Bibliothèque Nationale, Département de Manuscrits Occidentaux, Fonds Jean-Richard Bloch; Don 28448.

16 'J'use de l'histoire comme d'un aliment romanesque, et du roman comme d'une matière historique.' J.-R. Bloch. 'Au ralenti (Commentaire)'. *Europe*, 1933, No. 11 (122), p. 258.

17 Selected articles in *l'Humanité, Europe, Vendredi*, January–December 1936.

18 Malraux's unpublished interview for *Marianne*. In: J. Lacouture. *André Malraux: une vie dans le siècle*. Paris: Seuil, 1973, p. 214.

19 V. Cunningham. *British Writers of the Thirties*. Oxford, New York: Oxford University Press, 1988, p. 401.

20 *NRF*, 1930, p. 588.

21 R. Marchand, P. Weinstein. 'Le cinéma (L'art dans la Russie nouvelle)'. In: *l'Humanité*, 16 April 1926.

22 M. Arland. *NRF*, 1937, Vol. 49, p. 676.

23 P. Vaillant-Couturier. 'Avec qui êtes-vous, artistes et écrivains?'. *Commune*, 1934, 5–6: 484.

24 R. Rolland. 'Adieu à Gorki'. *Europe*, June 1936, p. 290.

25 His novel *The Second Day of Creation* was called 'roman-type de l'édification socialiste' by D. de Rougemont, *NRF*, 1933, Vol. 40, p. 927, and *Without Pausing for Breath* was called a portrayal of constructions in the days of industrialisation. Both novels were praised for their 'vertu d'évidence'. *NRF* published a translation of his *Jeunesse russe*, a selection of personal letters, confessions and diaries of young Soviet people.

26 I. Ehrenbourg. 'Jeunesse russe'. *NRF*, 1933, Vol. 40, pp. 5–35.

27 S. de Beauvoir. *La force de l'âge*. Paris: Gallimard, 1960, p. 146.

28 J. Prévost. 'Cinéma Soviétique' by Léon Moussinac. *NRF*, July–December 1929, p. 723.

29 P. Bost. On 'Les marins de Kronstadt'. *Vendredi*, 1936, No. 30.

30 Bost, ibid.

31 P. Bost. On 'Ceux du kolkhoze'. *Vendredi*, 1936, No. 24.

32 Bost, op. cit.

33 *Vendredi*, 1936, No. 24.

34 *NRF*, 1934, Vol. 43, p. 770.

35 Quoted by Cunningham, op. cit., p. 396.

36 Bloch to Ehrenburg, letter of 29 June 1934. Bibliothèque Nationale, Fonds Jean-Richard Bloch, Correspondance, Lettres à Jean-Richard Bloch, t. XVIII, f. 252.

37 L. Aragon. 'Message au Congrès des John Reed Clubs'. New York, April 1935. In *L'oeuvre poétique, 1927–1935*, Paris, Messidor, 1989, p. 1082.

38 W. Frank. *Dawn in Russia: The Record of a Journey*. New York, London: Charles Scribner's Sons, 1932.

39 F. Kupferman. *Au pays des Soviets: le voyage français en Union Soviétique 1917–1939*. Paris: Gallimard, 1979.

40 '[L]e front de refus'. In: M. Ferro. *L'occident devant la révolution Soviétique: l'his-toire et ses mythes*. Brussels: Edition Complexe, 1980.

41 H. Nizan, M.-J. Jaubert. *Libres mémoires*. Paris: Editions Robert Laffont, 1989, p. 204. According to Nizan's widow, he covered a vast area of the French province, including mining regions.

42 Bloch to Rolland, letter of 13 March 1935. Bibliothèque Nationale, Fonds Romain Rolland, pp. 347–50.

43 W. Klein. '*L'Homme du communisme. Portrait de Staline*, par Jean-Richard Bloch'. In: T. Gorilovich, ed. *Retrouver Jean-Richard Bloch*. Debrecen, Hungary: Kossuth Lajos Tudomanyegyetem, 1994, pp. 43–54.

44 Jean-Richard and Marguerite Bloch. *Journal du voyage en URSS.*

45 Francis Cohen, interview with the author, 10 December 1997, Paris.

46 See also Bloch's letters preceding his departure for the USSR. Bibliothèque Nationale Fonds, Département des Manuscrits Occidentaux, Fonds Jean-Richard Bloch; Don 28448.

47 *Journal du voyage en URSS*, letter of 10 September 1934, p. 49.

48 Ibid., 13 August 1934.

49 Ibid., 6 August 1934.

50 Ibid., 13 August 1934.

51 Ibid., 29 August 1934.

52 Ibid., 17 August 1934.

53 Ibid., 13 August 1934.

54 Ibid., 5 September 1934.

55 Ibid., 29 August 1934.

56 Ibid., 13 August 1934.

57 Ibid., 22–23 August 1934.

58 Ibid.

59 Ibid.

60 Ibid.

61 Ibid.

62 Ibid., 10 September 1934.

63 Ibid., 5 September 1934.

64 Ibid., 12 August 1934.

65 Ibid., 18 August 1934.

66 Ibid., 22 August 1934.

67 Ibid., 30 August 1934.

68 Ibid., 13 August 1934.

69 Ibid., 18 August 1934.

70 Ibid., 10 September 1934.

71 Ibid., 12 August 1934.

72 Ibid., 13 September 1934.

73 'Disques'. *Marianne*, 19 and 26 September 1934.

74 Ibid.

75 Before the trip, Bloch quoted Léon Moussinac's opinions on the USSR. *Journal du voyage en URSS*, 6 August 1934.

76 Ibid., 23 August 1934.

77 Ibid., 22 August 1934.

78 Ibid., 10 September 1934.

79 Ibid., 10 September 1934.

80 Ibid., 22 August 1934.

81 Ibid., 18 August 1934.

82 Ibid., 18 August 1934.

83 Ibid., 29 August 1934.

84 Ibid., 29 August 1934.

85 Ibid., 22 August 1934.
86 Ibid., 29 August 1934.
87 Ibid., 3 September 1934.
88 Ibid., 15 September 1934.
89 Ibid., 3 September 1934.
90 Ibid., 24 September 1934.
91 Ibid., probably 5 October 1934.
92 Ibid., 24 September.
93 Ibid., 2 October 1934.
94 Ibid., 27 September 1934.
95 Ibid., 17 September 1934.
96 Ibid., 27 September 1934.
97 Ibid.
98 Ibid.
99 Ibid., 17 September 1934.
100 Martin du Gard to Bloch, letter of 19 January 1935. Bibliothèque Nationale, Fonds Jean-Richard Bloch, Lettres à Jean-Richard Bloch, t. XXX, f. 425.
101 Maurer, op. cit., p. 49.
102 Claude Bloch, interview with the author, 12 December 1997, Paris.
103 Marguerite Bloch. *Carnet de voyage en URSS en 1934* (unpublished). Bibliothèque Nationale, Fonds Jean-Richard Bloch, Carnet 3.
104 R. Aron. *Mémoires*. Paris: Julliard, 1983, pp. 123–4.
105 C. Jelen. *L'aveuglement: les socialistes et la naissance du mythe soviétique*, preface by Jean-François Revel. Paris: Flammarion, 1984, p. 9.
106 Beauvoir, op. cit., p. 223.
107 During this trial, Soviet engineers were accused of creating an anti-Soviet organisation, the so-called Prompartiya, and of wrecking industry and transport.
108 Quoted in 'Wishful Disbelief', in *Yellow Rain Pavillion*, http://www.fortfreedom.org/y00.htm.
109 *L'Humanité*, 23 April 1935.
110 H.G. Wells. *Experiment in Autobiography*. New York: The Macmillan Company, 1934, p. 689.
111 *Carnet,* pp. 19 and 25–6.
112 W. Duranty. *I Write as I Please*. New York: Simon and Schuster, 1935, pp. 280–283. In: T. Hunszak. 'Walter Duranty: Liar for a Cause'. Commentary, http://www.ukrweekly.com/Archive/2003/090312.shtml#t02.
113 *Carnet*, p. 20.
114 Ibid., pp. 34–5.
115 See M. Carynnyk, L.Y. Luciuk. B.S. Kordan, eds. *The Foreign Office and the Famine: British Documents on Ukraine* and Walter Duranty, 'Russians Hungry, But Not Starving', *New York Times*, March 31 1933, http://www.colley.co.uk/garethjones/soviet_articles/russians_hungry_not_starving.htm.
116 Duranty, ibid.
117 Rolland to Bloch, letter of 15 November 1934, Fonds Jean-Richard Bloch, ff. 182–3.
118 Ibid., f. 182.
119 Bloch to Rolland, letter of 13 December 1934. Fonds Romain Rolland, f. 339.
120 Rolland to Bloch, letter of 3 August 1935. Fonds Jean-Richard Bloch, ff. 191–3.
121 Rolland to Bloch, letter of 29 December 1934. Fonds Jean-Richard Bloch, f. 184.
122 Bloch to Rolland, letter of 1 January 1935, Fonds Romain Rolland, f. 343.
123 Ibid.
124 Bloch to Rolland, letter of 26 July 1935, ff. 361–2.
125 The name of the first volume.
126 P. Istrati. *Vers l'autre flamme*. Paris: Gallimard, 1987, p. 52.
127 Maurer, *A. Gide et l'URSS*. Berne: Editions Tillier, 1983, p. 34.

128 Ibid., p. 67.
129 'Panaït Istrati est mort'. *L'Humanité*, 15 April 1935.
130 A. Sheridan. *André Gide: A Life in the Present*. London: Hamish Hamilton, 1998.
131 Maurer, op. cit., pp. 124–5.
132 B. Crémieux. *NRF*, 1936, p. 1071.
133 Beauvoir, op. cit., p. 296.
134 P. Nizan. 'Un esprit non prévenu'. *Vendredi*, 1937, No. 5.
135 'Je regrette qu'il n'ait pas entendu Boris Pasternac lire ses poèmes, qui ne sont pas faciles, devant quinze cent ouvriers', ibid.
136 G. Friedmann. 'André Gide et l'URSS'. *Europe*, 1937, p. 29.
137 *Commune*, March 1937, No. 43, p. 804.
138 'Une lettre de Romain Rolland à propos du livre d'André Gide'. *L'Humanité*, 18 January 1937.
139 Beauvoir, op. cit., p. 285.
140 P. Herbart. *En URSS 1936*. Paris: Gallimard, 1936, p. 153.
141 Aron, op. cit., pp. 123–4.
142 Aragon to Last. In: Sheridan, op. cit., p. 506.
143 Ferro, op. cit., p. 99.
144 E. Dabit. *Journal intime (1928–1936)*. Paris: Gallimard, 1989, p. 413.
145 Bloch to Rolland, letter of 26 July 1935. Bibliothèque Nationale, Fonds Romain Rolland, ff. 356–7.
146 '"I Am at Home," Says Robeson at Reception in Soviet Union'. Interview by Vern Smith. *Daily Worker*, 15 January, 1935.
147 D. Caute. *Le Communisme et les intellectuels français, 1914–1966*. Paris, Gallimard: 1967, p. 154.
148 'Le message du grand Romain Rolland'. *L'Humanité*, 6 January 1937.
149 S. Spender. *World within World*. London: Hamish Hamilton, 1951, p. 212.
150 See script for the documentary *Sartre* by A. Astruc and M. Contat. Paris: Gallimard, 1977.
151 Ibid., pp. 9–10.
152 Herbart, op. cit., p. 10.
153 S. McMeekin. *The Red Millionaire: A Political Biography of Willi Münzenberg, Moscow's Secret Propaganda Tsar in the West*. New Haven: Yale University Press, 2003, p. 297.
154 Ibid., p. 299.
155 J. Lacouture. *André Malraux*. Paris: Cahier de l'Herne, 1982, pp. 176–7.
156 Ibid., p. 267. On Malraux's silent disapproval also see M. Sperber. *Au-delà de l'oubli*. Paris: Calmann-Lévy, 1979, p. 141.
157 N. Racine. 'Malraux et la revue *Commune*'. *Europe*, November–December 1989, Nos 727–8, p. 41. Lacouture quotes 1938 as the date of Malraux's definite distancing, op. cit., p. 267.
158 N. Racine notes: 'Par la suite, il minimisera les faces sombres du régime stalinien et gardera pour sa correspondance privée avec Rolland, la gêne que lui inspirent les procès de Moscou, mis en scène par Staline.' Racine. 'Jean-Richard Bloch (1939–1941) ou les épreuves de la fidélité'. In: *Jean-Richard Bloch ou l'écriture et l'action*, eds. A. Angrémy et M. Trebitsch. Paris: Bibliothèque nationale de France, 2002, p. 256.
159 Bloch to Rolland, letter of 7 October 1936. Fonds Romain Rolland, f. 454.
160 Rolland to Bloch, letter of 3 March 1938. Fonds Jean-Richard Bloch, f. 250.
161 Ibid.
162 Ibid., ff. 250–1.
163 B. Duchatelet. 'Introduction'. In: R. Rolland. *Voyage à Moscou*. Introduction and notes by Bernard Duchatelet. Paris: Albin Michel, 1992, p. 95.
164 Bloch to Rolland, letter of 7 October 1936, Fonds Romain Rolland.
165 Ibid.

166 McMeekin, op. cit., p. 302.
167 Racine, 'Jean-Richard Bloch', p. 259.
168 P. Istrati. *Vers l'autre flamme*. Paris: Gallimard, 1987, p. 109.
169 S. Zweig. *The World of Yesterday*. London: Cassell, 1953, p. 337.
170 V. Serge. *Les Révolutionnaires*. Paris: Seuil, 1967, p. 14.
171 Quoted by P. Ory. *Nizan, destin d'un révolté*. Paris: Ramsay, 1980.
172 F.C. Barghoorn. *The Soviet Cultural Offensive. The Role of Cultural Diplomacy in Soviet Foreign Policy*. Princeton, New Jersey: Princeton University Press, 1960; F.C. Barghoorn. *Soviet Foreign Propaganda*. Princeton, NJ: Princeton University Press, 1964, p. 31.
173 S. Coeuré. *La grande lueur à l'est: les français et l'Union Soviétique*. Paris: Seuil, 1999; R. Mazuy. *Croire plutôt que voir? Voyages en Russie soviétique (1919–1939)*. Paris: Odile Jacob, 2002; and current work on VOKS by J.-F. Fayet and M. David-Fox.
174 Articles by Golubev and Nevezhin, Maximenkov, and A. Blum.

2 Comintern: the origins of Soviet cultural propaganda

1 J.-F. Fayet. *Karl Radek (1885–1939): biographie politique*. Bern: Peter Lang, 2004.
2 *Postanovleniye TsIK Soyuza SSR of 20/11/24 'O Komissii Prezidiuma Tsentral'nogo Ispolnitel'nogo Komiteta Soyuza SSR po organizatsii kul'turnoy svyazi s drugimi stranami'* (Decision of TsIK of the USSR of 20 November 1924 'On the Commission for the Establishment of Cultural Relations with Other Countries of the Praesidium of the Central Executive Committee of the USSR'). GARF, VOKS, f. 5283, op. 1a, d. 8, ll. 4–7.
3 It replaced the Permanent Commission of Foreign Aid of the Praesidium of TsIK of the USSR (*Postoyannaya komissiya zagranichnoy pomoschi pri Prezidiume TsIK Soyuza SSR*), created also, on 7 September 1923, by the Central Executive Committee of the USSR. GARF, VOKS, f. 5283, op. 1a, d. 8, l. 4.
4 Ibid., (a) l. 5.
5 Ibid., (b).
6 M. Drachkovitch. *The Revolutionary Internationals, 1864–1943*. Stanford: Stanford University Press, 1966, pp. 161 and 175.
7 Ibid., p. 170.
8 *Thèses et résolutions adoptées au IIIme congrès de l'Internationale Communiste* (Moscow, 1921), p. 42. Quoted by Drachkovitch, op. cit., p. 175.
9 Its task was to reach the working masses in the West via Communist parties and their organs by disseminating this information through the Press Sub-Department of the Agitprop of IKKI (*P/O pechati Agitpropa IKKI*). Comintern's complex and changeable structure is discussed in: V. Pyatnitsky. *Zagovor protiv Stalina* (*A Plot against Stalin*). Moscow: Sovremennik, 1998. It includes the origin and operations of Comintern's propaganda section (p. 153). Bela Kun to Mal'tsev (Agitprop of the Central Committee of the Russian Communist/Bolshevik/Party), letter of 24 November 1924. RGASPI, Comintern, f. 495, op. 30, d. 74.
10 Bela Kun to Mal'tsev, letter of 24 November 1924, ibid., and *Vypiska iz protokola N 143 zasedaniya orgburo TsK VKP(b)* (Excerpt from the Protokol N 143 of the Meeting of the Orgburo of the VKP(b) Central Committee). RGASPI, Comintern, f. 495, op. 99, d. 22, p. 164. (RKP(b) was renamed VKP(b) (The All-Union Communist Party (of the Bolsheviks)) at the XIV Party Congress in December 1925.)
11 To ensure close cooperation with and control by the latter, it was suggested that the Head of Agitprop would be a Politburo member or that Politburo would instruct one of its members to have control over Agitprop. See 'Draft theses regarding the functioning of Agitprop Departments of the Central Committee of the Comintern branches' of 11 August 1926. RGASPI, Comintern, f. 495, op. 18, d. 445, l.1.

12 *Dokladnaya zapiska ob organisatsii informatsii ob SSSR zagranichnykh kompartyy ot 25 maya 1926 g.* (Reporting notice on the provision of information about the USSR to foreign Communist parties). RGASPI, Comintern, f. 495, op. 30, d. 272, l. 7.
13 Not to be confused with MORP, the International Association of Revolutionary Writers.
14 *Proyekt rezolyutsii org. buro II po dokladu IK MORP of 20 avgusta 1926 g.* (IIK Organising Bureau draft resolution following the MORP Executive Committee report of 26 August 1926). RGASPI, Comintern, f. 495, op. 18, d. 447.
15 Bela Kun to Mal'tsev, op. cit., ll. 108–108a. For more information on the creation and functions of Inprekorr, see: V. Pyatnitsky. *A Plot against Stalin*, pp. 159–60.
16 Inprekorr was published in German, French and English but not in Russian. Bela Kun to Steklov, letter of 31 July 1924. RGASPI, Comintern, f. 495, op. 30, d. 74.
17 Reporting notice on the provision of information about the USSR to foreign Communist parties, op. cit., l. 2.
18 Bela Kun to Mal'tsev, letter of 24 November 1924, op. cit., ll. 108–108a.
19 Ibid., l. 108.
20 Mad'yar, Head of Sub-Department of Press of Agitprop IKKI, to Andreyeva, GPU, letter of 3 September 1924. RGASPI, Comintern, f. 495, op. 30, d. 39.
21 M. Goldovskaya (director). *The Solovki Power* (documentary). Mosfilm Studios, 1988.
22 'Maxime Gorky vous présente quelques criminels du Bielomorstroi'. *Commune*, 1933, No. 2, p. 3. According to Gorky, former kulaks and exploiters, thieves and other elements previously hostile to the regime and currently interned in a labour camp were learning how to read, and were already reading newspapers and showing an interest in politics.
23 Reporting notice on the provision of information about the USSR to foreign Communist parties, op. cit., l. 1.
24 Ibid., l. 5.
25 Ibid.
26 Ibid., l. 4.
27 IIK Organising Bureau draft resolution following the MOPR Executive Committee report of 26 August 1926, op. cit.
28 Ibid.
29 Ibid., l. 9.
30 Bela Kun to Mal'tsev, letter of 24 November 1924, op. cit., l. 108a.
31 Ibid.
32 Bela Kun to Chairman of the Gosizdat Editorial Board, letter of 28 August 1924. RGASPI, Comintern, f. 495, op. 30, d. 74, l. 32.
33 Bela Kun to Mal'tsev, letter of 24 November 1924, op. cit., l. 108a.
34 Bela Kun to Chairman of the Gosizdat Editorial Board, letter of 28 August 1924, op. cit.
35 Ibid., l. 32.
36 Ibid.
37 Lentsner to Petrovsky, letter of 1 August 1927. RGASPI, Comintern, f. 495, op. 30, d. 360, l. 10.
38 Ibid.
39 Kurella to Narkomtrud, letter of 19 August 1927 regarding Soviet artists' tours abroad. RGASPI, Comintern, f. 495 op. 30, d. 367, l. 329.
40 Ibid.
41 Ibid.
42 Ibid.
43 Ibid.
44 M. Drachkovitch, B. Lazitch. 'The Comminist International'. In: Drachkovitch M. *The Revolutionary Internationals, 1864–1943*, pp. 175–6.

45 M. Drachkovitch, ibid., p. 176.
46 IIK Organising Bureau draft resolution following the report of the MOPR Executive Committee of 26 August 1926, op. cit.
47 Bela Kun to Mal'tsev, letter of 24 November 1924, op. cit., l. 4.
48 *Agitprop Komintern – Proekt tezisa* (*Agitprop of Comintern – draft provisions*), 11 August 1926. RGASPI, Comintern, f. 495, op. 18, d. 445, ll. 3–4 and op. 30, d. 272, l. 9.
49 Ibid., f. 495, op. 18, d. 445, l. 7.
50 Ibid., f. 495, op. 30, d. 272, l. 9.
51 Directive pour le travail dans les organisations sympathisantes de masse, à but spéciaux, 12 July 1926.
52 Ibid. (p. 1 of the Directive).
53 Ibid.
54 Ibid., l. 82 (p. 3 of the Directive).
55 Ibid., ll. 82–3 (pp. 3–4 of the Directive).
56 Ibid (p. 1. of the said document).
57 Reporting notice on the provision of information about the USSR to foreign Communist parties, op. cit., l. 5, and ll. 8–9. This document proposes including, among its materials, a map of institutions for mother and child as well as other materials that would interest working women.
58 Directive pour le travail dans les organisations sympathisantes de masse, à but spéciaux, 12 July 1926, l. 82 (p. 3 of the document).
59 '[U]n grand nombre de médecins, d'instituteurs, d'artistes, de savants, d'économistes, d'hommes et de femmes de la petite bourgeoisie, sympathisants avec la Russie des Soviets'. Ibid.
60 Reporting notice on the provision of information about the USSR to foreign Communist parties, op. cit., l. 7.
61 Directive pour le travail dans les organisations sympathisantes de masse, à but spéciaux, op. cit., l. 81 (p. 2 of the said document).
62 Ibid., l. 83 (p. 4 of the said document).
63 Reporting notice on the provision of information about the USSR to foreign Communist parties, op. cit., l. 9.
64 Ibid.
65 Ibid.
66 Ibid.
67 The meeting was held in Cologne on 27–28 September 1928. *Dokladnaya zapiska politsekretaryu o zasedanii plenuma buro druzey SSSR, 27–28 sentyabrya* (The reporting notice to the Political Secretary about the meeting of the plenum of the Bureau of Friends of the USSR, 27–28 September). RGASPI, Comintern, f. 495, op. 99, d. 26, l. 63.
68 Ibid.
69 *Postanovleniye Sekretariata IKKI o rabote obshchestv druzey SSSR, 10.9.36* (Decision of the Comintern Executive Committee regarding the operation of the Associations of Friends of the USSR of 10 September 1936). RGASPI, Comintern, f. 495, op. 99, d. 39, l. 13.
70 Drachkovitch M. *The Revolutionary Internationals, 1864–1943*, p. 187.
71 See Lenin's alleged statement on 'deaf-mute' educated strata in Europe recalled by Yu. Annenkov in: B. Lazitch, M. Drachkovitch. *Lenin and the Comintern*. Stanford, CA: Hoover Institution Press, Stanford University, 1972, pp. 549–50.
72 For example, the All-Union Central Union of Trade Unions (VTsSPS) would receive trade unionists, the Central Union of Consumer Societies (Tsentrosoyuz) would receive cooperatives, and the League of Struggle against Imperialism would receive Oriental delegations.

73 See undated document on the reception of foreign delegations. RGASPI, Comintern, f. 495, op. 99, d. 22, l. 52.
74 Zinov'yev to A. France, letter of 6 February 1922. RGASPI, Comintern, f. 495, op. 30, d. 20, l. 17; Zinov'yev to H. Barbusse, letter of 6 February 1922, ibid., l. 18.
75 RGASPI, Comintern, f. 495, op. 99, d. 11.
76 H. Barbusse. Speech made on 10 November 1927. RGASPI, Comintern, f. 495, op. 30, d. 357, l. 3.
77 '[U]n genial organisateur', to quote J. Droz. 'A propos de la biographie de Willi Münzenberg'. In: *Willi Münzenberg, 1889–1940, un homme contre*. International conference, Aix-en-Provence, proceedings, 26–29 March 1992.
78 Palmier. 'Quelques remarques sur les techniques de propagande de Willi Münzenberg'. In: *Willi Münzenberg*, pp. 39–53.
79 Draft resolution of the IKK Orgbureau regarding the MOPR Executive Committee report of 20 August 1926, op. cit.
80 *Zadachi Zh* (Zh tasks), ibid.
81 According to Fritz Adler in Palmier, op. cit., p. 42.
82 G. Perrault. 'La légende Münzenberg vue à travers les écrivains de l'époque'. In: *Willi Münzenberg*, p. 60.
83 Palmier, op. cit.
84 Kurella to Barbusse, letter of 28 August 1926. RGASPI, Comintern, f. 495, op. 30, d. 357.
85 Kurella to Secretariat of the Central Committee of VKP(b), letter of 17 May 1927 regarding the creation of the magazine *Vestnik inostrannoy literatury*. RGASPI, Comintern, f. 495, op. 30, d. 367, l. 100.
86 Ibid.

3 MORP: propaganda through coercion

1 J.-P. Morel. *Le roman insupportable: l'internationale littéraire et la France*. Paris: Gallimard, 1985, p. 363. Other accounts say that delegates came from twenty-two countries. International Association of Revolutionary Writers. *Short Literary Encyclopaedia*, Vol. 4. Moscow: Soviet Encyclopedia Publishers, 1967, p. 728.
2 I have based my research on MORP documents kept in RGASPI. They include MORP's correspondence with Comintern, the Department of Culture and Propaganda (Kul'tprop) of the VKP(b) and the Soviet Writers' Union; correspondence between MORP's Soviet members and French writers; records of meetings of the MORP Secretariat and its French commission; and correspondence with other organisations. Some of the documents were received by MORP from related organisations (e.g. the Association des Ecrivains et Artistes Révolutionnaires (AEAR) and members of the French Communist Party (FCP)). In the absence of directive materials (*direktivnyye materialy* – in effect, instructions from above), these documents were used to identify MORP's policies and activities.
3 A.V. Lunacharsky's 'Report on the International Bureau of Communication of the Proletarian Literature', ed. L.K. Shvetsova. In: V.G. Bazanov, D.D. Blagoy, V.V. Vinogradov, A.N. Dubovikov, I.S. Zil'bershteyn, S.A. Makashin, K.D. Muratova, R.M. Samarin, L.I. Timofeyev, N.A. Trifonov, M.B. Khrapchenko, V.B. Shtcherbina, eds. *Iz istorii mezhdunarodnogo ob'yedineniya revolyutsionnykh pisateley (MORP)* (*From the History of the International Association of Revolutionary Writers (MORP)*). Literaturnoye nasledstvo (Literary Heritage), Vol. 81. Moscow: Nauka, 1969, p. 44, note 2.
4 The All-Russian Association of Proletarian Writers (VAPP), the Bureau of National Writers and the Proletkul't in 'International liaison bureau of the proletarian literature. A brief history of its origin and activities (July 1924–May 1925). The International Group'. RGASPI, MORP, f. 541, op. 1, d. 128.

5   O. Yegorov. 'International Organisation of Revolutionary Writers'. In: V.G. Bazanov *et al.*, op. cit., p. 15.
6   Ibid., p. 17.
7   'The International Bureau as a Comintern auxiliary organisation', in 'International liaison bureau of proletarian literature', op. cit.
8   In applying party policy towards literature, as set out in a resolution of the XIII Party Congress, ibid.
9   Morel, op. cit.
10 Yegorov, op. cit., pp. 18 and 23.
11 MORP's correspondence was often addressed to both the Kul'tprop of VKP(b) and IKKI.
12 See minutes of the meeting of the MORP Secretariat of 16 January 1932. RGASPI, MORP, f. 541, op. 1, d. 2, l. 3. Because of an increase in the number of countries involved, by 1935 they included: 1. Anglo-American, 2. French and Italian, 3. Spanish, 4. German, 5. Oriental, 6. Scandinavian, and 7. Baltic commissions (see M. Apletin, MORP Secretary, to the Director of MOSKANTSTORG, letter of 3 January 1935. RGASPI, MORP, f. 541, op. 1, d. 21.
13 Bela Illes (1895–1974). Hungarian writer and MORP Secretary until 1933.
14 Bruno Yasensky (1901–41). Author of *Je brûle Paris* and *L'homme change de peau*, and member of three Communist parties – Polish, French and Russian.
15 Ludkiwicz emigrated to the USSR in 1931 and worked initially for Mezhrabpom, then for MORP (1932–35) and finally for Goslitizdat.
16 Johannes Becher (1891–1959). German revolutionary poet and a Communist deputy in the pre-Hitler Reichstag.
17 Mikhail Apletin had been VOKS's Secretary General from 1932 and its Deputy Chairman from 1934.
18 Illes. 'Report of the Secretariat of the International Bureau of Revolutionary Literature on the preparatory work for the Broadened Plenum of the International Bureau of Revolutionary Literature'. In: V.G. Bazanov *et al.*, op. cit., p. 51.
19 A. Lunacharsky. 'Report on the International Liaison Bureau of proletarian literature', 9 January 1925. In: V.G. Bazanov *et al.*, op. cit., p. 41.
20 Illes. 'Report of the Secretariat of the International Bureau of Revolutionary Literature on the preparatory work for the Broadened Plenum of the International Bureau of Revolutionary Literature', p. 51.
21 Their task was to prepare materials about various countries for the members of their commissions. Minutes of a broadened meeting of the MORP Secretariat of 17 August 1932. RGASPI, MORP, f. 541, op. 1, d. 2. From January 1933, Germanetto was appointed Chairman of the Romance commission and Kamionskaya was appointed as Secretary, thus replacing Aragon, who previously represented France.
22 Ludkewicz and Illes (MORP Secretariat) to IKKI (Manuil'sky, Knorin, Bela Kun and Gopner), undated, possibly prior to the First Congress of the Soviet Writers' Union. RGASPI, Comintern, f. 495, op. 30, d. 988, l. 19.
23 Ibid., l. 17.
24 'It is imperative to point out to the Comintern apparatus the necessity of providing MORP with technical assistance in the above work/translations, rotary [press] work, etc.', ibid., l. 20.
25 'The MORP Secretariat requests the Comintern Executive Committee to review its attitude to MORP and the movement it heads, and to provide us with real assistance for our further work', ibid.
26 'Until now we have been working in close contact with RAPP. Now it is essential for us to establish the closest contact possible with the new Soviet writers' union.' Illes (undated speech following the liquidation of RAPP and its consequences for MORP, possibly May 1932). RGASPI, MORP, f. 541, op. 1, d. 1.
27 Yegorov, op. cit., p. 22.

28 Ludkewicz and Illes (MORP Secretariat) to Gronsky (Chairman of the Organising Committee), letters of 27 January 1933 and 25 May 1933. RGASPI, MORP, f. 541, op. 1, d. 12.

29 Ludkewicz (MORP Secretariat) to Gronsky, letter of 27 January 1933. RGASPI, MORP, f. 541, op. 21, d. 12.

30 Ibid. Also: 'The question of our budget still remains unresolved, and we don't know when it will be resolved. You know that we did not approach any other organisation on the matter of the MORP financing.' Ludkewicz (MORP Secretariat) to Gronsky (Chairman of the Organising Committee), letter of 27 January 1933. RGASPI, MORP, f. 541, op. 1, d. 21, l. 12.

31 Yegorov, op. cit., p. 22.

32 Illes (undated speech), op. cit.

33 Yegorov, op. cit., p. 23.

34 MORP Secretariat to IKKI (Manuil'sky, Knorin, Bela Kun, Gopner), undated letter (probably late 1933). RGASPI, Comintern, f. 495, op. 30, d. 988, l.15.

35 The journal was renamed twice, first as *Literatura mirovoy revolyutsii* (*Literature of the World Revolution*) and, second, as *Internatsional'naya literatura* (*International Literature*). Some of the members of its editorial board, for example Sergey Dinamov and Bruno Yasensky, remained on its staff through both name changes.

36 A. Kurella, Deputy Head Agitprop of IKKI, to Secretariat of the Central Committee of VKP(b), regarding publication of the magazine *The Herald of International Literature*, 17 May 1927. RGASPI, Comintern f. 495, op. 30, d. 367, l. 100. It was proposed in cooperation with the publishing house *Land and Factory*.

37 '*Napravleniye chteniya sovetskogo chitatelya v perevodnoy belletristike*', ibid., l. 101

38 Ibid., l. 102.

39 Ibid., l. 101.

40 Ibid.

41 Kurella to Secretariat of the Central Committee of VKP(b), regarding publication of the magazine *The Herald of International Literature*, op. cit., l. 100.

42 Ibid.

43 Ibid.

44 Ludkewicz and Illes (MORP Secretariat) to Gronsky, letter of 25 May 1933, op. cit.

45 Brief summary of the activities of MORP and its [foreign] branches: Attachment 1 to the 'Appeal' to IKKI; Ludkiewicz and Illes (MORP Secretariat) to IKKI (Manuil'sky, Knorin, Bela Kun and Gopner), undated, possibly prior to the First Congress of the Soviet Writers' Union. RGASPI, Comintern, f. 495, op. 30, d. 988, l. 21.

46 Ibid., l. 26.

47 Ibid., p. 21.

48 Ibid.

49 Ibid.; also Yasensky's report of 5 April 1932 on the restructuring of MORP. RGASPI, MORP, f. 541, op. 1, d. 15.

50 Ibid.

51 Brief summary of the activities of MORP and its [foreign] branches, op. cit., l. 25.

52 Ibid. l. 15.

53 Morel, op. cit., p. 394.

54 Jean Fréville (*l'Humanité*) to Berzina (MORP), letter of 23 February 1932. RGALI, Foreign Commission, f. 631, op. 14, d. 711.

55 Fréville to MORP, letter of 10 April 1932. RGALI, Foreign Commission, f. 631, op. 14, d. 711.

56 '[C]ar vous embrassez à Moscou toute la production littéraire soviétique, ce que nous, d'ici, ne pouvons pas faire'. Fréville to Berzina, letter of 23 February 1932, op. cit. Moscow communicated in response that providing French translations would be dif-

ficult if publication could not be guaranteed. Handwritten comment in the margin of Fréville's letter to MORP of 10 April 1932, ibid.

57 Fréville to Berzina, letter of 23 February 1932, op. cit..
58 Ibid.
59 Ibid.
60 Ibid.
61 Yegorov, op. cit., p. 18. For the background information on the creation of *Monde*, see Morel, op. cit., p. 173.
62 Illes. In: *The Herald of International Literature*, 1928, 6: 123. Quoted by Morel, op. cit., p. 176.
63 Barbusse to MORP, letter of 24 December 1929. RGASPI, MORP, f. 541, op. 1, d. 128.
64 Morel, op. cit., p. 174.
65 Ibid., p. 373.
66 Bruno Yasensky to Serafima Gopner (Agitprop), letter of 13 December 1930. RGASPI, MORP, f. 541, op. 1, d. 20.
67 See J.-P. Morel in his chapter 'Le procès de Barbusse', op. cit., pp. 373–8.
68 Open letter to Barbusse (undated, attached to Illes' letter to Gopner of 23 April 1929) signed by Becher, Illes, Libedinsky, Lunacharsky, Yasensky, Mikitenko and Serafimovich. RGASPI, MORP, f. 541, op. 1, d. 128.
69 'Statement of the AEAR Fraction (Literary Section) to the Politburo of the [F]CP' (in Russian). RGASPI, MORP, f. 541, op. 1, d. 6, ll. 38–40. This file contains only the Russian translation of the French writers' correspondence.
70 Yasensky to Gopner, letter of 13 December 1930, op. cit.
71 Communist Fraction of the MORP Secretariat to Bela Kun, undated letter (probably early 1932). RGASPI, MORP, f. 541, op. 1, d. 20, l. 23.
72 Ibid.
73 Reference to 'New Conditions – New Tasks in Economic Construction', a speech delivered by Stalin on 23 June 1931 at a Conference of Economic Executives, in which he stated six conditions for development of the Soviet economy.
74 Communist Fraction of the MORP Secretariat to Bela Kun, undated letter (probably early 1932), op. cit., l. 24.
75 Ibid.
76 Ibid., l. 23.
77 Ibid., l. 24 verso.
78 Ibid.
79 Ibid., l. 24.
80 Morel, op. cit.
81 Statement by S. Dinamov on 21 May 1931. Minutes of the meeting of the Communist fraction of the MORP secretariat. RGASPI, MORP, f. 541, op. 1, d. 1.
82 Illes. In: Morel, op. cit., p. 376.
83 Statement by S. Dinamov, 21 May 1931, op. cit.
84 In 1931 and 1932, Gorky requested that Barbusse have his name removed from the Board of *Monde*. F. Narquirière, '*Yezgenedel'nik Monde*' (the weekly *Monde*). In: V.G. Bazanov *et al.*, op. cit., p. 231.
85 Communist Fraction of the MORP Secretariat to Bela Kun, undated letter (probably early 1932), op. cit., ll. 23 verso.-24.
86 Barbusse to Vaillant-Couturier, letter of 11 March 1932. RGASPI, MORP, f. 541, op. 1, d. 6, l. 28 (in Russian).
87 Ibid.
88 Ibid.
89 'Statement of the AEAR Fraction', op. cit., ll. 38–40.
90 RGASPI, MORP, f. 541, op. 1, d. 6, ll. 28–40.
91 *Monde* being on the verge of bankrupcy, and Barbusse's own struggle against 'incred-

ible financial difficulties'. Barbusse to Vaillant-Couturier, letter of 8 April 1932, ibid., l. 29.

92   Barbusse to Vaillant-Couturier, undated letter, ibid., l. 30.

93   Vaillant-Couturier to Barbusse, letter of 9 May 1932, ibid., l. 31.

94   Ibid.

95   Ibid.

96   Barbusse to Vaillant-Couturier, telegram, ibid., l. 32.

97   Vaillant-Couturier to Barbusse, letter of 15 May 1932, ibid., l. 33.

98   Ibid.

99   Ibid.

100 'Statement of the AEAR Fraction', op. cit., l. 39.

101 Morel, op. cit., p. 426.

102 Ibid.

103 Ibid.

104 Ibid.

105 Vaillant-Couturier to Barbusse, letter of 15 May 1932, op. cit., l. 33.

106 Vaillant-Couturier. 'A letter in which Barbusse was supposed to break with his muddled past, on the basis of his discussions with Kirshon, Afinogenov and Moussinac' (undated, available only in Russian). RGASPI, MORP, f. 541, op. 1, d. 6, ll. 34–5.

107 V.G. Bazanov *et al.*, op. cit., p. 247.

108 Vaillant-Couturier. 'A letter in which Barbusse was supposed to break with his muddled past', op. cit., l. 34.

109 Ibid.

110 Ibid., l. 35.

111 Ibid.

112 Barbusse to Vaillant-Couturier, letter of 17 May 1932, RGASPI, MORP, f. 541, op. 1, d. 6, l. 36.

113 Ibid.

114 Ibid.

115 Ibid., l. 37.

116 Ibid.

117 Ibid., ll. 36–7.

118 Ibid., l. 36.

119 'Statement of the AEAR Fraction', op. cit., ll. 38–40.

120 Ibid., l. 39.

121 Ibid., l. 40.

122 Ibid.

123 Ibid.

124 Yegorov, op. cit., p. 22; Illes, undated speech regarding the liquidation of RAPP and its effects for MORP. RGASPI, MORP, f. 541, op. 1, d. 1.

125 Illes. Minutes of the meeting of the MORP Secretariat on 17 August 1932. RGASPI, MORP, f. 541, op. 1, d. 6.

126 Minutes of the meeting of the MORP Secretariat on 8 September 1932. RGASPI, MORP, f. 541, op. 1, d. 6, l. 83.

127 Statement by S. Dinamov, 21 May 1931, op. cit.

128 Illes. Minutes of the meeting of the MORP Secretariat on 8 September 1932, op. cit., l. 83.

129 Metallov. Minutes of the meeting of the MORP Secretariat on 20 May 1932. RGASPI, MORP, f. 541, op. 1, d. 1.

130 Ibid.

131 Illes. Minutes of the meeting of the MORP Secretariat on 8 September 1932, op. cit., l. 83.

132 Yegorov, op. cit., p. 18; Kurella to MORP, letter of 15 December 1932. RGASPI, MORP, f. 541, op. 1, d. 128.

133 Minutes of the meeting of the Secretariat on 26 November 1933. RGASPI, MORP, f. 541, op. 1, d. 7.
134 Ibid.
135 See his letter from Paris to MORP. Kurella to MORP, letter of 15 December 1932, op. cit.
136 Ibid.
137 According to Sarukhanyan, MORP made several attempts to encourage the creation of a British branch. See: A. Sarukhanyan. 'Rozhdeniye angliyskoy sektsii MORPa' ('The birth of the English MORP branch'). In: V.G. Bazanov *et al.*, op. cit., pp. 367–71.
138 Yegorov, op. cit., p. 20.
139 T. Balashova. 'The Association of Revolutionary Writers and Artists'. In: V.G. Bazanov *et al.*, op. cit., p. 221; Yegorov, op. cit., p. 18.
140 See: D. Pike. *German Writers in Soviet Exile, 1933–1945.* Chapel Hill: The University of North Carolina Press, 1982; Morel, op. cit.
141 Morel, op. cit., p. 401.
142 Ibid., p. 411.
143 *Literature of the World Revolution,* 1932, pp. 59–60. In ibid., p. 412–13.
144 Morel, ibid., p. 413.
145 Fréville to Berzina (MORP), letter of 23 February 1932, op. cit.
146 Fréville to MORP, letter of 10 April 1932, op. cit.
147 Ibid.
148 Minutes of the meeting of the MORP Secretariat on 8 September 1932, op. cit.
149 Morel, op. cit., p. 415.
150 Léon Moussinac (1890–1964). Film and theatre critic, and an active promoter of Soviet and revolutionary cinema in France. He visited the USSR several times, both as a MORP representative and as a theatre director of the Jewish theatre.
151 Minutes of the meeting of the MORP Secretariat on 13 January 1933. RGASPI, MORP, f. 541, op. 1, d. 7, l. 7.
152 Ibid.
153 Brief summary of the activities of MORP and its [foreign] branches, op. cit., l. 21.
154 Ibid., p. 22.
155 Ludkewicz, Illes and Becher (MORP Secretariat) to the Comintern Political Commission, letter of 13 January 1934. RGASPI, Comintern, f. 495, op. 30, d. 988.
156 D. Aaron. *Writers on the Left: Episodes in American Literary Communism.* New York: Harcourt, Brace and World, 1961, p. 283.
157 To com. Stetsky, the Central Committee of VKP(b), and to com. Pyatnitsky and com. Knorin, the Presidium of IKKI. RGASPI, Comintern, f. 495, op. 30, d. 952, l. 79.
158 Ibid.
159 Ibid.
160 Yegorov mentions the refusal by the PEN Club, then headed by Galsworthy, to negotiate with MORP in order to establish cooperation. Yegorov, op. cit., p. 20.
161 To com. Stetsky, the Central Committee of VKP(b), and to com. Pyatnitsky and com. Knorin, the Presidium of IKKI. RGASPI, Comintern, op. cit., l. 79.
162 Ibid., ll. 79–79 verso.
163 Ibid., l. 79 verso.
164 *Note au sujet d'une organisation internationale nouvelle d'écrivains.* RGASPI, Comintern, f. 495, op. 30, d. 988, ll. 31–6 (in French).
165 The Soviet writer Ilya Ehrenburg, who lived in Paris and was closely associated with French literary circles, was aware of Barbusse's intention of setting up and heading such an organisation and attributes the authorship of the letter to one of Barbusse's assistants. He wrote about it to Mikhail Kol'tsov, the first Head of the Foreign Commission of the Writers' Union. See A. Rubashkin, ed. ' "There are rumours that the money comes from Moscow. . .". Letters from Ilya Ehrenburg to Mikhail Kol'tsov, 1935–1937'. *Novyy Mir,* 1999, 3.

166 *Note au sujet d'une organisation internationale nouvelle d'écrivains*, op. cit.
167 Rubashkin, op. cit.
168 Ibid.
169 Ehrenburg confirms in his letters to Kol'tsov that one of Barbusse's associates considered the above members for the administration of the organisation.
170 Ehrenburg also mentions a reference to Soviet funds expected by this organisation, whereas he himself was unaware of the source of this finance.
171 J. Becher. Protocol of a meeting of the MORP Secretariat of 8 May 1935. RGASPI, Comintern, f. 495, op. 30, d. 1076, l. 12 (in Russian).
172 Ibid., l. 14.
173 Ibid.
174 Ibid., l. 15.

4 MORP: the closing years

1 Selected correspondence between Rolland and writers including the MORP members Kurella, Dinamov and Moussinac was published by V.G. Bazanov *et al.*, op. cit., pp. 279–330.
2 Rolland to Moussinac, letter of 17 October 1933, ibid., pp. 293–4.
3 Rolland to Kurella, letter of 16 December 1933, ibid., pp. 293–4, 308–9.
4 Rolland to Kurella, letters of 23 October 1933 and 21 December 1933, ibid., pp. 296 and 310 respectively.
5 Rolland to Upton Sinclair, letter of 27 December 1933, ibid., pp. 312–13.
6 Rolland to Illes, letter of 22 September 1932, ibid., pp. 286–9.
7 Rolland to Illes, letter of 21 June 1931, ibid., p. 279.
8 Illes to Rolland, telegram of, possibly, 1 March 1932. RGASPI, MORP, f. 541, op. 1, d. 114.
9 Rolland to Illes, letter of 1 March 1932 acknowledging the receipt of his telegram, ibid.
10 Illes. Undated speech following the dissolution of RAPP. RGASPI, MORP, f. 541, op. 1, d. 1.
11 Minutes of the meeting of the MORP Secretariat on 8 September 1932, op. cit.
12 Illes to Stetsky (Kul'tprop of the VKP(b) Central Committee), letter of 22 March 1932. RGASPI, MORP, f. 541, op. 1, d. 114.
13 In fact, one of MORP's earlier debts was the result of organising, on Comintern's instructions, the 1930 Kharkov Second World Conference of Revolutionary Writers. As it had not been financed properly, the newly created MORP was left with a debt of 7,000 roubles. Illes and Yasensky to A. Khalatov, the Chairman of the Board of the State Publishers (OGIZ), application of 9 December 1930. RGASPI, MORP, f. 541, op. 1, d. 22.
14 Ibid.
15 Ludkewicz and Illes (MORP Secretariat) to IKKI (Manuil'sky, Knorin, Bela Kun and Gopner), undated, possibly prior to the First Congress of the Soviet Writers' Union, op. cit., l. 13.
16 MORP Secretariat to Gronsky, letter of 27 January 1933, op. cit.
17 Anatol Hidas (MORP Communist fraction) to Belkin (Workers and Peasant Commission) (RKI), letter of 19 July 1932. RGASPI, MORP, f. 541, op. 1, d. 9, l. 4.
18 Ibid.
19 Ibid.
20 Ibid.
21 Elsa Triolet stayed in Moscow for extended periods during Aragon's work for Comintern, MORP and *Littérature internationale*. Her perceptions could have also been affected by benefits offered to her and Aragon by VOKS and the Soviet Writers' Union, as well as by her sister Lili Brik's privileged living conditions.

22 Brief summary of the activities of MORP and its [foreign] branches, op. cit., l. 18.
23 Ibid., l. 17.
24 W. Benjamin. 'Ya okhotno prinimayu priglasheniye k sotrudnichestvu' ('I am happy to accept your offer of collaboration'). W. Benjamin's correspondence with the editors of the journal *Das Wort*, 1936–37. *Istoricheskiy arkhiv* (*The Historical Archives*), 1998, 1: 103–23 (Russian translation).
25 Ibid.
26 M. Apletin to A.S. Shcherbakov (Head of Kul'tprosvetotdel of the Central Committee of VKP(b)), letter of 10 June 1935. RGASPI, Comintern, f. 495, op. 30, d. 1076.
27 Dinamov to Barbusse, letter of 27 April 1935. RGASPI, MORP, f. 541, op. 1, d. 113.
28 Barbusse to Dinamov, letter of 12 May 1935, ibid.
29 Morel, op. cit., p. 380.
30 See Aragon and Sadoul's statement at the Congress in M. Nadeau. *Documents surréalistes*, pp. 221–3, quoted in: P. Daix, *Aragon: une vie à changer*. Paris: Seuil, 1975, p. 251.
31 Morel, op. cit., p. 420.
32 'According to my agreement with the comrades from the Association of Revolutionary Writers and Artists [AEAR] of France, it seems to me that I have to clarify my position to you in writing' ('To the comrades of the International Association of International Writers'), minutes of the broadened meeting of the MORP Presidium of 19 June 1932. RGASPI, MORP, f. 541, op. 1, d. 6, l. 25 (in Russian).
33 Ibid.
34 Ibid., l. 26.
35 Ibid.
36 Ibid., l. 27.
37 Ibid.
38 Preface by *l'Humanité*, 3 March 1932, ibid. (Russian translation).
39 Rolland to Illes, letter of 6 March 1932, ibid. (Russian translation).
40 Minutes of the meeting of the MORP Secretariat on 8 September 1932, op. cit.
41 Serafima Gopner of Agitprop, Manuil'skiy and Bela Kun in Illes to Gopner, letter of 17 March 1932, ibid.
42 Illes to Stetsky, letter of 22 March 1932, ibid.
43 Illes to Gopner, letter of 17 March 1932, op. cit.
44 Ibid.
45 Minutes of the meeting of the MORP Secretariat on 8 September 1932, op. cit., ll. 83–84.
46 Ibid.
47 Ibid.
48 Ibid.
49 Ibid., l. 84.
50 Illes. Undated speech following the dissolution of RAPP, op. cit.
51 Rolland to Illes, letter of 29 March 1932. In: V.G. Bazanov *et al.*, op. cit., pp. 283–284.
52 Ludkewicz and Illes (MORP Secretariat) to IKKI (Manuil'sky, Knorin, Bela Kun and Gopner), undated, possibly prior to the First Congress of the Soviet Writers' Union, op. cit., l. 13.
53 Ludkewicz to Gronsky, letter of 27 January 1933, op. cit.
54 For example, com. Tret'yakov's report about MORP's operations and the task of establishing contacts with workers in the arts. Minutes of a broadened meeting of the MORP Secretariat on 17 August 1932. RGASPI, MORP, f. 541, op 1, d. 6, ll. 69–71.
55 M. Apletin, MORP Secretary to M. Kol'tsov, the Chairman of the Commission of Foreign Relations of the Soviet Writers' Union, letter of 19 April 1935. RGASPI, MORP, f. 541, op. 1, d. 27; Apletin to A.S. Shcherbakov, Head of Kul'tprosvetotdel

of the Central Committee of the VKP(b), letter of 10 June 1935, op. cit., ll. 20–20 verso.

56 Ludkewicz and Illes (MORP Secretariat) to IKKI (Manuil'sky, Knorin, Bela Kun and Gopner) (undated, possibly prior to the First Congress of the Soviet Writers' Union), op. cit., l. 13.

57 Ibid.

58 Ibid.

59 Ibid.

60 Com. Tret'yakov's report about MORP's operations and the task of establishing contacts among workers in the arts. Minutes of a broadened meeting of the MORP Secretariat on 17 August 1932, op. cit.

61 Minutes of the meeting of the MORP Secretariat on 23 May 1933, and minutes of the broadened meeting of the MORP Secretariat on 4 October 1933. RGASPI, MORP, f. 541, op. 1, d. 7.

62 Com. Tret'yakov's report about MORP's operations and the task of establishing contacts among workers in the arts, op. cit., l. 69.

63 Ibid., l. 70.

64 Ibid.

65 Ibid.

66 Morel, op. cit. p. 391.

67 Com. Tret'yakov's report about MORP's operations and the task of establishing contacts among the workers of the arts, op. cit., l. 70.

68 Ibid., l. 71.

69 Ibid.

70 See earlier references to *Journal de voyage en URSS* by Marguerite and Jean-Richard Bloch, Chapter 1. Another area of MORP's involvement suggested by Tret'yakov was the forthcoming Soviet Writers' Congress. Tret'yakov found the preparations for the Congress to be insufficient and proposed a number of topics for discussion by the Congress, including Soviet literary relations with the West (i.e. Soviet literature for the West), publication of foreign books and the collection of impressions of the USSR by foreign writers and their influence in the USSR and the West. Minutes of the meeting of the MORP Secretariat on 23 May 1933, op. cit.

71 Minutes of the broadened meeting of MORP Secretariat of 17 August 1932, Com. Tret'yakov's report about MORP's operations and the task of establishing contacts among the workers of the arts, f. 541, op. 1, d. 1.

72 Tret'yakov, Hidas and Vislyak to the Soviet Writers' Union, Tret'yakov to VOKS and Vandursky to Intourist. Minutes of the meeting of the MORP Secretariat of 20 August 1932. RGASPI, MORP, f. 541, op 1, d. 6.

73 Minutes of the meeting of the MORP Secretariat on 28 September 1932, ibid.

74 Minutes of the meeting of the MORP Secretariat on 13 January 1933. RGASPI, MORP, f. 541, op. 1, d. 7.

75 Minutes of the broadened meeting of the MORP Secretariat on 4 October 1933, ibid.

76 Illes and Ludkewicz (MORP Secretariat) to the Communist fraction of the Secretariat of the Soviet Writers' Union, letter of 25 May 1933. RGASPI, MORP, f. 541, op. 1, d. 21., l. 17.

77 Apletin to Kol'tsov (Chairman of the Commission of Foreign Relations of the Soviet Writers' Union), letter/proposal of 19 April 1935. RGASPI, MORP, f. 541, op. 1, d. 27, ll. 1–2.

78 Ibid.

79 Ibid.

80 Ibid.

81 Ibid.

82 Biographical information of French writers, 1934. RGALI, Foreign Commission, f. 631, op. 14, d. 716.

83 Apletin to Shcherbakov, Head of Kul'tprosvetotdel of the Central Committee of VKP(b), letter of 10 June 1935, op. cit., ll. 20–20 verso.
84 Ibid., l. 20 verso.
85 Ibid.
86 Ibid.
87 Postanovleniye Politbyuro TsK VKP(b) o likvidatsii Mezhdunarodnogo ob'yedineniya revolyutsionnykh pisateley (Decision by the Politbureau of the Central Committee of the VKP(b) to close the International Association of Revolutionary Writers), 10 December 1935. RGASPI, f. 17, op. 3, d. 973, l. 27. In: A. N. Yakovlev, ed. *Vlast' i khudozhestvennaya intelligentsiya. Dokumenty TsK RKP(b)-VKP(b), VChK-OGPU-NKVD o kul'turnoy politike. 1917–1953 gg.* (Power and artistic intelligentsia. Documents on cultural policies by TsK RKP(b)-VKP(b) and VChK-OGPU-NKVD). Moscow: Mezhdunarodnyy Fond 'Demokratiya', 1999.
88 D. Pike, op. cit., pp. 123–4.
89 Ibid., p. 125.

5 Laying the foundations of relations with Western intellectuals: VOKS in the 1920s

1 J.-F. Fayet. 'Entre culture, politique et lobbying diplomatique: la société pansoviétique d'échanges culturels avec l'étranger [V.O.K.S.]'. In: H.U. Jost, S. Przioso, eds. *Relations internationales, échanges culturels et reseaux intellectuals.* Lausanne: Antipodes, 2002, p. 2.
2 GARF, VOKS f. 5283, op. 1, d. 1, l. 1. In: Golubev and Nevezhin, op. cit., p. 313.
3 D. Caute. *The Fellow Travellers.* London: Macmillan, 1973; P. Hollander. *Political Pilgrims Travels of Western Intellectuals to the Soviet Union, China and Cuba: 1928–1978.* New York: Oxford University Press, 1981; P. Loffler. *Chronique de l'Association des écrivains et des artistes révolutionnaires (Le mouvement littéraire progressiste en France) 1930–1939.* n. p.: Subervie, 1971; Kupferman, op. cit.; Maurer, op. cit.; P. Labérenne. 'Le Cercle de la Russie Neuve (1928–1936) et l'Association pour l'étude de la culture soviétique (1936–1939)'. *La Pensée*, June 1979, pp. 13–25; Istrati, op. cit.; Duhamel, *Le Voyage de Moscou.* Paris : Mercure de France, 1927; Rolland, *Voyage à Moscou*, op. cit.
4 Barghoorn. The Soviet Cultural Offensive, op. cit.; S.R. Margulies. The Pilgrimage to Russia: The Soviet Union and the Treatment of Foreigners, 1924–1937. Madison, WI: The University of Wisconsin Press, 1968.
5 M. Kuz'min. *Deyatel'nost' partii i sovetskogo gosudarstva po razvitiyu mezhdunarodnykh nauchnykh i kul'turnykh svyasey SSSR (1917–1932)* (*The Activities of the Party and the Soviet State in the Development of Soviet International Scientific and Cultural Relations (1917–1919)*). Leningrad: Izdatel'stvo Leningradskogo Universiteta, 1971; A. Ioffe. *Internatsional'nyye, nauchnyye i kul'turnyye svyazi Sovetskogo Soyuza. 1928–1932* (*International, Scientific and Cultural Relations of the Soviet Union. 1928–1932*). Moscow: Nauka, 1969, pp. 9–10; A. Ioffe. *Mezhdunarodnyye svyazi sovetskoy nauki, tekhniki i kul'tury. 1917–1932* (*International Relations of Soviet Science, Technology and Culture. 1917–1932*). Moscow: Nauka, 1975.
6 *Postanovleniye i Ustav* (*Decision and Regulations*). *Ustav* published in *Pravda*, No. 184, on 14 August 1925 had been approved on 8 August 1925 by the Deputy Chairman of the Council of People's Commissars of the USSR, A. Tsyurupa, and Deputy Head of the Council of People's Commissars of the USSR, I. Miroshnikov. GARF, VOKS, f. 5283, op. 1 d. 1, ll. 1–2. They specify the operations and tasks of VOKS's sectors and departments as well as those of certain positions, for example *referenty* (officers-in-charge). See *Polozheniye o referenture* (*Regulations regarding officers-in-charge*), ibid., p. 4, l. 6 verso.
7 The documents mention the supervision of VOKS by the Agitprop of the Central Committee of the VKP(b). Kameneva mentions the name of Ol'khovyy, who super-

vised VOKS's operations (*slyedyaschego za rabotoy VOKS*). RGASPI, Comintern, f. 495, op. 99, d. 26, l. 208.

8 Despite the statement in the *Regulations regarding officers-in-charge* that the Executive Secretary was VOKS's top position, the position of ultimate power and decision making was undoubtedly its Chair.

9 In some cases they were employees of the People's Commissariat of Foreign Trade (NKVT).

10 *Regulations (Ustav)*, op. cit., (z) l.1 and (i) l. 2.

11 Ibid., (k) l. 2.

12 According to Soviet sources, the *VOKS* magazine covered socialist construction and cultural revolution, and spread Soviet literature in sixty-four countries through its Book Exchange Bureau. A. Arnte, 'Rol' vsesoyuznogo obschestva kul'turnoy svyazi s zagranitsey v ukreplenii internatsional'nykh svyazey s trudyaschimisya Latvii (1925–1940)' ('The Role of the All-Union Organisation for Cultural Relations with Foreign Countries in the strengthening of international relations with the workers of Latvia (1925–1940)'). *Izvestiya Akademii nauk Latviyskoy SSR*, 1984, 12 (449): 12.

13 Correspondence with the VOKS officer-in-charge in Paris regarding the sending of Soviet literature. GARF, VOKS, f. 5283, op. 9, d. 12.

14 'Soviet law', 'Social and legal protection of minors in the USSR', 'Physical education in the USSR'.

15 'Inventions and improvements in transport', 'Bacon production in the USSR', 'Agricultural cooperation', 'Forestry cooperation', 'Nizhny Novgorod fair', 'Our oil industry'.

16 'Soviet literature over seven years', 'Exhibitions in the USSR', 'French literary studies in the USSR', 'Art and theatre in the USSR', 'The path of development in Soviet cinema', 'Film education in the USSR', 'Society of Friends of the Soviet Film-making Industry', 'Science in the USSR', 'Russian Academy of Sciences'.

17 'Russian Academy of Sciences', 'The main achievements of anthropology since the Revolution'.

18 *L'amour de l'art* also received 'Museum construction up to time the October Revolution' as well as articles on Soviet art: 'Moscow exhibitions in the 1925–1926 season', 'From the new spectator to the new artist', 'Our sculpture'.

19 'Lenin on Art and Science' by Lunacharsky.

20 'Infectious diseases in the USSR up to the time of 1926', 'Schools in the Leningrad region up to 1925'.

21 'On the economy of national republics (Azerbaijan, Georgia, Armenia, Kazakhstan)'.

22 Films sent for the exiled Spanish revolutionary, Soriano. Correspondence with the VOKS representative (1925–26) regarding the sending of materials/literature on the USSR. GARF, VOKS, f. 5283, op. 9, d. 12.

23 Korinets (VOKS Executive Secretary) and Sorokin to Divil'kovsky, letter of 13 August 1927. GARF, VOKS, f. 5283, op. 7, d. 6.

24 Correspondence between Zamenhof and Korinets of 1927. GARF, VOKS, f. 5283, op. 7, d. 6, ll. 150–5.

25 Ibid., l. 150.

26 GARF, VOKS, f. 5283, op. 7, d. 6, l. 143.

27 Letters by Korinets of 1927. GARF, VOKS, f. 5283, op. 7, d. 6.

28 Korinets and Karzhansky (VOKS) to VOKS Paris representative, correspondence of July 1926, ibid.

29 Ibid.

30 GARF, VOKS, f. 5283, op. 7, d. 34.

31 Report from the editor of the information bulletin A. Dikgof-Derental' to the VOKS Chair Petrov of 19 October 1929. GARF, VOKS, f. 5283, op. 1 d. 126, l. 9 verso.

32 Ibid., l. 10 verso.

33 Ibid, l. 9.
34 *Regulations (Ustav)*, op. cit., (b) l. 1.
35 M. Kuz'min. 'Angliyskoye obschestvo kul'turnykh svyazey s SSSR' ('The English society of cultural relations with the USSR'). *Voprosy istorii*, 1966, 2: 203–6.
36 Yu. Murav'yov. 'Sovetsko–germanskiye kul'turnyye svyazi v period Veymarskoy respubliki' ('Soviet–German cultural relations in the period of the Weimar Republic'). *Vestnik istorii mirovoy kul'tury*, 1960, 5: 55–63; G. Rosenfel'd. 'Nauchnyye i kul'turnyye svyazi mezhdu SSSR I Veymarskoy respublikoy' ('Scientific and cultural relations between the USSR and the Weimar Republic'). *Voprosy istorii*, 1963, 10: 71–83.
37 V. Shishkin. 'Iz istorii chekhslovatsko–sovetskikh kul'turnykh svyazey. 1918–1925 gg.' ('From the history of Czechoslovak–Soviet relations. 1918–25'). *Vestnik istorii mirovoy kul'tury*, 1960, 6: 84–99.
38 L. Zhila. 'Ustanovleniye kontaktov mezhdu organizatsiyami druzey SSSR v Bolgarii i VOKSom (1932–1939)' ('The establishment of contacts between organisations of Friends of the USSR in Bulgaria and VOKS (1932–39)'). *Vestnik Moskovskogo Universiteta*, 1989, Ser. 8, History, 1: 42–53.
39 M. Kuz'min. 'Kul'turnyye svyazi mezhdu SSSR i Yaponiyey posle Oktyabrya (1925–1932)' ('Cultural relations between the USSR and Japan after [the] October [revolution] (1925–32)'). *Narody Azii i Afriki*, 1967, 5: 133–43.
40 Arnte. 'Rol' vsesoyuznogo obschestva kul'turnoy svyazi s zagranitsey v ukreplenii internatsional'nykh svyazi s trudyaschimisya Latvii (1925–1940)' ('The Role of the All–Union Organisation for Cultural Relations with Foreign Countries in the strengthening of international relations with the workers of Latvia (1925–40)'). *Izvestiya Akademii Nauk Latviyskoy SSR (The news of the Latvian SSR Academy of Sciences)*, 1984, 12 (449): 11–25.
41 A.N. Solov'yov. 'Iz istorii franko–sovetskikh kul'turnykh i nauchnykh svyazey v 1931–1935 gg.' ('From the history of French–Soviet cultural and scientific relations in 1931–35'). *Vestnik istorii mirovoy kul'tury*, 1960, 1: 80–91.
42 Arnte, op. cit. Mazuy notes this period as that of the widespread creation of pro-Soviet friendship societies with the purpose of spreading 'the truth on the USSR'. See Mazuy, op. cit., p. 109.
43 GARF, VOKS, f. 5283, op. 7, d. 34, l. 14.
44 Ibid., l. 15.
45 Olga Kameneva to the Secretariat of the Central Committee of the VKP(b), copy to the Agitprop of the Central Committee of the All-Russian Communist (Bolshevik) Party, presumably prior to November 1928. RGASPI, Comintern, f. 495, op. 99, d. 26.
46 Correspondence with the plenipotentiary representative of the USSR in Germany regarding the creation of a representation of the Special Commission of Foreign Aid in Germany (Central Relief Committee USSR), 15 December 1924. GARF, VOKS, f. 5283, op. 1 d. 41, ll. 2–4.
47 VOKS correspondence with its representative in the USA, 1925. GARF, VOKS, f. 5283, op. 1a d. 42.
48 Report by *referent* Livent-Levit about cultural relations with Germany, 17 July–25 October 1929. GARF, VOKS, f. 5283, op. 1 d. 126, l. 4 verso.
49 Ibid., l. 210.
50 Ibid., l. 208.
51 Ibid.
52 Ibid., l. 209.
53 GARF, VOKS, f. 5283, op. 2, d. 81, l. 100.
54 GARF, VOKS, f. 5283, op. 2, d. 233.
55 Ibid.
56 Kameneva to Tikhomenev, undated letter (before May 1927). GARF, VOKS, f. 5283, op. 7, d. 6, l. 15.

57 Ibid., l. 17.
58 Ibid., l. 26.
59 Ibid., l 26.
60 GARF, VOKS, f. 5283, op. 7, d. 6, l. 3.
61 Ibid., l. 18 (original in French).
62 Invitation to attend the first inaugural meeting of the French–Soviet rapprochement society. GARF, VOKS, f. 5283, op. 2, d. 81, l. 93.
63 GARF, VOKS, f. 5283, op. 7, d. 6, l. 5.
64 Ibid., l. 38.
65 Ibid., l. 56.
66 Ibid., l. 57.
67 He may have been referring to the assassination of P.L. Voykov, a Soviet ambassador to Poland. Another possibility is a series of international scandals to do with revelations about Soviet spying in Poland, Turkey and China, which came to light in 1927.
68 GARF, VOKS, f. 5283, op. 7, d. 6, l. 61.
69 Ibid. (original in French).
70 'Memorandum regarding the Society for Cultural Relations between Russia and Great Britain known as CRS' (only available in its translation from English into Russian). GARF, VOKS, f. 5283 op. 10, d. 127, l. 12.
71 Moussinac to Kameneva, letter of 1 July or August 1927, VOKS, f. 5283, op. 7, d. 6, l. 62.
72 Ibid.
73 Ibid.
74 Rabinovich, late 1927. GARF, VOKS, f. 5283, op. 7, d. 34, l. 28.
75 Ibid.
76 Ibid.
77 Ibid.
78 Ibid.
79 Duhamel's own notes in his diary and correspondence regarding his participation in the creation of the society are fleeting. He paid much less attention to the creation of the society than the VOKS documents suggest. See: G. Duhamel. *Les espoirs et les épreuves 1919–1928. Lumières sur ma vie.* Paris: Mercure de France, 1953; *Le livre de l'amertume. Journal 1925–1956.* Paris: Mercure de France, 1983.
80 Rabinovich, GARF, VOKS, f. 5283, op. 7, d. 34, l. 28.
81 Report from the editor of the information bulletin A. Dikgof-Derental' to the VOKS Chair Petrov of 19 October 1929, op. cit., l. 11.
82 Ibid.
83 Ibid.
84 Ibid.
85 *Regulations regarding the VOKS staff*, op. cit., l. 5.
86 'Provisions regarding the Bureau for the Reception of Foreigners, Area of competence (*Krug vedenia*)'. *Regulations regarding the VOKS staff*, ibid., p. 4, l. 6.
87 Kameneva's correspondence with the Comintern, 6 and 17 May 1927. RGASPI, Comintern, f. 495, op. 99, d. 22, l. 22.
88 An internal letter by VOKS's Bureau for the Reception of the Foreigners expresses the hope that 'undoubtedly Prof. Mazon will be very valuable in the strengthening of our scientific links with France', 11 February 1927. GARF, VOKS, f. 5283, op. 7, d. 7.
89 In the 1920s, Victor Serge was working for the Comintern. See: *Mémoires d'un révolutionnaire: 1901–1941*. Paris: Seuil, 1978.
90 Report of 3 April 1927. GARF, VOKS, f. 5283, op. 7, d. 7.
91 Letter of 29 April 1927, ibid.
92 G. Duhamel. *Le voyage de Moscou*. Paris: Mercure de France, 1927.

93 Th.P. Riggio, J.L.W. West III, eds. *Dreiser's Russian Diary*. Philadephia: University of Pennsylvania Press, 1996.
94 *Dreiser's Russian Diary*, ibid, pp. 193 and 195.
95 *Dreiser's Russian Diary*, ibid., pp. 90–1, 95 and 98.
96 Tsekubu – The Central Commission for the improvement of scholars' conditions.
97 GARF, VOKS f. 5283, op. 7, d. 7.
98 *Dreiser's Russian Diary*, op. cit., 1996, pp. 90–1 and 98.
99 Ibid., pp. 88, 90 and 98.
100 GARF, VOKS, f. 5283 Op. 6 d. 24, l. 24.
101 *Regulations regarding the VOKS staff*, op. cit., p. 4, l. 6.
102 Duhamel came on the invitation of the Academy of Fine Arts. *Le Voyage de Moscou*, op. cit., p. 12.
103 GARF, VOKS, f. 5283, op. 7, ll. 7–8.
104 Ibid., l. 103.
105 Ibid., l. 8.
106 VOKS Moscow office to Leningrad section, letter of 23 November 1927. GARF, VOKS, f. 5283, op. 7, d. 6, l. 207.
107 'About Dreiser's stay in the USSR'. GARF, VOKS, f. 5283, op. 7, ll. 62.
108 GARF, VOKS, f. 5283, op. 2 d. 81, ll. 79–82.
109 This indicates a period before he joined the FCP in 1927. The period prior to December 1930, when the writer severed ties with the surrealists, is another possible date.
110 GARF, VOKS, f. 5283, op. 2 d. 81, ll. 79–82.
111 *Le voyage de Moscou*, op. cit.
112 Letters of thanks from foreigners who visited VOKS, 11 December 1925–28 October 1928. GARF, VOKS, f. 5283, op. 8 d. 53.
113 Reports by foreigners who visited the USSR, published in the press, 1928. GARF, VOKS, f. 5283, op. 8 d. 52.
114 Dinamov to Kameneva, letter of 19 January 1928. GARF, VOKS, f. 5283, op. 1, d. 142. Dreiser is mentioned on l. 9.
115 GARF, VOKS, f. 5283, op. 7, d. 6, ll. 114 and 123.
116 Ibid., ll. 121–2.
117 Ibid., l. 169.
118 *Actualités*, 24 August 1927 – review of *Seule en Russie*; *Information*, 26 August 1927 – *Courrier des livres*; *L'impartial français*, 30 August 1927; *Oeuvre*, 30 August 1927. GARF, VOKS, f. 5283, op. 7, d. 6, ll. 159–60.
119 *Regulations regarding the VOKS staff*, op. cit., p. 4, l. 6 verso.
120 Report of the VOKS *referent* of Romance countries. GARF, VOKS, f. 5283, op. 7, d. 34.
121 Ibid.
122 'About Dreiser's stay in the USSR', op. cit., l. 62.
123 Ibid.
124 Davidovskaya. 'On the American writer Theodore Dreiser's trip to N. Novgorod', 11 December 1927. GARF, VOKS, f. 5283, op. 7, ll. 66–8.
125 'About Dreiser's stay in the USSR', op. cit., l. 64.
126 Sergey Dinamov, ENI, *Literary Encyclopedia*, vol. 3, 1930, http://feb-web.ru/feb/litenc/encyclop/le3/le3–4171.htm.
127 M. Lewin. *The Making of the Soviet System*. London: Methuen, 1985, p. 100.
128 Ioffe. *International scientific and cultural relations of the Soviet Union. 1928–1932*, op. cit., pp. 226–7. Kameneva was still in her position in 1929 – a letter was sent to her in this year by Prof. Ye. Spal'vin, VOKS plenipotentiary in Japan. In his letter of 10 May 1929, he states that he had received her letter of 23 March. GARF, VOKS, f. 5283, op. 1 d. 142.
129 *International, Scientific and Cultural Relations of the Soviet Union. 1928–1932*, op. cit., pp. 226–7.

130 The last reference about Kameneva is found in the report of Livent-Levit, *referent* for Central Europe, of 17 July 1929, in which he says, 'Two weeks ago when O.D. [Kameneva] was still here'. Report by *referent* Livent-Levit, 17 July–25 October 1929, op. cit., l. 1.

131 V.V. Katanyan, ed. *Imya etoy teme: lyubov'! Sovremennitsy o Mayakovskom* (*Love is the Name of this Theme. Contemporaries on Mayakovsky*). Moscow: Druzhba Narodov, 1993, pp. 44–85 and p. 77.

132 Istrati, letter to GPU of 4 December 1928 in the attachment to *Vers l'autre flamme*, op. cit., p. 198.

133 Report from the editor of the information bulletin A. Dikgof-Derental' to the VOKS Chair Petrov of 19 October 1929, op. cit., l. 11.

134 GARF, VOKS f. 5283, op. 8, d. 62.

135 See previous reports on Dreiser, op. cit.

136 GARF, VOKS f. 5283, op. 7, d. 13, ll. 199–201.

137 Ibid., l. 199.

138 Ibid., l. 201.

139 Ibid., l. 201.

140 Item (4), 'Bureau's tasks', in 'Provisions regarding the Bureau for the Reception of Foreigners, *Staff Regulations*, op. cit., p. 4.

141 The Program of cultural service of a Dr Weinstein (*Programma kul'turnogo obsluzhivaniya d-ra Vainshtein*). GARF, VOKS, f. 5283, op. 1 d. 142, l. 141.

142 Davidovskaya. 'On the American writer Theodore Dreiser's trip to N. Novgorod', 11 December 1927, and 'About Dreiser's stay in the USSR', op. cit, ll. 62–8.

143 GARF, VOKS, f. 5283, op. 7, d. 13.

144 Ibid., p. 159.

145 Ibid., 5 July 1929.

146 Ibid.

147 Undated and unsigned. GARF, VOKS, f. 5283, op. 7, d. 13, ll. 159–61.

148 Ibid.

149 Ibid.

150 Ibid.

151 Ibid.

152 Ibid.

153 Ibid

154 Ibid.

155 Ibid.

156 Ibid.

157 *Vendredi*, 29 May 1936 and 17 July 1936. In: *André Gide et l'URSS*, op. cit., p. 102.

6 Manufacturing support: VOKS in the 1930s

1 Petrov to VOKS representatives, including Ioel'son, 21 March 1930, l. 13, and 'VOKS activities regarding the campaign of response to the statements of foreign clerics', 14 March 1930, ll. 8–12. Petrov to VKP(b) in GARF, VOKS, f. 5283 op. 1a d. 143. Correspondence between VOKS and NKID regarding Britain, 15 March 1930–26 December 1930.

2 The Director of the Museum of Western Art suggested that all enquiries about cooperation be exercised through VOKS. 'C'est la prérogative de VOKS de cultiver les relations intellectuelles et artistiques entre nos pays; je ne doute pas que VOKS étudiera avec une grande attention et sympathie la question du voyage du peintre Le Fauconnier.' B. Ternowets, Director of the Museum of Western Art, to Barbusse, letter of 26 February 1935. RGASPI, MORP, f. 541, op. 1, d. 113.

3 Arosev to member of TsK VKP(b) Ya. A. Yakovlev, 23 November 1936. GARF, VOKS, f. 5283 op. 1a d. 308, l. 118.

4   Information on tourists from France, Italy and Spain who visited the USSR from late 1935 to 1936, and the records of conversations with them, 5 October 1935–8 October 1936. GARF, VOKS, f. 5283, op. 2, d.260, l. 130.

5   Ibid., l. 159.

6   VOKS correspondence (1932). GARF, VOKS, f. 5283, op. 7, f. 48.

7   Information on tourists from France, op. cit., ll. 159–90.

8   VOKS listed the 'bourgeoisie' separately from professionals and students.

9   Andre Gide. *Afterthoughts: A Sequel to Back from the USSR*, translated by Dorothy Bussy. London: Martin Secker, 1938, pp.102–3. In: L. Maximenkov, C. Barnes. 'Boris Pasternak in August 1936 – an NKVD Memorandum'. *Toronto Slavic Quarterly*, 2003, 6 (Fall), http://www.utoronto.ca/tsq/06/pasternak06.shtml.

10   Information on tourists from France, op. cit.

11   Arosev's speech at the meeting of the VOKS active nucleus, 14 May 1937. GARF, VOKS, f. 5283, op. 1, d. 357, l. 67. In: Golubev and Nevezhin, op. cit., pp. 349–50.

12   R. Orlova. *Memoirs of Times not Bygone*. Ann Arbor: Ardis, 1983, pp. 103–18.

13   Presumably Chamson referred to their fear of Fascism. Information on tourists from France, op. cit., l. 11.

14   Malraux to VOKS Chairman, letter of 3 September 1935 (in Russian). GARF, VOKS, f. 5283, op. 7, d. 287.

15   Ibid., l. 149.

16   Information on tourists from France, op. cit., ll. 30 and 179.

17   Ibid., l. 26.

18   Barbusse to Petrov, letter of 20 August 1932. GARF, VOKS, f. 5283, op. 7, d. 269.

19   VOKS, in turn, sent Friedmann to the Comintern. Letter from I. Roytman (the Acting Head of the Romance sector) to Manuil'sky (Secretariat of IKKI), 16 September 1932, ibid.

20   Information on tourists from France, op. cit., l. 180.

21   Ibid., ll. 120, 139 and 171.

22   Ibid., ll. 20 and 29.

23   Ibid., l. 185.

24   Ibid., l. 117.

25   Ibid., l. 103.

26   Ibid., ll. 87–9.

27   Ibid., l. 165.

28   Ibid., l. 130.

29   Ibid., ll. 76–82.

30   Ibid., l. 185.

31   Ibid., l. 180.

32   Ibid.

33   Ibid., l. 164.

34   Ibid., ll. 140–2.

35   Interpreter Ghilyarevskaya on Pierre Herbart and his wife, ibid., l. 102.

36   Ibid., l. 164.

37   Ibid., l. 180.

38   Ibid., l. 93.

39   For example, a visitor who was shown photos and given a description of the Institute of Mother and Child, instead of being allowed to sit in on appointments at the Institute, ibid., l. 162.

40   This visitor is unrelated to Marguerite and Jean-Richard Bloch.

41   Information on tourists from France, op. cit., l. 162.

42   Ibid., l. 161.

43   Ibid., l. 162.

44   Ibid., l. 91.

45   Ibid., l. 37.

46 Skavronskaya, interpreter (Leningrad), to Grasberg, Head of the First Western Department (Moscow), report regarding the visit of René Arcos; his correspondence with Arosev of 5 February 1935 and 17 February 1935. GARF, VOKS, f. 5283, op. 2, d. 292.
47 Interpreter Gladkova's report of 27 April–5 May 1935, ibid.
48 Information on tourists from France, op. cit., l. 190.
49 Ibid., l. 188.
50 Ibid., l. 190.
51 Ibid., l. 98.
52 Ibid., l. 96.
53 Ibid.
54 Ibid., l. 71.
55 Ghilyarevskaya's report about work with Mme Duchêne (France), 23 May 1936. GARF, VOKS, f. 5283, op. 1a, d. 307, l. 120 (Secret Department, 1936).
56 Ibid.
57 Gladkova quotes Jacques Meyer, the Secretary General of the newspaper *Intransigeant*. Information on tourists from France, op. cit., l. 117.
58 Ibid., l. 44.
59 Frantz Masereel in a conversation with Melnikov, the Head of the First Western Department, ibid., l. 80.
60 René Arcos' visit; his correspondence with Arosev of 5 February 1935 and 17 February 1935, op. cit.
61 Information on tourists from France, op. cit., l. 73.
62 Ibid., l. 45.
63 Ibid., l. 38.
64 Ibid., l. 129.
65 Paul Gsell to Arosev, 10 Sept 1934. GARF, VOKS, f. 5283 op. 9 d. 129, l.74.
66 Ibid., l. 190.
67 Gladkova, record of conversation with visitors (George Friedmann, 24 August 1936). GARF, VOKS, f. 5283 op. 1 d. 334, l. 30.
68 Information on tourists from France, op. cit., l. 113.
69 Ibid., l. 104.
70 Malraux to VOKS Chairman, letter of 3 September 1935, op. cit. (in Russian).
71 Ibid.
72 Arosev to Pokhitonov, note of 23 September 1934, ibid.
73 List of expenses of the First Western Department, 31 October 1935–4 March 1936. GARF, VOKS, f. 5283, op. 2, d. 259.
74 Letter to VOKS of 22 October 1935 requesting information on extra-curricular, professional, artistic and technical education of adolescents, and leisure for adults (clubs, courses, libraries). Information on tourists from France, op. cit., l. 66.
75 Student Jean Tren asked VOKS to send information to a Paris school, ibid., l. 182.
76 Broun to VOKS, report of 10 February 1937. GARF, VOKS, f. 5283, op. 7, d. 452.
77 VOKS correspondence (1935–1937). GARF, VOKS, f. 5283, op. 2, f. 288, l. 81.
78 Ibid., l. 69, ll. 74–6.
79 Broun to Melnikov, Head of the First Western Department, letter of 24 April 1936. GARF, VOKS, f. 5283, op. 7, d. 364.
80 Broun to VOKS, report of 10 February 1937, op. cit.
81 Report of the Romance sector, July–December 1932. GARF, VOKS, f. 5283, op. 2, d. 100, l. 21.
82 Broun to VOKS, report of 10 February 1937, op. cit.
83 Melnikov, Head of the First Western Department, to Broun, letter of 19 May 1936. GARF, VOKS, f. 5283, op. 7, f. 364.
84 D. Novomirskiy, the Head of the Anglo-American sector in Moscow, to Ioelson, 7

March 1930. Correspondence between VOKS and NKID regarding England, March–December 1930. GARF, VOKS, f. 5283, op. 1a, d. 143 1.2.

85 'Kak druz'ya SSSR vystupayut zarubezhom v yego zaschitu' ('How friends of the USSR act abroad in its defence'), April 1931 (author unknown). GARF, VOKS, f. 5283, op. 1 d. 168, ll. 1–19.

86 Ibid.

87 Ibid. l. 1.

88 Petrov to VOKS representatives, including Ioel'son, 21 March 1930. Correspondence between VOKS and NKID regarding England, op. cit., l. 13.

89 D. Lilleker. *Against the Cold War: The History and Political Traditions of Pro-Sovietism in the British Labour Party, 1945–1989.* London: Palgrave IB Tauris, 2004, p. 14.

90 Soviet sources refer to it as the Society of Friends of the New Russia. See: S. Kuz'min. 'The English society of cultural relations with the USSR', op. cit., pp. 203–6.

91 I. Maysky. *B. Shou i drugiye: Vospominaniya (B. Shaw and the Others: Memoirs).* Moscow: Iskusstvo, 1967.

92 Anglo-American Department, correspondence with the London society for cultural relations. GARF, VOKS, f. 5283, op. 3, d. 325.

93 From 12 November to 8 December 1928, the SCR assisted in arranging an exhibition of Soviet graphic art in London, and VOKS commented that 'the success of the show with the public was beyond any doubt whatsoever'. Bloomsbury Gallery, London, to VOKS, 29 October 1929. GARF, VOKS, f. 5283 op. 1a, d. 127, l. 8.

94 In his letter of 14 February 1929 to F.V. Linde, VOKS Secretary General, ibid., l. 5.

95 D. Novomirskiy, Head of the Anglo-American Sector, to Ioel'son, VOKS plenipotentiary in England, 7 March 1930. Correspondence between VOKS and NKID regarding England, op. cit., l. 2.

96 Ibid.

97 Catherine Rabinovich, Honorary Secretary, to Novomirskiy, 7 May 1930, ibid., l.40.

98 Novomisrskiy to Ioel'son, 17 May 1930, ibid., l. 37.

99 Ioelson to Petrov, 4 April 1930, ibid., ll. 30–1.

100 Ibid., l. 2 (verso).

101 Ioelson to Novomirskiy, 3 June 1930, ibid., l. 76.

102 Ioelson to Novomirskiy, 24 June 1930, ibid., l. 88.

103 Novomirskiy to Ioelson, 7 June 1930, ibid., l. 45.

104 Petrov to Sokol'nikov, Soviet Plenipotentiary in England, 26 August 1930, ibid., l. 57.

105 Ingulov to Petrov (possibly), 13 November 1930, ibid., ll. 95–7.

106 Ibid., l. 97.

107 Ibid., l. 96.

108 Ingulov to Petrov, 24 November 1930, ibid., l. 101.

109 Petrov to Sokol'nikov and (possibly) VOKS representative, 26 November 1930, ibid., ll.100–1.

110 Ibid., l. 103.

111 Ibid.

112 Ye. L. (Lerner?) to Svirskiy, representative in USA, undated, filed 1932. GARF, VOKS, f. 5283 op. 1a, d. 190, l. 5 (verso).

113 Anglo-American Sector, reports of VOKS departments for 1935. GARF, VOKS, f. 5283 op. 1, d. 278, l. 7.

114 'Le Cercle de la Russie Neuve (1928–1936), op. cit.

115 Cultural rapprochement society Cercle de la Russie Neuve. GARF, VOKS, f. 5283, op. 7, d. 34, l. 96.

116 Broun to VOKS, report of 10 February 1937, op. cit.

117 Cultural rapprochement society Cercle de la Russie Neuve, op. cit., l. 96.

118 Ibid., l. 80.

119 Talks presented by the cultural rapprochement society Russie Neuve, 30 July–31 October 1934. GARF, VOKS, f. 5283, op. 9, d. 121.
120 Cultural rapprochement society Cercle de la Russie Neuve, op. cit., l. 80.
121 Report of the Romance sector, July–December 1932, op. cit., ll. 1–6.
122 Talks presented by the cultural rapprochement society Russie Neuve, op. cit.
123 Broun to Polyakova, senior officer-in-charge (*starshiy referent*) of the First Western Department, letter of 10 February 1937, f. 5283, op. 7, d. 452.
124 Cultural rapprochement society Cercle de la Russie Neuve, op. cit., l. 80.
125 Notification of the opening of the Association pour l'étude de la culture soviétique (in French). Broun to VOKS, letter of 22 July 1937. GARF, VOKS, f. 5283, op. 7, d. 452.
126 Report on the situation in France. GARF, VOKS, f. 5283, op. 2, f. 259, l. 31.
127 Report of the Romance sector, July–December 1932, op. cit., l. 99.
128 Talks presented by the cultural rapprochement society Russie Neuve, 30 July–31 October 1934, op. cit.
129 Broun to VOKS, report of 10 February 1937, op. cit.
130 Ibid.
131 Arosev's visit to France. GARF, VOKS f. 5283, op. 7, d. 205. Arosev's trip to France, in December 1934, was included in his tour of Eastern Europe and the Baltic States.
132 Arosev requested that the VOKS representative give the poets the 'utmost assistance to what would be the best and most beneficial use of their time in Paris'. Arosev to Ye. Girshfeld, letter of 16 November 1935. GARF, VOKS, f. 5283, op. 7, d. 364.
133 A. Bezymensky to A. Shcherbakov, letter of 11 December 1935. In: A. Rubashkin, ed. 'Writers who wrote to Shcherbakov', letters by I. Ehrenburg, M. Kol'tsov, A. Bezymensky and A. Shcherbakov, 1935–36. *Neva*, 1999, 2: 177–8. Rubashkin stresses Shcherbakov's powerful position, ensured by his personal contacts with Stalin, p. 171.
134 Broun to VOKS, report of 10 February 1937, op. cit.
135 Broun to Nikolayev, Deputy Chairman of VOKS, letter of 25 February 1937, ibid.

7 VOKS and the 'famous foreigners'

1 List of expenses of the First Western Department, 31 October 1935–4 March 1936, op. cit.
2 Pokhitonov. 'Dlya pamati' ('Memory list'). GARF, VOKS, f. 5283, op. 2, d. 259, ll. 21–2.
3 Reports of VOKS Departments for 1935. GARF, VOKS, f. 5283, op. 1, d. 278.
4 Tsentrosoyuz, England, Ltd to Tsentrosoyuz, Moskva, and Lerner, VOKS, 20 September 1932. GARF, VOKS, f. 5283 op. 1a, d. 190, l. 64.
5 Hollander, Margulies, Coeuré, Mazuy.
6 Arosev to Ravel, invitation of 17 February 1935. GARF, VOKS, f. 5283, op. 7, d. 286. Ravel did not come to the USSR because of illness.
7 Vildrac to Arosev, letter of 24 May 1935. GARF, VOKS, f. 5283, op. 5, f. 836.
8 Arosev to Vildrac, letter of 14 June 1935 to Vildrac, ibid.
9 Chernyavskiy to Angarov, TsK VKP(b), 5 July 1936. GARF, VOKS, f. 5283 op. 1a, d. 308, l. 75.
10 Shut'ko, member of the Bureau of the Board of VOKS, to Hotel Metropol, letter of 9 September 1935, ibid.
11 Karen Michaelis. GARF, VOKS f. 5283, op. 8, d. 230, l. 2–5.
12 Ibid., ll. 24–8.
13 G.B. Shaw. GARF, VOKS f. 5283, op. 12, d. 328, l. 2.
14 Ibid., l. 2–2 (verso)
15 Ibid., l. 2 (verso) (quoted in the original).
16 Lunacharsky's speech, ibid., ll.3–7.
17 Ibid., l. 7 (verso).

18 Ibid., l. 8.
19 Programme of service provided to Marquet. GARF, VOKS, f. 5283, op. 7, d. 313.
20 Unknown author (possibly Broun) to Chernyavsky, letter of 31 July 1934, ibid., l. 57.
21 Chernyavsky to V.V. Pokrovsky, Leningrad VOKS, ibid., l. 54.
22 Ibid., ll. 56–7.
23 Overko to Chernyavsky, ibid., l. 51.
24 Ibid.
25 Report by com. Kravchenko on the reception of the French artist Albert Marquet, ibid., ll. 35–6.
26 Ibid.
27 Ibid.
28 Report by com. Kravchenko, ibid., l. 35.
29 Kravchenko, conclusion, 19 August 1934, ibid.
30 I. Ehrenburg. *Lyudi, gody, zhizn'* (*People, Years, My Life*). Memoirs in three volumes. The amended and completed edition. Moscow: Sovetskyy pisatel' Publishing house, 1990, Vol. II, p. 208.
31 Indicated, for instance, in the balance of expenses for the reception of Barbusse in 1935 – room in Metropol, secretary, interpreter. List of expenses of the First Western Department, op. cit.
32 Ye. Lerner (Deputy Chairperson of VOKS) to Ye. Gelfer, Head of the Department for the Reception of Foreigners, letter of 16 September 1932, ibid.
33 Telegrams from Lerner to Kharkov and to Dneprostroy notifying them of Barbusse's arrival and requesting that he be given good hotel rooms, provisions, a car and that he be met at the station, 4 and 7 October 1932, ibid.
34 M. Ingber, Head of the Press Bureau, to Sergiyevsky, the All-Union Lenin Library, letter of 27 September 1932, ibid.
35 Apletin to Pokrovsky, Leningrad VOKS, letter of 11 September 1934. GARF, VOKS, f. 5283, op. 7, d. 118.
36 Telegram to Leningrad, 19 September 1934, ibid.
37 Pokhitonov and Pokrovsky, undated telegram, ibid.
38 Pessis, the editor of Foreign Press, to Défélipon (*Monde*), letter of 16 August 1930, ibid.
39 Barbusse to Pessis, letter of 3 March 1930. GARF, VOKS, f. 5283, op. 7, d. 269.
40 Barbusse to VOKS, letter of 3 March 1930, ibid.
41 Ibid.
42 Barbusse to Pessis, letter of 6 July 1929, ibid.
43 Barbusse to Pessis, letter of 25 April 1929, ibid.
44 Barbusse to Pessis, letter of 25 April 1929, ibid.
45 Barbusse and Défélipon to Pessis, correspondence of January–February 1930, ibid.
46 Pessis to Défélipon, letter of 15 January 1930, ibid.
47 Pessis to Défélipon, letter of 14 February 1930, ibid.
48 Barbusse to Pessis, letter of 23 February 1930, ibid.
49 Défélipon to Pessis, letter of 22 January 1930, ibid.
50 Barbusse to Pessis, letter of 23 February 1930, ibid.
51 Barbusse to Pessis, letter of 23 August 1930, ibid.
52 Ibid.
53 Pessis to Barbusse, letter of 7 October 1930, ibid.
54 Barbusse to Arosev, letter of 4 June 1934. GARF, VOKS, f. 5283, op. 7, d. 269.
55 Annette Vidal's telegram to VOKS (undated) following Barbusse's death, ibid.
56 Berlin, 17 December (1930 or 1931). GARF, VOKS, f. 5283, op. 2, d. 81, ll. 45–6.
57 Rolland to VOKS, letter of 29 August 1930. GARF, VOKS, f. 5283, op. 7, l. 118.
58 Rolland to Arosev, letter of 24 December 1934, ibid.
59 Rolland to Arosev, letter of 8 February 1932, ibid.

60 Rolland to Rabinovich, letter of 2 May 1930, ibid.
61 Rolland to Petrov, letter of 5 June 1932, ibid.
62 Petrov to Rolland, letter of 26 June 1932, ibid.
63 Arosev to Rolland, letter of 7 February 1935, ibid.
64 *Voyage à Moscou*, op. cit.
65 Apletin to Rolland, letter of 17 March 1934, with letters by Panferov and Novitch attached. Bibliothèque Nationale, Fonds Romain Rolland, Lettres d'Aplétine, f. 1.
66 Rolland to Rabinovich, letter of 2 May 1930. GARF, VOKS, f. 5283, op. 7, d. 118.
67 M. Kudasheva to VOKS, letter of 12 June 1933, ibid.
68 Apletin to Rolland, letter of 4 April 1938. Bibliothèque Nationale, Fonds Romain Rolland, Lettres d'Aplétine, f. 7.
69 *Des hommes d'influence,* op. cit.
70 Arosev to Yezhov, Secretary of TsK VKP(b), 15 May 1936. GARF, VOKS, f. 5283 op. la, d. 308, l. 47.
71 Ibid., l. 47 (verso)
72 Secret Department, 1936. GARF, VOKS, f. 5283 op. 1a, d. 307.
73 Ibid., l. 39.
74 To decline VOKS's request regarding the organisation of exhibitions of Lithuanian artists, American art and French paintings in the USSR. A. Andreyev, Secretary of TsK VKP(b), regarding foreign exhibitions of 5 May 1936. TsK VKP(b), GARF, VOKS, f. 5283 op. la, d. 308 l. 48.
75 Secret Department, 1936, ibid., l. 19.
76 Ibid., l. 86.
77 Ibid., l. 91.
78 Ibid., l. 90.
79 Letter by Polyakova of 17 May 1936, ibid., l. 106.
80 Arosev to Yagoda, People's Commissariat of Internal Affairs, Commissar General of State Security, People's Commissar of Internal Affairs, 21 August 1936, ibid., ll. 148–50.
81 Report by Shpringer (undated), ibid., l. 150.
82 Arosev to com. Yezhov, Secretary of TsK VKP(b), 5 May 1936. GARF, VOKS, f. 5283 op. la, d. 308 l. 42.
83 *Proyekt dokladnoy zapiski v Politbyuro TsK VKP(b) o VOKS'e* (*Draft Proposal regarding VOKS [for the consideration] of the Politburo of the Central Committee of the VKP(b)*). GARF, VOKS, f. 5283 op. la, d. 308, l. 59.
84 Arosev to Ya. Yakovlev of TsK VKP(b), 23 November 1936. GARF, VOKS, f. 5283, op. 1a, d. 307 d. TT l. 187, copy to N. Yezhov, People's Commissar of Internal Affairs.
85 Arosev, regarding proposal of 3 December 1936 to merge Intourist and VOKS, to Angarov, Secretary of TsK VKP(b), copy to Andreyev and Yezhov, ibid., l. 129.
86 Ibid., l. 119.
87 Arosev to Stalin, Molotov, Yezhov and Andreyev, TsK VKP(b), 13 December 1936. GARF, VOKS, f. 5283, op. la, d. 308, ll. 133–9.
88 Ibid., l. 135.
89 Ibid., ll. 133–9.
90 Telegram of invitation from Arosev to Gollancz, 15 April 1937. Victor Gollancz's stay in USSR. GARF, VOKS, f. 5283 op. 3, d. 1070, l. 28.
91 J. Lewis. *The Left Book Club: An Historical Record.* n.p.: Gollancz, 1970.
92 Kislova to Leningrad VOKS, 23 April 1937. Victor Gollancz's stay in USSR, op. cit., l. 43.
93 Ibid., l. 39.
94 Ibid., l. 38.
95 Regarding conversation with Gollancz, Leningrad Section. Orlov to Arosev, 14 May 1937, ibid., l. 37.

96 Ibid., l. 34.
97 Ibid.
98 Ibid., l. 34 (verso).
99 Ibid., l. 26.
100 Gollancz to Kislova, Anglo-American Department, 5 July 1937, ibid., l. 23.
101 Left Book Club's groups' stay in USSR, 24 June 1938–7 August 1938. GARF, VOKS, f. 5283, op. 3, d. 1087.
102 Umansky, A.O. Litagentstvo, to Kislova, 19 May 1937, ibid., d. 1070, l. 29.
103 Ibid., ll. 9–11.
104 VOKS reprentative Grinyov, Soviet Embassy, to Milikovskiy, Head of Anglo-American sector, 22 December 1937, ibid., l. 16.
105 Gollancz's form (Anketa), ibid., ll. 2–4.
106 Ibid., l. 3.
107 L. Maximenkov, C. Barnes. 'Boris Pasternak in August 1936 – an NKVD Memorandum'. *Toronto Slavic Quarterly*, 2003, 6 (Fall), http://www.utoronto.ca/tsq/06/pasternak06.shtml.
108 L. Feuchtwanger. 'Foreword. Aim of the book'. In: *Moscow 1937*, Published 1937, http://www.kuzbass.ru/moshkow/koi/INPROZ/FEJHTWANGER/moscow1937.txt
109 Ibid.
110 Some of them were published earlier and the others, kept in separate files, are being added in this section. I.A. Altman 'L. Feuchtwanger in Moscow (from the reports of a VOKS employee)' in *Sovetskiye arkhivy* (*Soviet Archives*), 1989, 4: 55–63. Other VOKS reports on Feuchtwanger are contained in GARF, VOKS, f. 5283, op. 8, d. 290, op. 5, d. 745, op. 1, d. 334, and op. 8 d. 292.
111 Karavkina, 13 December 1936. GARF, VOKS, f. 5283, op. 5, d. 745, l. 22.
112 Karavkina, 11 December 1936, ibid., l. 21.
113 Karavkina, 29 December 1936. GARF, VOKS, f. 5283, op. 1, d. 334.
114 Karavkina, 13 December 1936, op. cit., l. 22.
115 Karavkina, 7 December 1936. GARF, VOKS, f. 5283, op. 8, d. 290, l. 16.
116 Karavkina, 11 December 1936, op. cit., l. 21.
117 24 December 1936. GARF, VOKS, f. 5283, op. 1, d. 334, l.5.
118 Karavkina, 13 December 1936, op. cit.
119 This meeting took place on 28 December.
120 Karavkina, 15 December 1936. GARF, VOKS, f. 5283, op. 8, d. 290, l. 11.
121 Karavkina, 25 December 1936. GARF, VOKS, f. 5283, op. 1, d. 334, l. 4.
122 Karavkina, 3 January 1937. GARF, VOKS, f. 5283, op. 5, d. 745, l. 19.
123 Karavkina, 14 December 1936. GARF, VOKS, f. 5283, op. 8, d.290, l. 9.
124 Karavkina, 16 December 1936. GARF, VOKS, f. 5283, op. 1, d. 334, l. 9.
125 Karavkina, 25 December 1936, ibid., l. 4.
126 Karavkina, 27 December 1936, ibid., l. 3.
127 Karavkina, 17 December 1936, ibid., l. 8.
128 Karavkina, 19 December 1936, ibid., l. 7.
129 Karavkina, 14 December 1936, op. cit.
130 Karavkina, 16 December 1936, op. cit.
131 Karavkina, 17 December 1936, ibid. l. 8.
132 Karavkina, 25 December 1936, ibid. l. 4.
133 Karavkina, 22 December 1936, ibid. l. 6.
134 Karavkina, 11 December 1936, op. cit., l. 21.
135 Karavkina, 4 January 1937, ibid., l. 20.
136 Ibid.
137 Karavkina, 22 December 1936 op. cit., l. 6.
138 Karavkina, 29 December 1936, ibid., l. 1.
139 The full text is available in 'Beseda s Lionom Feykhtvangherom (1937)' ('Conversa-

tion with Lion Feuchtwanger (1937)'). *Al'manakh Vostok*, 2004, 6 (18), http://www.situation.ru/app/j_artp_447.htm.

140 Lion Feuchtwanger's *Moscow 1937* was first published in Amsterdam in 1937 in German and immediately translated into Russian and published in the Soviet Union. The English quotations are my own translation from the Russian version of the 1937 Soviet edition, http://www.kuzbass.ru/moshkow/koi/INPROZ/FEJHTWANGER/moscow1937.txt.

141 'Accusations caused by the lack of comfort', *Moscow 1937*.

142 Ibid.

143 Chapter 1, 'Weekdays and holidays', *Moscow 1937*.

144 'A picture of today's Moscow' in Chapter 1, ibid.

145 Ibid.

146 'Frankness for frankness' in Introduction, ibid.

147 'Bolshevist self-criticism' in Chapter 2, 'Conformism and Individualism', ibid.

148 'Construction of a Soviet State or the freedom of abuse?' in Chapter 3, 'Democracy and Dictatorship', ibid.

149 'Conversation with Lion Feuchtwanger (1937)', op. cit.

150 Chapter 6, *Moscow 1937*.

151 Chapter 6, 'Stalin and Trotsky', *Moscow 1937*.

152 Chapter 7, 'The Obvious and the Covert in the Trotskyite trials', *Moscow 1937*.

153 Ibid.

154 In: Roy Medvedev. 'Western Writers Meet Stalin. Why the Generalissimo Liked Foreign Litterateurs'. *The Moscow News*, 2005, 48, http://english.mn.ru/english/issue.php?2002–30–11.

155 GARF, VOKS, f. 5283, op. 14, d. 292, l. 167. In: Golubev and Nevezhin, op. cit., p. 317.

8 The bond of friendship

1 Archives of the Foreign Commission of the Soviet Writers' Union are kept in the Russian State Archive of Literature and Arts (RGALI, formerly TsGALI), Fond 631. Information on its creation and tasks is contained in *opis'* 14.

2 It was led by Party functionaries A. Shcherbakov (1934–36), V. Stavsky (1936–39) and A. Fadeev (1939–44). D. Babichenko, ed. *'Schast'ye literatury' Gosudarstvo i pisateli. 1925–1938. Dokumenty ('The Happiness of Literature' The State and the Writers. 1925–38. Documents)*. Moscow: Rosspen, 1997.

3 Barghoorn reports that, by 1956, sixty people were employed by the Commission's section for Polish literature. *The Soviet Cultural Offensive*, p. 169.

4 Although I will be examining pre-war materials, some of my information will include the wartime and post-war period to illustrate the Foreign Commission's further adjustment to the changing circumstances.

5 RGALI, Foreign Commission, f. 631, op. 13, d. 118 and op. 11, d. 302.

6 M. Apletin, the Deputy Chairman of the Foreign Commission of the Soviet Writers' Union, to V.F. Smirnov, the Chairman of VOKS, letter of 2 June 1939. RGALI, Foreign Commission, f. 631, op. 14, d. 23. The meeting was held in the office of A. Shcherbakov at the Board of the Soviet Writers' Union.

7 Minutes of the meeting of the Foreign Commission of the Soviet Writers' Union on 29 May 1936. RGALI, Foreign Commission, f. 613, op. 14, d. 5, l. 16.

8 M. Apletin's statement regarding visits of foreign writers during the meeting of the Foreign Commission of the Soviet Writers' Union of 29 May 1936, ibid., l. 14.

9 Ibid., ll. 15–16.

10 Gide's travels in the USSR including his route, sightseeing and reactions, as well as newspaper reports, are best documented in Maurer's *André Gide et l'URSS*, op. cit.

11 Maurer lists all the statements made by Gide during his visit and the occasions that triggered them, op. cit., pp. 107–13.

12 Kol'tsov's statement regarding visits of foreign writers made during the meeting of the Foreign Commission of the Soviet Writers' Union of 29 May 1936. RGALI, Foreign Commission, f. 613, op. 14, d. 5, l. 16.

13 Pil'nyak's comments made during the meeting of the Foreign Commission of the Soviet Writers' Union, 29 May 1936, ibid., l. 17.

14 Ibid.

15 Lev E'lbert ('Snob') – a 'special designation officer' of the VChK Foreign Department (*osoboupolnomochennyy inostrannogo otdela VChK*) in Vaksberg, *Lilya Brik*, p. 121. The Foreign Department of VChK and, later, OGPU and the NKVD, were tasked with spying abroad. In: J. Rossi. *Spravochnik po GULAGu* (*The GULAG Handbook*). London: Overseas Publications Interchange, 1987, p. 136.

16 Kudasheva-Rolland to Apletin, letter of June 1936. RGALI, Foreign Commission, f. 631, op. 14, d. 729.

17 Georges Friedmann to Apletin, letters of 20 June 1939 and 19 July 1939. RGALI, Foreign Commission, f. 631, op. 3, d. 117, ll. 47 and 53 respectively.

18 Chamson to Apletin, 1936, undated letter. RGALI, Foreign Commission, f. 631, op. 1, d. 293.

19 Marcel Cohen to Apletin, letter of 25 October 1938. RGALI, Foreign Commission, f. 631, op. 11, d. 257, l. 4.

20 Apletin to Cassou, letter of 4 March 1936. RGALI, Foreign Commission, f. 631, op. 11, d. 256, l. 2.

21 Apletin to Bogdanov, the Central Committee of the International Organisation for Assistance to Revolutionaries (MOPR), letter of 14 August (year unstated). RGALI, Foreign Commission, f. 613, op. 14, d. 23, l. 98.

22 Apletin to Yaroslavsky (*Istorik marksist*), letter of 26 May 1939, ibid., l. 22.

23 Apletin to Erlich (*SSSR na stroyke*), letter of 25 May 1939, ibid., l. 25.

24 Ibid.

25 Apletin to The Soviet Writers' Union, letter of 31 July 1939, ibid., l. 82.

26 Apletin to Kudasheva and Rolland, letter of 31 May 1938. Bibliothèque Nationale, Fonds Romain Rolland, Lettres d'Aplétine, f. 12.

27 Apletin to Aragon, letter of 20 June 1939. RGALI, Foreign Commission, f. 631, op. 11, d. 233.

28 Kol'tsov to Bloch, letter of 22 May 1935. Bibliothèque Nationale, Fonds Jean-Richard Bloch, Lettres à Jean-Richard Bloch, t. XLI, ff. 187–8.

29 Chamson to Apletin, 1936, undated letter, op. cit.

30 Apletin to Aragon, letter of 17 February 1938. RGALI, Foreign Commission, f. 613, op. 11, d. 233.

31 Apletin to Petrosyan, Department of Propaganda and Agitation of the VKP(b) Central Committee, letter of 1 June 1939. RGALI, Foreign Commission, f. 631, op. 11, d. 257, l. 24.

32 'L'anniversaire de Romain Rolland'. RGALI, Foreign Commission, f. 631, op. 14, d. 735.

33 RGALI, Foreign Commission, f. 631, op. 14, d. 729.

34 RGALI, Foreign Commission, f. 631, op. 14, d. 735.

35 Apletin to Aragon, telegram of 15 December 1936. RGALI, Foreign Commission, f. 613, op. 11, d. 233.

36 Apletin to Bloch, letter of 23 November 1936. Bibliothèque Nationale, Fonds Jean-Richard Bloch, Lettres à Jean-Richard Bloch, op. cit., f. 64.

37 Apletin to Vaillant-Couturier, letters of 29 February 1936 and 26 March 1936. RGALI, Foreign Commission, f. 631, op. 11, d. 239.

38 Apletin to J.-R. Bloch, letter of 22 May 1937. Bibliothèque Nationale, Fonds Jean-Richard Bloch, Lettres à Jean-Richard Bloch, t. III, f. 67.

39 Apletin to Francis Jourdain, letter of 8 December 1936. RGALI, Foreign Commission, f. 631, op. 11, d. 254, l. 1.
40 Dnepropetrovsk workers to the Soviet Writers' Union, Moscow. RGALI, Foreign Commission, Apletin to Malraux, letter of 5 April 1936, f. 631, op. 11, d. 266.
41 Apletin to Francis Jourdain, letter of 8 December 1936. RGALI, Foreign Commission, f. 631, op. 11, d. 254, l. 1.
42 Apletin to Aragon, letter of 21 December 1937. RGALI, Foreign Commission, f. 613, op. 11, d. 233, l. 55.
43 Apletin to Cassou, letter of 14 May 1938. RGALI, Foreign Commission, f. 631, op. 11, d. 256, l. 4.
44 Apletin to Nizan, letter of 11 April 1937. RGALI, Foreign Commission, f. 631, op. 11, d. 274.
45 Dinamov to Nizan, letter of 1 June 1937, ibid.
46 *International Literature* (possibly Rokotov) to Nizan, letter of 10 January 1938. RGALI, *International Literature*, f. 1397, op. 2, d. 140.
47 Apletin to Bloch, letter of 23 November 1936. Bibliothèque Nationale, Fonds Jean-Richard Bloch, Lettres à Jean-Richard Bloch, f. 64.
48 Apletin to Kudasheva and Rolland, letter of 4 April 1938. Bibliothèque Nationale, Fonds Romain Rolland, Correspondance, f. 7.
49 Apletin to Cassou, letter of 4 March 1936. RGALI, Foreign Commission, f. 631, op. 11, d. 256, l. 2.
50 Apletin to Chamson, letter of 10 October 1936. RGALI, Foreign Commission, f. 631, op. 1, d. 293.
51 Dinamov to Chamson, letter of February 1937, ibid.
52 Apletin to Malraux, letter of 5 April 1936, op. cit. Factory newspapers: *Martenovka, Proletarskaya pravda, Postroyka*. Village newspapers: *Bol'shevistskiy put', Krasnyy Oktyabr'*. District newspapers: *Proletarskaya pravda, Zvezda, Severnyy rabochiy, Gor'kovskaya kommuna, Literaturnyy Leningrad, Orenburgskaya kommuna*. Republic newspapers: *Kommunist, Komsomolets Dagestana, Krasnyy Krym*. Moscow newspapers: *Pravda, Izvestiya, Literatunaya gazeta, Journal de Moscou, Moscow Daily News, Vechernyaya Moskva, Rabochaya Moskva, Komsomol'skaya pravda, Krasnyy sport, Za industrializatsiyu, Trud, Ekonomicheskaya zhizn', Krasnyy voin, Za kommunisticheskoya presveshcheniye*.
53 Dinamov to Chamson, letter of February 1937, op. cit.
54 'Par ailleurs, j'ai trouvé une somme rondelette, ce matin, pour mes trois anciens volumes parus en 1926 et complètement épuisés depuis longtemps; les éditions d'état m'ont demandé de signer un contrat d'ensemble pour tous mes bouquins passés, présents et à venir.' J.-R. Bloch. *Journal du voyage en URSS*, lettre du 29 août 1934, op. cit., ll. 32–3.
55 Arosev to Vildrac, letter of 14 June 1935. GARF, VOKS, f. 5283, op. 5, d. 836.
56 Rolland to Kerzhentsev, letter of 1 April 1936 (in Russian). RGALI, Foreign Commission, f. 631, op. 14, d. 729.
57 Apletin to Aragon, letter of 21 December 1937. RGALI, Foreign Commission, f. 631, op. 11, d. 233, l. 55.
58 Apletin to Aragon, letter of 7 April 1938, ibid.
59 Dinamov to Chamson, letter of 4 February 1936, op. cit.
60 Galperin to Nizan, letter of 2 March 1936. RGALI, Foreign Commission, f. 631, op. 11, d. 274.
61 Apletin to Kudasheva and Rolland, letter of 27 May 1938. Bibliotèque Nationale, Fonds Romain Rolland, f. 9.
62 Apletin to Aragon, letter of 17 March 1938. RGALI, Foreign Commission, f. 631, op. 11, d. 233.
63 Apletin to Julien Benda, letter of 3 April 1939. RGALI, Foreign Commission, f. 631, op. 11, d. 231, l. 4.

64 Apletin to Julien Benda, letter of 19 March 1939. RGALI, Foreign Commission, ibid., l. 3.
65 Thus, in 1939, one batch dated between 17 and 19 March, and the second between 2 and 3 April.
66 Friedmann to Apletin, letter of 2 February 1939. RGALI, Foreign Commission, f. 631, op. 3, d. 117.
67 Apletin to Historical Institute of the Academy of Sciences, letter of 26 August (year not stated). RGALI, Foreign Commission, f. 613, op. 14, d. 23, l. 110.
68 Apletin to Aragon, letter of 7 April 1938. RGALI, Foreign Commission, f. 631, op. 11, d. 233.
69 Apletin to Marcel Cohen, letter of 25 October 1938. RGALI, Foreign Commission, f. 631, op. 11, d. 257, l. 4.
70 Apletin to Cassou. RGALI, Foreign Commission, f. 631, op. 11, d. 256, l. 6.
71 Apletin to Aragon, letter of 1 February 1938. RGALI, Foreign Commission, f. 631, op. 11, d. 233.
72 Apletin to Nizan, letter of 7 February 1939, RGALI, Foreign Commission, f. 631, op. 11, d. 274.
73 Apletin to Bloch, letter of 10 March 1937. Bibliothèque Nationale, Fonds Jean-Richard Bloch, Lettres à Jean-Richard Bloch, t. III, l. 65.
74 Apletin to Malraux, letter of 16 June 1937. RGALI, Foreign Commission, f. 631, op. 11, d. 266.
75 Dinamov to Nizan, letter of 20 May 1937. RGALI, *International Literature* f. 1397, op. 2 d. 140.
76 Ibid.
77 Ibid.
78 Apletin to Bloch, letter of 10 March 1937, op. cit.
79 Apletin to Aragon, letter of March 1937. RGALI, Foreign Commission, f. 631, op. 11, d. 233.
80 Dinamov to Chamson, letter of 4 February 1936, ibid.
81 Apletin to Vaillant-Couturier, letter of 9 February 1936. RGALI, Foreign Commission, f. 631, op. 11, d. 239.
82 *International literature* (possibly Rokotov) to Nizan, letter of 10 January 1938, op. cit..
83 Friedmann to Apletin, letter of 23 July 1937. RGALI, Foreign Commission, f. 631, op. 13, d. 117.
84 Dinamov to Aragon, letter of 5 May 1936. RGALI, Foreign Commission, f. 631, op. 11, d. 233.
85 Friedmann to Apletin, letter of 2 February 1939, op. cit.
86 Friedmann to Apletin, letter of 23 July 1937, op. cit.
87 Record of Malraux's statements about the film *We of Kronstad* on 4 March 1936. RGALI, Foreign Commission, f. 631, op. 15, d. 80 (in Russian).
88 Ibid.
89 Ibid.
90 Editions sociales internationales to *Mezhdunarodnaya kniga*, letter of 8 June 1938. RGALI, Foreign Commission, f. 631, op. 13, d. 117, ll. 34–5 (in French).
91 R. Maghidov to Rokotov, letter of 2 January 1939, ibid., ll. 40–1 (in French).
92 Ibid.
93 Ibid., l. 41.
94 Apletin to Fadeev, the Bureau of the Board of the Soviet Writers' Union, letter of 25 January 1939. RGALI, Foreign Commission, f. 631, op. 14, d. 22.
95 Ibid.
96 Raisa Orlova speaks of the unfulfilled attempts by Vladimir Kemenov, VOKS's chairman in 1939, to take over the magazine as VOKS's printed organ. In: R. Orlova, op. cit., p. 110.

97   Barghoorn. *The Soviet Cultural Propaganda*, p. 169.
98   Apletin to Aragon, letter of 20 June 1939, op. cit. Apletin makes a reference to Prof. Mazon's article in *Mois*.
99   'How friends of the USSR act abroad in its defence', April 1931, author unknown, op. cit.
100 Friedmann to Apletin, letter of 5 January 1937. RGALI, Foreign Commission, f. 631, op. 13, d. 117, l. 9.
101 Friedmann to Apletin, letter of 25 February 1937, ibid., l. 10 (verso).
102 Friedmann to Apletin, letter of 22 March 1939, ibid.
103 Blech to Apletin, letter of 8 February 1939. RGALI, Foreign Commission, f. 631, op. 14, d. 771 (in Russian).
104 Ibid.
105 Babichenko, op. cit., p. 126.
106 RGASPI, MORP, f. 541, op. 1, d. 128.
107 *Romanskaya Komissia MORP* (MORP Romance Commission). RGALI, Foreign Commission, f. 631, op. 14, dd. 714, 715 and 726; and f. 631, op. 2, d.121.
108 MORP Romance Commission, op. cit. Summary report 19, 15 January 1934. RGALI, Foreign Commission, f. 631, op. 14, d. 715.
109 *Obzory literaturnoy zhizni Frantsii* (Reviews of French Literary Life). RGALI, Foreign Commission, f. 631, op. 14, d. 778.
110 In *NRF*, January 1940, entry of 29 January 1940, ibid.
111 Summary report, entry of 16 December 1939, ibid.
112 Summary report, entry of 10 February 1940, ibid.
113 The American *Daily Worker* of 27 November 1939, entry of 29 January 1940, ibid. Documents of the Association still have not been recovered and their whereabouts remain unknown.
114 The article was published in the Copenhagen magazine *Die Welt* on 21 March 1940, entry of 14 April 1940, ibid.
115 *Obrashcheniye frantsuzskikh uchenykh v zaschitu belofinnov* (The address of French scholars in support of the White Finns), *Temps*, 31 January 1940. RGALI, Foreign Commission, f. 631, op. 14, d. 778 and 783.
116 For example, his talk 'Finland, its example, its suffering' in a military club in Paris, entry of 1 February and 3 March 1940, ibid., d. 778.
117 Published in *NRF* in February 1940, entry of 3 March 1940, ibid.
118 Although, on Stalin's instructions, Comintern called on all Communist parties to support the 'winter campaign', public opinion in the UK and France was strongly supportive of Finland. See: Yu. Afanas'yev, ed. *Drugaya voyna. 1939–1945 (Another War. 1939–45)*. Moscow: Moskovsky Gosudarstvennyy Gumanitarnyy Universitet, 1996, pp. 46–7.
119 RGASPI, Comintern, f. 495, op. 18, d. 1292, l. 47. In Yu. Afanas'yev, ibid., p. 44.
120 Friedrich to Lubarsky, letter of 30 December 1939. RGALI, Foreign Commission, f. 631, op. 14, d. 21, l. 1.
121 Dinamov to Nizan, letter of 28 May 1937. RGALI, *International Literature*, f. 1397, op. 2, d. 140 (in French).
122 Friedmann to Apletin, letter of 2 February 1939. RGALI, Foreign Commission, f. 631, op. 13, d. 117, l. 42.
123 Rolland to Apletin, letter of 18 May 1939. RGALI, Foreign Commission, f. 631, op. 14, d. 23, l. 56.
124 Quoted from Apletin's letter to Sheverdin (OVIR) of 8 July 1939, ibid., l. 57 (in Russian).
125 Apletin to Rolland, letter of 9 June 1940. Bibiothèque Nationale, Fonds Romain Rolland, ff. 16–17.
126 See Triolet's correspondence with the Director of Gosizdat, e.g. Lettre du Directeur

des Editions littéraires d'Etat à E. Triolet du 19 avril 1938. CNRS, Centre Louis Aragon–Elsa Triolet, Fonds Elsa Triolet.

127 Elsa Triolet to Rokotov, *International Literature*, letters of 25 March and 24 July 1939. RGALI, *International Literature*, f. 1397, op. 1, d. 760, pp. 3 and 7.

128 Bruno Yasensky to Elsa Triolet, letters of 13 August 1935 and 1 September 1935. CNRS, Centre Louis Aragon–Elsa Triolet, Fonds Elsa Triolet.

129 Lev Kuleshov to Elsa Triolet, letters of 29 December 1930 and 23 January 1931, ibid.

130 Triolet to Vishnevsky, letters of 8 June 1937, May 1937, April 1937, 10 November 1936, 6 March 1937. RGALI, f. 1038, op. 1, d. 3140.

131 Yasensky to Triolet, letter of 13 August 1935, op. cit.

132 Triolet to Fadeev, letter of 11 October 1933. RGALI, f. 602, op. 1, f. 1593, f. 2; Triolet to Vishnevsky, letters of April–July 1937. RGALI, Vishnevsky, f. 1038, op. 1, d. 3140.

133 Triolet to Vishnevsky, letters of 29 April 1937, May 1937 and 8 June 1937 regarding *Les Beaux Quartiers*, op. cit. Triolet to Fadeev, op. cit. regarding the delays with *Busy*.

134 Triolet to Vishnevsky, letter of 16 March 1937 regarding the silence in the Soviet press about *Les Beaux Quartiers*. RGALI, f. 1038, op. 1, d. 3140.

135 Triolet to Rokotov, letter of 24 July 1939 on Triolet being a Russian writer as well as French. RGALI, *International Literature*, f. 1397, op. 1, d. 760, pp. 3 and 7.

136 Ibid.

137 L. Stern. '*Journal du voyage en URSS* de Marguerite et Jean-Richard Bloch', *Jean-Richard Bloch, ou l'écriture et l'action*, eds A. Angrémy and M. Trebitsch. Paris : Bibliothèque Nationale de France, 2002, pp. 231–41.

138 Claude Bloch, interview with the author on 9 December 1997.

139 Ibid.

140 Gulyayev. *Spravka* (Certificate), 17 October 1940. IKKI, f. 495, op. 270, d.736, ll. 19–20 (a copy of this document has been kindly provided to me by Nicole Racine).

141 See Bloch's correspondence with Ehrenburg prior to his visit in 1934, 8 June–13 July 1934. Bibliothèque Nationale, Fonds Jean-Richard Bloch, Lettres à Jean-Richard Bloch.

142 See Bloch's correspondence with Mil'man, December 1934–May 1936, ibid., t. XXXIV, ff. 218–26 and 228–9.

143 M. Bloch. *Carnet*, p. 30.

144 See Kol'tsov's letters to Bloch, May 1935–May 1936. Bibliothèque Nationale, Fonds Jean-Richard Bloch, Lettres de Koltsov, t. XXVI, ff. 185–8.

145 Tret'yakov to Bloch, letter of 6 July 1935, ibid., Lettres à J.-R. Bloch, t. XLI, f. 30.

146 Lidine to Bloch, letter of March 1935, ibid., t. XXVIII, f. 458.

147 See Vishnevsky's letter of 23 September 1935 regarding the French production of *The Optimistic Tragedy*, ibid., t. XLVIII, f. 28.

148 El'bert asked Bloch's advice on the new *Revue de Moscou* and encouraged him to return to Moscow. Lettre d'El'bert du 193[?] after the 1934 Writers' Congress, ibid., t. XVIII, f. 274.

149 Gulyayev, op. cit., l. 20. See also N. Racine. 'Bloch, Jean-Richard', *Dictionnaire biographique du mouvement ouvrier français*, eds. J. Maitron, C. Pennetier, t. XLIV, *Supplement to vols 1–43: 1789–1939*, Supplement to Vol. 1–9. New biographies. Paris: Les Editions de l'atelier, 1997.

150 Bloch to Stalin, letter of 1 May 1941. Bibliothèque Nationale, Fonds Jean-Richard Bloch, t. XLIV, f. 250.

151 Ibid.

152 Professor Vladimir Andreevich Uspensky, personal correspondence with the author, December 2005.

153 Apletin to M. Bloch, letter of 18 December 1943. Bibliothèque Nationale, Fonds Jean-Richard Bloch, Lettres à Jean-Richard Bloch, t. III, f. 68.
154 Apletin to Bloch, letter of 25 May 1944, ibid., f. 69.
155 Bloch to Molotov, Tehran, letter of 26 December 1944, ibid.
156 Ibid.
157 Bloch to Nikolay Tikhonov, Chairman of the Soviet Writers' Union, letter of 25 May 1944, ibid., f. 23.
158 Apletin to J.-R. Bloch, letter of 30 May 1945, ibid., f. 73.
159 Bloch to Apletin, letter of 13 July 1945, op. cit., f. 81.
160 Ibid., f. 82.
161 Tikhonov to Bloch (à la rédaction de *Ce soir*), letter of 20 May 1946, ibid. Lettres à J.-R. Bloch, f. 24.
162 Klein. '*L'Homme du communisme. Portrait de Staline*, par Jean-Richard Bloch', op. cit., pp.43–54.

Epilogue

1 The first Congress was held in Breslau, 1948, followed by Paris and Prague in 1949.
2 Fayet. *Karl Radek* (1885–1939), p. 719, n. 364.
3 http://en.wikipedia.org/wiki/Olga_Kameneva#endnote_Conquest
4 Artyom Yermakov. 'Nozhnitsy nebytiya' ('The scissors of non-existence'), http://www.ug.ru/?action=topic&toid=2885.
5 V.F. Kolyazin, ed. (in cooperation with V.A. Goncharov of the Central Archives of the FSB of RF), '*Vernite mne svobodu!' Deyateli literatury i iskusstva Rossii i Germanii – zhertvy stalinskoro terrora. Memorial'nyy sbornik dokumentov iz arkhivov byvshego KGB* ('Give me back my freedom!' Russian and German artists and writers – victims of Stalin's terror. A memorial collection of documents from the archives of the former KGB). Moscow: Medium, 1997, pp. 46–68.
6 V. Shentalinsky. 'Pulya vmesto tochki' ('Bullet instead of full stop'). In: *Raby svobody (Slaves of freedom)*. Moscow: Parus, 1995, pp. 185–207.
7 V. Shentalinsky. 'Proshu menya vyslushat' ('May I have the floor'), ibid., pp. 26–81.
8 Kolyazin, ibid., pp. 220–40.
9 Ibid., pp. 284–301.
10 '*Vernite mne svobodu!*', pp. 288–90, 293–6.

Bibliography

Archives

Archives Nationales: Série F7 – Police Générale (Paris).

Bibliothèque Nationale, Département de Manuscrits Occidentaux: Fonds Jean-Richard Bloch, *Correspondance*, *Journal du voyage en URSS, Carnet de voyage en URSS en 1934* and Fonds Romain Rolland, *Correspondance*; Fonds Marcel Cohen, *Correspondance* (Paris).

CNRS, Centre Louis Aragon–Elsa Triolet: Fonds Elsa Triolet, *Correspondance* (Paris).

GARF (*Gosudarstvennyy arkhiv Rossiyskoy Federatsii*, State Archive of the Russian Federation): VOKS, Fond 5283 (Moscow).

RGALI (*Rossiyskiy gosudarstvennyy arkhiv literatury i iskusstva*, Russian State Archive of Literature and Art): The Foreign Commission of the Soviet Writers' Union, Fond 631; *International Literature*, Fond 1397; Ilya Ehrenbourg, Fond 1204 (Moscow).

RGASPI (*Rossiyskiy gosudarstvennyy arkhiv sotsial'no-politicheskoy istorii*, Russian State Archives of Socio-Political History): Comintern (Agitprop), Fond 495; MORP, Fond 541 (Moscow).

Magazines and newspapers of the 1920s–1930s

Clarté
Commune
Europe
l'Humanité
International Literature (Russian, French and English editions)
Marianne
NRF
Russie d'aujourd'hui
Vendredi
VOKS

Books, articles and published documents of associations

Aaron, D. *Writers on the Left: Episodes in American Literary Communism*. New York: Harcourt, Brace and World, 1961.

Adereth, M. *The French Communist Party – a Critical History (1920–1984): From*

Comintern to 'the Colours of France'. Manchester: Manchester University Press, 1984.

AEAR. *Ceux qui ont choisi*. Paris: Edité par l'AEAR, circa 1932.

Afanas'yev, Yu., ed. *Drugaya voyna: 1939–1945 (Another War: 1939–45)*. Moscow: Moskovsky Gosudarstvennyy Gumanitarnyy Universitet, 1996.

Alberti, R. *The Lost Grove*, trans. and ed. by G. Berns. n.p.: University of California Press, 1959.

Albertini, J. *Avez-vous lu Jean-Richard Bloch?* Paris: Editions sociales, 1981.

Amis de la vérité sur l'URSS. *Bilan de la terreur en URSS (Faits et chiffres)*. Paris: Librairie du travail, 1936.

Aragon, L. *L'oeuvre poétique, 1927–1935*, tome II. Paris: Messidor, 1989.

Arnte, A. 'Rol' vsesoyuznogo obschestva kul'turnoy svyazi s zagranitsey v ukreplenii internatsional'nykh svyazey s trudyaschimisya Latvii (1925–1940)' ('The role of the All-Union Organisation for Cultural Relations with Foreign Countries in the strengthening of international relations with the workers of Latvia'), *Izvestiya Akademii Nauk Latviyskoy SSR (The news of the Latvian SSR Academy of Sciences)*, 1984, 12 (449): 11–25.

Aron, R. *Mémoires*. Paris: Julliard, 1983.

Aroseva, O., Maksimova, V. *Bez grima (Without Makeup)*. Moscow: Tsentrpoligraf, 1998.

Association Française des Amis de l'Union Soviétique. *Le guide de l'Ami de l'U.R.S.S. Indispensable à tout adhérent des 'Amis de l'URSS'*. Paris: AUS, 1936.

Association des Amis de l'Union Soviétique. *Journées françaises pour la paix et pour l'amitié avec l'URSS*. Unabridged text of the presentations delivered at the Grand amphitheatre of the Sorbonne on 23–24 October 1937. Paris: Edition du Secrétariat Général des Journées, Librairie AUS, 1937.

—— *Pour la paix. Pacte Franco-Soviétique*. Reports and presentations at the VI National Congress of the French Association of Friends of the Soviet Union in Lyon, 30, 31 October and 1 November 1938. Paris: Les éditions AUS, 1938.

Association Internationale des Ecrivains. *Conférence extraordinaire tenue à Paris du 25 juillet 1938*. Publication of the International Writers' Association for the Defence of Culture. Paris: Denoel.

Astruc, A., Contat, M. *Sartre* (Film script). Paris: Gallimard, 1977.

Babel, I. *Sochineniya v dvukh tomakh (Collected work in two volumes)*. Moscow: Khudozhestvennaya literatura, 1992.

Babichenko, D., ed. *'Schast'ye literatury' Gosudarstvo i pisateli. 1925–1938. Dokumenty ('The Happiness of Literature' The State and the Writers. 1925–38. Documents)*. Moscow: Rosspen, 1997.

Bakhrakh, A. 'Po pamyati, po zapisyam' ('From my memory, from my notes'). *Kontinent*, 1976, 8: 349–386.

Balakhonov, V. 'SSSR glazami frantsuzskikh pisateley' ('USSR through the eyes of French writers'). Introduction and annotated publication of excerpts from letters by Romain Rolland and Henri Barbusse. *Zvezda*, 1987, 11: 147–54.

Balle, F. *Médias et societes*. Paris: Montchrestien, 1990.

Bance, A.F., ed. *Weimar Germany: Writers and Politics*. Edinburgh: Scottish Academic Press, 1982.

Barghoorn, F. *The Soviet Cultural Offensive. The Role of Cultural Diplomacy in Soviet Foreign Policy*. Princeton, NJ: Princeton University Press, 1960.

—— *Soviet Foreign Propaganda*. Princeton, NJ: Princeton University Press, 1964.

Bark, D.L. *The Red Orchestra: Instruments of Soviet Policy in Latin America and the Caribbean.* Stanford, CA: Hoover Institution Press, Stanford University, 1986.

Bayac, J. Delperrié de. *Histoire du Front Populaire.* Paris: Fayard, 1972.

Bazanov, V., Blagoy, D.D., Vinogradov, V.V., Dubovikov, A.N., Zil'bershteyn, I.S., Makashin, S.A., Muratova, K.D., Samarin, R.M., Timifeyev, L.I., Trifonov, N.A., Khrapchenko, M.B., Shtcherbina, V.B., eds. *Iz istorii mezhdunarodnogo ob'yedineniya revolyutsionnykh pisateley (MORP). Literaturnoye nasledstvo (From the History of the International Association of Revolutionary Writers (MORP).* Literaturnoye nasledstvo (Literary Heritage), Vol. 81. Moscow: Nauka, 1969.

Beauvoir, S. de. *Mémoires d'une jeune fille rangée.* Paris: Gallimard, 1958.

——— *La force de l'âge.* Paris: Gallimard, 1960.

Benjamin, W. *Moscow Diary.* Cambridge, MA: Harvard University Press, 1986.

Benn, D.W. *Persuasion and Soviet Politics.* Oxford: Basil Blackwell, 1989.

Berard, E. *La vie tumultueuse d'Ilya Ehrenbourg.* Paris: Ramsay, 1991.

Berezhkov, V. *Ryadom so Stalinym (Next to Stalin).* Moscow: Vagrius, 1998.

Berl, E. *Présence des morts.* Paris: Gallimard, 1977.

Berlin, I. 'Meetings with the Russian Writers, 1945 and 1956'. *Slavica Hierosolymitana*, 1981, 5–6: 593–639.

Bernard, J.-P. *Le parti communiste français et la question littéraire: 1921–1939.* n.p.: Presses Universitaires de Grenoble, 1972.

Bettinghaus, E.P. *Persuasive Communication.* New York: Holt, Rinehart and Winston, 1968.

Bloch, J.-R. *Correspondance (1921–1939) de Jean-Richard Bloch et Andre Monglond.* Selected and annotated by Tivadar Gorilovics. Debrecen, Hungary: Kossuth Lajos Tudomanyegyetem, 1989.

——— *Destin du siècle.* Paris: Presses Universitaires de France, 1996.

Bodek, R. *'We are the Red Megaphone!': Political Music, Agitprop Theatre, Everyday Life and Communist Politics in Berlin During the Weimar Republic.* Ann Arbor: The University of Michigan, 1990.

Bona, D. *Stefan Zweig: L'ami blessé.* Paris: Plon, 1996.

Borland, H. *Soviet Literary Theory and Practice During the First Five-Year Plan 1928–1932.* New York: Greenwood Press, 1969.

Brown, J.A.C. *Techniques of Persuasion.* Harmondsworth: Penguin Books, 1963.

Burger-Roussennac, A. '1932: L'année incertaine. Deux politiques communistes de rassemblement des intellectuels et de lutte contre la guerre. L'Association des écrivains et artistes révolutionnaires et le mouvement d'Amsterdam', *Communisme*, 1993, 32–4: 129–40.

Cadot, M. *La Russie dans la vie intellectuelle française: 1839–1856.* Paris: Fayard, 1967.

Carr, E.H. *Twilight of the Comintern, 1930–1935.* New York: Pantheon Books, 1982.

Caute, D. *Le Communisme et les intellectuels français, 1914–1966.* Paris: Gallimard, 1967.

——— *The Fellow Travellers.* London: Macmillan, 1973.

——— 'The Literature of the Left' in *The Modern World: Reactions.* London: Aldus Books, 1976, Vol. III, p. 409.

Chernobayev, A. *V vikhre veka (In the Whirlwind of the Century).* Moscow: Moskovskiy Rabochiy, 1987.

Chklovski, V. *Voyage sentimental*, trans. V. Pozner. Paris: Simon Kra, 1926.

Cody, M.J., McLaughli, M.L., eds. *The Psychology of Tactical Communication.* Clevedon: Multilingual Matters, 1990.

Coeuré, S. '... comme ils disent SSSR. Louis Aragon et l'Union soviétique dans les années 1930'. In: Bernard Lecherbonnier and Jacques Girault (eds). *Les Engagements d'Aragon*. Paris: L'Harmattan, 1998, 24: 59–67.

—— *La grande lueur à l'est: les français et l'Union Soviétique*. Paris: Seuil, 1999.

Cohen-Solal, A., with the collaboration of Nizan, H. *Paul Nizan, Communiste impossible*. Paris: Bernard Grasset, 1980.

Le Congrès des Amis de l'URSS (Novembre 1927). Paris: Bureau d'éditions, n.d.

Corbet, C. *L'opinion française face à l'inconnu russe (1799–1894)*. Paris: Librairie Marcel Didier, 1967.

Cunningham, V. *British Writers of the Thirties*. Oxford: Oxford University Press, 1988.

Dabit, E. *Journal intime (1928–1936)*. Paris: Gallimard, 1989.

Daix, P. *Aragon: une vie à changer*. Paris: Flammarion, 1994.

Davies, R.W. *Soviet History in the Yeltsin Era*. London: Macmillan, 1997.

Daniels, M.F., Walch, T., eds. *A Modern Archives Reader: Basic Readings on Archival Theory and Practice*. Washington, DC: National Archives and Records Service, US General Services Administration, 1984.

Desiriaux, R. *URSS: Pays des peuples frères*. n.p.: L'Association des amis de l'Union Soviétique, 1936.

Dewey, J. *Impressions of Soviet Russia and the Revolutionary World: Mexico, China, Turkey, 1929*. Bureau of Publications, Colombia University, 1964.

Dominique, P. *Oui, mais Moscou*. Paris: Librairie Valois, 1931.

Donald, R.R. *Hollywood and World War II: Enlisting Feature Films as Propaganda*. Amherst: University of Massachusetts, 1987.

Dovring, K. *Road of Propaganda. The Semantics of Biased Communication*. New York: Philosophical Library, 1959.

Drachkovitch, M., ed. *The Revolutionary Internationals, 1864–1943*. Stanford: Stanford University Press, 1966.

——, Lazitch, B., eds. *The Comintern: Historical Highlights. Essays, Recollections, Documents*. New York: Praeger, 1966, for The Hoover Institution on War, Revolution and Peace, Stanford University.

Dreiser, T. *Dreiser Looks at Russia*. London: Constable, 1928.

Drobashenko, S. 'Soviet documentary film, 1917–1940'. In: N. Pronay, D.W. Spring, eds. *Propaganda, Politics and Film, 1918–1945*, pp. 249–69.

Dubief, H. *Le déclin de la IIIe République: 1929–1938*. Paris: Edition du Seuil, 1976.

Dubinskaya-Dzhalilova, T. 'Velikiy gumanist (Po materialam perepiski M. Gor'kogo i I.V. Stalina)' ('The Great Humanist (Based on the correspondence between V. Gorky and I.V. Stalin)'), *Novoye Literaturnoye Obozreniye*, 1999, 40: 223–50.

Duhamel, G. *Le voyage de Moscou*. Paris: Mercure de France, 1927.

—— *Les espoirs et les épreuves 1919–1928: lumières sur ma vie*. Paris: Mercure de France, 1953.

—— *Le livre de l'amertume: journal 1925–1956*. Paris: Mercure de France, 1983.

—— *Témoins d'un temps troublé. Roger Martin du Gard – Georges Duhamel, correspondance 1919–1958*, ed. A. Lafay. Paris: Minard, 1987.

Dullin, S. *Des hommes d'influence: les ambassadeurs de Staline en Europe, 1930–1939*. Paris: Payot, 2001.

Duranty, W. *I Write as I Please*. New York: Simon and Schuster, 1935.

Ehrenbourg, I. *Duhamel, Gide, Malraux, Mauriac, Morand, Romains, Unamuno: vus par un écrivain d'URSS*. Paris: Gallimard, 1934.

—— *Lyudi, gody, zhizn'* (*People, Years, My Life*). Memoirs in 3 vols. The amended and completed edition. Moscow: Sovetskyy pisatel', 1990.

Ellul, J. *Propaganda: The Formation of Men's Attitudes*. New York: Alfred A. Knopf, 1966.

Fauchereaux, S., ed. *Moscow 1900–1930*. London: Alpine Fine Arts Collection, 1988.

Fayet, J.-F. 'Entre culture, politique et lobbying diplomatique: la société pansoviétique d'échanges culturels avec l'étranger [V.O.K.S.]' in H.U. Jost and S. Przioso (eds). *Relations internationales, échanges culturels et reseaux intellectuals*, Lausanne: Antipodes, 2002.

—— *Karl Radek (1885–1939): biographie politique*. Bern: Peter Lang, 2004.

Ferro, M. *L'Occident devant la Revolution soviétique*. Brussels: Editions Complexe, 1980.

Fitzpatrick, S., ed. *Cultural Revolution in Russia, 1928–1931*. Bloomington and London: Indiana University Press, 1978.

Fitzpatrick, S., Rabinovich, A., Stites, R., eds. *Russia in the Era of NEP*. Bloomington: Indiana University Press, 1991.

—— *The Cultural Front: Power and Culture in Revolutionary Russia*. Ithaca: Cornell University Press, 1992.

—— *Everyday Stalinism. Ordinary Life in Extraordinary Times: Soviet Russia in the 1930s*. New York: Oxford University Press, 1999.

Feuchtwanger, L. *Moscow 1937*. London: Victor Gollancz, 1937.

—— *Moskva 1937*, Published 1937, Moscow (in Russian), http://www.kuzbass.ru/moshkow/koi/INPROZ/FEJHTWANGER/moscow1937.txt (last checked on 22 December 2005).

Fleishman, L. *Boris Pasternak v dvadtsatyye gody* (*Boris Pasternak in the Twenties*). Munich: Wilhelm Fink Verlag, 1980.

—— *Boris Pasternak v tridtsatyye gody* (*Boris Pasternak in the Thirties*). Jerusalem: The Magnes Press, The Hebrew University, 1984.

Foulkes, A.P. *Literature and Propaganda*. London: Methuen, 1983.

Frank, W. *Dawn in Russia. The Record of a Journey*. New York: Charles Scribner's Sons, 1932.

Frezinsky, B. 'Parizh nachinalsya v Odesse' ('Paris began in Odessa'). *Nevskoye Vremya*, 27 June 1995.

Frezinsky, B. '"Andre Deren udivlyon i razobizhen'. Kak frantsuzskikh khudozhnikov ne pustili v Sovetskiy Soyuz' ('"André Derain is surprised and offended." How French artists were not allowed into the USSR'). *La pensée russe* Australian issue, 1996, 1 (31 October–6 November): 11.

Gak, A.M. 'V.I. Lenin i razvitiye mezhdunarodnykh kul'turnykh i nauchnykh svyazey Sovetskoy Rossii v 1920–1924 godakh' ('V.I. Lenin and the development of international cultural and scientific relations in 1920–24'). *Voprosy istorii*, 1963, 4: 196–204.

George, A.L. *Propaganda Analysis: A Study of Inferences Made from Nazi Propaganda in World War II*. Evanston, IL: Row, Peterson and Company, 1959.

Gide, A. *Retour de l'URSS* et *Retouches à mon retour de l'URSS*. Paris: Gallimard, 1950.

Gide, A., Levesque, R. *Correspondance (1926–1950)*. Selected, presented and annotated by Pierre Masson. n.p.: Presses Universitaires de Lyon, 1995.

Gide, A., Martin du Gard, R. *Correspondance (1913–1934 et 1935–1951)*. Paris: Gallimard, 1968.

Goldovskaya, M. (director). *The Solovki Power* (documentary). Mosfilm Studios, 1988.

Golubev, A., Nevezhin, V. 'VOKS v 1930–1940-e gody' ('VOKS in the 1930s–1940s').

Minuvsheye. Istoricheskiy al'manakh 14. Moscow: Antheneum-Fenix, 1993, pp. 313–366.

Gorilovich, T. (ed.) *Retrouver Jean-Richard Bloch*. Debrecen, Hungary: Kossuth Lajos Tudomanyegyetem, 1994.

Gorky, M., Auerbach, L., Firin, S., Williams-Ellis, A. *Belomor: An Account of the Construction of the New Canal between the White Sea and the Baltic Sea*. New York: Harrison Smith and Robert Haas, 1935.

Gray, C. *The Great Experiment: Russian Art*. London: Thames and Hudson, 1962.

Hagen, M. von. 'The Archival Gold Rush and Historical Agendas in the Post-Soviet Era'. *Slavic Review*, 1993, 1 (Spring): 96–100.

Hanrez, M. *Céline*. Paris: Gallimard, 1961.

Hasluck, N. 'Waiting for Ulrich: The Kisch and Clinton Cases'. *Quadrant*, 1999, April: 28–33.

Heller, M., Nekrich, A. *Utopiya u vlasti: istoriya Sovetskogo Soyuza s 1917 goda do nashikh dney* (*Utopia in Power: the History of the Soviet Union from 1917 to the Present*). London: Overseas Publications Interchange Ltd, 1982.

Herbart, P. *En URSS 1936*. Paris: Gallimard, 1937.

Hingley, R. *Nightingale Fever, Russian Poets in Revolution*. London: Weidenfeld & Nicolson, 1982.

Hogenhuis-Seliverstoff, A. *Les relations franco-soviétiques 1917–1924*. Paris: Publications de la Sorbonne, 1981.

Hollander, P. *Political Pilgrims Travels of Western Intellectuals to the Soviet Union, China and Cuba: 1928–1978*. New York: Oxford University Press, 1981.

Holquist, P. '"Information Is the Alpha and Omega of Our Work": Bolshevik Surveillance in Its Pan-European Context'. *The Journal of Modern History*, 1997, September: 415–450.

International Association of Revolutionary Writers. *Short Literary Encyclopaedia*, Vol. 4. Moscow: Soviet Encyclopedia Publishers, 1967.

Ioffe, A. *Internatsional'nyye, nauchnyye i kul'turnyye svyazi Sovetskogo Soyuza: 1928–1932* (*International, Scientific and Cultural Relations of the Soviet Union: 1928–32*). Moscow: Nauka, 1969.

Ioffe, A. *International Scientific and Cultural Relations of the Soviet Union: 1917–1932* (*International scientific and cultural relations of the USSR: 1917–1932*). *Voprosy istorii*, 1969, 4: 50–66.

Ioffe, A. *Mezhdunarodnyye svyazi sovetskoy nauki, tekhniki i kul'tury: 1917–1932* (*International Relations of the Soviet Science, Technology and Culture: 1917–1932*). Moscow: Nauka, 1975.

Istrati, P. *Vers l'autre flamme*. Paris: Gallimard, 1987.

Jean-Richard Bloch. Special issue of *Europe,* revue mensuelle. June 1966, No. 446.

Jelen, C. *L'aveuglement: les socialistes et la naissance du mythe soviétique*. Paris: Flammarion, 1984.

Jowett, G.S., O'Donnell, V. *Propaganda and Persuasion*. Beverly Hills: Sage, 1986.

Judt, T. *Marxism and the French Left: Studies in Labour and Politics in France, 1830–1981*. Oxford: Clarendon Press, 1986.

—— *Past Imperfect: French Intellectuals, 1944–1956*. Berkeley, CA: University of California Press, 1992.

Katanyan, V.V., ed. *Imya etoy teme: lyubov'! Sovremennotsy o Mayakovskom* (*Love is the Name of this Theme! Contemporaries on Mayakovsky*). Moscow: Druzhba Narodov, 1993.

—— *Prikosnoveniye k idolam* (*Touching the Idols*). Moscow: Izdatel'stvo Zakharov-Vagrius, 1997.

Kemp-Welch, A. *Stalin and the Literary Intelligentsia, 1928–39*. London: Macmillan, 1991.

Kharlamov, M., Ioffe, A., *et al.*, eds. *Leninskaya vneshnyaya politika sovetskoy strany 1917–1924* (*Lenin's Foreign Politics of the USSR 1917–24*). Moscow: Nauka, 1969.

Khlevnyuk, O. *Politbyuro: Mekhanizmy politicheskoy vlasti v 1930-ye gody* (*Politburo: Mechanisms of Political Power in the 1930s*). Moscow: ROSSPEN, 1996.

Knapp, W. *France: Partial Eclipse Library of the 20th Century*. London: Macdonald/American Heritage Press, 1972.

Koch, S. *Double Lives: Spies and Writers in the Secret Soviet War of Ideas Against the West*. New York: Maxwell Macmillan International, 1994.

Kolesnikova, N. *Bruno Jasenski: His Evolution from Futurism to Socialist Realism*. Waterloo, ON: Wilfrid Laurier University Press, 1982.

Kriegel, A. *Aux origines du communisme français*. Paris: La Haye, Mouton, 1964.

Kupferman, F. *Au pays des Soviets: le voyage français en Union Soviétique 1917–1939*. Paris: Gallimard, 1979.

Kuz'min, M. 'Angliyskoye obschestvo kul'turnykh svyazey s SSSR' ('The English society of cultural relations with the USSR'). *Voprosy istorii*, 1966, 2: 203–6.

—— 'Kul'turnyye svyazi mezhdu SSSR i Yaponiyey posle Oktyabrya (1925–1932)' ('Cultural relations between the USSR and Japan after [the] October [revolution] (1925–32)'). *Narody Azii i Afriki*, 1967, 5: 133–43.

—— *Deyatel'nost' partii i sovetskogo gosudarstva po razvitiyu mezhdunarodnykh nauchnykh i kul'turnykh svyasey SSSR (1917–1932)* (*The Activities of the Party and the Soviet State in the Development of the USSR International Scientific and Cultural Relations (1917–32)*). Leningrad: Izdatel'stvo Leningradskogo Universiteta, 1971.

Labérenne, P. 'Le Cercle de la Russie Neuve (1928–1936) et l'Association pour l'étude de la culture soviétique (1936–1939)', *La Pensée*, 1979, June: 13–25.

Lacouture, J. *André Malraux: une vie dans le siècle*. Paris: Seuil, 1973.

—— *André Malraux*. Paris: Cahier de l'Herne, 1982.

Larson, C.U. *Persuasion. Reception and Responsibility*. Belmont, CA: Wadsworth Publishing Company, 1973.

Lazitch, B., Drachkovitch, M. *Lenin and the Comintern*, Vol. 1. Stanford, CA: Hoover Institution Press, Stanford University, 1972.

Lewin, M. *The Making of the Soviet System*. London: Methuen, 1985.

Leal, B. *Drieu la Rochelle: Decadence in Love*. Brisbane: University of Queensland, 1973.

Lilleker, D. *Against the Cold War: The History, Traditions and Strategies of Pro-Sovietism in the British Labour Party, 1945–89*. London: IB Tauris, 2004.

Loffler, P. *Chronique de l'Association des écrivains et des artistes révolutionnaires (Le mouvement littéraire progressiste en France) 1930–1939*. Rodez: Editions Subervie, 1971.

Lottman, H. *The Left Bank: writers in Paris from Popular Front to Cold War*. London: Heinemann, 1983.

Mazuy, R. *Croire plutôt que voir? Voyages en Russie soviétique (1919–1939)*. Paris: Odile Jacob, 2002.

McCauley, M. *The Soviet Union 1917–1991*. London: Longman, 1993.

McClung Lee, A., Briant Lee, E. *The Fine Art of Propaganda*. New York: Octagon Books, 1972.

McMeekin, S. *The Red Millionaire. A Political Biography of Willi Münzenberg, Moscow's Secret Propaganda Tsar in the West*. New Haven, CT: Yale University Press, 2003.

Marcou, L. *Ilya Ehrenbourg: un homme dans son siècle*. Paris: Plon, 1992.

Margulies, S.R. *The Pilgrimage to Russia: The Soviet Union and the Treatment of Foreigners, 1924–1937*. Madison, WI: University of Wisconsin Press, 1968.

Maurer, R. *André Gide et l'URSS*. Bern: Editions Tillier, 1983.

Maximenkov, L., Barnes, C. 'Boris Pasternak in August 1936 – an NKVD Memorandum'. *Toronto Slavic Quarterly*, 2003, 6 (Fall), http://www.utoronto.ca/tsq/06/pasternak06. shtml (last checked on 22 December 2005).

Maximenkov, L. 'Ocherki nomenklaturnoy istorii sovetskoy literatury: Zapadnyye piligrimy u stalinskogo prestola (Feykhtvanger i drugie)' ('Sketches of the nomenclature history of the Soviet literature: Western Pilgrims at Stalin's throne (Feuchtwanger and the others)'). *Voprosy literatury*, 2004, 1–2, http://magazines.russ.ru/voplit/2004/2/max13.html (last checked on 17 August 2006).

Mayakovsky, V., Brik, L. *Correspondence 1915–1930*, ed. B. Jangfeldt. Stockholm: Almqvist & Wiksell International, 1982.

Maysky, I. B. *Shou i drugiye: Vospominaniya (B. Shaw and the Others: Memoirs)*. Moscow: Iskusstvo, 1967.

Maxwell, D.E.S. *Poets of the Thirties*. London: Routledge and Kegan Paul, 1969.

Mazuy, R. 'Les "Amis de l'URSS" et le voyage en Union Soviétique. La mise en scène d'une conversion'. *Politix*, 1992, 18: 108–28.

—— *Croire plutôt que voir? Voyages en Russie soviétique (1919–1939)*. Paris: Odile Jacob, 2002.

Medvedev, R. 'Western Writers Meet Stalin. Why the Generalissimo Liked Foreign Litterateurs'. *Moscow News*, 2005, 48, http://english.mn.ru/english/issue.php?2002–30–11 (last checked on 22 December 2005).

Modiano, P. *L'interrogatoire*. Paris: Gallimard, 1976.

Morand, P. *Je brûle Moscou*. Paris: Flammarion, 1928.

Morel, J.-P. *Le roman insupportable: L'Internationale littéraire et la France*. Paris: Gallimard, 1985.

Morel, J.-P. ' "Le monstrueux tissu d'équivoques" A propos d'Aragon et de l'Internationale des Ecrivains révolutionnaires (1928–1932)'. In: Bernard Lecherbonnier and Jacques Girault (eds). *Les Engagements d'Aragon*. Paris: L'Harmattan, 1998, 24: 47–58.

Mortimer, E. *The Rise of the French Communist Party 1920–1947*. London: Faber and Faber, 1984.

Moussinac, L. *Le cinéma soviétique*. Paris: Gallimard, 1928.

Myuller, R., Kolyazin, V.F., eds. 'Ya okhotno prinimayu priglasheniye k sotrudnichestvu.' Perepiska V. Ben'yamina s redaktsiyey zhurnala 'Das Vort'. 1936–1937 gg.' ('I am happy to accept your invitation of collaboration.' W. Benjamin to editorial board of the magazine *Das Wort*. 1936–1937'). *Istoricheskiy arkhiv*, 1998, 1: 103–23.

Murav'yov, Yu. 'Sovetsko–germanskiye kul'turnyye svyazi v period Veymarskoy respubliki' ('Soviet–German cultural relations in the period of the Weimar Republic'). *Vestnik istorii mirovoy kul'tury*, 1960, 5: 55–63.

Nantell, J. *Rafael Alberti's Poetry of the Thirties: The Poet's Public Voice*. Athens, GA: University of Georgia Press, 1986.

Nichol James, P. 'Soviet Propaganda and Active Measures'. *Problems of Communism*, 1990, 39 (1): 93–9.

Nikulin, L. *Lyudi i stranstviya: Vospominaniya i vstrechi (People and Wanderings: Memoirs and meetings)*. Moscow: Sovetskiy pisatel', 1962.

254   Bibliography

Nizan, H., Jaubert, M.-J. *Libres mémoires*. Paris: Editions Robert Laffont, 1989.

Nizan, P. *Paul Nizan, intellectuel communiste*, unpublished articles and correspondence. Paris: Maspéro, 1967.

Olkhovyy, B. 'O poputnichestve i poputchikakh' (Stat'ya vtoraya) ('About fellow-travelling and fellow travellers' (Article Two)), *Pechat' i revolyutsiya. Zhurnal literatury i iskusstva, kritiki i bibliografii*, kniga shestaya, iyun'. Moscow: Gosizdatel'stvo, 1929, p. 15.

Orlova, R. *Vospominaniya o neproshedshem vremeni* (*Memoirs of the Times not Bygone*). Ann Arbor, MI: Ardis, 1983.

Ory, P. *Nizan, destin d'un révolté*. Paris: Ramsay, 1980.

—— *La belle illusion: Culture et politique sous le signe du Front populaire, 1935–1938*. Paris: Plon, 1994.

Paris–Moscou 1900–1930. Catalogue of the Paris–Moscou exhibition, Georges Pompidou Centre, revised and amended edition, 1979.

Pascal, P. *Pages d'amitié 1921–1928*. Paris: Editions Allia, 1987.

Pasternak, B. *Perepiska Borisa Pasternaka* (*Correspondence*). Moscow: Khudozhestvennaya literatura, 1990.

Pasternak, Ye. *Boris Pasternak: Materialy dlya biografiyi* (*Boris Pasternak: Materials for a Biography*). Moscow: Sovetskiy Pisatel', 1989.

—— *Boris Pasternak: The Tragic Years 1930–1960*. London: Collins Harvill, 1990.

Pennetier, C., ed. *Le Komintern: l'histoire et les hommes. Dictionnaire biographique de l'Internationale communiste en France, à Moscou, en Belgique, au Luxembourg, en Suisse (1919–1943)*. Dictionnaire biographique du mouvement ouvrier international, Paris: Collection Jean Maitron, 2001.

Peters, I. *Chekhoslovatsko–Sovetskiye otnosheniya (1918–1934)* (*Czechoslovak–Soviet Relation (1918–1934)*). Kiev: Naukova Dumka, 1965.

Pike, D. *German Writers in Soviet Exile, 1933–1945*. Chapel Hill: University of North Carolina Press, 1982.

Pirozhkova, A. *I. Babel': vospominaniya* (*I. Babel: Souvenirs*). Moscow: Sovetskiy pisatel', 1972.

Piscator, M., Palmier, J.-M. *Piscator et le théâtre politique*. Paris: Payot, 1983.

Popov, V., Frezinskiy, B. *Il'ya Erenburg: Khronika zhizni i tvorchestva v dokumentakh, pis'makh, vyskazyvaniyakh i soobscheniyakh pressy, svidetel'stvakh sovremennikov* (*Ilya Ehrenburg: The Chronicle of Life and Work in documents, letters, statements and press reports, and testimonies of his contemporaries*), Vol. 1, 1891–1923. St Petersburg: Lina, 1993.

Pozner, V. *Anthologie de la prose Russe contemporaine*. Paris: Hazan, 1929.

—— *Panorama de la litterature Russe contemporaine*, preface by Paul Hazard. Paris: Editions Kra, 1929.

—— *U.R.S.S., les oeuvres représentatives*. Presentation by Luc Durtain. Paris, 1932.

—— *Vladimir Pozner se souvient . . .* Paris: Julliard, 1972.

Pratkanis, A.P., Aronson, E. *Age of Propaganda. The Everyday Use and Abuse of Persuasion*. New York: W.H. Freeman, 1992.

Prochasson, C. *Les intellectuels et le socialisme XIXe-XXe siècle*. Paris: Plon, 1997.

Pronay, N., Spring, D.W., eds. *Propaganda, Politics and Film, 1918–45*. London: Macmillan, 1982.

Pyatnitsky, V. *Zagovor protiv Stalina* (*A Plot Against Stalin*). Moscow: Sovremennik, 1998.

Racine, N., Bodin, L. *Le Parti Communiste français pendant l'entre-deux-guerres*, 2nd edition. Paris: Presse de la fondation nationale des sciences politiques, 1982.

Racine, N. 'Malraux et la revue *Commune*'. *Europe*, 1989, November–December, Nos 727–8, pp. 29–42.

—— 'Bloch, Jean-Richard'. In J. Maitron and C. Pennetier (eds). *Dictionnaire biographique du mouvement ouvrier français*, Vol. 44, Supplement to Vols 1–43: 1789–1939, New biographies. Paris: Les Editions de l'atelier, 1997.

—— 'Aragon, militant du mouvement communiste international (1930–1939)'. In: Bernard Lecherbonnier and Jacques Girault (eds). *Les Engagements d'Aragon*. Paris: L'Harmattan, 1998, 24: 77–86.

—— 'Jean-Richard Bloch (1939–1941) ou les épreuves de la fidélité'. *Jean-Richard Bloch, ou l'écriture et l'action*, eds. A. Angrémy and M. Trebitsch. Paris: Bibliothèque nationale de France, 2002, pp. 253–73.

Read, C. *Culture and Power in Revolutionary Russia: The Intelligentsia and the Transition from Tsarism to Communism*. London: Macmillan, 1990.

Remington, T.F. *The Truth of Authority. Ideology and Communication in the Soviet Union*. Pittsburgh: University of Pittsburgh Press, 1988.

Remington, T.F., ed. *Politics and the Soviet System: Essays in Honour of Frederick C. Barghoorn*. London: Macmillan, 1989.

Riggio, T.P., West III, J.L.W., eds. *Dreiser's Russian Diary*. Philadelphia: University of Pennsylvania Press, 1996.

Rigoulot, P. *Les paupières lourdes*. Paris: Editions Universitaires, 1991.

Robrieux, P. *Histoire intérieure du Parti communiste*. Paris: Fayard, 1980–84.

Rolland, R. *Voyage à Moscou*. Paris: Albin Michel, 1992.

Romanovsky, S. *Mezhdunarodnyye kul'turnyye i nauchnyye svyazi SSSR* (*International Cultural and Scholarly Connections of the USSR*). Moscow: Mezhdunarodnyye otnosheniya, 1966.

Rosenfel'd, G. 'Nauchnyye i kul'turnyye svyazi mezhdu SSSR i Veymarskoy respublikoy' ('Scientific and Cultural Relations Between the USSR and the Weimar Republic'). *Voprosy istorii*, 1963, 10: 71–83.

Rossi, J. *Spravochnik po Gulag'u* (*The Gulag Handbook*). London: Overseas Publications Interchange, 1987.

Rubashkin, A., ed. 'Pisateli pishut Shcherbakovu' ('Writers who Wrote to Shcherbakov'). Letters by I. Ehrenbourg, M. Kol'tsov, A. Bezymensky, and A. Shcherbakov (1935–1936). *Neva*, 1999, 2: 171–82.

Rubashkin, A., ed. '"Poshli tolki, shto den'gi moskovskiye . . ." Pis'ma Il'yi Erenburga Mikhailu Kol'tsovu, 1935–1937' ('"There are rumours that the money comes from Moscow . . ." Letters from Ilya Ehrenburg to Mikhail Kol'tsov, 1935–37'). *Novyy Mir*, 1999, 3.

Russell, B. *The Autobiography of Bertrand Russell*. London: George Allen and Unwin, 1967.

Sadoul, G. 'Une femme, un homme', in *Elsa Triolet et Aragon*. Special issue of *Europe*, 454–455 (February–March 1967): 104–123.

Serge, V. *Les révolutionnaires*. Paris: Seuil, 1967.

—— *Mémoires d'un révolutionnaire: 1901–1941*. Paris: Seuil, 1978.

——, Sedova Trotsky, N. *The Life and Death of Leon Trotsky*, trans. by A.J. Pomerans. London: Wildwood House, 1975.

Shentalinsky, V. *Raby svobody. V literaturnykh arkhivakh KGB* (*Babel', Bulgakov, Floren-*

skiy, Pil'nyak, Mandel'shtam, Klyuyev, Platonov, Gor'kiy). (*The Slaves of Freedom. In the KGB Literary Archives*). Moscow: Parus, 1995.

Sheridan, A. *André Gide: A Life in the Present*. London: Hamish Hamilton, 1998.

Shirer, W.L. *The Collapse of the Third Republic*. London: William Heinemann, Secker & Warburg, 1970.

Shishkin, V.A. 'Iz istorii chekhslovatsko–sovetskikh kul'turnykh svyazey: 1918–1925 gg' ('From the history of Czechoslovak–Soviet relations: 1918–25'). *Vestnik istorii mirovoy kul'tury*, 1960, 6: 84–99.

Shultz, J.R.H. 'Soviet Strategy and Organisation: Active Measures and Insurgency', in D.L. Bark, ed. *The Red Orchestra: Instruments of Soviet Policy in Latin America and the Caribbean*. Stanford, CA: Hoover Institution Press, Stanford University, 1986.

Skoryatin, V. *Tayna gibeli Mayakovskogo* (*The Mystery of Mayakovsky's Death*). Moscow: Zvonnitsa-MG, 1998.

Slonimsky, M. *Kniga vospominaniy* (*The Book of Souvenirs*). Moscow: Sovetskiy Pisatel', 1966.

Smith III, T.J., ed. *Propaganda: A Pluralistic Perspective*. New York: Praeger, 1989.

Smith, V. '"I Am at Home," Says Robeson at Reception in Soviet Union'. *Daily Worker*, 15 January, 1935.

Solonevich, T. *Zapiski sovetskoy perevodchitsy* (*Notes of a Soviet Interpreter*). Sofia: Golos Rossii, 1937.

Solov'yov, A.N. 'Iz istorii franko-sovetskikh kul'turnykh i nauchnykh svyazey v 1931-1935 gg' ('From the history of French–Soviet Cultural and Scientific Relations in 1931–1935'). *Vestnik istorii mirovoy kul'tury*, 1960, 1: 80–91.

Souvarine, B. 'Posledniye razgovory s Babelem' (My Last Conversations with Babel). *Kontinent*, 1980, 23: 343–78.

—— *A contre-courant. Ecrits 1925–1939*, introduction by J. Verdès-Leroux. Paris: Denoël, 1985.

Spender, S. *The Thirties and After: Poetry, Politic, People (1933–75)*. London: The Macmillan Press by agreement with Fontan Paperbacks, 1978.

—— *World Within World: The Autobiography of Stephen Spender*. London: Hamish Hamilton, 1951.

Sperber, M. *Au-delà de l'oubli*. Paris: Calmann-Lévy, 1979.

Stalin–Wells *Talk. The Verbatim Record and a Discussion by G. Bernard Shaw, H.G. Wells, J.M. Keynes, Ernst Toller and others*. London: The New Statesman and Nation, 1934.

Stalin I. *Pis'ma I. V. Stalina V. M. Molotovu, 1925–1936. Sbornik dokumentov* (*I.V. Stalin's Letters to V.M. Molotov, 1925–36. Collected documents*). Moscow: Rossiya Molodaya, 1995.

Stalin, J.V. Talk With the German Author Emil Ludwig, December 13, 1931. First Published: Bolshevik, April 30, 1932, No. 8. Source: Works, J.V. Stalin, Foreign Languages Publishing House, Moscow, 1955, Volume 13, pp. 106–25; Transcription/HTML Markup: Hari Kumar for Alliance Marxist-Leninist (North America)/Charles Farrell. Online Version: http://www.marxists.org/reference/archive/stalin/works/1931/dec/13. htm (last checked on 22 December 2005).

Stern, L. 'The background history of creation of the French rapprochement society *The New Russia* (based on unpublished VOKS documents)'. *Australian Slavonic and East European Studies*, 1997, 11 (1/2): 143–60.

—— 'The creation of French–Soviet cultural relations. VOKS in the 1920s and the French intelligentsia', *AUMLA. Journal of the Australasian Universities Language and Literature Association*, 1998, 89 (May): 43–67.

—— 'The All-union Society for cultural relations with foreign countries and French intel-lectuals, 1925–1929' *Australian Journal of Politics and History*, 1999, 45 (1): 99–109.
—— '*Journal du voyage en URSS* de Marguerite et Jean-Richard Bloch'. *Jean-Richard Bloch, ou l'écriture et l'action*, eds. A. Angrémy and M. Trebitsch, Paris: Bibliothèque nationale de France, 2002, pp. 231–41.
Struve, G. *Russian Literature under Lenin and Stalin 1917–1953*. Norman: University of Okalahoma Press, 1971.
Sworakowski, W.S. *The Communist International and its Front Organisations*. Stanford, CA: The Hoover Institution on War, Revolution, and Peace, 1965.
Trebitsch, M. 'Jean-Richard Bloch ou l'optimisme du pessimisme'. In: J.-R. Bloch. *Destin du siècle*. Paris: Presses Universitaires de France, 1996.
Vaksberg, A. *Neraskrytye tayny* (*Unresolved Mysteries*). Moscow: Novosti, 1993.
—— *Lilya Brik* (*Lila Brik*) Moscow, Smolensk: Rusich, 1998.
—— *Val'kiriya revolyutsii* (*The Valkyrie of the Revolution*). Smolensk: Rusich, 1997.
Vildrac, C. *Pages de journal (1922–1966)*. Paris: Gallimard, 1968.
Vorob'yova, Ye. 'Obrazovaniye i deyatel'nost' chekhoslovatskogo obschestva ekonom-icheskogo i kul'turnogo sblizheniya s Novoy Rossiyey' ('The establishment and activi-ties of the Czechoslovak society of economic and cultural rapprochement with the New Russia'). *Sovetskoye slavyanovedeniye*, 1965, 2: 33–43.
Wells, H.G. *Experiment in Autobiography*. New York: Macmillan, 1934.
Whitton, J.B., ed. *Propaganda and the Cold War: A Princeton University Symposium*. Washington, DC: Public Affairs Press, 1963.
Willi Münzenberg, 1889–1940, Un homme contre. International conference, Aix-en-Pro-vence, proceedings, 26–29 March 1992.
Yakovlev, A., ed. *Vlast' i khudozhestvennaya intelligentsiya. Dokumenty TsK RKP(b)-VKP(b), VChK-OGPU-NKVD o kul'turnoy politike. 1917–1953 gg.* (*Power and Artistic Intelligentsia. Documents on Cultural Policies by TsK RKP(b)-VKP(b) and VChK-OGPU-NKVD*). Moscow: Mezhdunarodnyy Fond 'Demokratiya', 1999.
Zhila, L. 'Ustanovleniye kontaktov mezhdu organizatsiyami druzey SSSR v Bolgarii i VOKSom (1932–1939)' ('The establishment of contacts between organisations of Friends of the USSR in Bulgaria and VOKS (1932–1939)'). *Vestnik Moskovskogo uni-versiteta*, 1989, Ser. 8, History, 1: 42–53.
Zweig, S. *The World of Yesterday*. London: Cassell, 1953.

Unpublished interviews conducted by the author

Interviews with Claude Bloch, 11 September 1995 and 12 December 1997, Paris.
Interview with Francis Cohen, 10 December 1997, Paris.
Interviews with Irina Ehrenburg, 10 and 22 July 1995, Moscow.
Interview with Boris Frezinsky about Ilya Ehrenburg, 21 July 1995, Moscow.
Interview with Arlette Lafay about Georges Duhamel, 12 September 1995, Paris.
Interview with Antonina Pirozhkova, 6 August 1995, Moscow.
Interviews with Vladimir Pozner, December 1983–January 1984, Paris.

Index

Lightning Source UK Ltd.
Milton Keynes UK
UKOW032141230513

211164UK00001B/11/P